NAMIBIA
THE VIOLENT HERITAGE

To Greta

NAMIBIA
THE VIOLENT HERITAGE

David Soggot

REX COLLINGS

LONDON
1986

Soggot, David
  Namibia: the violent heritage.
  1. Namibia—Politics and government
  I. Title
  968.8   DT714

ISBN 0-86036-210-8 (UK)

Typeset by Rapidset and Design Ltd, London WC1
Printed and bound in Great Britain by
Biddles Ltd, Guildford and King's Lynn

CONTENTS

PREFACE

The political and insurgent battles in Namibia have in recent years come to be fought with increasing ferocity; so too the propaganda war in which truth has all too often figured as the prime casualty. It is therefore not surprising that western readers have been baffled by the clamour of reciprocally destructive claims put out by the warring parties.

Since the early seventies my work as a defence lawyer has brought me into close collaboration with many of the main actors in the conflict. This contact together with political trials which were often focal points of political and social confrontation were for me a discovery. It was this precious ongoing experience which afforded irreplaceable insights into Namibia's political evolution, the changes in the legal and constitutional architecture and, above all, the subjective faith and sorrow of men and women who had dared to participate in history. This book is not offered as an academic treatise on the historical chain of events nor does it purport to be comprehensive. Some whole chapters have been devoted to the personal ordeal of individual political leaders and churchmen; I have done this in an attempt to convey, not only the dimension of their struggle, but also through the prism of their experience, some felt understanding of a people's dilemma.

What follows has been written in the hope of helping to salvage fundamental historical truths from the welter of contradiction; it has also been written in the belief – however quixotic – that some revelation of the truth might one day contribute to political sanity.

This book's ambitions have driven it to span an immense canvas; they have, by the same token, exacted long hours of labour and research. The entire venture would have remained unrealizable but for the grants awarded to me by the Field Foundation and the Swedish International Development Authority. Their generosity fostered the book's creation without in any way touching its formulation and drift. My thanks are also due to Dr Leslie Dunbar, Judge Justine Wise Polier, Birgitta Berggren and Carin Norberg for their staunch encouragement and support; to Dr Carl Mau, Dr Elizabeth Landis, Bill Johnston, Ralston Deffenbaugh Jnr and Ronnie Selvan S.C. for their salutary criticism and helpful suggestions, and to Sue Cullinan for her documentary exploration. I would also express my deepest gratitude to those many Namibians who were prepared to take me into their confidence and impart plainspoken segments of Namibian history that had survived in their memories.

London   D. S.
June 1985

INTRODUCTION

It is all too often the comfortless lot of small nations to remain in obscurity until plucked from history's shadows by the hand of calamitous fate. Namibia, a new flashpoint in the perilous game of global strategy, has not been spared this destiny. From the beginning of the eighties the name Namibia has infiltrated our common vocabularly to take up its place of doubtful honour alongside Korea, Vietnam, Afghanistan and other names that have come to haunt this planet in the latter half of the twentieth century. This accession to notoriety has, alas, not been achieved without lavish slaughter in Namibia and neighbouring Angola. In the hope of destroying insurgent sanctuaries the South African Defence Force has strafed and invaded Angola's southern provinces, clashed with guerrillas and Angolan regulars and laid waste to towns and villages. The ferocity of attack has stimulated yet more Soviet aid to the Angolan government thus raising the spectre of super-power confrontation on the African subcontinent. Namibia has now become fashionable in debates amongst diplomats, theorists in global dominoes, military experts and political scientists, while the dimension of the bloodletting – and the promise of more to come – has excited the interest of the western press. It is only now that Namibia, in spite of a past rich in significance for this globe's history if not its survival, has entered into the focus of public awareness.

Almost a hundred years have passed since Bismarck's fateful telegram authorised the hoisting of the German flag over Angra Pequena on Namibia's Atlantic coast. The establishment of this historical bridgehead was the prelude to a century of political turbulence, revolts and their bloody repression, ventures in extermination, guerrilla warfare and war. And yet, after so much painful history, the Territory's names, Namibia and South West Africa – both are recognised by the Windhoek Post Office – remained so obscure until recently, that journalists and authors introduced their themes with prefatory glosses on the land and its people together with maps to demonstrate the country's domestic and international layout. For western readers Namibia used to conjure up indistinct images of regional turmoil and violent resistance to Apartheid. Few were aware of Namibia's wider implications and its complicity in an awesome trinity of scourges which has fascinated the twentieth century – genocide, totalitarianism and war.

There is today intriguing evidence that the entry of the German War Office into the field of conflict in Namibia ten years before the outbreak of the First World War may have been of far reaching importance in the shaping of German military and political initiatives in the decades which were to follow. In the wake of German conquest, the seizure of Herero land and cattle and the subjection of the Hereros to conditions of semi-serfdom and the *sjambok* (rhinoceros hide whip) led to the predictable reflex of revolt. Less foreseeable was the scale of reprisal for the injury to German life and property and the insult to German dignity. In a mood of omnipotence the German expeditionary force prepared its onslaught upon the Hereros whose few antiquated Victorian rifles were no match for German cannons and quick firing Maxim machine guns. After the Hereros were crushed at the battle of Waterberg in August 1904, General von Trotha, the German Chief of Staff, issued his *Vernichtungsbefehl* (extermination order). This was delivered in an aura of Gothic megalomania which decades later found its resonance in the frenzied declamations of a different *Führer*. von Trotha's edict, prefaced by the words 'I, the Great General of the German soldiers', doomed the Herero people to destruction. The order was implemented with relentless and systematic energy as the German soldiery shot and bayoneted thousands of Herero men, women and children, then clubbed them to death to 'help them die'. This first grandiose Germanic essay in twentieth century genocide was reversed by Berlin before the fulfillment of von Trotha's vision of annihilation – for economic reasons. The Hereros were needed as a labour force for the period of post-war reconstruction.

The sentiment of omnipotence lived on. In the aftermath of the revolt, the debris of the Herero people found themselves stripped of land and cattle and subject to comprehensive new regulations – structured with Teutonic thoroughness – whose grand design was the wiping out of the Herero culture and national character. The lawgivers, unwilling to exterminate the Hereros, had every intention of burying their national identity to achieve the ultimate product: a coalescence of the Hereros and other indigenous groups in a single anonymous conforming work force. What is of interest is that the all embracing authoritarian regime thus imposed upon the Hereros enjoyed the approval of most Germans, affording corroboration for Hannah Arendt's theory that the processes of colonial rule in Africa fostered the germinal beginnings of totalitarianism in our time.

If ever a museum should one day be consecrated to the memory of the United Nations Organisation (UN) the single exhibit Namibia/S.W.A. will be entitled to pride of place for nowhere has the World Body been more tried, nor its helplessness more poignantly exposed. Although the UN's predecessor, the League of Nations, awarded the Territory to South Africa in terms of a 'sacred trust' to promote the moral and material welfare of the inhabitants, the League did little to impose its authority when the South African Government introduced its own style of laws and provided the legal vaulting to the Apartheid system. The UN, since the sixties, has been dominated by Third World countries. It has become the theatre of much vehemence directed against South African policy. The UN has decreed South Africa's continued occupation to be illegal and has, in a plethora of resolutions, agitated and battled to put pressure on South Africa through trade and arms embargoes. It sees South African intransigence as a living affront to itself. Dispossessed of its very own ward, the UN's response has been one of fulmination and ineffective anger which the South Africans, armed with legal arguments, have brushed aside with impunity. It is precisely this defiance, seasoned with impunity and indifference, which is so illustrative of the paralysis at the UN, its incapacity to protect itself, as well as its tragic impotence to affect world conflict and war.

Though political science cannot claim the gift of prophecy Namibia's political record in recent times has offered Delphic glimpses of things to come in South Africa itself. Namibia in the seventies, in the forefront of the struggle against Apartheid, became South Africa's testing ground for the latest in its political strategies and military gadgetry. It was in Namibia that the South African Government set out on a course of constitutional tinkering that implied a form of power sharing with Blacks; it was in Namibia that the South African Defence Force tried out its counter insurgency techniques and military prototypes; it was in Ovamboland, in northern Namibia, that a new breed of guerrillas proved ineradicable in the face of Southern Africa's most redoubtable army. If this is South Africa's quandary in sparsely populated Namibia what are Pretoria's long term prospects in confrontation with its own Black millions?

What do South Africa's new policies signify? Does the partial dismantling of Apartheid in Namibia possibly herald a new era of South African enlightenment? For the Afrikaners and their Government there is no diaspora; to evade a southern *Götterdämmerung* they will, according to their own prime minister's cliché, need to adapt or die. Yet it was paradoxically in Namibia, the home of extremist *verkrampte* (conservative Afrikaner) racism and marching Hitler Jugend, that hotels and restaurants and White suburbs were opened to all races. By 1980 a National Assembly with a Black majority had been endowed with significant legislative power. For most Blacks who cannot afford the luxury of hotels and restaurants and affluent White property, the changes are unfulfilling palliatives. It is all very different however in the world of Afrikaner politics: there the retreat from absolute racial axioms is interpreted as a heretical betrayal of Apartheid faith. While Black Namibians, with their heritage of poverty and illiteracy may shrug off the sound and fury over seemingly incidental gestures, the bitter internecine struggles now being fought out in White ranks may provide some mirror to destiny's purposes in Southern Africa, reflecting a prevision of peace or its alternative – Kruger Square in Pretoria, shattered and smoking in the image of the Reich Chancellory's wartime ruins.

Where is the truth? Can it be rescued from the welter of confusion and manichean contradiction? Is SWAPO yet another of Moscow's marxist proxies or are its members overwhelmingly christian by committment and democratic by temperament? Is SWAPO support the function of terror or the natural legacy of conquest and discrimination? Are significant enclaves within Ovamboland under the *de facto* control of SWAPO's forces? Have Government death squads been deployed against them and are the accusations of systematic torture put out by some churchmen and SWAPO yet another exercise in the propaganda game? Who controlled the National Assembly? Had it a just claim to legitimacy or was it spawned in doubtful elections contaminated by intimidatory electoral technology? And was it South Africa or SWAPO who thwarted the efforts of the western Contact Group to achieve a peaceful settlement at the polls? Who after all fears the people?

Many of the troublesome questions which I have posed invite other questions as well as answers. The facts are often elusive, often entertwined with myth and organised falsehood. But human life survives as an unsmotherable reality; beneath the clash of arms and stridently disputing voices and the shadows of carrion seeking wings there remains a people's dilemma. While diplomats and politicians manoeuvre and fumble their way towards the *ignis fatuus* of a settlement, the statistics of death and injury – fictitious and real – mount in their thousands. It is now more than six years that the negotiations have been under way. But to what purpose? Despite the Lusaka and Nkomati accords there is no glimmer of a meaningful peace in southern Africa. In retrospect the succession of pleas, diatribes and conferences might figure as little more than a theatre of shadows doomed to repetitious sterile gestures. Perhaps. But what hope exists for Namibia's bloodless salvation beyond this vilified process of negotiation? What else will stop the beckoning holocaust?

Abbreviations

AG	Administrator General
AKTUR	Action Committee for the Maintenance of Turnhalle Principles
AMEC	African Methodist Episcopalian Church
ANC	African National Congress
BBC	British Broadcasting Corporation
BLANKSWA	White South West Africa
BOSS	Bureau of State Security
BPC	Black People's Convention
DEMKOP	Democratic Co-operative Development Party
DRC	Dutch Reformed Church
DTA	Democratic Turnhalle Alliance
DUF	Damara United Front
ELC	Evangelical Lutheran Church
ELOC	Evangelical Lutheran Ovambo-Kavango Church
GELC	German Evangelical Lutheran Church
HNP	Herstigte Nasionale Party (Reconstituted National Party)
ICJ	International Court of Justice
IG	Interessengemeinschaft
LWF	Lutheran World Federation
MPLA	Popular Movement for the Liberation of Angola
NC	National Convention
NCDP	Namibian Christian Democratic Party
NIP	National Independence Party
NNC	Namibia National Convention
NNF	Namibian National Front
NP	Nasionale Party (National Party)
NUDO	National Unity Democratic Organisation
OAU	Organisation for African Unity
OIP	Ovamboland Independent Party
OPC	Ovambo People's Congress
OPO	Ovambo People's Organisation
PLAN	People's Liberation Army of Namibia
RMS	Rhenish Mission Society
SADF	South African Defence Force

SASO	South African Students' Organisation
SWA	South West Africa
SWANU	South West Africa National Union
SWAPO	South West Africa People's Organisation
SWAPO-D	South West Africa People's Organisation – Democrats
UDI	Unilateral Declaration of Independence
UNITA	National Union for the Total Independence of Angola
UN	United Nations
UNTAG	United Nations Transitional Assistance Group
WWB	White Resistance Movement

C'est que la force at la violence sont des dieux solitaires. Ils ne donnent rien au souvenir.

– Albert Camus

1

Pax Germanica

Although a latecomer in the scramble for Africa, Germany hesitated at length before committing itself to the annexation of Namibia – then known by the geographical expression South West Africa – and the expense and burden of securing control over the indigenous tribes in the interior.

The discovery of diamonds in Griqualand West, in geological surrounds not dissimilar to those of the coastal areas around Angra Pequena,[1] undoubtedly deepened the German Reich's imperialist hankerings and contributed to the upsurge of pressures exerted upon the German Government by missionaries, settlers and powerful business interests. Then on the 24th April 1884 Bismarck's telegram declared Angra Pequena, a small bay on Namibia's Atlantic coast, subject to the protection of the Reich and sanctioned the hoisting of the German flag. The irony of this historical prelude to Germany's brand of conquest, subjugation and colonial enterprise, was that it could just as easily not have taken place.

Bismarck's declaration was the sequel to the purchase by Bremen businessman, Adolf Lüderitz, of Angra Pequena and a twenty mile broad coastal strip extending from the mouth of the Orange River to the 26th parallel.[2] This acquisition, an indispensable precondition for German expansion, was concluded in a deal with a minor Nama Chief, Joseph Fredericks of Bethanie who, bereft of title to the Namibian coastline, could with equal facility have sold off the city of Capetown. The contract of purchase, formulated in German legalese, referred to a twenty mile strip defined in terms of 'geographical miles'; neither Luderitz nor Rhenish missionary Bam, who helped put through the deal, cared to explain the difference between 'geographical miles' (7.4 kilometres) and English miles.

Lüderitz cherished the hope that the coastal strip embodied a veritable El Dorado of mineral wealth. Nothing of the sort was then found, neither diamonds nor gold nor any other deposits of precious metals, so that the German Government, weighing imperial pride against Namibia's putative poverty, was tempted for some time to surrender its interest in the territory. Neither Lüderitz nor the German Foreign Office had knowledge that under the stark windswept coastal desert lay enormous deposits of diamondifer-

1

Namibia the Violent Heritage

THE HOMELANDS

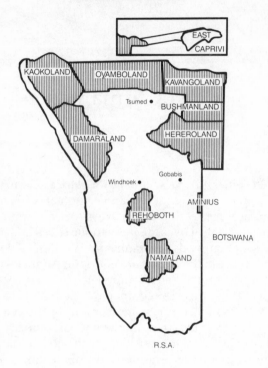

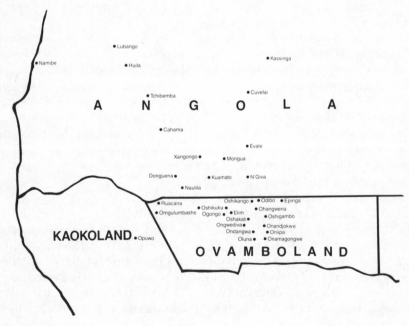

2

ous soil and that Namibia as a whole was endowed with legendary quantities of mineral wealth in the form of silver, manganese, copper, tin, lead, vanadium, uranium, zinc, wolfram and cadmium.

At the Berlin Conference convened by Bismarck in 1885 the coastline between the Orange and the Kunene Rivers – with the exception of Walvis Bay – was proclaimed a German interest. The colonial powers represented at the Conference acknowledged their collective 'sacred duty' to preserve the aboriginal races of Africa, care for their interests and cultivate their material advancement. Overnight the Territory became the *Sudwestafrikanische Schutzgebiet* (South West African Protectorate); with a stroke of a pen the Namibian population was placed under the legal tutelage and control of the German Emperor.

The penetration of German power into the interior presented more difficulties.

On the 21st October 1885 Imperial Commissioner, Dr. Heinrich Goering – father to Herman Goering who was destined to become a Nazi war leader – landed together with a secretary and a police superintendent. With the help of missionary Karl Büttner, Goering set out to procure unauthorised protection agreements from indigenous chiefs.[3] The timing of his negotiations turned out to be rather felicitous as the Hereros were embroiled in a struggle for ascendancy with the Nama tribes under the leadership of Hendrik Witbooi on their southern flank.[4] In the belief that German protection meant the deployment of some of Germany's might against his enemies, the Herero paramount chief readily entered into a treaty with Germany; in so doing he bound himself to make no concessions to foreign interests, to consent to German jurisdiction over all Europeans and to protect the life and property of German Nationals. But with the passage of time it became more than evident to the Hereros that the German presence, comprising a mere trinity of civil servants under Goering's direction, could provide little more than fictional military help. Egged on by British traders – according to the Germans with 'schnapps, promises and all sorts of lies'[5] – the Hereros repudiated Goering's treaty and at a meeting at Okahandja, the seat of Herero power, warned Goering to clear off and be well on his way to Germany 'before sunset'.

On his return to Berlin Goering appealed for the establishment of a German military presence to protect German business interests then embodied in the *German Colonial Company for South West Africa* and to realise the expansion of German power into the interior. Goering's appeal, heavily supported by the Rhenish Mission Society (RMS) and German business interests, bore fruit in the form of an expeditionary force of twenty-one German soldiers under the command of Captain Curt von Francois. Since the detachment was dependent on English ships for their transport, the soldiers went on board posing as a group of explorers. Goering now pressed for war and boldly predicted the certainty of a German victory over Hendrik Witbooi.

3

Goering's demands that Witbooi terminate his attacks on the Hereros were rebuffed with contempt. As the Germans reinforced their troop strength, Witbooi came to perceive von Francois' men as a prime danger to himself and the Hereros and in 1892, to Goering's and von Francois' disappointment, made peace with the Hereros. A year later in April 1893 von Francois, though unfortified with the remotest *casus belli*, carried out a surprise early morning attack on Witbooi's capital at Hornkranz. This debut, Germany's first military assault on the indigenous population, aimed at the 'destruction' of the Witboois, did scant honour to the German armed forces. Witbooi and his men escaped encirclement but seventy-eight women and children and some elderly men were killed. Witbooi homes were destroyed and eighty women and children were taken prisoners and transported together with the booty which, gathered and inventoried with meticulous care, was made up of household articles, horse-shoes, three violins, dentures and a pair of opera glasses.[6] Witbooi's riposte was the immediate capture of a large number of von Francois' horses. The majority of cavalrymen now found themselves without their mounts. Within a few months Witbooi, at the head of swift equestrian possés, carried out successful attacks on a German convoy and an experimental farm which the *Colonial Company* had unilaterally established in Witbooi territory. The tarnished German military image – it had been reduced to 'zero' according to von Francois' successor Major Leutwein – provoked comment in the Reichstag and furious complaints that Witbooi was the real master of the country. It was not long before von Francois was replaced by Major Leutwein who set out to consolidate German influence through a combination of political and military manoeuvres. Given the rivalry between different tribal chiefs, Leutwein's persuasive voice was not ineffective in securing contractual loyalty to the Kaiser, but when reason was ineffective the approach was blunter. As retribution for attempting to escape from German 'protection' Andries Lambert, chief of the Khaua tribe, was prosecuted on a murder charge – Lambert's followers had killed a German trader – 'tried', convicted and executed. For his next target Leutwein chose a minor chief, Simon Kooper, whom he felt would be susceptible to demonstrations of power through Prussian military parades with trumpets and the rumble of drums. During three days of negotiation, Kooper resisted Leutwein's offer of protection until the moment of confrontation with Leutwein's *Machtpolitik:*[7] a plain ultimatum to depart or face German rifles and the field gun. Kooper signed; it was only afterwards that Leutwein explained that the treaty – the document was couched in German and there were no copies – signified Kooper's acceptance of German sovereignty in perpetuity.

The decentralised structure of Herero power also enabled Leutwein to exploit tensions between Samuel Maherero, the young and inexperienced successor to the Herero paramountcy, and powerful rivals within the Herero tribe. Maherero was persuaded to allow the establishment of a garrison at Okahandja and to put his signature to a treaty defining the southern frontier of Herero territory. Though the tribe itself did not and would not have consented to any shrinking of their land the treaty would at some future time be used to strengthen Leutwein's legal and political hand.

Witbooi alone held out. Witbooi's statesman's intellect towered over his rivals; from the outset he refused protection and opposed a German influx; his intelligence divined the ominous intentions of German imperial power. When the Hereros, in the hope of securing German assistance against Witbooi, had entered into a treaty with Germany, Witbooi wrote to the paramount chief: 'Do you imagine that you will retain all the rights of your independent chieftanship after you shall have destroyed me (if you succeed)? That is your idea, but dear Captain, in the end you will have bitter remorse, you will have eternal remorse, for this surrender of your land and sovereignty to the White people.'[8] At the head of hundreds of veteran mounted marksmen who were thoroughly familiar with the domestic terrain, Witbooi represented a redoubtable enemy. He had fought a modest though successful war against a military giant; he became a legend in his own time and had inspired the solidarity and support of other Nama tribes. Leutwein's attempts to persuade Witbooi were in vain; his final ultimatum – the choice between unconditional submission and the 'destruction'[9] of the Witbooi tribe – went unheeded.

Leutwein decreed Witbooi territory to be the property of the German Government and declared Witbooi an outlaw. After reinforcements arrived, Leutwein attacked in the Naukloof mountains. Though the Germans sustained heavy casualties, their superior fire power which included the use of artillery destroyed Witbooi defences and forced a surrender. Ill-equipped to attempt the promised destruction of the Witbooi tribe, Leutwein held back from the attempted enforcement of his ultimatum. Haunted by prospects of chronic guerilla activity which might follow the dispersion of Witbooi's forces, Leutwein settled for a political solution. Witbooi's surrender was accepted; his followers, who were not disarmed, submitted to settle on Crown land under the surveillance of a German garrison near to Gibeon. This agreement later flowered into an alliance with Witbooi and a period of temporary military collaboration with the German Army.

While the Witboois survived the battle of Naukloof intact and possessed of their cattle, their Herero neighbours endured significant inroads into their land and livestock. From the commencement of von Francois' Governorship the great Herero cattle herds excited the interest of German traders and settlers (von Francois had held out the incentive of massive confiscations in his attempts to persuade the German Government to reinforce his troop strength). By 1896 thousands of Herero cattle had been confiscated by the Germans on the pretext that they had crossed agreed frontiers. (No amount of legal sophistry could persuade the Hereros that the confiscation was not cattle theft.) In one single raid thousands of beasts were seized. As the possession of cattle was basic to the Herero economy and culture the seizures

5

provoked anxiety and agitation throughout Hereroland and early in 1896 the tribes under chiefs Kahimema and Nikodemus of the Mbanderus revolted. This revolt was speedily suppressed by Leutwein with the assistance of Samuel Maherero. Nikodemus and Kahimema were court-martialled, Samuel Maherero and other headmen acting as jurors procured the defendants' execution.

Leutwein later explained his policy: 'The war with Witbooi had, at the very beginning of my colonial activity, opened my eyes to the difficulties of suppressing native risings in South West Africa. Since that time I used my best endeavour to make the native tribes serve our cause and play them off one against the other. . . . it was more difficult, but also more useful, to influence the natives to kill each other for us than to expect streams of blood and streams of money from the Old Fatherland for their suppression. . . .'[10]

The policy, aimed at the reciprocal destruction of Namibian tribes, was accompanied by the practice of taking no prisoners. Demands in the Reichstag for the extension of the Geneva Convention to colonial wars were opposed by Leutwein; colonisation, Leutwein reasoned, 'is always inhumane'; the humanitarian ethos of the Convention was, he said, incompatible with his 'humanitarian concern' for fellow Germans.[11] The extermination of prisoners was noted with uneasiness by tribal chiefs; they were also troubled by the succession of military parades and exercises. Leutwein meant these as demonstrations of power; the chiefs interpreted them as intimidatory signals and a chronic provocation. Witbooi alone protested: he did not need repeated reminders that the Emperor was more powerful.

Ravaged by the rinderpest epidemic and German encroachment the Herero community bowed – for the time being – to plunder, dispossession and to acts of ill treatment which at times embraced the murder or rape of Hereros of royal extraction. Samuel Maherero, debilitated by an attachment to alcohol, facilitated access to Herero territory by selling off land at Okahandja. A flood of German settlers, remarked Leutwein, poured into Hereroland, and behaved like a 'conquering army, even though we had conquered nothing'.[12] Traders took advantage of Herero unworldliness and put arbitrary prices on their goods. They gave credit in the knowledge that the debts could not be repaid; they compensated themselves by the seizure of cattle and entered kraals and took beasts sacred to the Herero ancestral cult.

The White settlers, convinced of their *herrenvolk* capacities, set out to establish a purely White society. While Leutwein feared the long term effects of their rapacity, he grappled with the task of restructuring the populations under his control in separated Black and White communities. This arrangement was to Leutwein, the theoretician and architect of apartheid in the *Schutzgebiet*, the just solution to racial conflict.

The settlers, imbued with racial pride, scorned their Herero and Nama workers who were vilified as indolent, uncivilized and in need of centuries of strict training. Workers on White farms were flogged for carelessness or inefficiency; a whip was usually on hand. Offences against Blacks were seldom investigated and radical amendments to the imperial German criminal code were made to legalise the flogging of 'natives'. Prior to the amendment the code provided a precise definition of criminal offences and their prescribed punishments: corporal punishment was excluded. This was modified by an imperial ordinance of 1896[13] in terms of which men and youths were judicially flogged with as many as forty strokes – sometimes delivered in two instalments. The *sjambok*, a rhinoceros hide lash, became the traditional instrument for refractory servants who were punished with twenty-five lashes or more in addition to fourteen days in chains. Hans, a Nama, was sentenced in a district court to forty lashes and two months in chains for ill-treating an animal; Jan Thomas – twenty-five lashes for 'repeated negligence'; Lukas – fifty lashes and fourteen days in chains for 'gross negligence and drunkenness'; Charlie, a Herero – twenty-five lashes for 'telling a lie'. Other sentences were twenty-five lashes for 'desertion', twenty-five lashes for 'disobedience', fifty lashes and six months hard labour for 'vagrancy' and six lashes for 'milking strange goats'.[14]

Under German law masters were authorised to punish their servants under the authority of the *Väterliche Züchtigungsrecht* – the paternal right of correction. The punishment was presumed to be moderate and no official record or notification to any judicial authority was required. Amongst the settlers in the *Schutzgebiet* this institution became the pretext for flogging and assault on men and women to the point of death. Offenders were rarely brought to court; if there were prosecutions against the settlers the outcome was usually acquittal or the imposition of nominal sentences. Leutwein feared the cumulative effect of injustices and the gathering resentment amongst Blacks; racial discrimination he observed, had become rooted in the practices of the law courts.[15] In trials against White defendants the Black witnesses were effectively disregarded. The *Deutsche Kolonialbund*, in order to confirm the practice, issued an edict which provided: '1. Every coloured person must regard a White man as a superior being. 2. In court the evidence of one White man can only be outweighed by the statements of seven coloured persons.' During the years 1894 to 1903, fifteen Blacks were prosecuted and executed – six for the death of a German soldier in 1895. In the same period there were only four prosecutions for murder by Whites on Blacks.[16] The sentences of imprisonment were: one year, two years, three months (for the murder of two Namas), and three years (for the murder of a chief's daughter). In prosecutions for murder against White farmers after the Herero revolt, evidence emerged of the practice of insensate brutality on many White farms: servants were killed when they tried to defend themselves against beatings; whips were studded with iron; young shepherd boys and girls and women in advanced stages of pregnancy were not immune; death frequently followed the extraction of 'confessions' after investigations into cattle losses. The courts themselves were impregnated – in Leutwein's language – with 'racial hatred'. White defendants, supported by the settler population, boldy justified the extremity of punishment as necessary to protect their assets. A German farmer, Schneidewind, beat a woman shepherd to death because her herd had scattered; Kisker flogged a naked pregnant woman until she collapsed; Baas shot and killed a woman who had stolen sheep. Cramer had beaten two women who miscarried; two others died from their *sjambok* injuries. For his assault on eight victims Cramer was sentenced to twenty-one months' imprisonment; an appeal judge, after declaring that Cramer's conduct recalled the blackest deeds of the epoch of slavery, reduced the sentence to four months' imprisonment and a fine. The defendants not only enjoyed the sympathy of the bench – they also had the professional and moral support of their advocates whose vocabulary extended to naming Black workers 'vermin' in need of drastic punishment. The columns of the Windhoek newspaper, the *Südwestbote*, spoke up in solidarity with the defendants. The entire German population of Windhoek appeared to be 'behind' Cramer and his co-defendants. German intellectuals added their encouragement; Dr. Karl Dove, the Director of Land Settlement at Windhoek, wrote epigrammatically: 'Leniency towards the natives is cruelty to the Whites'.[17]

Goaded by fears for their survival as a people and incensed by German punitive practices and the scandalous inequality before the courts, the Hereros decided to act, before the processes of dispossession and displacement had broken them as a people. In January 1904, Samuel Maherero, with the unanimous support of his chiefs, decided on rebellion. Maherero called upon Witbooi to join in the revolt: 'Rather let us die together and not die as a result of ill-treatment, imprisonment, or all the other ways. . . . Make haste that we may storm Windhuk – then we, shall have enough ammunition. I am furthermore not fighting alone, we are all fighting together.'[18]

The Hereros rose; but they were alone. The message never reached Witbooi; Maherero's courier, a Baster chief, in a critical act of betrayal handed it to Leutwein instead. The Nama decision to rise in rebellion took place later – after the destruction of the Hereros as a military force.

All the Herero tribes joined in the attack; wherever they were in the Territory workers left their employment to take part in the fighting. Armed settlers and German soldiers were attacked. Under orders from Maherero, women, children, Englishmen and missionaries were to be spared.[19] The casualty lists of soldiers and settlers grew as the Hereros succeeded in fighting their way towards complete repossession of their land. In Germany public indignation was inflamed by atrocity reports and strident attacks on the Hereros for their affront to German imperial majesty. The Army Chief of Staff, Graf Schlieffen, was put in command of military operations by Kaiser Wilhelm; from Berlin, thousands of miles from the battle front, Graf Schlieffen directed German military responses and ordered Leutwein to take the offensive even before the arrival of reinforcements. An unwilling Leutwein attacked; the first engagement with Herero fighting men was indecisive, the second battle, at Oviumbo, brought Leutwein forces near to disaster. An infuriated German military command, now calling for blood, procured the appointment of General von Trotha as Military Governor and Supreme Commander of the Armed Forces in the *Schutzgebiet*. In a decree styled 'Order of the All Highest' von Trotha declared a state of martial law. Leutwein's fears that military victory uncrowned by political settlement would degenerate into a wearying conflict with guerillas were dismissed. Von Trotha's solution was final and absolute: the extermination of the Herero people.

Maherero awaited the onslaught in the Waterberg mountains where he had concentrated his fighting men. But the indecisive engagements with Leutwein's troops which had so upset the German military command, had taken their toll: Herero soldiers, armed with primitive Victorian rifles, were now in dire need of ammunition. Reinforced by thousands of fresh troops, the German Army, supported by thirty artillery pieces and quick-firing Krupp and Maxim machine guns, and guided by von Moltke's principles of attack, encircled the Hereros. The unequal combat soon turned to disaster. Their military power broken, the Hereros retreated with their cattle and small livestock into the mountains of the Waterberg and the Sandveld to the north of Gobabis. The Herero chiefs, led by Samuel Maherero and a thousand followers fled through the Kalahari desert in search of safety in Botswana – then the British Protectorate at Bechuanaland. With their ammunition boxes empty, the Hereros, leaderless, defeated and exhausted, were ripe for surrender on any terms.

The fate of eighty thousand routed defenceless Herero men, women and children was sealed by von Trotha's *Vernichtungsbefehl* (extermination order): ' . . . Within German Territory every Herero, with or without arms, with or without cattle, will be shot. Herero women and children will not be allowed; they shall be driven back to their own people or else they shall be fired upon. This is my declaration to the Herero people. Signed: von Trotha the Great General of the mighty Kaiser.'

Day after day von Trotha's men pursued Herero refugees. To cut off escape into the desert the water holes were poisoned; they soon became the centres of congregations of corpses. Wherever they were, across Hereroland, in the Waterberg or in the Sandveld, throngs of Hereros were destroyed by the soldiery; detachments sent out to purge Hereroland pursued the slaughter with vigour, burnt and destroyed Herero kraals and seized cattle. Stricken groups of women and children who had in their thousands fallen behind the exodus, were killed where they were, huddled along the roadside; they were shot and bayonetted, then clubbed to death to 'help them die'. In the Sandveld the pursuers hunted out nests of starving refugees and slayed them where they were found, whether asleep, walking or burrowing for wild roots. Thousands were hanged; since rope was not available in sufficient quantities the victims were often suspended with fencing wire in a slow process of strangulation. Those who were hanged were left suspended; those who were shot or bayoneted were left in their blood. There were no burials – according to witnesses merely fields of corpses, a mass of carrion, the aftermath of an African *Götterdämmerung*. No one was taken prisoner. von Trotha's explanation: the women and children were, 'for the most part sick' so they were left to perish rather than to 'infect' the German soldiers.

von Trotha's groom, Manuel Timbu, was present during the campaign:

' . . . The soldiers shot all natives we came across. It did not matter who they were. Some were peaceful people who had not gone into rebellion; others, such as old men and women, had never left their homes; these were all shot. . . We came on two very old Herero women. They had made a small fire and were warming themselves. They had dropped back from the main body of Hereros owing to exhaustion. von Trotha and his staff were present. A German soldier dismounted, walked up to the old women and shot them both as they lay there. . . A young Herero woman came walking out of the bush. She looked tired and hungry. von Trotha asked her several questions but she did not seem inclined to give information. von Trotha then ordered that she should be taken aside and bayonetted. . . '[20]

Hendrik Campbell, Commandant of the Baster contingent that fought alongside the Germans, described a sequel to the battle at Katjura:

'. . . We discovered eight or nine sick Herero women who had been left behind. Some of them were blind. The German soldiers burnt them alive in the hut in which they were lying. The Baster soldiers intervened and tried to prevent this . . . by complaining to the German Commander. He said to me "That does not matter they might have infected us with some disease".'[21]

Those Herero soldiers who had managed to break away from the German pincers were systematically pursued. Official Army reports related with pride 'the ruthless energy of the German command in pursuing their beaten enemy'. No effort and no sacrifice was too great in the task of eliminating the last of the Hereros. They were hunted 'like a wounded beast' from water hole to water hole until death overtook them in the waterless Omaheke desert. Army reports portrayed an awesome picture of 'armies that had died of thirst. The death rattle of the dying and the shrieks of maddened people – these echoed through the solemn silence of eternity. The Judgment had now concluded its work of punishment. The Hereros have ceased to exist as an independent tribe.'[22]

After the outbreak of the Herero uprising the Namas, in an agony of uncertainty, adopted a wait and see policy. They too had lost cattle and land though on a lesser scale. After the battle of Waterberg, fears that they too had been earmarked for extermination were strengthened by reports from

Nama fighters who had fled from their German allies. German soldiers and officers, whose feelings towards Namas and Hereros were indistinguishable, had warned that 'next time' it would be the turn of the Namas. In Hereroland itself German death squads made little effort to distinguish between Hereros, Berg-Damaras and Bushmen.

Under the leadership of Hendrik Witbooi the Namas revolted in October 1904 with an initial attack against settlers in Namaland. The Namas had learnt from the Hereros' disaster at Waterberg and avoided major confrontations. Nama leaders Witbooi, Cornelius and Morenga, struck out with swift elusive commandos. The war took on a guerilla dimension with fourteen thousand German soldiers embroiled in a costly and for the German Reich humiliating two-year struggle. Peace would spell death was Witbooi's reply to von Trotha's demands for surrender. After Witbooi's death in action at the end of October the war was continued by Cornelius, Johannes Christian, Simon Kooper and Morenga, and was eventually ended by negotiation with the help of German missionaries and officers of the British Cape police.

A policy of extermination was pursued against the Namas and Hereros in the prisoner-of-war camps. Thousands of Namas, deported to Shark Island on the Atlantic coast, perished from neglect and disease.

In a country mauled by war, carnage and destruction, the rulers of the German Protectorate were faced with forbidding obstacles. The threatened liquidation of the Herero and Nama people had serious implications for the future development of industry, mining and agriculture. It was thanks to this consideration, unaffected by glimmerings of compassion, that Vice Chancellor von Bulow partly repudiated the *Vernichtungsbefehl*. Neither the Hereros nor the Witboois were to be exterminated: the Hereros were needed as workers; the Witboois were too insignificant. In the case of the Namas the Chancellor pronounced himself in favour of a genocidal solution for they were creatures without a *raison d'être* – they were 'useless as workers'.[23]

The final statistics of war: sixteen thousand Hereros survived out of a population of eighty thousand. Amongst the Namas the death toll was 10,000 in a population estimated at 20,000.[24]

The war had brought havoc in other forms: those Namas and Hereros who survived were stripped of their livestock and land. The transfiguration of a pastoral population into landless labourers was accompanied by the promulgation of new regulations whose purpose was the destruction of tribal society. These regulations, unlike the processes of extermination, were consistent with sound economics: their design was to efface the Herero's personality and culture and alienate him from the memory of collective loyalty. Cattle, central to the Herero culture, could henceforth neither be possessed nor raised. Foreshadowing the ambitions of twentieth century totalitarian regimes, the authorities set out to divest the survivors of the social and cultural fabric which had nurtured them. In the last resort the planners in Berlin and Windhoek sought to fashion from the residual human material in their possession a single anonymous malleable working class which understood the iniquity of idleness and the indissoluble link between their welfare and the well-being of their masters.

2

Sacerdotal Conquerors

The history of German missionary activity, from the earliest years of conquest, was inseparably bound up with the expansion of German imperial control into the Territory. Within the ranks of the German clerics the RMS instigated and fostered this process; it encouraged and abetted the physical and legal conquest of the interior and developed an identity of interest with the German Reich which brought it into conflict rather than a bond of Christian brotherhood with Namibia's indigenous people. Their role in later years revealed symptoms of a dramatic reversal of policy, but whether the Churches acted as accomplices in conquest or as militant challengers to the conquerors, their role, to this day, has remained intensely political.

Four years after raising the Prussian flag over their Mission at Otjimbingwe in 1864, the RMS applied to the Prussian Government for protection. When this was not forthcoming the Society began to campaign for intervention and propounded the necessity of colonial acquisition. Major German business interests were invited to develop trade and invest in the Territory and in 1873 a limited company, the Missions-Handels-AG. was floated to carry out trading operations in the 'mission field' of the RMS. (The Society received fifty per cent of the net profits.) Once the Company got going it specialised in the importation of weapons and ammunition into the Territory.

The process of establishing a colonial foothold was sedulously nurtured by the missionaries who used their best offices as interpreters, advisers and agents. We have already noted missionary Bam's complicity in the Angra Pequena 'purchase'; mission Inspector Dr. C.G. Büttner succeeded in coaxing reluctant chiefs to enter into protection treaties with Lüderitz after the purchase; in an attempt to persuade Willem Christian of the Bondelswarts tribe to accept protection, Büttner, not without some unsavoury agility, hinted at the possibility that Bismarck might declare war. Missionary Rust, on Imperial Commissioner Goering's instigation, presented Hendrik Witbooi and his father, Moses Witbooi, with a protection agreement for their signature. This so enraged the Witboois that they shut down Rust's Mission, forbade further services and started up their own independent church. It was the assurances of RMS missionaries that drew Samuel Maherero into an acceptance of German protection on the understanding that meaningful aid would be forthcoming. When it finally dawned on him that protection was an empty gesture, he barred the RMS from further religious activity. Threatened with the prospect of having to close down, many missionaries clamoured openly for war, and when war came they provided invaluable assistance to the *Schutztruppe*: they furnished useful intelligence information, prodded feuding chiefs into a military alliance with the Germans, and even ventured to offer their military opinions. Dr. Büttner pressed for a military strike against Hendrik Witbooi on the ground that Damaraland was the key to Southern African penetration which 'we should not allow to pass out of our hands'. The attack, he suggested, should be launched during Witbooi's retreat to the South after a battle with the Hereros.

Early missionary zeal lost its innocence as indigenous Blacks showed a disinclination to embrace the proffered exports of German faith and culture. The sacerdotal conquistadors had stepped ashore with fixed value systems and unbending preconceptions of their tasks. They viewed the indigenous lifestyle and economic practices with disapproval. The missionaries complained that a major tenet of the Gospel – that man should work by the sweat of his brow – was not comprehended; in reports, Blacks were characterised as indolent, hedonistic and adulterous.[2] The missionaries took in African customary practices with puritanical eyes; they objected to the institution of polygamy as a species of whoring; the simplicity of tribal life and the unwillingness of tribesmen to take up under-paid employment was presented as unashamed parasitism. The Hereros and the Namas were in short a breed that needed to be saved from themselves by godliness and an effective colonial administration. The clergy brought with them a brand of Christianity which reflected an alien and elitist form of Christian consciousness; they preached with severity and disapproval; the perspectives shaped in conformity with this vision fostered amongst the converted and unconverted a suspicion of divinely ordained alienation.[3] Together with their trading centres the missionaries established craft industries; they induced a dependence on mission enterprise and cultivated new needs in an uncomplicated pastoral population and in so-doing prepared the way for the conversion of a self reliant pastoral community into a labour force at the service of White employers. But the clerics were unable to realise their goals. Their activities met with hesitation, unwillingness and resistance to the point where exasperated missionaries began to perceive the necessity for destructive war and the associated remedies of dispossession, decomposition and the disappearance of tribal cohesion.[4] These were powerful reasons for favouring war as an unavoidable step in the direction of a *Pax Germanica* to be established on the triple foundations of faith, obedience and law.

No public outcry greeted the publication of von Trotha's extermination order; many clerics rendered willing assistance to the *Schutztruppe*. The holocaust was justified in the minds of some missionary leaders as a terrible but just punishment for the Herero attack on the divinely ordained government of the Protectorate.[5] Like prodigal sons the Hereros had covered themselves with guilt; they had betrayed the love of the Mission and had forfeited the 'right' to be addressed as 'Beloved in Jesus Christ'.[6] In the wake of the devastation the missionaries found rich pickings; in the year after the revolt there were mass conversions to Christianity amongst the Hereros and Namas. The work of spiritual colonisation was immensely facilitated in the concentration centres where thousands of Hereros and Namas lived and died in conditions of misery and total dependence. A great campaign of social assistance was unfurled by the RMS and other Churches in a competitive crusade to impregnate the victims of war with a new faith and a salvational spirit of humility.[7]

The RMS welcomed the encroachment of German settlers onto Herero and Nama land but fought for the retention of some reserves to protect their Missions from obliteration. They raised no protests against land dispossession as such, nor the award of prospecting rights to mining companies, nor the imposition of draconian labour regulations.

In 1905 the Administration under Governor Lindequist prohibited marriages between Blacks and Whites; in a later amendment all partners to mixed marriage regimes were deprived of the vote and their civic rights. The RMS voiced its opposition, though not on the ground of the law's racist assumptions. The Roman Catholic Mission on the other hand issued its own ecclesiastical prohibition against mixed marriages, even though this prohibition was nowhere authorised by divine law. In Windhoek, settler associations excluded the children of mixed marriages and Protestant Churches shut their kindergartens to children of mixed descent.[8] In the field of education the Churches diligently supported the policies of the colonial administration aimed at the inculcation of a sense of allegiance – deemed to be more effective than the *sjambok* and the Mauser. Boarding schools were proposed to provide an antiseptic atmosphere freed from the influence of African home life; it was axiomatic that scholars be taught industriousness and obedience – inseparable companions to productivity and servility.

With the advent of the South African administration in 1915 the racist axioms underlying the policy of the Churches required no adjustment. The RMS refused to train Blacks as pastors and the Churches found no obstacle to allowing their clergy to act as marriage officers under a South African legal system which prevented marriages across the racial divide.

But whatever the objective alliance between nineteenth century church leaders and the processes of conquest in Namibia might have been, many missionaries pursued their evangelical task in the spirit of pan-racial Christian brotherhood. It was this spirit which was in later years to germinate and grow and finally take possession of the RMS transfigured in the twentieth century in the form of the Evangelical Lutheran Church (ELC). It was this

Church and its Finnish Lutheran counterpart in the north, the Evangelical Lutheran Owambo-Kavango Church (ELOC) which stepped out into the twentieth century, reshaped their heritage, reinterpreted their christian duty and in so doing became redoubtable protagonists of change in Namibia.

3

The Sacred Trust

The discovery of diamonds at Lüderitz Bay in 1908 added a new dimension to economic prospects in German South West Africa. Investment and White settlement increased sharply: the White population, numbering 3,700 before the rebellion, increased to 15,000 by 1913. Agricultural development advanced to the stage of requiring heavy investment in irrigation; roads and railways were built with the expansion of mining and industrial activity. The wild atmosphere of a boom changed to a rhythm of steady production and a diamond market was established in Berlin. Exports rose from 0.4 million Marks in 1906 to 34.7 million in 1910.

The *Schutzgebiet* seemed destined to prosper and realise Luderitz's dream of inexhaustible wealth and never-ending commercial expansion.

History alas had other thoughts for the burgeoning successes of the *Schutzgebiet* and decreed that the precious fruit of decades of German enterprise and toil should fall, as it began to ripen, into the hands of Germany's enemies.

With the outbreak of the First World War the South African Government under General Louis Botha joined the Allied Powers in their conflict with Germany. In July 1915 a force of some 60,000 South African troops invaded the territory, drove the outnumbered German regular and reservist forces northwards until their surrender at Khorab on the 9th July 1915. The terms of surrender were magnanimous: the reservists were permitted to resume civilian life; a small number of German regular officers were interned; martial law was declared and the population was encouraged to resume its normal peacetime activities.[1]

After the defeat of Germany, the Union of South Africa proposed to the League of Nations that South West Africa, also referred to as the Territory, should be incorporated as a fifth province of the Union of South Africa. The proposal was rejected and on the 17th December 1920 the former German Protectorate was entrusted to South Africa as a mandated territory. South Africa's obligation was now to govern the Territory and promote to the best of her ability the moral and material welfare of the inhabitants.

Herero and Nama hopes that the outcome at the League of Nations would lead to a restoration of their land were disappointed. Although the mandate empowered the South African Government to confiscate the property of German nationals, the South African Administrator – the new Governor over the Protectorate – decreed that an attack on 'vested interests' would not be countenanced and ruled out the possibility of an expropriation of German farms.[2] But the resettlement of landless Hereros and Namas remained a vexed problem. The South Africans recommended the allocation of an extensive area on the eastern side of the Gobabis and Waterberg districts contiguous with the Bechuana border. The Hereros, now led by Hosea Kutako, were appalled by this gesture; the recommended land was none other than the Kalahari Sandveld and the Omaheke Desert in which thousands of their countrymen perished in flight from von Trotha's soldiers. Large segments of what was once Hereroland, good farmland in the hardveld, were not opened to Herero resettlement. The creation of 'black islands' was contrary to South Africa's policy of segregation, in later years more bluntly described as apartheid.[3] Under the South African administration the practice of flogging was curbed and Blacks were permitted the possession of small herds of cattle, but the new Administration failed to break with the spirit of German labour policies. Numbers of measures were introduced to cope with the labour shortage. A Vagrancy Proclamation No. 25 of 1920 exposed the homeless and jobless to imprisonment and fines under the criminal law. Magistrates were empowered to compel defendants to work for farmers at a predetermined wage; this discretionary power developed into a fruitful source of farm labour. The Masters and Servants Proclamation No. 34 of 1920 imposed criminal punishment on servants guilty of negligence, breach of duty, desertion and disobedience; the withholding of wages and unlawful dismissal were also penalised. The Native Administration Proclamation No. 11 of 1922 established the South African 'Pass Law' system: Blacks, on pain of imprisonment, were compelled to carry a form of identity document; movement in or out of the Territory and travel within the Territory was forbidden without special permits. Proclamation No. 33 of 1922 authorised the imposition of a curfew. No Blacks could enter into the streets at night-time unless armed with the written consent of their employers.

The levying of taxes contributed to pressures on Blacks to enter the labour market; money now had to be earned to meet taxation demands. This brought the Administration on to a collision course with the very wards whom it was presumed to care for in the exercise of a 'sacred trust'.[4] In the extreme south, the Bondelswart Namas, burdened by an increased dog tax – their dogs were vital for their survival as hunters – withdrew into a hilltop laager after an abortive attempt by the authorities to arrest their leader, Abraham Morris, who had returned from exile. No parleying took place. The Administrator at the head of a force of 370 mounted riflemen with machine guns attacked the laager after South African military aircraft had bombed and straffed the Bondels community inside it. One hundred men, women and children were killed. Bondels leader Jacobus Christian, indicted on a charge of engaging in active hostilities against the armed forces, was later sentenced to five years' imprisonment with hard labour.

At the League of Nations the Permanent Mandates Commission deplored the failure to negotiate with the Bondels and the unnecessary bloody retaliation against their essentially defensive manoeuvre. The Commission censured the Administration for its perspective that the Blacks were there chiefly as a labour force for the Whites.[5]

Conscious of the Mandate Commission's scrutiny the South Africans reacted to the Rehoboth Baster rebellion in 1924 with circumspection. Under the German colonial administration the Rehobothers, faithful allies at the time of the Herero and Nama uprisings, were granted a measure of independence. Under South African rule a large section of the community campaigned for complete independence; when this was refused the Basters proclaimed a Republic, defied the Administrator and made an appeal to the League of Nations. A massive show of force and a surprise encirclement of the Baster Rehoboth capital by Army, Police and Air force units provided sufficient bloodless persuasion.

Though the German Government had in 1908 entered into an official treaty with Ovambo tribal heads and, in exchange for recruiting rights, guaranteed German protection, no administrative inroads were made into Ovamboland. Situated in the tropics, Ovamboland, contiguous with Portuguese Angola, remained outside the area of police surveillance – the police zone – and Whites were not allowed access. The Ovambos were more numerous than the entire population of the police zone; armed and coherently organised, they were far too serious a military obstacle to be challenged with the limited military power that had been available to the German Governor.

The South Africans facilitated the extension of their administration over Ovamboland by the despatch of a military force against Chief Mandume shortly after the occupation of the Territory. Threatened by more attacks from Portuguese forces which had reportedly killed between 4,000 and 5,000 Blacks, Mandume swore allegiance to the South African regime. Mandume was later informed that the Portuguese had agreed to a boundary between Angola and the Territory. The new frontier ran through Mandume's territory thus isolating two thirds of its tribesmen who found themselves on the Portuguese side. Charged with violations of the boundary Mandume was ordered to appear before the Administrator in Windhoek. When Mandume did not turn up – his headmen, in terms of tribal custom, had vetoed his departure – South Africa determined on a show of force. With the assistance of the Portuguese army – their field guns were put at the disposal of the South Africans – the South Africans attacked and killed and wounded one hundred of Mandume's fighting men. Mandume himself, no more than twenty-one years old, was killed by machine gun fire.

Military aircraft were once again used in 1932 against Chief Ipumbu of the Ukuambi tribe. The ostensible motive was a claimed reluctance on the part of the Chief to submit to the authority of the South African Commissioner. This attack was supervised by the Administrator himself and was designed both as a gesture of domination and as a means of removing an intractable Chief. Ipumbu put up no resistance to the attack; he was captured and sent into exile. His replacement was more compliant.

The terms of the Mandate imposed on South Africa were couched in solemnly phrased woolly formulae. Article II of the Mandate for the Territory read: 'the Mandatory shall promote to the utmost the material and moral wellbeing and the social progress of the inhabitants of the Territory subject to the present Mandate.' A further problem which bedevilled the work of the Mandates Commission was its powerlessness on the fundamental issue of the League's authority over the Mandatory Government. The League itself had no definite power; it did not enjoy sovereign capacity, and lacked power to exact compliance on the part of a Mandatory.

The relationship between the League and South Africa deteriorated during the 1920's when it became clear that the South Africans were interested in the Territory as suitable for White settlement, to be dealt with as South Africa's own colony. During the first year of the Mandate land was allocated to two hundred White settlers; at the end of 1925 the figure had risen to 1,106 settlers. In the following year the White population was double its pre-war strength – in spite of the repatriation of 6,000 Germans. Considerable incentives and financial assistance were made available for new farmers. What was evident was the determination of Pretoria to secure the Territory for White occupation. Within the police zone 4,250 White farmers owned 600,000 large stock against 60,000 owned by Blacks. The average White farm was 37,000 acres.[6] The Mandates Commission formally deplored the absence of 'social progress' of Blacks in the Territory; the disparity in wealth troubled the Commission, as also the importation into Namibia of South Africa style pass laws and apartheid legislation.

The Commission's anxiety that Blacks ought to have been gaining some insight into the work of self-Government and administration was not appeased. A measure of self-Government was introduced in the Territory in 1925, but for Whites only. The South West Africa Constitution Act No. 42 of 1925 established a Legislative Assembly of which six members were appointyed and eighteen elected by White voters. The Assembly was endowed with limited legislative capacity: Native Affairs, Justice, Defence and other legislative fields were reserved for the South African Parliament. An Executive Committee and an Advisory Council to assist the Administrator were simultaneously brought into being. An enquiry from Lord Lugard, a member of the Commission, as to how the interests of Blacks were represented in the Legislative Assembly, elicited the explanation that a member of the Advisory Council would be selected on the grounds of his acquaintance with the reasonable wants and wishes of the 'non-White races' in the Territory. The 'native', the Commission was told, should not be pressed beyond his capacity for absorbing European political institutions; he should be allowed to develop quietly.

On the South African side, little effort was made to hurry that development. The Administrator's report of 1926 reads: 'Any attempt to force him (the native) to abandon his native customs and give him instead the aspirations and outlook on life of Europeans is to be deprecated.' A Government Commission of 1933 found that Black education was largely in the hands of foreign missionaries; it was limited to instruction in the rudiments of reading, writing and arithmetic, 'a method of education which experience has shown to be inadequate by itself to raise a primitive race to civilization'. The Administrator's report the following year was revealing: £95,000 was devoted to the education of 31,600 White scholars while £12,000 was paid for 235,000 Black scholars – representing £3.0.0. per capita expenditure for Whites and 12 pence for Blacks (These statistics did not deter the Government from maintaining that Whites and Blacks were treated alike.) Government policy for Black areas outside the police zone required the poor to pay for their own services; expressed differently this meant that the poor had to do without them. The *total* sum contributed by the Government to Owambo schooling rose to £200 in 1935. Medical services for Blacks in the north were described by the 1933 Commission as 'primitive and inadequate'. The finding of the Mandates Commission was harsher: it criticised the sluggish pace of economic and educational development, objected to an educational system which threw the responsibility on the communities themselves and accused the Administration of aiming to perpetuate the status quo.

With the dissolution of the League of Nations in April 1946 and its reincarnation as the United Nations Organisation (UN), the various mandatory powers, except for South Africa, submitted to the new UN trusteeship system. South Africa resisted on the grounds that her mandate had lapsed with the demise of the League – that was the legal justification – and on the ground that the majority of the Territory's inhabitants favoured incorporation into South Africa. In order to bolster this claim South Africa carried out a 'consultation' amongst Blacks in the Territory on two issues: did they favour incorporation with South Africa or did they prefer the trusteeship to continue under the supervision of the UN? This consultation, referred to as a 'referendum' was not addressed to individuals; pre-printed petitions which called for incorporation were distributed by Native Commissioners for favour of signature by chiefs, headmen and counsellors on behalf of their followers. No counting of heads took place and there cannot be certainty that the headmen and chiefs themselves understood the true significance of the petitions which began with the preamble 'that our people have been happy and have prospered under the rule of the Government of the Union of South Africa and that we should like that Government to continue to rule us'

21

and 'that we do not wish any *other government or people* to rule us'. Apart from the printed panegyrical comment on government rule, a Government attempt to overreach its wards may be inferred from an explanatory document addressed 'To the natives' which the Commissioners put out:

'She (Germany) began to be more and more aggressive, and for the past six years she made war, and one which was more serious than that which took place thirty years ago. Countries such as Japan, Italy and Austria stood on her side. She was terribly strong and well armed. Within a very short time she nearly conquered the whole of Europe and robbed the smaller nations of their possessions and made them slaves. As you know she was again defeated. The Nations which fought her are England, Russia, France, America, South Africa and the other Dominions. This time she suffered a serious defeat, and the troops of the Allies are still in Germany. These Nations will now take decisions over the former German and Italian Colonies.'

The 'explanation' gives the context of the Second World War but shrinks from providing a definition of the real choices; though the major powers are referred to, the supra-national quality of the UN, its autonomy and its trusteeship organisms are ignored. The document concludes:

'They will perhaps like to know now whether you yourselves the inhabitants of the Mandated Territory would like to be under the Union and retain your rights, and whether you would like to be governed by another nation or nations whose names I have named and which want now to constitute the United Nations. It is about that that you must now decide. On that I want to have your answers. Do not be in a hurry, there is a lot of time today.'

This paragraph has a regrettable capacity to mislead: the choice is between 'retaining your rights' as citizens 'under the Union' or submission to the Government of 'another nation' or the great powers. It was a vote for the preservation of the status quo or domination by some mysterious power – no one knew what sort of horrors the French or the Russians might have been tempted to import – or the great powers themselves.

The South African report on the outcome of the exercise revealed a poll of 208,850 in favour of incorporation; 33,520 voted against; 56,870 were not consulted. The UN delegates – except for the British – were suspicious. The report stated:

'If there was one question that recurred more than others it was whether any change in the administration of the Territory would remove them from under the shadow of the Crown of King George of England. Once assured that the change implied no departure from South Africa's partnership in the British Commonwealth of Nations, the Natives declared themselves fully satisfied on this point.'

This assurance was misleading in law as the South African Government had every right then and in future to withdraw from the British Commonwealth. The parliamentary opposition, the National Party destined to take office in 1948 – had already announced its firm republican intentions. The role of the chiefs in the procurement of a massive 'Yes' aggravated suspicions. The Anglican Bishop of Damaraland pointed to the dependence of the chiefs on the Administration, their ignorance of trusteeship under the UN and the fact that Blacks in the police zone – removed from the pressure of chiefs and headmen – resisted incorporation. (A similar pattern of voting responses was to emerge in subsequent elections in Ovamboland.) Hosea Kutako and the Herero Chiefs Council called for a UN supervised referendum. Kutako's attempt to send four Herero spokesmen to address the UN was thwarted by South Africa on the pretext that the Hereros did not have their own government. The Reverend Michael Scott went in their place. After making his own investigations, he petitioned the UN and produced evidence before the Trusteeship Committee against the vehement opposition of South African representatives. His evidence, evocative of the passion and felt resentment of those who implored UN intervention, brought to an end an epoch of legal wrangling and evasion and transformed the Namibia question into an issue of world concern. Whatever hopes the South Africans cherished for their 'referendum' were dashed by the Scott papers which depicted many chiefs as being under the impression that a 'yes' vote was a vote for remaining under the British Crown; one Native Commissioner had said that UN control would lead to an influx of starving Indians who would deprive Whites and Blacks of their livelihood while Nama chief David Witbooi was offered money for the preservation of ancestral graves as an incentive to co-operate.

In the face of strong UN opposition South Africa did not proceed with its incorporation plans but, with the promulgation of the South West Africa Affairs Amendment Act of 1949, provided for the Territory's Whites to be represented – out of all proportion to their numbers – by six members in the House of Assembly and four senators in the South African Parliament. In the same year South Africa decided to submit no further reports or information to the world body. It was, however, not to be left alone and on the 3rd July 1950 the International Court of Justice (ICJ) ruled that the international status of the Territory could not be unilaterally altered by South Africa; in short South Africa's obligation as mandatory power persisted.

Impugned before the International Court of Justice in July 1966 South Africa was to enjoy some respite until 1968 when the Security Council declared South Africa's continued presence in Namibia a violation of law and in terms of Resolution 264 exacted South Africa's withdrawal. Later in 1971 the International Court of Justice was to return to the issue with a finding that South Africa had breached its mandatory obligations.

South Africa's obstinate hopes that the UN would 'go away' were not destined to be fulfilled.

4

Political Awakening

From the inception of the South African Native Congress – later known as the African National Congress (ANC) – in 1912 the tide of Black resistance in South Africa swelled consistently in its assault on the bastions of White supremacy. The movement, nurtured by disparate influences, represented the evolution towards a single national consciousness amongst the diverse racial, cultural and class divisions amongst the voteless. Early radicalisation was initiated by Mahatma Gandhi. The memory of his campaigns of passive resistance was to inspire thousands to court arrest and imprisonment in the Defiance Campaign of 1952. Nationwide militancy became, during the 20's, incarnate in the Industrial and Commercial Workers' Union (ICU), a countrywide trade union which pressed demands for national liberation. A succession of strikes helped to mould a militant tradition. In 1918 sanitary workers came out on strike in Johannesburg; later in 1920 40,000 Black miners mounted a strike until it was broken by police attack. A passive resistance campaign against the Pass Laws in the same year led to the arrest of 700 demonstrators. The massive industrialisation of the second world war created a giant Black worker population and provided the mass basis of national struggles across South Africa during the 50's. The 1952 Defiance Campaign against racist laws led to the jailing of 8,000 volunteers; under the leadership of Chief Albert Luthuli, the ANC supported the campaign against the forced removal of Blacks from their freehold homes in Johannesburg's Sophiatown and against the implementation of the Bantu Education Act. In the rural areas peasants in Sekhukhuniland and Zululand attacked chiefs who collaborated with a Government attempt to impose its authority through the Bantu Authorities Act. At Zeerust violent confrontation between pass-burning women and the police erupted; in Pondoland a major peasant revolt broke out. The Pan-African Congress (PAC) a breakaway body from the ANC pursued its own course of militant demonstrations, until the entire epoch of overt resistance to apartheid rule was abruptly terminated by the shooting down of 200 demonstrators at Sharpeville in 1960 followed by the definitive suppression of the ANC and the PAC.

Political Awakening

In Namibia Blacks watched and waited in silent decades of slow maturation towards a new awakening.

The historical convulsions in South Africa could not fail to make episodic impact in Namibia. During the 1920's a branch of the ICU survived briefly in the workers compounds at Lüderitz. A Union of railway workers, the Non-European Railway Staff Association, founded in 1949, distinguished itself by its docility: it demanded no increments, confined its grievances to minor complaints and combatted absenteeism. This association likewise died out. Later in 1952 Ray Alexander of the Food and Canning Workers' Union in Capetown helped to lay the foundation for a parallel union in Lüderitz Bay. This initiative petered out after Alexander was banned and police officers appeared on the scene to question union officials. In 1952 and 1953 Ovambo Contract Workers struck for better pay. This action, confined to Lüdertiz, led to the shooting of three workers; it also fostered an awareness which was not forgotten in the general strike of 1971, of the futility of isolated strikes. One other achievement was the promulgation of the Factories Machinery and Building Work Ordinance of 1953 which limited working hours to 46 a week.

In the early 50's Namibian students studying in South Africa were exposed during the Defiance Campaign to the radical ideas percolating on student campuses.

At Fort Hare Univeristy, Jariretundu Kozonguizi participated in the activities of the ANC student branch. On his return to Namibia he, together with Mburumba Kerina and Zedekia Ngavirue, founded in 1952 the South West African Student Body;[1] this was later reconstituted as the South West Africa Progressive Association (SWAPA) with a membership open to all 'Non-Whites' in the Territory. SWAPA published the first Black newspaper in the Territory, *South West News*. SWAPA members later linked up with the Herero Chiefs Council under the leadership of Hosea Kutako; in 1954 Kozonguizi was co-opted onto the Council but later went into exile to act as spokesman at the UN alongside Michael Scott. Shortly after his departure in May 1959 the South West African National Union (SWANU) was founded by members of SWAPA and the Chiefs Council under the presidency of Uatja Kaukuetu. SWANU's purpose was the creation of a national political movement capable of leading the struggle for freedom and independence. Early dissension set in; there were disputes between the radically-minded intellectuals and the influential Chiefs Council; some students offended Kutako's secretary Clemens Kapuuo by opposing his election as Deputy Chief. In the years that followed SWANU's inauguration it proved itself unable to consummate its aims. The initiative for the establishment of a national organisation with a mass base came from a different direction.

With the outbreak of the second world war. Andimba Herman Toivo Ja Toivo, a student at the Finnish Mission Industrial School in Ovamboland,

25

left the classroom and entered into service with the Native Military Corps of the South African Defence Force (SADF). At the end of the war he emerged from the army with the rank of corporal and returned to school where he completed standard six and obtained a teacher's diploma. He then taught for one year. Then in the hope of furthering his education he travelled to South Africa where he worked as a clerk in a manganese mine, thereafter as a constable in the South African Railway Police and finally as a clerk for a furniture dealer in Salt River, Capetown. The memory of war, the internment of a large part of the German population by the South African Government during the war, Kutako's appeal to the United Nations and the accession to power of the National Party in South Africa on an apartheid platform in 1948 quickened the sense of grievance in Ja Toivo and his companions in the north, Sam Nujoma and Eliaser Tuhadeleni. In Windhoek a seminal contact with Kutako and David Witbooi – both survivors of a historical strain of resistance – heightened their political awakening and their intuitive grasp that something had to be done. To avoid the detested *odalate* – the contract work which 'chained' them – Ja Toivo, Solojmon Mifima, Emile Appollus, Maxton Joseph, Peter Mweshihange and others took up employment in Cape Town. Stimulated by a milieu of political and intellectual discussion and contact with members of the African National Congress the Liberal Party and the Communist Party, Ja Toivo and his close collaborators set out in 1957 to attack the contract labour system and founded the Ovambo People's Congress in Cape Town. Their preoccupation with the contract system was a response to a struture of bureaucratic constraints which burdened Ovambo men seeking to take up employment. Labour regulations forbade departure from Ovamboland without special permission; visitors to Windhoek or other centres were under a duty to leave on the expiry of their permits or face arrest and imprisonment; workers were not permitted to bargain for better wages, nor were they entitled to choose their place of employment; on the expiry of their contract their return to the Ovambo homeland was compulsory.[2] Workers were not permitted to change employment. Huge barrack-like compounds housing thousands of male workers served as accommodation for the period of a contract. Many who had found work in the south outside of the contract system – unless they were government employees or ex-service men who were given preferential treatment – were driven to affect a Herero identity. Gottlieb Maxuilili, a co-founder of the organisation, was a railway policeman; Nujoma, married to a Herero wife and employed as a messenger on the railways, also survived in Windhoek, however precariously. The decision, therefore, to form an organisation, conceived of as a machine to mount an attack on the *odalate*, was an adaptive response of men who were themselves trapped in a uniquely oppressive web of bureaucratic control. The then limited programme of its organisers, and its confinement to Ovambos – the only tribe significantly affected by the *odalate* – provides evidence that the OPC initiative was a reaction to an existential predicament rather than the fruit of ideological impregnation. Early in 1959 the OPC was renamed the Ovambo People's Organisation (OPO).

In December 1958, Ja Toivo, after smuggling a taped message to the UN to his friend and collaborator Mburumba Kerina, in a bogus copy of *Treasure Island* was ordered to return to Namibia by the Salt River Native Commissioner.[3] On his return to Ovamboland Ja Toivo was confined to a radius of ten miles around Ondongwa. The official choice of Ondongwa was a curious blunder: in an attempt to neutralise Ja Toivo, officials compelled him to settle at the hub of the contract labour system. There Ja Toivo started a shop which became the centre of OPO activity in the north. Ja Toivo's shop was built a short distance from the South West African Native Labour Association's (SWANLA) recruiting grounds where men gathered, and loitered, sometimes for days waiting for jobs. Political meetings were held under the trees; if the contract workers were unable to pay for their membership cards on the spot, details of OPO organisers in the compounds were passed on to them. In the police zone OPO field workers led by an indefatigable Nujoma organised workers in the factories and in the mines. The organisation grew apace.

In April 1959 Nujoma assumed leadership of OPO in Windhoek and became its full-time organiser; meetings were held in townships and in compounds and, with the help of Jacob Kuuhangua and Louis Nelengani, a network of branches was established. A successful go-slow strike in a fish cannery at Walvis Bay reinforced OPO's credibility. Field workers found unanimous support for OPO's central objective – the abolition of the *odalate*; thousands joined in Walvis Bay and, according to Vinnia Ndadi, the Secretary for the branch, an undreamt of amount of £800 was collected by way of subscriptions.[4]

During December of 1959 the first grim flash of social unrest marked the entry of Namibia's Blacks into the cockpit of Southern African turmoil. Plans for the compulsory removal of the entire population of Windhoek's Old Location to a new township named Katutura – the municipal fathers were unaware that the name signified 'we have no fixed abode' – became a rallying point for joint action by members of OPO, SWANU and the Herero Chiefs Council. For Katutura's opponents it represented an evil geometry of apartheid designed to separate Blacks into separate ethnic ghettos. A joint campaign of opposition was mounted with deputations, demonstrations and meetings. In the last meeting before calamity struck, more than four thousand attended at 'Freedom Square' to hear Nujoma, Kutako and his aide, Clemens Kapuuo. Katutura was condemned: it was intended as a concentration camp; it looked like a concentration camp; all movements in and out of the township and all residence and accommodation were to be controlled by municipal bureaucrats; the ethnic separation was an evil device to encourage inter-tribal conflict; the residents of the Old Location were too poor to pay the new rents and the transport costs.

The protests were ignored. On the 9th December the women of the Old Location defied police orders and marched to the residence of the Administrator where they demonstrated. On the same day OPO called for a retaliatory boycott of municipal services, buses and the beer hall – prime sources of municipal profit. The following day pickets were out; the call was heeded. At a meeting in the location, officials demanded an end to the boycott. A number of units from the police force intervened armed with sten guns. Three pickets were arrested. Confronted by indignant crowds the police opened fire. When the clatter of guns had died down and the smoke had cleared the unbelieving residents found that eleven amongst their number had died; there were fifty four wounded.

The police claimed that the shootings were justified. One month later a judicial commission carried out by Mr. Justice Hall, then Judge President of the Territory, exonerated the police force.

After the shooting Nujoma was ordered to return to Ovamboland. He chose exile instead; with Kutako's help Nujoma escaped across the border to Botswana and made his way to Tanzania where Julius Nyerere urged him to present his testimony to the UN as soon as possible.

On the 9th April 1960 OPO was formally dissolved and reconstituted as the South West African People's Organisation (SWAPO). From its inception OPO had attracted members of other ethnic groups; in Windhoek the conflict with the Administration had broadened the field of political combat while Kerina, writing from New York, had urged the conversion of OPO into a non-ethnic national organisation. The themes of national unity and self-reliance in the struggle for independence became the twin platforms of SWAPO campaigning in the 60's; organisers set out to channel the grievances and aspirations of Blacks in the reserves, towns and compounds, and for the first time in its history Ovamboland witnessed the phenonemon of the modern political mass meeting.

Beyond the borders the ranks of the external wing increased as more and more refugees fled the Territory. The organisation grew; offices were established in Dar es Salaam, New York, London, Helsinki, Stockholm, Dakar, Algiers, Cairo and Lusaka. Determined to steer a non-aligned course, the organisation began to receive support from the West, Scandinavian countries and the Socialist countries. Attempts to unify SWAPO and SWANU activities faltered; leadership quarrels and policy differences impeded a *rapprochement*. Kozonguizi's attack on the West and the UN while on a visit to China provoked SWAPO criticism: the speech could be interpreted as an attempt to seek an alignment with Communist countries which could only be prejudicial to the Namibian cause in the West. SWAPO's caution paid off and enabled it, by dint of industrious lobbying to exert its influence in Europe and America and at the UN; this was to culminate in official recognition by the UN and the OAU of SWAPO as the sole authentic representative of the Namibian people in 1973.

SWAPO's National Conference reviewed progress on the political and diplomatic fronts, at its meeting in Windhoek in 1961. At the UN Nujoma and Kerina had submitted petitions and applied diplomatic pressure to spur the UN into meaningful action against South Africa. But the impunity with which the South Africans had killed off demonstrators in December 1959 had brought home the sobering message of the UN's impotence; SWAPO's faith in the ability of the UN to alter the course of Namibian history began to fade. The realisation set in that nothing but the argument of counter-violence could prevail. This sombre conclusion had already been reached by the ANC in South Africa. In 1962 SWAPO's external wing initiated a military training programme and dispatched two hundred volunteers to Egypt for training. In 1963 Algeria gained independence and the OAU was founded. Both pledged their aid. In October 1964 the Caprivi National Union (CANU) merged with SWAPO thus extending SWAPO's grip to remote areas in the north. In the same year trained guerrillas infiltrated the northern stretches of Namibia to set up rural bases.

The emergence of the OAU on the international scene in 1963 led to vigorous African intervention in the UN. Two member states, Liberia and Ethiopia, charged with the task of taking justiciable action against South Africa applied for an ICJ ruling that South Africa's failure to promote 'the material and moral well-being and the social progress' of the Territory's inhabitants constituted a breach of the mandate. This failure, they submitted, was compounded by the application of apartheid and repressive measures in conflict with the spirit of the mandate. South Africa replied on a point of procedure: Liberia and Ethiopia, they argued, had no standing in law. South Africa's submission was upheld in July 1966. South Africa was jubilant but the judgment was immediately impugned by international jurists. Animosity in the General Assembly to the ICJ's finding gave birth to a resolution terminating South Africa's mandate. A Council for Namibia was established to govern the Territory from the outside and lead it to independence. On the 12th June 1968 the Territory, in terms of General Assembly Resolutions 2372 was formally baptised Namibia; in the same year the Security Council declared South Africa's continuing presence in Namibia a violation of law. Security Council Resolution 264 exacted South Africa's withdrawal; Resolution 276 called upon member states to suspend diplomatic, consular and economic ties with South Africa in so far as she acted on behalf of her former ward.

Later in 1971 the ICJ was to return to the issue with a finding that South Africa had indeed breached its mandatory obligations. But its 1966 ruling produced one serious irreversible consequence. Its decision in favour of South Africa confirmed both SWAPO's disillusionment with the international community and its nagging belief in the necessity of armed struggle.

In the same year SWAPO grasped the nettle and declared from Dar-es-Salaam: 'We have no alternative but to rise in arms to bring about our own liberation. . .'[5]

Events followed swiftly. Preparations for action had been made long in advance; guerrillas returning in 1965 and 1966 had made contact with Ja Toivo and Tuhadeleni in the north. Though at first opposed to the armed struggle, Ja Toivo agreed to give assistance. Later, on the 26th August 1966, South African security forces attacked a guerrilla base camp at Omgulumbashe in Ovamboland. One month afterwards SWAPO retaliated with a surprise attack on government buildings at Oshikongo.

The Omgulumbashe débacle led to the death of two guerrillas and the capture of twenty-seven, among them Tuhadeleni who was to become the first defendant in the trial that followed. After a round-up of SWAPO leaders throughout Namibia, Gottlieb Maxuilili, the acting President, Johnny Ja Otto, the Secretary General, Jason Mutumbulua, Secretary for Foreign Affairs, and Ja Toivo were detained under the Suppression of Communism Act. This was the first application of the Act to the Territory.

Ten SWAPO leaders including Ja Toivo and Tuhadeleni and twenty-seven guerrillas were secretly flown to Pretoria for interrogation.

The interrogators set out to establish a link between the guerrillas and SWAPO executive leaders. Ja Toivo, like his co-prisoners, was detained in solitary confinement at the Pretoria local jail. Security police officers brought him to Compol, the Security Police headquarters in Pretoria. Preliminary interrogation by some policemen was accompanied by blows to the head. When he fell he was kicked. He was taunted with, 'Where is the United Nations now?' Blindfolded and handcuffed, he was suspended by the attachment of handcuffs to hot water pipes by other interrogators for four days and nights; his toes were only just able to touch the ground. The questions were both confusing and penetrating; the questioners changed shifts, there was no time for sleep; he was shocked with electricity and threats were made to crush his genitals until he was driven to confess his complicity and more: 'confessions' to personal guilt, adultery, usury and theft – with thanks to the Colonel for 'trying your best to save me from going to jail'. When his bloated legs were eventually incapable of supporting him he was taken down. Similar techniques – and others – were used on his co-detainees. The process continued until the interrogators, armed with a formidable pile of 'confessions' called a halt to the questioning and returned the detainees to their cells where they remained, each one locked in isolation, until brought to court for trial before Judge Ludorf of the Transvaal Supreme Court. During preparations for trial a secret message to say that the police had assaulted him was smuggled from a SWAPO detainee, sixty-eight year old Gabriel Mbindi, who was being kept as a witness, to the defendants' human rights attorney Joel Carlson. Carlson launched an urgent application for an injunction to protect Mbindi, using the defendants' affidavits to prove the investigation team's system of unlawful assault. The security officers denied the accusations; an attempt was made to corroborate their denials with the reports of magistrates who had visited the detainees but a medical specialist found evidence of fresh injury – two perforations of Mbindi's eardrum – testimony more eloquent than the totality of affidavits. A day before the injunction proceedings were to be heard Mbindi was released.

The episode at Omgulumbashe was followed by a proliferation of ministerial warnings against the terrorist conspiracy on South Africa's borders. This facilitated the promulgation of the draconian Terrorism Act No. 83 of 1967 by the South African Parliament (only one representative, Helen Suzman, voted against it). The Act was made retroactive to June of 1962 and was expressly extended to the Territory as well as the Republic of South Africa.

The trial opened in the Pretoria Supreme Court on the 3rd August 1967 and proceeded in the face of demands from the General Assembly of the UN for the withdrawal of the prosecution. The Association of the Bar of the City of New York described the Terrorism Act as an offence to the basic concept of justice, due process and the rule of law, and protested against its application to Namibia. US Ambassador Goldberg spoke of the 'atrocious Terrorism Act' while Vice-President Hubert Humphrey strongly condemned the trial during his African tour.[7] The defence team led by N. Philips Q.C. objected to the jurisdiction of the court on the ground that South Africa's title to the Territory was in international law illegal. After the hearing of evidence and argument in the trial was completed, the court rejected this contention and convicted the defendants.

In an august address to the court Ja Toivo expressed the defendants' credo:

'My Lord, we find ourselves here in a foreign country, convicted under laws made by people who we have always considered as foreigners. We find ourselves tried by a judge who is not our countryman and who has not shared our background.

We are Namibians and not South Africans. We do not now and will not in the future, recognize your right to govern us, to make laws for us, in which we had no say; to treat our country as if it were your property and us as if you were our masters. We have always regarded South Africa as an intruder in our country. This is how we have always felt and this is how we feel now and it is on this basis that we have faced this trial.'

' . . . I am a loyal Namibian and I could not betray my people to their enemies. I admit that I decided to assist those who had taken up arms; I know that the struggle will be long and bitter. I also know that my people will wage that struggle whatever the cost.'

' . . . We believe that South Africa has a choice – either to live at peace with us or to subdue us by force. If you choose to crush us and impose your will on us, then you not only betray your trust but you will live in security for only so long as your power is greater than ours.'

Ja Toivo and nine co-defendants were sentenced to twenty years' imprisonment; twenty defendants were sentenced to life imprisonment; Maxuilili, Ja Otto, and Mutumbulua, convicted under the Suppression of Communism Act, were each jailed with an effective sentence of three months. Ja Toivo like his South African counterpart Nelson Mandela was henceforth confined in South Africa's maximum security political prison on Robben Island.[8]

5

The Churches Stir

In 1954 a little noticed domestic constitutional event with far-reaching implications took place without fuss or publicity in the Finnish Lutheran Churches in northern Namibia: the Finnish Mission Society granted autonomy to their congregations which were gathered together in the Evangelical Lutheran Ovambo-Kavango Church (ELOC). In 1960 Leonard Auala a shy, shambling pastor from the north, whose matter-of-fact gentleness shrouded an immense capacity for leadership, stepped into the office of Moderator; three years later he was consecrated the first Bishop of the Church.

Under pressure from the Lutheran World Federation (LWF) the United Evangelical Mission in Germany – formerly the Rhenish Mission – adopted a policy of self-determination in 1957 and established the Evangelical Lutheran Church (ELC) whose congregations embraced the central and southern areas. Pastor Gowaseb became the Moderator and Doctor Lukas de Vries, a quick-thinking voluble theologian with a politician's intuition, became head of the Church in 1972, graced with the old German title of *Präses*. (White German members remained entrenched in their separate Church, the German Evangelical Lutheran Church (GELC) which had started in 1960.)

The latent promise inherent in these silent transformations can only be understood against the immensity of numbers and the Churches' organisational coherence; by dint of their size and solidarity ELOC and ELC represented the most powerful social organisms in the Territory; by 1960 ELOC's membership was 200,000, that of ELC 100,000. It is the sheer mass of popular support in the two Lutheran Churches which provides, in the Southern African context, a unique feature of consolidation. ELOC's domain comprises the Ovambo and the Kavango masses in the north; in the south the far-flung support for ELC is to be found amongst the Damara, Nama, Herero and Baster segments of the population. The Churches, as a vast institutional common denominator, provide far-reaching immunity against the pernicious effects of ethnic division which have so often blemished the cause of liberation and democracy in Africa. The Churches, by their very existence, are a living bulwark against the fulfilment of the

33

South African thesis that the eleven 'tribes'[1] of Namibia – excluding the White 'tribe' would, left to themselves, descend into a state of squalid confrontation or live in peril of oppression under the yoke of Ovambo hegemony.

The proliferation of the Lutheran confession in Ovamboland and Kavangoland in the nineteenth century and the social milieu in which the Finnish Mission operated made for a development different from that of the RMS in the South. The Germans never 'took on' Ovamboland with its considerable population and forbidding distances so that the north of Namibia was spared the ravages of conquest, dispossession and subjugation. The Finnish missionaries were left free to spread the Gospel without complicity in the unpalatable dialectic of military violence and political deception;[2] their missions distinguished themselves by the strength of their pietism, the absence of judgmental arrogance and their unconcern with the creation of a Finland outside of Finland.[3] Under South African rule ELOC submitted to Government policies and complied with the educational demands of the Bantu Education Department.

The first timid political stirrings in the Churches took place in the 1960's, a decade of deepening ferment. But even faint protest required a rupture with a tradition of servility if not complicity with repressive official policies, more so amongst ELC leaders who were not that far removed in time from the Rhenish Mission's encouragement to the contract system and labour regulations under the German and South African regime, its acceptance of Bantu education, its connivance with the provisions of the Mixed Marriages Act, its submission to the general principles of apartheid and – as recently as 1959 – its detachment in the face of bloodshed in the Old Location.

The shock wave produced by South Africa's Odendaal plan for the uprooting of Black populations finally broke the chrysalis of ecclesiastical silence. The scheme projected the establishment of a Bantustan administration within the Black areas on the lines evolving in the Republic. The plan spelt out the drastic implications ordained by the major resettlement of population groups after the allocation of areas as ethnic 'homelands' to nine separate Black groups (the Coloureds in the Territory, persons of mixed racial descent, were not awarded a homeland). The remainder of all land in the Territory was deemed to be a 'White area'. At that stage, 100,000 Whites – no more than ten per cent of the total population – held sixty per cent of the Territory's land surface. The plan was a blueprint for an all-embracing grand design of apartheid, the separation of Whites from Blacks, the fragmentation of the Black population into non-viable economically dependent rural labour reservoirs whose lands were overcrowded, overpopulated, often waterless, often unsuitable for raising livestock and equipped only with rudimentary amenities.[4] Its main impact was directed at the Damaras, Namas and Hereros; between eighty and ninety per cent were to be affected. The ostensible constitutional purpose – later implemented by the Native Nations Act

No. 54 of 1968 – was the creation of uni-ethnic entities whose people would advance from simple tribal administrative structures to 'self-government' and eventually 'independence'. Only citizens of the homelands would enjoy citizenship rights there; this meant that Blacks would be deprived of a common Namibian citizenship; their legal status was to be degraded to that of rightless aliens. They would in reality be guest workers in the White areas. The plan in addition provided for the Territory's Legislative Assembly to be downgraded to the status of a South African provincial council.

Sharing the mood of uncertainty and fear in the Black communities, the Black Lutheran Churches formulated their analysis and critique of the plan and drew up a memorandum. Their proffered solution was not separation, but unity and collaboration amongst the inhabitants. The memorandum was at first not handed in as the Churches were led to believe that the plan would not be implemented; this belief was reversed in 1967 when the Government's intention to go ahead had become clear. A new memorandum was now formulated; it reflected the Churches' disquiet over the Odendaal plan's implications but it now went further, protested against the denial of the right of free movement and levelled accusations of interrogational brutality against the police force. These were outspoken charges, but there was no challenge; the memorandum was submitted with discretion; its contents were withheld from the Press. In the same year ELOC and ELC joined with the Anglican Church in a request to the Commandant of the South African Police in Ovamboland to put an end to the administration of electric shock on prisoners. Their representations were formal, polite and discreet. There was as yet no confrontation.

Under the leadership of American-born Bishop Bob Mize elements in the 50,000 strong Anglican Church were likewise beginning to grope towards confrontation. Though eight-five per cent of the diocese were Black, they were not welcome in the Anglican Cathedral, the mother Church of the diocese in Windhoek. It was a Church dominated at first by White congregants. Mize's predecessors had been men cast in the mould of English-style country parsons, more at home in the Officers' Mess and at Church fêtes organised by the colonial settlers than in the dusty kraals of the Black reserves. Bishop John Vincent, who preceeded Mize, held office in the style of a White patriarch; he was and felt distant from his Black flocks; Ovamboland, where most Anglican support was to be found, figured as remotely in his consciousness as it was geographically removed. He was well received amongst White Anglicans in Windhoek. He was a widely read man; he was popular in the White community and developed a reputation for being a splendid emergency speaker for Rotary and like-minded associations.

The expulsion of Bishop Robert Mize in July 1968 remains after many years, an enigma. Benign and by temperament accepting to the point of naiveté, he launched no attack on Government policies, expressed no public criticism of apartheid, remained apparently unconcerned with political developments and offered no provocation. Imbued with Christian charity and natural kindness, Mize was, if anything, inclined towards a promiscuous affection towards Whites and Blacks. He had nothing of the panache, nor the rhetorical flair, nor the intellectual concrescence which embroiled his successors in the social and political maelstrom exterior to the practices of the Church. His concern was devoted to work in the Church dimension, to congregations and members; a ubiquitious traveller, he made numerous trips to Black congregations in the north. His one frailty, in the perspective of White Namibians, was an artless love which embraced Blacks and Whites; during his travels this led him to bring along Black congregants or priests to attend services at White congregations in towns such as Walvis Bay and Otjiwarongo. As he saw it the gesture was nothing but banal conformity with ordinary standards of civilization. To his astonishment he saw White hackles rise – on clergymen and congregants alike. In this way his simple humanity presented an unconscious though perhaps far-reaching challenge to the conscience of White Christians within and exterior to his Church; he himself, not without an element of comedy, noted the passion which he aroused with incredulity and only the faintest notion as to what had gone wrong. His house was open to all comers, much to the resentment of White neighbours who feared that the presence of Blacks might depress property values.[5] The character of his ministry was one of simplicity; as a result of his initiative American priests were imported to assist in the diocese; more Blacks were ordained than ever before in the Church's history and schools were opened. Under him the Namibian diocese – called the Diocese of Damaraland – was allowed autonomy. The Synod was constituted in 1966, with which power in the Church passed to Black control. (There were schismatic mutterings amongst the Whites but they did nothing about it.) One of the immediate legacies of this constitutional mutation was the decision, after the expulsion of Mize, by a majority of Black delegates to elect Colin Winter as successor in the face of White opposition.

Dean Colin Winter was under no illusion when he preached of racial equality as a divinely commanded condition in Windhoek's Anglican Cathedral. For him theological duty and political action were inseparably intertwined. Winter's allusions to Communist and Nazi power and the dangers of 'rendering to Caesar the things that belong to God' were not lost on the White congregation; they did not enjoy the reminder that there was a higher power which was God's. They listened and they seethed; they damned his theologically motivated attacks on apartheid as up-dated blasphemy; they resented his literacy classes for Blacks in the Cathedral and the home prayers and Bible study designed to encourage meetings of Black and White Anglicans. 'Do this' Winter pleaded 'because Christians have been doing it right from the beginning to express their common brotherhood in Christ. This is an urgent thing in a land where contact between race and race seems to have broken down'.[6] They accused him of arrogance, of an indifference to their needs and sensibilities and complained futilely to Mize. Mize did not interfere: it got worse. Winter laid hands on a truck and drove Blacks from Katutura and Khomasdal to join services in the Cathedral.

Was it his failure to intervene which led to Mize's expulsion? No official reasons were given for the refusal to renew his residence permit. Was it that the Security Police believed that he had communication with SWAPO 'terrorists' in Tanzania? They accused him of complicity after he wrote a letter in an attempt to dissuade a SWAPO member from taking up arms. His vigorous pacifism would have allowed no other course. According to Mize the Security Police chose to disregard the contents of his letter and persisted in their accusation though he was never prosecuted.

Did the Security Police believe that Mize was behind Winter's campaigning? Did they espouse the hope that the expulsion of Mize would deprive Winter of his guardian Bishop, leaving the Church a free hand to dispose of Winter?

The true reasons which motivated the Administration might never be known. Whatever they were, Mize was forced to leave in July 1968 thus establishing the beginnings of a conflict in which the Anglicans missed no opportunity to discountenance an apartheid administration.

After Winter's consecration as Bishop, a different form of attack was directed against the Anglican Church. Backed by the security police and the Administration, rebel Anglican clergyman Peter Kalangula attempted to cut off Winter's authority in the north by engineering a split in the Church. Kalangula criss-crossed Ovamboland in police vehicles campaigning for an autonomous Ovambo diocese. Boasting of Government support, Kalangula made accusations that Winter had stolen Church funds from the north. Together with armed bodyguards he moved around Ovamboland – there were even reports that he was in possession of a machine gun – in an attempt to persuade priests to join his schismatic church. He was not successful. Kalangula's amalgam of reproach and nimble oratory failed to win over a single priest.[7]

Though led by White Bishops until the ordination of Bishop James Kaluma in 1977, the Anglican Church grew into a fundamentally Black peasant Church with the overwhelming mass of its support in the north. It was and continued to be a poor Church whose clergy, sharing a common experience and an endemic poverty in the villages of the north, understood the material and spiritual crises amongst their congregants. These were men of little education: few had gone beyond primary school, many were without fluency in English or Afrikaans; in spite of the dignity of their office, they lived in poverty and the cloth, supposedly black, was all too often a shade of faded dark green.

From 1966 it was these men who determined the destiny of their Church and what was to be done about Caesar.

6

From Bonhoeffer to Auala –
Spiritual and Temporal Conflict

South Africa's legal administration of the mandate had become an illegal occupation and South Africa was obligated to withdraw its Administration from the Territory – this was the ICJ's ruling handed down in an Advisory Opinion on June 21, 1971. Namibian Blacks celebrated the ruling throughout the Territory; in Katatura township dwellers danced in the streets. The churchmen saw it as an answer to their prayers. Some Whites were disappointed – most were indifferent.

It was paradoxically a Security Police initiative which led to the Black Lutheran broadside of 1971 and their intrusion onto the historical rostrum. After the publication of the World Court's decision, members of the South African Security Police visited Bishop Leonard Auala and asked for his opinion. This took place at a time when the South African Government had put forward a proposal to hold a referendum to determine whether Namibians wanted South African rule or not. (The positive results of the 1946 'referendum' were not forgotten.) The South Africans were confident that dissenting votes in the south could once again be dwarfed by the immense acceptance which Chiefs and Native Commissioners – now described as Bantu Affairs Commissioners – would be able to orchestrate in the north where more than half the population lived.

It was not long before the South Africans found themselves obliged to face new facts and revise their perception of the Bishop and his assistants who, with their well-worn image of docility, seemed ill-equipped to resist pressure in the labyrinths of power. The Government was to learn that their strands of love and conciliation were intertwined with a less manageable stubborn faith.

Characteristically Auala answered that his single opinion was of little avail and suggested that a questionnaire, distributed among Lutheran congregations in the north, would be more to the point. The officials approved, a questionnaire was composed, reproduced and circulated through the Church network. The outcome which the Police and the Administration did not predict was a tidal vote of rejection; Auala's referendum was a clear expression of popular denunciation of South Africa's presence; it was a direct clamorous contradiction of South African claims that most Blacks and Whites wanted them.[1]

The referendum had another effect: it propelled the Lutheran leaders to a new vision of their majestic responsibility with all its attendant toil and risk.

The preamble to their Open Letter was cast in language which, bearing the imprint of solemnity and concern, allowed no room for accusations of irresponsible demagogy nor Leninist subversion. Almost apologetically it explained how Church leaders had been approached by the authorities and that this had encouraged the Churches to express their opinions. Hard on the heels of their diffidence followed five categorical denunciations of Government policy:

1. The government maintains that by the race policy it implements in our country, it promotes and preserves the life and freedom of the population. But in fact the non-white population is continuously being slighted and intimidated in their daily lives. Our people are not free and by the way they are treated, they do not feel safe. In this regard, we wish to refer to Section 3 of Human Rights.
2. We cannot do otherwise than regard South West Africa, with all its racial groups, as a unit. By the Group Areas Legislation, the people are denied the right of free movement and accommodation within the borders of the country. This cannot be reconciled with Section 113 of Human Rights.
3. People are not free to express or publish their thoughts or opinions openly. Many experience humiliating espionage and intimidation which has as its goal that a public and accepted opinion must be expressed, but not one held at heart and of which they are convinced. How can sections 18 and 19 of the Human Rights be realised under such circumstances?
4. The implementation of the policy of the government makes it impossible for the political parties of the indigenous people to work together in a really responsible and democratic manner to build the future of the whole of South West Africa. We believe that it is important in this connection that the use of voting rights should also be allowed to the non-white population. (Sections 20 and 21 of the Human Rights.)
5. Through the application of Job Reservation the right to a free choice of profession is hindered and this causes low remuneration and high unemployment. There can be no doubt that the contract system breaks up a healthy life – because the prohibition of a person from living where he works, hinders the cohabitation of families. This conflicts with sections 23 and 25 of the Human Rights.

In clear language the Lutherans directed their attacks against the architecture of Government policy: they rejected apartheid and its consequence of humiliation and insecurity; they rejected the homelands policy – that most sacred of National Party cows. Each grievance, in a reproachful litany, was contrasted with the 1948 Universal Declaration of Human Rights.

The Churches' five-point attack launched them onto the stage of on-going public confrontation. They condemned South Africa for its systematic betrayal of a sacred trust. In retrospect the temerity of these men who for years had held their peace and muted their protests is grasped with difficulty; no one in Namibia expected the bland and somewhat portly Auala to challenge

Pretoria's unbending authority, a challenge which would inevitably produce national and international repercussions. The Namibian issue was for the planners of policy in Pretoria one of the most sensitive. It did not take much imagination to visualise the anger and the passion which might be provoked – and the retribution. The Church through its document had become a major and inerradicable witness in political issues where South Africa's credibility was at stake.

True courage is not without its innermost fears. In South Africa the cloth had never conferred immunity against official attack. The danger of retaliation by incensed Whites and the passionate responses of Blacks were both unpredictable. A dominee of the Dutch Reformed Church was to compare the Open Letter to the explosion of a bomb, and accuse the churchmen of incitement to violence. As a precaution against precisely this sort of eventuality, Auala and Lutheran Pastor Gowaseb put out a companion explanatory letter to their congregants recording both their faith and trepidation. The letter concluded:

'We also want to inform the members of our congregations that we are determined to inform the Government of the state of affairs and our conviction of what changes must occur. We appeal to you to maintain the peace and with a peaceful disposition to continue seeking our brothers in all racial groups. We want to advise you also to build bridges and not to break down contact. Our purpose is to stand for the truth and for a better future for our people and races, even when it involves suffering for us.'

The White press reacted with a barrage of criticism against the Open Letter. Auala was slated as naive and irresponsible. Officials were angry and the Commissioner General for the Indigenous People of South West Africa, Jannie de Wet, summoned the offending clerics. Feelings ran high amongst Windhoek Whites who were not slow to see in the Open Letter a *Doppelgänger* to SWAPO propaganda; they viewed the Letter as an incitement to violence, a bitter perception which was to find aggravating confirmation in the strike crisis six months later. They read into the Open Letter a double cause of mischief: it livened the embers of Black resentment while on the international front it became a manifesto with harsh implications for long term Government policy in Namibia. On the carpet before Jannie de Wet the Churchmen were told that they had overstepped the mark and would be responsible for the very serious consequences which might follow. This was a well used ploy in South Africa, whose officialdom would warn that the expression of grievances was *per se* in the historical circumstances of the time a criminal incitement to civil commotion and violence. In July 1971 when the hint of reprisal was strongest, Colin Winter took up the crucial but dangerous theme of violence and called on other Churches to rally to the Black Lutherans.[2]

Auala and Gowaseb were not brought before the Criminal courts nor subjected to retaliatory house arrest and banning orders. The South Africans, as we have noted, were at the time rethinking their response to the UN; it was going to be a game in which Auala's and Gowaseb's support would be as beneficent as their candour was undermining. De Wet's long term purpose was to draw Auala into a stable entente with the regime. The official mind was one of both benevolence and condescension. Whether the Administration imagined Auala to be a 'push over' or not, it did not shrink from cavalier responses. Shortly after the announcement of the World Court's decision officials of Ovambo Radio interviewed Auala; in a later broadcast Ovambo Radio – reversing the Bishop's sentiments – announced that he was not in favour of the ICJ decision. When Auala heard the broadcast in his car he almost broke the radio in anger. He afterwards telephoned the SABC, pointed out that they were in possession of a tape-recording of the interview and, with much asperity, insisted on an immediate correction.[3] Even after this outburst the official approach did not change.

After some attempt to 'soften up' Auala, Jannie de Wet proposed a joint meeting with Prime Minister Vorster. Auala went along with the suggestion.

The meeting with Vorster in Windhoek in August 1971 turned out to be more of a confrontation than a conference. Auala led the ELOC delegation; ELC was represented by Pastors Paulus, Gowaseb, Albertus Maasdorp, Eiseb and Reeh. The delegation of churchmen, as yet untried in the world of Ministries, found itself in conference with a redoubtable phalanx of Ministers and officials: flanking the Prime Minister were M.C. Botha, Minister of Bantu Administration and Development, the Administrator of South West Africa, Jannie de Wet and other high officials.

The Prime Minister listened carefully while the clergymen spoke, undeflected by Vorster's bluntness and incisive interruptions. Gowaseb spoke of the pathos of resettled populations in the homelands, their bewilderment and confusion and how the less adaptive elderly, unable to survive the forced removal, died in 'poverty and misery'.

Vorster was visibly not won over; he underscored his personal belief in separate development as a keystone in the architecture of Government policy. The Government, he said, was determined to maintain law and order – a lightly veiled warning to the churchmen. It would brook no defiance and would continue to govern the different 'nations' of the Territory in consultation with the nations of the world.

Neither the delegations nor the Churches they represented were subdued by the Prime Minister's warning. They had taken risks and had thus far got away with it. An obscure future with predictable and unknown dangers lay ahead but they were prepared to face up to it. Politically speaking the Lutherans had come to stay.

What was it which prompted the Black Lutherans to break from the meekness of the past and their tradition of submission to Governmental power?

What had happened to the Lutheran view of the two kingdoms and the God-given right of Government?

In the years which followed the second world war a process of questioning and self-examination swept the Lutheran Churches in Germany. Memories of Lutheran complicity with the Hitlerian Reich and Bonhoeffer's new vision – he died in heroic struggle against the Nazi regime – inspired a renaissance of humanist values and a gathering belief that it was the Church's duty to intervene in history on the side of the voteless and the repressed. At its General Assembly in Helsinki in 1963 the LWF took up the great issues of racial repression and discrimination and concluded that theological principle authorised and commanded resistance to racism. Later in 1967 Lutheran pastors from Namibia, including Auala, took part in a Lutheran seminar at Umpumulo in the Republic, whose theme was the struggle against apartheid; in a published memorandum the doctrine of the two kingdoms was reinterpreted and apartheid policy was denounced as a scourge of the human experience.[4]

The traditional thinking in the Namibian Churches was also affected by Black theological doctrines; Professor James Cone[5] had already written his seminal tome on Black theology: any affirmation of God must also be an affirmation of the uniqueness of every individual; since God affirmed individuality He also affirmed Blackness. This theology was a theology of liberation as well, interpreted as a passionate call to freedom, the sloughing off of a slave mentality, an inferiority complex and self-hatred. In the doctrine's perspective Christ's liberation was also to be understood as a liberation from the circumstances of external bondage.

At the Fifth Assembly of the LWF at Evian in 1970 the organisation spoke out with emotion against the 'horrendous system of apartheid and colonialism'; racism it urged remained as an 'insidious method' of accomplishing the denial of human rights.

But the question remains: what distinguished the churchmen from their brethren in the Republic? And did it require the Umpumulo manifesto to inform Black congregations in Namibia of their suffering and the need to do something about it? Undoubtedly the official backing and the doctrinal prodding from the LWF with its world-wide authority, helped the awakening. But other Churches in the Republic survived the South African reality with a similar availability of theological inspiration and overseas support. And yet it was left to the Churches in Namibia to throw down the gauntlet and speak out in tones which, in bureaucratic eyes, bordered on treason.

If there were winds of change in Southern Africa they blew with particular ferocity across Namibian plains. In 1959 Namibians had a taste of their own Sharpeville; 1966 saw the debut of SWAPO's armed struggle and in the same year the capture of Tuhadaleni and his comrades in the Ovambo bush. In the trial which followed in Pretoria a thousand miles away, Ja Toivo's speech reverberated through the courtroom to stir, not only Ja Toivo's listeners in court, but the souls of clerics throughout Namibia. Ja Toivo's speech came to them as a reminder of the living solidarity of Christian thought and liberatory aspiration amongst Namibia's Blacks. The defendants had been accused, said Ja Toivo, of a vocabularly commonly found in Communistic documents. Ja Toivo disagreed:

'But My Lord in the documents produced by the State there is another type of language. It appears even more than the former. Many documents finish up with an appeal to the Almighty to guard us in our struggle for freedom. It is the wish of the South African Government that we should be discredited in the Western World. That is why it calls our struggle a Communist plot; but this will not be believed by the world.'

Ja Toivo explained: 'I tried to do what I could to prevent my people from going into the bush. In my attempt I became unpopular . . . '

Were not the processes which compelled Ja Toivo to help his comrades not also to grapple Black Lutheran leaders to the same national cause? Was it not inevitable that the clerics, living in the villages and little towns of Namibia, would themselves be inspired and propelled by the awakened aspirations of those around them? In the north the cohesion of Ovambo society had never been broken; with a common idiom, a common fate, and a pandemic experience of poverty, they had begun to share a single vision of the tasks that lay ahead. Auala and his assistants, Pastors Dumeni and Gowaseb – they too were steeped in the knowledge and frustration of those around them; they had to speak out or face oblivion. They saw at first hand the unrewarding waste of youthfulness in the factories and mines; Auala's own sons worked as contract labourers in a system that exacted degrading anal examinations. Ja Toivo and Auala had an established friendship. Auala went, as a friend and pastor, to visit the defendants in Pretoria; he was turned back at the prison – permission could not be granted.[6] With all its backing, its hospitals, its clinics, schools, colleges and printing presses, the Lutheran Church was also a peasant Church with the strength and frailty of a peasant Church, slow to gather momentum, but once on the move an unsmotherable force. It was the interpenetration of Church and people which bestowed on Church leaders their awareness and their strength and drove them into the open to recreate the 'prophetic role' of the Church. In common with their brethren in the Anglican Church, Lutheran leaders began to understand that the crises generated by neo-colonialism and a police state presented the Churches with choices not dissimilar to those faced under German colonialism. The final decision to act was the culmination of prolonged self-questioning as to the contemporary tasks of a Christian society and whether the Church had in fact, in its cloister of silence, come to disobey its own Lord. Their imperative duty, they decided, was to break out of a silence which an obsolescent pietistic doctrine had imposed upon them. Churchmen searched into their consciences; Lutheran workers of the United Evangelical Mission publicly 'confessed' in September 1971 that they were often tempted to yield to the secular authorities to the detriment of their 'native brothers and sisters'. It was not without reason that in conversations with the Prime Minister Auala had said 'we must recognise that the Church is the conscience of the people and that equally also must be conscience of the authorities . . . ' This 'conscience' was to give the Churches their strength in the years to come amidst the numerous perils inherent in a course of public confrontation; it also enabled them both to restrain their followers and alert the Government to their diminishing capacity to do so. The Government too understood their potentiality for restraint. If in the agitated years which followed the Churches enjoyed some apparent immunity, the explanation may lie in the Government's fear that drastic official retaliation against the Church could kindle the fires of unrest.

In the Republic the Churches' condemnation of official attacks on individual freedoms was largely ignored by the Government. The same Churches, at the time, voiced their opposition to grants made to guerrilla movements in Southern Africa by the World Council of Churches but held back from opposing increased South African military expenditure and compulsory military service with the South African Defence Force. They were out of sympathy with the aims and methods of the ANC and the PAC; they were reluctant to face South Africa's institutional violence and looked forward with some doggedness to a change of heart in the White community. As late as 1975, a deputation of Canadian Anglicans, sent out to investigate the condition of the Churches in an apartheid state, reported the South African Churches to be 'deeply enmeshed in the racist complicities of Southern Africa . . . while an overriding note of White paternalism debilitated many in the Christian community. Others more sensitive and calculating are unprepared to move or to stand out for fear of alienating their fellow Whites[7] . . . ' The Churches, ensnared by White money and White politics, foreswore a theology capable of grappling with one of the gravest contemporary threats to Christianity. The Catholic Church's complicity with the Portuguese colonial government in Mozambique ravaged its credibility. Protest against the parade of authoritarian injustices would have dragged it towards confrontation, brutality, imprisonment and banishment. In the belief that the Church should safeguard itself for the tasks of preaching, baptizing, building and maintaining its membership, it opted for silence – the Church's life lingered but its God became irrelevant.

Within a few months of the Open Letter the machinery of state was turned against the Churches: work permits were refused for visiting priests and Church workers and visas were withheld. No reasons were given. In November 1971, Auala returned to the attack. After an audience with Jannie de Wet was granted, the churchmen complained of the official impediments to their work: they objected to the refusal of work permits and visas without reasons being given; they could understand the Government's offensive against Communism but asked themselves how the Churches were viewed when the Government curbed their activities with such severity.

The Lutheran delegation had other items on the agenda: one of them was the contract labour system which they referred to as forced slavery.

They did not bargain with history's obscure purposes nor could they have envisaged that their representations over the *odalate* would indirectly lead to a turning point in Namibian twentieth century history.

7

General Strike

The talks with De Wet led to a renewed stalemate. Upon their conclusion De Wet issued a public statement denying that the contract labourers were under any compulsion to engage themselves; the Ovambos, he announced, were quite happy with the contract labour system. With hindsight this utterance may be dismissed as farcical, but for the 40,000 Ovambo workers operating in the mines and factories and farms, De Wet's declaration served notice that the system would be never-ending. That notice, in the historical context, acted as a detonator in a vast socio-economic timebomb.

The advent of the 1971 strike was the moment of political metamorphosis in Namibian political development. The concatenation of succeeding events, the return home of Ovambo workers in their thousands, the new schemes which helped break the strike and the influx of police reinforcements, transferred the hitherto muted conflict into one of blunt violence, civil war and war.

Compound buildings in Namibia were sprawling and windowless with high penitentiary walls surrounded by networks of barbed wire draped over stout posts; under roofs of iron, men slept in cavernous, sombre dormitories on cement slabs for beds separated by concrete bulkheads – like cattle stalls stripped of amenities and privacy. Some months after the strike, an American jurist Judge William Booth, brought out as an observer to the trial of the alleged strike leaders, carried out an inspection of the Katutura compound. He found the buildings barrack-like in construction cut off by barricades of barbed wire, broken glass parapets and the stench of urine; conjugal living was not allowed; washing hung from lines strung across the courtyards while men washed in concrete troughs; the dormitories were grimy, the kitchen unsanitary – flies had settled on food which was served through openings in a wire fence; the mealie porridge was slapped into bowls with a shovel containing a conglomeration of 'liquified vegetables'. Meat was a 'hunk of bone' with little trace of meat – a matter of interest he observed in a country where butchers sell meat for people, meat for 'boys' and 'cats' meat.'[1]

The *Windhoek Advertiser* referred to the compound as 'little less than a filthy ghetto' and pointed to the thousands of men compacted into 'a place which is totally inadequate'.[2] The secretary for the Windhoek Chamber of Commerce condemned it for its inadequacy. For years prior to the strike the quality of life in the compound deteriorated; there were no recreation facilities; workers relaxed on cement steps. In November 1971 workers rioted during the construction of watchtowers around the buildings.[3]

Under the *odalate* the men complained that they were treated like so much cattle. At the recruiting centres workers were ordered to strip; they were examined, classified and subjected to an anal examination; a copper ring bearing each worker's contract number was clasped around his wrist. Contracts varied from twelve to eighteen months; to quit work was a criminal offence; before the strike wages varied between R5 and R15 per month[4]; some employers only paid out the full wages at the end of the contract period to ensure that workers did not 'escape'. After years of prolonged absences from home many workers found themselves estranged from their own children.[5]

On termination of contract the worker was obliged to return to Ovamboland whether he wished to carry on or not. Back in Ovamboland he had no right to renew employment with the same firm. Over 40,000 workers laboured in a system which reduced them to work units; its distinctive feature was the mask of anonymity imposed upon each hand whether in mining, industry or business. The workers came and, as they went, they were replaced. The migrant worker, caught up in impersonal relationships with new employers or managers was alone as a worker and – but for the solidarity, frustration, and violence of life in the compounds – alone as an individual. Some formed relationships with women in the south; the hitherto little known phenomenon of divorce and illegitimacy was imported into Ovamboland together with the contagion of venereal diseases. The International Commission of Jurists referred to the system as being 'akin to slavery'. Those who profited most from the system were giant US, British and South African corporations.

De Wet's statement, reinforced by a parallel declaration by the Minister of Bantu Administration and Development, confirmed workers' suspicion that the Administration would not listen to reason. Throughout the compounds of Namibia debate congealed into demands: the demand for freedom to travel, to work where they liked, to live where they liked, and to work where the pay was highest. In the compound of Walvis Bay, SWAPO students who had joined workers' ranks after dismissal from school explained newspaper articles of De Wet's speech to their fellow workers; the notion of an all-or-nothing strike spread in the compound; a meeting of thousands of workers on the town soccer field was addressed by various speakers; one of them was Thomas Komati, a boyish untried SWAPO student whose youthful charisma was soon to pluck him from obscurity. A committee was elected to represent the workers; when their demands were not met they demanded

47

repatriation to Ovamboland. The cry for reform was taken up in towns and mines throughout Namibia. In Windhoek workers contacted SWAPO leaders David Merero and Axel Johannes who encouraged strike action. They did not organise it. Their counsel was elementary – to strike on a national basis or not at all. Then on the 13th December the White population of Windhoek, until then reassured by comforting pronouncements from De Wet, was stunned by a sudden strike by 6,000 workers. Strike paralysis spread to other centres. There was panic in the White community when businesses became affected, goods piled up on the railways, building construction stopped and heaps of garbage encroached onto pavements. On December 15th the compound at Katutura was cordoned off by police carrying sten guns; a unanimous work force held out in the compound. The arrest of thirteen suspected strike leaders made no impact on the momentum of the strike. Strikes spread to Klein Aub, Oamites copper mine, the Berg Aukas lead and vanadium mines, and the Uis tin mine. By mid-January most of the larger centres and mines were in the grip of a general strike and eight mines were driven to close down temporarily.

In an attempt to put an end to the spreading industrial rot, the Administration called in headmen from Ovamboland to persuade the workers at Walvis Bay to return to work. They also appealed for Auala's help – an inexplicably maladroit move after all that had happened in the year. When the headmen tried to speak, there was pandemonium and a *charivari* of cat-calls; only Auala was allowed to speak. Over the microphone Auala explained that he too, in his way, was attempting to change the system. But they were being cheated shouted a voice from the crowd; the Whites were trying to stop the strike; all they wanted to do was arrest leaders and continue with the system. Auala listened and understood. Namibia in that moment of decision paused at destiny's threshold. Then in the presence of the Security Police he blurted out: 'Very well then, you have no choice but to strike.'[6]

Surrounded by armed police, the workers packed their belongings in the compounds and awaited the arrival of the trucks. The Administration bowed with surprising speed to the strikers' demands for repatriation; officials feared that to do otherwise might, in the strained atmosphere, lead to bloody clashes. But there was another motive – to get rid of the strikers as soon as possible and replace them with new recruits. If this could be accomplished, the strikers' own tactics would transform their spectacular initiative into defeat.

But the Administration had not reckoned with the strikers' mood and strategy. Prior to taking action, letters had gone back and forth between the different compounds and Ovamboland. When the first call went out the strikers knew that their brethren stood behind them.[7] The solidarity proved durable. No scabs were forthcoming from Ovamboland. The Administration's hasty efforts to draw replacements from elsewhere in Namibia and neighbouring states succeeded in the recruitment of a 1,000 workers. In Walvis Bay workers imported from South Africa drifted away from their jobs; the work was too exacting while many were put off when they came to understand their strike-breaking role. Officials blamed 'agitators' for the impasse but no agitators were found and, as we shall see, no leaders were uncovered amongst those who had been arrested. Confiscated letters produced in court proved no web of conspiracy: they reflected instead a wistful longing for fair play and the readiness on the part of anonymous labour units to make sacrifices.

The letters reflect no ideological influences. On the contrary: 'The Bible says that Christ died to free all men, but I am not free under contract . . . ' and ' . . . some are cowards. I was in Ongwediva. Do you want to go to the Kingdom of God? Don't be afraid. There are many hands.'

At a mass meeting at Oluno in the north Johannes Nangutuuala, a passionate democrat, was elected chairman of a 'Contract Committee'. The committee put out a manifesto which pin-pointed their grievances. Officials made oblique promises of a new deal but neither M.C. Botha nor the directors of SWANLA nor the homelands government were prepared to negotiate with the workers' committee. After a meeting between Ovambo Ministers and Government officials sweeping reforms were announced: recruitment would not longer be carried out by SWANLA; labour employment offices would be organised henceforth by the Ovambo Government, workers would know beforehand the amount of their wages and fringe benefits and they would be permitted to maintain contact with their families. Johannes Nangutuuala was persuaded to go on Radio Ovambo to put his seal of approval on the new scheme. But when workers turned up for jobs, they discovered that, but for two incidental changes, and the substitution of the Ovambo Government for SWANLA, nothing had changed.

The Government's ambitions for the newly formed Ovambo Government were painfully undermined by the role which the Ovambo executive was driven to enact in the execution of the supposed new deal. The disappearance of SWANLA merely led to the recrudescence of the contract system with faintly disguising touches. Where SWANLA had operated the Ovambo Government stepped in; no changes of any significance were introduced; the resounding phrases and promises that the worker would be allowed to maintain contact with his family became, in the eyes of the workers, proven falsehoods;[8] the entire change, celebrated as an historic breakthrough, was interpreted as nothing more than a gigantic fraud designed to break strike solidarity. Those Ovambo Ministers who claimed to represent and protect the workers, were seen to be active accomplices in deception, worse still they discredited themselves by stepping into SWANLA's role with no other purpose than to preserve the *odalate*. Infuriated workers broke down the Angolan border fence and held meetings. In an atmosphere of crisis the Ovambo Government called for police and troop reinforcements. In Oshakati De Wet focused attention on the fact that the entry of police and troops reinforcements had been requested by the Ovambo Legislative Council. What had started as a non-violent strike led to the transfiguration of Ovamboland into an occupied zone. Large reinforcements of police were drafted to the Territory in convoys together with units of the SADF. With patrols of troops and police, road blocks and searches across Ovamboland, the stage was set for a qualitative change in the character of confrontation. This was the beginning of Ovamboland in the 70's with its army camps, fearsome high axled anti-landmine armour, its troop carriers, airstrips, fighter bombers, prisons and its daily toll of fatalities where Ovambo resistance and SWAPO insurgency converged.

The Ovambo people were not to forget the Ovambo Government's call for police reinforcements, troops, and the warlike paraphernalia they brought with them. From 1972 onwards the Ovambo Government, rightly or wrongly, was deemed in Ovamboland to be an accomplice of the security forces.

The pent up anger now turned against the Ovambo Government and collaborating chiefs. Groups of workers attacked the kraal of Philipus Kaluvi, a headman directly concerned with the contract system and burnt down his general dealer's shop; the homes of other chiefs and headmen were damaged or destroyed and official buidings were burnt down; headman Samuel Kaulinge was assaulted and seriously injured – his wife was killed after she intervened. Defence force units and policemen patrolled Ovamboland to put an end to meetings and to protect the border fence. The Government conceded that a serious state of tension prevailed and put out assurances that everything was under control. In several areas soldiers and police clashed with workers. By the end of January six men had been shot and killed by soldiers according to official news hand-outs. Reports from churchmen and SWAPO leaders suggested a much higher mortality rate. Three policemen were injured at Etomba and another three at Oshakati.

On the 4th February 1972 Proclamation R17 introduced emergency regulations, akin to martial law in their stringency. Political meetings were effectively prohibited[9]; it became an offence to undermine the authority of the State, the Ovambo Government, or any chief or headman; individuals could be arrested without a warrant and detained for questioning; detention was incommunicado with no right of access to legal advisers. Failure to obey the lawful order of a chief or headman was punishable; it also became a criminal offence to treat them with disrespect or boycott any meeting called by them.

The regulations were implemented with alacrity; throughout Ovamboland police sprang into action. Corrugated metal cubes, described by churchmen as 'cages', were erected at various centres; numbers of detainees were crowded into the enclosures; there was often standing room only and a single bucket for toilet requirements. At check points men and women, ordered to dismount from vehicles, were questioned at gunpoint. Clergymen were treated no differently. In Oshakati there were reports of interrogation, beatings and electric shock administration. Lutheran and Anglican priests heard the screams of detainees at Oshikongo. On the 27th January a news black-out was imposed in the north; unauthorised persons were not permitted to enter and officials were prevented from issuing statements to the press. U.S. observer Judge Booth requested permission to enter Ovamboland. This was turned down so he made his own investigations. The witnesses that he had examined, he said, 'saw soldiers and police shooting down people, loading them on trucks and hauling them away. They saw people who were under arrest packed in trucks since the jails are too full. They saw and heard groans, yells and other evidence of torture at jails in Oshikongo, Ondongua and Oshakati.'[10]

After the arrest of Anglican priest Olavi Nailenge, Colin Winter set off for Ovamboland. (He was unable to see Nailenge who was detained incommunicado for a hundred and thirty-seven days; after his release Nailenge claimed he had been shocked with electricity under interrogation.) Then on the 30th January a group of Anglicans returning from service at Epinga fled from an armed police patrol after a youth had been shot down; the police opened fire. Four were killed and two were seriously injured. Winter broke the Ovambo silence by releasing a report on the Epinga slayings to the world press. Winter spoke of an all-pervasive fear in Ovamboland: no one felt safe; trivial infringements gave rise to arrests and shootings. The day after the Epinga shooting, Winter's permit to enter Ovamboland was withdrawn on instructions from Pretoria.[11]

On the 25th January 1972, thirteen prisoners, each one of them numbered, appeared before the magistrate of Windhoek on charges, brought under the Master and Servants Legislation, of having incited workers to strike. Winter attended court, met the strikers, and tried to arrange their defence. Winter had no benign eye for the judges and many of the advocates in Windhoek. He judged them to be partisans of the regime and hostile to his Church.[12] His search for a sympathetic advocate – the man had to be a 'fighter' – led him to Bryan O'Linn of the Windhoek Bar. Winter and the thirteen defendants were encouraged by O'Linn's first sour appraisal that the prosecution should never have been brought in the first place: 'It just won't stand up in open court'. When the trial opened, O'Linn appeared for the defence while Winter watched with two overseas observers, Judge William Booth of the New York Supreme Court and Alex Lyon a British Member of Parliament. In the press there were accusations and innuendos of an Anglican Church conspiracy to discredit South Africa; journalists who unashamedly cleared their stories with the security police highlighted the role of the Church in playing host to Lyon and Booth; the discovery of a 'Church document' – the press never identified it – in the possession of one of the defendants was seized upon to interlard reports with hints of Anglican complicity in the strike.[13]

Apart from the evidence of an informer, the State produced no meaningful proof of incitement or intimidation. The prosecution evidence was either

indifferent or it was broken down; the defendants were confident. One of them was asked 'Who told you to strike?'. The defendant paused triumphantly and replied 'God did'. O'Linn did not hesitate to take the offensive. A gasp went up in the court room when O'Linn's cross examination extracted from the paymaster of Pupkewitz Stores details of their employees' salary: R 1.54 was paid per six-day working week. In this one line of evidence lay the heart of the matter. The tragedy was that the wages of Pupkewitz Stores were not unusual. [14]

To accusations of being an agitator Winter replied: 'From the Government's point of view, I should confine myself to what it calls 'preaching the Gospel'. From my point of view, I cannot confine myself to a Gospel which excludes the widows and the oppressed, together with the despised and downtrodden.' [15] But Winter's spirited public defence and its postulates brought about a rift amongst White church-goers who felt notoriety and priestly dignity to be incompatible. In Windhoek's White community there were whispers of 'Communist'; threatening telephone calls started up; callers promised violence – the less venturesome breathed heavily. The successful defence of the strike leaders who were subsequently ordered to pay nominal fines did not help.

Winter lasted till the end of February 1972. On the eve of UN Secretary General Waldheim's visit to South Africa, the Administration issued a deportation order in terms of the Undesirables Removal Proclamation No. 50 of 1920 which provides for the deportation of individuals if the Administrator 'is satisfied that any person within the Territory is dangerous to the peace, order or good government of the Territory . . . '. Winter rushed to the Supreme Court for an urgent injunction staying the Administrator's Order on the ground that he had used his statutory powers unlawfully and with an improper purpose.

The application was dismissed. As a parting shot Winter flew to Capetown to present UN Secretary General Waldheim with a memorandum. Winter was expelled together with his dedicated diocesan treasurer David de Beer and the Rev. Stephen Hayes. But the expulsions did not eradicate Anglican opposition, nor was Winter stifled. After he left, the Church determined that he should continue as Bishop in Exile. From overseas the sounds of Winter's voice continued to trouble the South Africans. The banishment, far from silencing the Church, only served to strengthen its vociferous dissent.

It was to Richard Wood that the Anglican Synod in its wisdom decided to allot the office of Suffragen Bishop, also known as the 'hot seat'.

8

The UN – Illusion and Reality

The ICJ's Advisory Opinion of 1971 was reaffirmed by Security Council Resolution 301 (1971): South Africa was under an obligation to withdraw its administration; its continued presence in the Territory was an 'internationally wrongful act, for which it remained accountable to the international community'. South Africa's persistent refusal to withdraw could, in the view of the Security Council, create conditions 'detrimental to the maintenance of peace and security in the region'.

The ICJ's decision and the Security Council's endorsement brought relief and a renewal of hope that South Africa's withdrawal was merely a matter of time. In Windhoek, David Meroro, SWAPO's National Chairman, declared however that Namibia's freedom was dependent on the struggle for national liberation in the Territory itself, irrespective of the international community's plans. Meroro's views were broadly shared by the Herero Chiefs Council, SWANU, Clemens Kapuuo and his supporters in the National Unity Democratic Organisation (NUDO), the Damara Tribal Executive led by Justus Garoeb and other groups. At a meeting in Rehoboth in November 1971 representatives of these organisations formed the National Convention (NC), an alliance under the chairmanship of J.S.A. Diergaardt. They opposed apartheid without qualification as also the fragmentation of Namibia into different ethnic homelands, and looked forward to the replacement of the Administration by the UN as an indispensable step in the direction of democratic elections leading to independence in a unitary state.

South Africa's response to the ICJ's ruling was one of sovereign indifference. Prime Minister Vorster dismissed the decision, charged the court with hypocrisy, double standards and the betrayal of its own logic.

At its meeting in Addis Ababa in February 1972 the Security Council appraised its own impotence. In a review of the strike it criticised South Africa's 'brutal repression' and the intervention of a 'sham settlement'; the contract labour system, it resolved, was in conflict with the Universal Declaration of Human Rights. The Council called on South Africa to abolish the system immediately.

In an attempt to break away from a pattern of unfruitful verbal salvos the

Security Council directed Secretary General Waldheim, 'to initiate as soon as possible contacts with all parties concerned with a view to establish the necessary conditions so as to enable the people of Namibia, freely and with strict regard to the principles of human equality, to exercise their right to self-determination and independence . . . '. Vorster followed up this move by inviting Waldheim to visit South Africa. Later in March 1972, Waldheim flew to South Africa and so brought to an end years of acrimonious exchanges on the legality of South Africa's title to the Territory. In a meeting with Waldheim, Vorster declared South African policy to be one of self-determination and independence for the *peoples* of Namibia. Waldheim stressed the need for independence in terms of national unity and territorial integrity; in so far as the South African proposal foreshadowed fragmented legally independent but factually ensnared ethnic states, no agreement was possible. Towards the end of Waldheim's stay Vorster forwarded a memorandum which, in ambiguous language, avoided reference to the word 'peoples'. Shortly before his departure Waldheim, somewhat over-optimistically, characterised his visit as a 'break through'.[1]

Waldheim's visit was followed by that of his representative Dr. A. Escher, who together with a multi-racial staff began a further round of negotiations in October. After three weeks in Namibia, Escher reported that the majority in the Territory favoured the creation of a united independent state.[2] Vorster resisted his invitation to enter into discussion on South African plans for 'self-determination' and 'independence'. This debate, Vorster suggested, could usefully remain in abeyance until the inhabitants had more administrative and political experience. The art of self-government, Vorster urged, could best be achieved on a regional basis.

At the most, the negotiations revealed an ambiguous suggestion that the South Africans did not exclude the possibility of constitutional developments other than those based on the homelands formula and that it was their belief that the exercise of self-determination could appropriately be attempted after the elapse of one decade of preparation. Other heartening concessions were foreshadowed – freedom to carry on legitimate political activities, freedom of speech and freedom to hold meetings. The negotiations produced one other conciliatory gesture from Vorster: his willingness to establish an Advisory Council made up of representatives from various regions and ethnic groups in Namibia. Rightly or wrongly Escher interpreted this gesture as evidencing a willingness to deal with the Territory as a whole.

After Escher's departure Vorster held an 'off the record' discussion with newspaper editors in Pretoria. In his mind South Africa had triumphed in the negotiations; the demand for a unitary constitution had been abandoned; as for 'one man one vote' – that, he said, was 'dead'.[3]

Vorster was wrong. Neither Waldheim nor Escher intended such concessions but his comment – a matter of interest for later development – highlighted South Africa's preoccupation with electoral mechanisms.

On his return from the Territory Escher expressed enthusiasm for further contact with South Africa. The African States did not approve and branded Vorster's response as a delaying tactic to which Escher had been a party. Escher disappeared from the scene.

In May 1973 South Africa formally signified its intentions to allow freedom of speech, political activities and meetings, provided public security was not disturbed; to allow greater freedom of movement, and to take such measures in cooperation with the Secretary General as would ensure the attainment of self-determination and independence.[4] It was not envisaged, read the declaration, that any individual population group would become independent as a separate entity.

The physical intrusion of the UN into Namibia, through its representatives Waldheim and Escher, aroused hopes and passion and the confident expectation that sooner or later Blacks would be led to independence by the UN. Expectations were jarred when, in the welter of assurances and conciliatory gestures, the South Africans brought the Development of Self-Government for Native Nations in South West Africa Amendment Bill before Parliament in February 1973. In language uncontaminated by arch circumlocution that Bill and its introductory White Paper defined the purpose of the legislation: to empower the State President to proclaim any segment of Namibia set aside for an ethnic group to be a 'self-governing area'. The White Paper affirmed the Government's irrevocable intention to lead 'individual nations' in South West Africa and the eastern Caprivi to self-government and independence. Hard on the heels of the Bill came the announcement that Ovamboland was to become self-governing and that elections for a Legislative Assembly would be held in August of 1973.

SWAPO and its Youth Wing the SWAPO Youth League (SYL) mounted a boycott campaign in Ovamboland and in the south. Clemens Kapuuo, SWAPO Chairman David Meroro, and other orators, under the banner of the National Convention, addressed meetings at Katutura with calls for an immediate end to the development of Bantustans. The first meeting of the Prime Minister's Advisory Council in March 1972 was the subject of mordant criticism in Katutura. The Advisory Council was caricatured as a collection of 'stooges'. Most of the representatives, collaborators in tribal government bodies, were described as illiterate, foolish or corrupted nonentities who represented no one. The whole exercise, said the speakers, was a retrograde step: the South Africans, they pointed out, were prepared to establish a multi-racial council only because it suited their divisive policies. The crowds at Katutura applauded but when Dr. Romanus Kampuga, a Kavango Legislative Councillor, attempted to sing the praises of the Advisory Council in the Ovambo compound, upset workers went on the rampage and set administrative offices on fire.[5]

On the 30th April, the day before the grant of self-government to Ovamboland, SWAPO Regional Chairman John Ja Otto, Johannes Nangutuuala and others made representations to Chief Philemon Elifas, the head of the Ovambo Government; after an address to a meeting of thousands of supporters they were arrested and detained under proclamation R17.

In the run up to the August elections, the Ovambo Legislative Council ruled that only approved parties could participate in the elections. Meetings by SWAPO and Johannes Nangutuuala's organisation DEMCOP (Democratic Co-operative Party) had become automatically disbarred in terms of Proclamation R17. One party alone was permitted to contest the elections: the Ovamboland Independence Party (OIP) largely composed of semi-educated traditionalists and government supporters. The members of the OIP controlled the Legislative Assembly which issued the decree in the first place. Tribal policemen, armed, undisciplined and poorly trained, intervened to prevent SWAPO meetings. In May six SYL leaders were arrested including Thomas Komati and Ezekiel Maxiulili, son of Gottlieb Maxiulili. Tear gas was thrown at a demonstration of over 3,000 men and women gathered outside the Ondongua magistrate's court where John Ja Otto and his co-defendants were being tried for holding an illegal meeting. The police moved in with batons; twenty-six were arrested and numbers of spectators were injured.[6] Students at the Ongwediva Training College were given corporal punishment for having attended the demonstration.

With the approach of the elections, units of the South African police and tribal police carried out scores of arrests. In July a new tactic was evolved: tribal policemen armed with *epokolo* sticks, derived from the central rib of the makalani palm branch, forcibly dispersed Youth League protest meetings. The Ovambo cabinet requested additional police assistance to stamp out unauthorised meetings. In the Ongandjero district Chief Makundi, the Minister of Justice in Ovamboland, confronted SWAPO speakers with a revolver while tribal policemen attacked and clubbed Youth League leaders and supporters and smashed their loudspeaker in the presence of South African policemen. After Youth League threats to call a general strike, no intervention took place at their next meeting at Engela but nine leaders were later arrested. A blackout of news was imposed and only specially authorised representatives of the South African Press Association were allowed in. In the hope of restraining the police from major confrontation Bishop Auala publicly warned of unrest. Young SWAPO leaders, he said, were holding meetings because the whole world had been told that there was an election, when in fact there was no possibility of a real election.

At the election in August, the Ovamboland Independence Party won eighteen of the twenty-one elected member seats in the Legislative Assembly. Despite Ovambo Radio's unqualified support for the OIP, three independent candidates succeeded in winning seats.

Given the one-party quality of the election the official results were unimportant; but one fact of overriding importance to Government planning pained the official mind – the percentage poll of only 2.5 for the entire election.

Unless drastic action could, at some time in the future, reverse the voting trend, the Government's grandiose strategy for the creation of Bantustans was in jeopardy. Since the Ovambos constituted almost half the population of Namibia, it was fundamental that their projected homeland government should be graced with legitimacy. In practical terms effective measures had to be formulated before the next round of elections.

It was against this background that the Administration carried out a post-mortem of the Ovambo election and prepared their blueprint for the next one.

9

Vengeance at Oniipa

In the rectangle of 16,220 square miles of land making up Ovamboland, police and military activities were concentrated in the areas around Ondongua and Oshakati. With their headquarters and printing presses at nearby Oniipa and their hospital complex at Onandjokwe the Lutherans were strategically placed to monitor police and army activity. With the arrest and detention of hundreds of detainees in 1972 and 1973 numerous complaints of brutality on the part of the security forces were passed onto Auala.

Conscious of their earlier failure to persuade Vorster to appoint a judicial commission of enquiry, Auala and his assistant Kleophas Dumeni now drew up lists of complainants and recorded their allegations and injuries.

On the 30th April 1973, Auala and De Vries led a delegation of clergymen to a conference with Vorster and Jannie de Wet. Their complaints were not new: they objected to official impediments to the movement and residence of church workers; they complained of the unexplained refusal of residence permits and visas to visiting clergymen; they put their anxious views of the ill effects of apartheid, the corrosion of family life caused by the pass laws and the migratory labour system and once again complained of brutality by policemen and soldiers. But this time they broke from generalities: a list of thirty-seven complainants and their specific allegations against the security forces – soldiers and policemen – was handed to the Prime Minister. The accusations were now strengthened by the authority of the clergymen themselves; Auala and his collaborators had personally investigated many of the allegations and had noted the symptoms of injury. A number of priests, Auala added, had themselves heard the screams of detainees in police stations and detectives' offices.

The Prime Minister's response was courteous; he took note of the deputation's request for a judicial commission and promised that the complaints would be investigated.

No judicial commission of inquiry was established. Five months after the interview the Lutherans received an official communication from the Prime Minister's office: investigations into all the allegations had led to the finding that they were without substance. The churchmen were astonished. Both they and the complainants had not been contacted during the intervening five months, neither by the police, nor the army, nor any government official. It was to them inconceivable that a bona fide inquiry could have taken place without some consultation if not cross-examination of witnesses and complainants. The Bishops were not to be fobbed off by a letter drafted, it seemed, in contempt for their intelligence. Their reply spurned the 'investigation'. They themselves, they wrote, were unaware of any commission's investigation and had therefore to assume that the inquiry must have been made by the security forces – the same people who, as far as they were concerned, had been responsible for the brutality in question.

Once again the Bishops had confronted Pretoria; they impugned the security forces on a most sensitive issue: they had made their points with force and had got away with it, or so it seemed. Far from being imprisoned, banned or prosecuted – all of which had seemed eminently feasible – they had been received with dignity by the Prime Minister himself.

Nine days after the meeting with Vorster, ELOC's printing press at Oniipa was singled out for attack in the Ovambo parliament where the Minister of Education referred to the 'evil things' that emerged from Oniipa.

The illusory colour of immunity came to an end on the morning of the 12th May 1973 when a bomb, fashioned and implanted with professional dexterity, annihilated ELOC's printing works at Oniipa. The damage to the works which had turned out printed Bibles, religious literature and a Church monthly *Omukwetu*, was estimated at R600,000.[1] Such was the calibre of the device that the explosion was heard in a radius of forty kilometres. Police officers were awakened in their quarters seven kilometres away. Church bells rang out their alarms and hundreds gathered to fight the flames. Amidst the charred remains of prayer books and ruined machinery, milling crowds lamented the calamity. When the police arrived three hours later and began to disperse the crowds, Auala intervened. People, he said, should not be hounded away from a 'funeral'.[2]

The bombers were mistaken if their intention was to cut down ELOC's strength. Supporters were not frightened away; their hurt and the Churches' injury became consubstantial; the consequence of the destruction was contrariwise to promote anger rather than fear. An instantaneous popular belief sprang up that it was police handiwork designed to strike the Church dumb.

The general assumption in Lutheran congregations that the Security Police were responsible was encouraged by the discrepancy in the security forces' reaction to the explosion. Against the backdrop of guerrilla warfare, insurgent activity habitually provoked reflex counter strikes by policemen and soldiers. On this occasion, as the next issue of *Omukwetu* pointed out, no women and children were evacuated; neither helicopters nor armoured cars nor policemen nor soldiers nor police dogs and their handlers appeared on the scene. Some uniformed policemen turned up three hours after the conflagration and then only after they had been fetched by a missionary.

On June 3rd 1973 Bishop Auala led a procession of 8,000 congregants to a ceremony amidst the ruins and debris. During the service a Lutheran pastor urged the throng to join in with the construction of the new presses; the disaster, he proposed, was God's test of their faith. Two years later another service, attended by over 10,000 people, was held in thanksgiving for a new press risen from the ashes of the old.

10

The Law of the Epokolos

Within days of the Ovambo election fiasco, scores of SWAPO and Youth League office bearers were caught in a Security Police sweep in the north. Amongst those seized were Skinny Hilundwa, an active SWAPO executive in the north, Nestory Shanjengana, a school principal, and Phillip Alweendo and his brother Nicky, the owners of *Jo's Restaurant* at Ondongua. Some time later DEMCOP's chairman Johannes Nangutuuala and Thomas Komati, who had led the strike in Walvis Bay were, together with Andreas Nuukwawo, a Church worker, and Franz Nangutuuala, Johannes's brother, also taken in.

The detentions were effected under Proclamation R17; all the detainees were kept incommunicado in police cells. No contact with their families was permitted. Some detainees afterwards reported police assaults. Nicky Alweendo alleged that he had been made to stand for seven hours during questioning on the identity of SWAPO leaders. He was also interrogated on his reasons for demonstrating at the time of Dr. Waldheim's and Dr. Escher's visits.

The detainees were subjected to interrogations which were curiously devoid of direction. They were not accused of any offence; no attempt was made to extract proof of conspiracy or crime, no charges were laid and, in the event, no one was prosecuted. Johannes Nangutuuala, well known for his pacifist beliefs, was asked about his discussions with Dr. Waldheim and Dr. Escher without any suggestion of impropriety. A Lt. Steyn investigated Nuukwawo's political background and the possibility of SWAPO contact with the external wing. The remainder of the detainees were questioned in similarly broad terms. There was no hint that the detentions were motivated by ulterior considerations. Nothing presaged what lay in store.

At the time of his arrest by security police Captain Grobler, Johannes Nangutuuala presumed that he would be kept for interrogation until the police thought fit to release him; apprehensive shadows crossed his mind at the idea of what might happen during interrogation. A teacher by profession Nangutuuala, aged forty-one, with a high corrugated intellectual's forehead, stood out as a respected personage in the north. A fervent believer in communication and the power of the written word, he was one of the first to meet with Dr. Waldheim and Escher, written memoranda in hand. (He made representations after receiving clear assurances that there would be no official comeback.) He had dedicated himself and his group to pacifist goals and law-abiding political activism.[1]

Despite the existence of differences, a broad agreement prevailed between Nangutuuala and SWAPO. Unlike SWAPO, he did not wish to boycott the Ovambo Legislative Council; he kept out of the elections because he was driven to do so – his party was not 'recognised'. He presented more as a mild intellectual than as a radical figure, and at the time of the strike, when his popularity and power were at their height, he offered his cautious leadership to the strike committee and faithfully pursued the strikers' demands.

Nangutuuala made no protest when Grobler detained him. His replies to the Captain's questions were polite and cooperative – he was cordial towards the security police to the point of servility. (Before he attended the opening session of the Legislative Council, he, quite unnecessarily, sought Captain Strauss's permission to enter the Council Chamber). Grobler made no mention of any suspected offence, nor did he, during the weeks that Nangutuuala was kept in a dark corrugated iron cell, make any allusion to the possibility that he had transgressed the law; even so, Captain Strauss's announcement on the morning of the 24th October that he was to be released without charges came as a considerable relief.

But he was not allowed to walk out of the police station to his freedom. With his habitual submissiveness he complied with Strauss's order to mount a waiting police vehicle where he found Andreas Nuukwawo. No explanations were offered by Captain Strauss, nor his subordinate Constable Kahwedi as they drove off in the direction of the Ondongua Tribal Authority offices. Nangutuuala's perplexity grew as a ragged group of tribal policemen clutching rifles moved towards them on their arrival and surrounded the police van. Strauss unlocked the door at the back. A tribal policeman grasped Nangutuuala's jacket with a monosyllabic 'Out!' It was a grunt which brooked neither delay nor denial. Nangutuuala obeyed, followed by Nuukwawo. In the hall they found Chief Minister Philemon Elifas waiting with his brother Emanuel and Tribal Authority headmen. No one greeted Nangutuuala on his entry into the hall; a crowd of men and women in addition to some thirty armed tribal policemen were looking on. Elifas and his councillors in an animated mood stared at him without greetings, as if at a stranger; at that moment it occurred to Nangutuuala that he had, unannounced, became a defendant in a judicial theatre where familiar faces made up the tribal court. The policemen milled around in an expectant mood. Then in rapid succession the confusion of voices died down, Nuukwawo was led out, and tribal secretary Julius Ngaikukuete stood up with a notebook in hand and called for silence. 'This honourable Ondongua tribal court' he began solemnly 'has found you guilty of many offences of which only four are now mentioned'. He then elaborated:

'At a gathering in the tribal offices you said that the honourable Mr. Jannie de Wet should feel ashamed of himself: you were prohibited from attending the opening of the Legislative Council at Ongwediva but you attended none the less; in an unpleasant manner you walked out with the Prime Minister and then moved around asking if you could see the Chief even though he was busy; you wrote a letter to the tribal authority requesting the release of prisoners without punishment. That is contempt of the authority and you are sentenced to twenty strokes of the *epokolo* to be administered by tribal messenger Victor Nuukwawo. In addition you are ordered to leave the tribal area of Ondongwa within four days.'[2]

Victor Nuukwawo with his *epokolo*, a two-metre long tapered instrument of archaic punishment, moved nearer. Nangutuuala struggled to grasp the unconvincing nightmare.

'Will the honourable chiefs and headmen allow me to defend myself?' he inquired with timidity.

'You are allowed to say nothing,' answered one of the headmen with impatience. The Chief Minister and his councillors were mute, watching, content to wait. The tribal policemen crowded closer.

Nangutuuala's eyes searched for Captain Strauss who had disappeared.

The secretary ordered him to remove his trousers. Nangutuuala, now very afraid, obeyed with awkwardness, conscious of the scores of men's and women's eyes concentrated on him. No, that was not enough, indicated Julius Ngaikukuete; the underpants, useless against trauma but so protective of Nangutuuala's morale, had to come down. A naturally shy man, a father of seven and a respected pedagogue, Nangutuuala, naked and at a loss before his political opponents and onlookers, struggled against his inward panic and pangs of humiliation. The stool lay ready. The secretary with a gesture told him to lie across it. Nuukwawo, with ceremonial precision, took up position and immediately struck downwards with all the apparent force of his musculature. Nangutuuala's body arched and writhed and from that moment never stopped its trembling. Some of the onlookers cried out and covered their eyes while the tribal policemen, restless and amused, smoked and laughed. Nangutuuala's body quivered, awaiting the flagellator's next move. Nuukwawo paused for a minute, leaving his victim to come to terms with his pain and the agony of uncertainty. The blows followed, swung with wild force from the top of Nuukwawo's reach. After the second blow Nangutuuala believed that his buttocks were already raw, a mass of exposed nerve endings. It was only when Nuukwawo changed his grip and struck down with the narrow edge foremost, that the *epokolo* broke the skin and sank into the flesh. Nangutuuala wanted to pray but found himself choked by pain. Tireless, with a woodcutter's exactitude, the flogger focused on the bloody area of exposed flesh. Most of the councillors looked on with interest, some with relish. Nangutuuala fought his urge to scream and, as the blows followed pitilessly, struggled to remain conscious. At last with the twentieth blow the torment came to an end. He moved to raise himself but Nuukwawo ordered him to lie still. A twenty-first blow was delivered. Then the secretary intervened and allowed him to gather himself in his bloodstained disarray.

Ten days later Nangutuuala was examined by a medical specialist who found his flesh discharging serum; with the destruction of skin the trauma had devastated the underlying tissues which had become necrosed and swollen. Despite treatment at the Onandjokwe Mission Hospital there was no sign of healing. There was danger of spreading infection, cellulitis and septicaemia, a potentially fatal blood condition; his necrosis could also lead to uraemia, a diminished capacity to pass urine and eventual death.

Tribal policemen were waiting outside the Ondongua Police Station when Thomas Komati emerged from detention under Proclamation R17. During his stay in the Ondongua cells episodic questioning took place on the subject of his Youth League activities. His answers were straight forward. He had nothing to conceal; all his political work, since his expulsion from Walvis Bay, had been overt. Since the police were already aware of the details, the interrogation did seem a waste of time.

The tribal policemen, before driving off in their van, handcuffed him to Nestory Shanjengana and Tulipohamba Ngidiniwa. Though their journey was unexplained the three prisoners were overjoyed to find themselves at last liberated from the dark airless suffocatingly hot cells at Ondongua.

Their journey ended at the tribal offices at Ohangwena where the three captives were, without explanations, ordered to wait, handcuffed to one another, on the verandah of the building. From the hall came the sounds of unidentified activity. Komati, inordinately youthful for his dual roles of strike leader and political theoretician, looked around with interest and conversed with Nestory Shanjengana, a neat bespectacled school-head who shared Komati's appetite for religious and political studies. Shanjengana's preoccupation centred on the higher primary school at Okalongo where he was principal; three months earlier the security police had led him away from school in the sight of staff and 280 boys and girls; at that time he had no suspicion that he would be away for so long. While in jail – also under Proclamation R17 – a hit and miss interrogation was, contrary to his expectations, unaccompanied by violence.

Komati was the first to be taken into the hall where he found the tribal councillors assembled under Headman Kautwima. Headman Gabriel Katamba asked whether it was Komati's intention to remain a SWAPO member. A little surprised, Komati answered with a simple 'Yes'. He was returned to the verandah while the other two went for an interview. A crowd of men, women and children watched from a distance; no one spoke to them.

The Law of the Epokolos

Towards five o'clock in the afternoon the three were escorted back to the hall where headmen Kautwima brusquely announced the tribal court's decision. Komati and Shanjengana were to be flogged: 'Thirty cuts from the *epokolo*' was his formula. Tulipohamba Ngidiniwa was fined R60 only, as he was not in good health. The appalled headmaster cried out that he had done no wrong, that there was no reason for punishment. His composure had vanished. In a voice of desperation he pleaded that they wanted 'to fight our case'. Kautwima interrupted: the 'court' had no wish to listen to arguments. Tribal policemen surrounded him and mocked 'Where is Namibia now?'. Four of their number then seized Shanjengana and their sergeant ordered him to lie over the stool; one of the headman ordered him to remove his 'doctors' glasses'. The headmaster begged them 'I have done no wrong' and said that he had undergone recent surgery for appendicitis, and that he was still not well. Four policemen pulled him over the stool. Someone assumed the role of flagellator, and, *epokolo* in hand, said 'I am going to hit you now, so hard, that the whole of SWAPO is going to hear'.[3] Men, women and children were watching, amongst them one of Shanjengana's teachers from the Okalongo school. The blows were delivered with long intervals between them; after the tenth stroke he fainted. He later found himself lying over the stool paralysed with a burning pain; he thought that his spine had been broken. Later, at the hospital, injuries were found on his buttocks but also on his upper legs – they came close to damaging his urethra – and on his lower back. His injuries bled for several days afterwards; it was difficult to pass urine and each time he did so he was left with searing pain.

During Shanjengana's ordeal, Komati sat and watched impotently. The intolerable waiting, with its undefined fears and the sounds of Shanjengana's uncontrollable screams, rivalled the physical woe which threatened. His turn came when a squad of armed men descended on him and pulled him to the hall where he was pinned down tightly over a stool. A policeman with a dagger in his belt took up the *epokolo*. Amongst the spectators some women were crying and averted their eyes. Aged twenty-one, 1. 9 metres tall, slender in build and scholarly in appearance, Komati was a fragile victim. He submitted with resignation; the blows were not always on target and his right leg was hit and bled. He screamed until he lost consciousness.

Phillip Alweendo and his brother Nicky, the owners of *Jo's Restaurant* in Ondongua were ordered to be stripped and beaten – they were to receive fifteen strokes each – as punishment for being 'SWAPOs' and allowing their restaurant to be used as a rendezvous for SWAPO supporters.

'Before I am punished I want to know the case against me,' Phillip demanded stoutly.

Headman Philimon Shilongo cut him short: 'A decision has been taken – that's all'. He spoke with the impatience of someone with many tasks ahead. But there were delays. Tribal policeman Nakwafila, entrusted with the work of chastisement, had mislaid the keys to the handcuffs and now lay drunk on the ground. Unable to extract intelligible replies from him, a messenger was sent off in search of the keys. Alweendo waited for nemesis in the oppressive heat of the afternoon. Later in the day the messenger returned. Alweendo's trousers and underclothing were taken away from him by the tribal police. They laughed when he screamed out 'O God O God!' with each blow. With the fifteenth he thought that it was all over; the *epokolo*-wielding policeman believed otherwise and added two more strokes because he had been so 'noisy'. Then the four councillors turned on his brother Nicky and his sister Hilda. Heedless of Nicky's objections that they would be ruined the councillors ordered Hilda to close down the restaurant immediately. Sentenced to fifteen strokes for being a SWAPO member and for teaching SWAPO songs to children, Nicky too received seventeen blows. 'You didn't lie properly,' was the chastiser's explanation for the unsolicited bonus.

Not all the beating was quite so summary. Andreas Nuukwawo was told at the tribal offices that the 'statement' from the South African police had not yet arrived. For two days he was detained by a tribal policeman. Nathaneel Homateni's 'case' was also postponed. He and Franz Nangutuuala, committed to Nakwafila's custody, were locked in a room – a crude boarding concealed the windows – chained together with four criminals on a floor which, covered with filth, stank fetidly of vomit and urine. Nakwafila was unaccountably angry and vowed to hurt them 'terribly' the following day; breathing alcoholic fumes he attached the leg irons with such ferocity that Homateni's ankles bled.[4] That night he burst into the room bellowing 'You SWAPOs are going to shit this year! I will make you both burn and give you plenty of pain. I have got a gun' he added, 'it's specially to shoot Johannes Nangutuuala and you – meaning Franz – if you ever take part in politics again!'[5] The next day Homateni was ordered to undress in the courtroom immediately after sentence was passed. Aged forty-seven years, a family man and a senior member of his congregation, he seethed with hatred and humiliation:

'I lay down over a chair and the blows descended. They were agonising. There were long pauses between the strokes. It was NAKWAFILA who flogged me. I know him well. He is a person who is usually under the influence of alcohol. He is a heavy drinker. That day, as also the previous day, his breath smelt of liquor and from his speech and his red eyes and his behaviour, I thought that he was under the influence of alcohol. I was terrified that he would not only strike my buttocks but possibly injure my spine. The pain was terrible and produced open injuries. By the eighth stroke I lost consciousness and when I came to my senses I found myself lying over the chair with a feeling of unbearable pain. I have in all my life never suffered such pain.'

Franz Nangutuuala's punishment was also delayed. The councillors were waiting for a 'letter' from the South African police to say how he should be punished, Nakwafila added by way of a clarification. In the courtroom the proceedings started with Nakwafila removing Franz Nangutuuaka's

'SWAPO shirt', a garment of bright red, blue and green fabric; the headman clapped and Chief Elifas laughed. 'Off!' ordered Nakwafila, nudging Nangutuuala's trousers with his stick. Now entirely uncovered, Nangutuuala submitted that he was not well and that the South African police had beaten him severely on the day of his arrest. The headman shouted 'lie down' and told him to prepare himself.

Before Nakwafila went to work a White official of the Bureau of State Security (BOSS) appeared on the scene; he was offered a chair from where he took in the reactions of victims and onlookers.

Uncooperative victims earned greater retribution. Petrus Pedjelenga, sentenced to twenty strokes, was awarded twenty-eight 'because he had asked questions'. He nearly fainted from the first blow; a tribal policeman held his throat so tightly during the scourging that he could not scream; a Government minister Cornelius Ndjoba looked on and asked why the youth had made Sam Nujoma their idol.

Exemplary punishment was not confined to leadership echelons. Elise Nghilwamo together with three other student nurses from the Anglican Mission Hospital at Odibo were arrested and brought like bewildered schoolgirls before the councillors at Ondongua. When questions were fired at them they replied awkwardly and tried to conceal their smiles of embarrassment. Theirs was the one 'case' where the councillors put questions.

'Why are you here?' was the first enquiry.

Elise: 'I do not know why I have been brought here.'

Councillor: 'You are here because you have been arrested. Are you a SWAPO member?'

Elise replied with sincerity that she was indeed a member.

Councillor: 'Why did you join SWAPO?'

Elise: 'Well it struggles for our betterment.'[6]

There were no accusations, merely a patchwork interrogatory: Were SWAPO meetings held at Odibo? Who taught SWAPO politics at the hospital? Who had recruited them? Elise answered in a soft voice and they were then ordered out. They made their exits with an air of amused deference for the semi-literate councillors whom most nurses thought to be old bunglers; despite the presence of Nakwafila and his now bloody *epokolo*, they felt secure in the knowledge that no woman had in living memory been subjected to that instrument.

The sequence of events which followed was later set out in Elise Nahilwamo's Affidavit.

'Together with the three other girls I was then recalled before the Tribal Court and we were informed that we had been found guilty of being absent from duty without leave. Sentence of the Tribal Court was that we each receive six strokes of the *epokolo* which is the central rib of the makalani palm.

We were told to accompany two members of the South African Police whom I know personally as Johannes Hitolus and Thomas Kandova, to a police vehicle which we then entered. I know the said two persons to be members of the Security Branch. I recognised the vehicle as one belonging to the South African Police in view of the letters SAP appearing before the numerals on the number plates of the vehicle.

We were driven a short distance away and taken from the vehicle one at a time. I noted that there were some two hundred onlookers in the vicinity.

I was wearing a jacket over a pair of slacks. My jacket was lifted up and I was held over a low stool.

Six strokes were administered on the buttocks. It was extremely painful. It is still painful to date hereof.

We were taken back to the Mission Station at Odibo by Rev. Philip Shilongo in his vehicle. We had to stand all the way as our buttocks were too painful to sit on.'[7]

After news of the imminent flagellation of Johannes Nangutuuala and Andreas Nuukwawo was passed on to Richard Wood, the Anglican Suffragen Bishop in Windhoek, Wood immediately telephoned his lawyers and, on the 25th October 1973, lodged in the Supreme Court an urgent application for a protective injunction. At the moment that the Court granted its order, Nakwafila was preparing to wield his instrument on Nuukwawo. (Nangutuuala's chastisement was already over). By the time the Court's order was conveyed to the Tribal Authority five hundred miles away in Ondongua the punishment of Nuukwawo was a thing of the past. The futility of Wood's injunction only served to confirm the Tribal Councillors' sense of immunity. The rate of thrashings soared. A large number of SWAPO supporters were still in custody; since most were held under Proclamation R17 they did not figure in official statistics; seventy had been arrested in the Ondongua and Oshakati area alone.

Newspaper reports of barbarous punishments in the north sparked off a furoré. Early in November 1973 Wood moved a resolution in the Anglican Synod at Johannesburg calling for the Prime Minister's urgent intervention to prevent a form of punishment 'repulsive to the Christian conscience'. (A number of protesters, ignorant of the Security Police involvement, appealed to the Commandant of the South African Police Force). No action was taken: both the Minister of Bantu Affairs and Jannie de Wet washed their hands of the scandal claiming that the matter was not within the Administration's jurisdiction, that the regulation of punishment was wholly within the province of the Ovambo Legislative Council which had acceded to self-government.

A considerable vocabulary of indignation and humanitarian protest was expended on the chiefs and headmen in the north who were themselves indifferent to the wave of fulminations. Few observers understood where the true responsibility lay. Few observers were in possession of a synoptic grasp of the facts; few realised that a succession of police swoops had been followed by a carefully metered release of detainees into the hands of tribal policemen or that numbers of detainees, liberated from detention under Proclamation R17, found tribal policemen waiting at the gates of the police station. None of the victims was aware of any preconceived joint strategy on the part of the Security Police and the chiefs and headmen. No one enjoyed an overview of the erratic system of interrogation which, orientated neither to the discovery nor proof of crime, had in most cases presumably been pursued in order to lend an investigatory colour to the detentions. The police kept away from the proceedings though on one occasion an official from BOSS stayed to observe Homateni's tribulation. None of the security officers lingered at the Tribal Offices after delivering their human cargo. There is some evidence that the Tribal Councillors merely rubber-stamped the orders of the Security Police and imposed sentences which had been fixed beforehand; a number of 'trials' were delayed while the councillors awaited undisclosed documentation from the Security Police; Andreas Nuukwawo was told that a 'declaration' was to arrive from the police while Franz Nangutuuala heard from Nakwafila – once again in his cups – that a letter from the police 'to say what the punishment should be' was expected.

Were the floggings not timed by the police to allow Cabinet Ministers in Pretoria to shelter behind legal forms? However urgent the need to break SWAPO it needed little prescience to forecast that a flogging campaign of this dimension was bound to unleash a protesting storm. Were the floggings not delayed until the Ovambo Government, now labelled 'self-governing', was firmly in the saddle, enabling Cabinet Ministers in Pretoria to maintain with some plausibility that the matter was entirely within the province of the Ovambo Government?

Finally the timing of the flogging campaign deserves comment. The beatings were carried out shortly after the August elections where the 2.5 per cent poll represented nothing less than a disaster for South Africa's political and constitutional strategy.

What was the purpose if not, once and for all, to break SWAPO in the north?

11

Fiat Justitia

A first impression of Richard Wood might have been gratifying to South African officials who hoped that Winter's deportation had cleared the way for the installation of a more amenable incumbent. Deceptively bland, the new occupant of Bishop's House, the Anglican residence in Windhoek, wore that sort of clergyman's altruistic halo which is easily confused with gullible kindliness.

Wood made his first entry into Windhoek clad in a safari suit and the entirety of his worldly possessions stuffed into a haversack. On his way into Namibia to meet Winter, he hitch-hiked through large stretches of desert and semi-desert visiting poverty-stricken communities and Ovambo migratory-labour camps. His purpose was to minister to the poor in a nomadic existence à la John the Baptist and to offer his talents to ameliorate, however humbly, the ravages of an apartheid society. His ministry was not entirely conventional: he wore safari suits and no clerical collars. (People, he said, do not swear at men in clerical garb – they preferred to say things which were completely untrue). After joining Winter he toured Namibia preaching and selling Bibles from the back of a converted combi affectionately baptised 'Father Wood's Rectory'. People listened to his form of saintliness without suspicion that they were in the presence of a champion pistol shot, a former electrical engineer in the Royal Air Force, an ex-serviceman from the British Expeditionary Force in France and a Dunkerque evacuee.

It was perhaps fortunate that Wood's temperament was of a kind that gathered strength in adversity. After the double failure of his injunction and his call upon the Prime Minister, he opted for the somewhat quixotic initiative of writing a letter to the chiefs and headmen at Ondongua and Ohangwena whom he hailed 'Brothers in Christ'. His missive – a composition of appeals to their humanitarian good sense and warnings against the misuse of power and the growing hatred against their authority – produced no visible effect. No one bothered to reply.

Once again Wood looked to the legal fraternity, only to be told that he was impotent to intervene. His belated manoeuvre to save Nangutuuala and Nuukwawo through the courts had to fail: legal procedure was too sluggish;

Ondongua was too far away; the railway stopped short of Ovamboland and no air services existed; telephonic communication was 'difficult' to 'impossible', especially from the Mission Stations whose lines were officially 'down' as often as they were 'up'. Once seized by tribal policemen no victim could telephone Windhoek and, even if he managed to do so, he was likely to reach the casualty wards before the lawyers made the courts. Nothing but a blanket injunction which paralysed the whole system of flogging could provide meaningful protection, but this, went the advice, was not feasible in law; there were no legal precedents for such sweeping remedies and the problem of *locus standi* (legal standing) remained insurmountable: no court could concede *locus standi* to a Bishop who was himself not threatened, to launch injunction proceedings for the protection of thousands of congregants in the far north.

Wood was alone in Windhoek's White suburbs. Most Whites viewed SWAPO as a dangerous alien grouping which threatened to undermine present prosperity and poison their future; many would have preferred SWAPO's political extermination. Wood himself, with all his bonhomie and his soldier's forthrightness, was received with crabbed suspicion; beyond an incorrigibly optimistic wife Cathy and a small band of helpers and friends, Wood remained isolated. Nor could he turn to his attorney, Von Biljon, who had refused to defend SWAPO members for the reason that 'we have information that these persons have associated themselves with mass violence and therefore in our opinion are no longer within the law'. The flogging scourge, according to prevailing sentiment, was the only language which militant Blacks might understand – a harsh though necessary remedy.

With all its metropolitan if not international flavour, Windhoek remained a small town with a knot of 30,000 Whites whose culture was at once polyglot and parochial. Rooted in von Francois' trespass upon Herero territory, Windhoek has ever since remained under a question mark. But whatever divisions of opinion might have existed, the overwhelming majority of Whites have faced domestic and external threat with remarkable solidarity; in this milieu the social ostracism of Winter, Wood and their ilk, was fairly inevitable. There were thus few to whom Wood could look for guidance and help. But in Johannesburg it was different; with its huge population of Whites and Blacks, dissident enclaves shrugged off hostile White opinion. It was to Johannesburg that Wood hastened, ignoring pessimistic legal advice and the dour commentaries of SWAPO analysts who warned him that Windhoek's judiciary would not put a stop to the reign of the *epokolos*. Wood's enquiries soon led him to Attorney Raymond Tucker who received him with warmth and, without a trace of hesitation, undertook to represent him. The following day Wood and Tucker arrived at my chambers where we carried out a hasty review of the facts and the law. In the meantime information of more floggings and arrests had come in; there were now fears that top SWAPO leaders including John Ja Otto would soon be taken in. Legal action was imperative. Time was now of the essence. The following day Wood and I flew to Windhoek.

In Bishop's House there was confusion without disorder. The manse was congested with victims and witnesses who had hurried to Windhoek to make their affidavits and show their injuries after word had gone out to Ovamboland. Thomas Komati, dishevelled but irrespressible, eagerly agreed to become SWAPO's applicant in spite of the headmen's warning that any further signs of opposition would be visited by more beatings. Archdeacon Phillip Shilongo, cordially detested by the chiefs – he had remained on at the Odibo Mission after an order to quit – also volunteered his affidavit. But Komati and Shilongo were not the only ones who were endangered. Everyone knew that his or her affidavit might be interpreted as an affront to the dignity of tribal councillors; the councillors had warned of the danger of a second 'installment'. There was no certainty that the application would succeed; its failure would well inflame the councillors' urge for further retribution. And yet it was a festive mood which prevailed over the bustle, the hum of conversation and the general movement in the rooms and passages at Bishop's House. Those whose injuries remained raw had an evident propensity to pace up and down rather than remain seated, while the student nurses helped Cathy Wood with the manufacture and distribution of sandwiches. During consultations an Afrikaans speaking secretary who had frankly declared herself to be against SWAPO turned up to man the typewriter; the pin money had triumphed over her reluctance but within an hour her frigidity disappeared amongst the infectiously optimistic faces. On the telephone, Wood pursued Auala around the world until he caught up with him in Geneva; Auala was instantaneously forthcoming and supportive. The application, now led by Richard Wood, would be presented to court as the joint initiative of the Anglican and Lutheran Churches and SWAPO.

On the morning of the 19th November 1973 their urgent application was presented to Mr. Justice Hoexter in the Supreme Court. Since the application was *ex parte* – launched without notice to the respondents – our submissions were unopposed. After hearing argument, Hoexter interdicted the Tribal Authorities from flogging any person on the ground that he or she was suspected of being a member or sympathiser of SWAPO or DEMCOP, until the expiry of fourteen days after the Territorial magistrate at Ondongua had received the names and addresses of the defendants. The injunction which the applicants had sought and obtained was therefore not absolute: the protective mechanism was the fourteen day delay which would enable Wood, Auala or SWAPO to intervene with a specific injunction. Judge Hoexter's order, though provisional and later reversed, effectively ended the pseudo-judicial campaign of punishments in the north.

The provisional injunction came up for confirmation before Judge President Badenhorst and Judge Strydom in March 1974. (Judge Hoexter had in the meantime been transferred to a post in the Republic.) The applicants' case and the respondents' answers were before the court. Our research had unearthed Roman-Dutch law authority on the issue of standing; our case was further strengthened by the decision of the Transvaal courts in *Bozzoli v. Station Commander John Vorster Square*[1] which acknowledged the standing of a university principal to intervene on behalf of detained students. Through the affidavit of ELOC pastor David Shihepo – born in the same year that Bismark annexed the Territory – we proved the nature and development of criminal procedure under tribal law and custom: corporal punishment was unknown until introduced by Hahn, a Government Official dubbed Shongola Hahn (Sjambok Hahn); the strokes never exceeded six; the judicial flogging of women was unknown and all trials envisaged allegation and counter allegation, evidence, some form of cross-examination and argument. The venerable Shihepo's propositions were stiffened by an affidavit from Auala who affirmed that flogging was never public: 'I never saw the imposition of corporal punishment on a single person for the reason that such punishment was administered in private.' Professional anthropologist, Robert Gordon, and Joe Muashekele, a B. Juris graduate member of the Kwanyama tribe, provided expert confirmation. The affidavits of a physician and a gynaecologist and photographs of suppurating injuries proved the fatal possibilities inherent in tissue destruction and the likelihood of a miscarriage.

Two hundred pages of affidavits and documentation were met with the blunt reply that the procedures were proper: there was no limit to the number of strokes in tribal law; women could be flogged and victims could be stripped. The overall description of the 'trials' and punishments embodied in our affidavits was not disputed.

The Judges were not invited to depart from precedent; they accepted the decision in the *Bozzoli* case but concluded that it was distinguishable. The university students whom Bozzoli wanted to protect had been in custody and were therefore incapable of making the application themselves. SWAPO members on the other hand, reasoned the Judges, could apply for an injunction when they felt threatened – a line of reasoning which ignored the undisputed reality: that the victims had no grounds for apprehension until the moment of their arrest. But even if the applicants did have *locus standi*, the Judges stated, the victims had an automatic right of appeal under tribal law once they were sentenced – a proposition which swept aside our uncontradicted evidence of 'trials' which were a mockery of judicial proceedings, where defendants were warned off argument on pain of added violence. Above all the Judges ignored the atmosphere in which the proceedings took place – the smoking, the sadistic exaltation, the air of festive vengefulness and disregard for public decency.

The judgment – brief, concise and wrong – dismissed the application with costs. For the applicants, the judgment's silence on the crudity of chastisement and the exaltation of the councillors was difficult to believe in a community of ingrained Calvinism with its horror of public nakedness. Public exposure in South African law was a criminal offence; photographs of women's naked breasts were not allowed – unless they were Black – while reproductions of male pudenda were strictly taboo. Apart from the Judges' duties to uphold morality and public decency, the tribal courts, exercising powers in terms of Proclamation R348 of 1967, fell within the Judges' review jurisdiction; the judiciousness and propriety of the proceedings were therefore the responsibility of the Judges. In their own courts, the Judges conducted proceedings with punctilio (counsel were even supposed not to rest their hands on their hips while addressing the Judges). The effect of the judgment was to allow vengeance to abuse the forms and powers of legal proceedings.

An application to the Judges in Windhoek for leave to appeal to the Appellate Division was turned down on the ground that there were no reasonable prospects of success. It was now over to the applicants to petition the Chief Justice in Bloemfontein. If this procedure was successful and leave was granted, more than six months could elapse before the hearing in the Appeal Court. In the meanwhile a temporary injunction pending the outcome of a petition to the Chief Justice was required to prevent further flogging. An application was brought before Judge Strydom; it was dismissed, once again on the ground that the applicants had not shown *locus standi* and had no reasonable prospects of success on appeal. The legal test for a temporary injunction was crisp and easily understood: what was the balance of convenience? In terms of law an injunction should be ordered where its refusal would result in irreparable harm to the applicants. So much for the general rule; in our case an injunction would at worst delay the execution of sentence fourteen days. It seemed axiomatic that this inconvenience was far outweighed by the crude violence which imperilled the lives and safety of the defendants. Judge Strydom was not persuaded by this argument. His words were: 'Such temporary relief may seriously hamper the administration of justice in Ovambo and would far outweigh any consideration of hardship on individuals who in any event are not precluded from applying to this court where they personally are affected'. But how could the Judge talk of 'hardship' to individuals when the undisputed evidence proved the risks inherent in the necrosis and spreading cellulitis which supervened after trauma? Johannes Nangutuuala's injuries were suppurating even after he had received medical treatment. What would happen to bleeding defendants who were illiterate, unaware of the need for medical treatment and at great distances from the nearest clinic? On the evidence Nakwafila, the main flagellator, was as often under the influence of alcohol as he was not. Some of the blows went too low and encroached dangerously in the vicinity of the urethra while others edged upwards threatening spinal injury. And finally what administration of justice was it that the Judges wished to protect? Was not the hooligan disregard for individual rights and dignity not calculated to be destructive of the very foundation of judicial administration in Ovambo-land?

After Judge Strydom's refusal of a temporary injunction on the 5th April 1974 a petition was lodged with the Chief Justice as a matter of urgency. Chief Justice Rumpff reacted swiftly and granted leave to appeal – implicitly but incontestably on the grounds that there were reasonable prospects of success. Armed with this ruling we urgently moved a second application for a temporary interdict. Since the Chief Justice, we argued, considered that there were reasonable prospects of success, the Windhoek Supreme Court should now bow to the most authoritative judicial voice and as a matter of course grant a temporary injunction. This reasoning and the Chief Justice's order were of no avail. Judge Strydom, unaffected by the obvious, persisted in the view that there were no prospects of success. Further protection was refused.

The Judges in Windhoek were wrong. On the 24th February 1975 the Appeal Court upheld the Appeal with costs and reimposed the injunction on the tribal authorities.[2] Chief Justice Rumpff, acting in accordance with the highest judicial traditions, found that the applicants *did* have standing, that the tribal authorities had acted with a callous disregard for the rights of individuals and that it would be wholly inappropriate to insist that the applicants had to hold back until the moment the prospective victims had been seized.

12

The Young Prophets

The year 1973 ushered in a startling efflorescence of SWAPO and SWAPO Youth League (SYL) activity. From the time of its formation in the sixties the SYL acted as an auxiliary to the parent body until the latter part of 1972, when in the aftermath of the general strike it struck out on its own with growing confidence. Inspired by Dr. Waldheim's visit and determined to take advantage of the Prime Minister's concessions on the issues of free movement and political activity, the SYL leadership, mingling seasoned activists and politically callow young men, started to find its feet in the troubled theatre of political action.

After the departure of Dr. Escher, the SYL held meetings in Walvis Bay, an important industrial and fishing centre with a major concentration of Ovambo contract labour. The forceful voices of Thomas Komati and Franz Nangutuuala generated an immediate response from the thousands of workers and township inhabitants who heard them out in open fields and sports grounds. Their success confirmed the widening belief in the SYL that their destiny was to propel them into the historical arena, not confine them to a humdrum factotumship. In Windhoek, SYL chairman David Shikomba and Shindabi Naudile penetrated the workers compound at Katutura to hold illegal meetings. They were caught, prosecuted and jailed for four months. This was for Shikomba an acceptable baptism; he was not to be so lucky in his next confrontation with South African justice.

The SYL's campaigning coincided with SWAPO plans to lay siege to the elections in Ovamboland in August 1973; meetings were held across the country with varying success; many were broken up by squads of helmeted police who would turn up with machine pistols and dogs. In Ovamboland thousands assembled to absorb the anti-election rhetoric and bitter attacks on the Chiefs and the Ovambo Government. For the handful of collaborators on the Prime Minister's Advisory Council they had nothing but derision. Reflecting the illusion and reality of their power the SYL boldly proclaimed their non-recognition of the Chiefs and Government.

The audiences in the South were equally responsive, a fact overlooked by SWAPO critics who would insist that SWAPO is primarily a tribalistic

Ovambo-based organisation. Without doubt the Ovambos both in the North and in the workers' compounds of the South reacted to SWAPO themes with a distinctive fervour; they did so because it spoke up for them, shared their risk and gave guidance, nor is it difficult to understand why this was so. In the South the Ovambo contract labourers were objectively the most exploited, the most restricted and politically threatened amongst the workers, so that the warmth if not extremity of their reactions, their volatility and their militancy were, in the prevailing climate of misery, not unnatural; the Ovambos were in the forefront of resistance and equally in the forefront of the news. It is this imbalance which has been exploited by SWAPO's detractors as proof that SWAPO is an Ovambo tribal organisation. They prefer to overlook the fact that SWAPO chairman, David Meroro, and other leading figures in the SWAPO and Youth League hierarchy, have emanated from other ethnic groups. The notion also underrates the powerful pan-tribal political forces at work in Southern Africa and the unique potential for unity in Namibia through the shared ardour of Christian belief.

The way the Youth Leaguers went about their work was particularly memorable: they presented their listeners with a remarkable mélange of prophecy and challenge. Though not given to the mystical belief that freedom would fall from heaven, many members were gripped by the certainty that 1974 was to be the definitive year of freedom in Namibia. They argued that the UN and other international bodies should be prompted to action through countrywide mobilisation and demands for freedom shouted with sufficient force across the plains of Namibia; then only would the UN, and indeed the World, finally compel the Republic to let loose the Namibian shackles. All this, in the context of world trade boycotts and arms embargoes, seemed eminently probable. The introduction of fuel restrictions in South Africa and Namibia was interpreted as satisfying evidence of gathering pressures on the Republic; for the young Turks in the Youth League the time was near when their Arab sympathisers would cut off the fuel lines to the Republic; and so with a mixture of interpenetrating fact and optimism, fantasy and political pragmatism, many SYL leaders came to believe and to put out the idea that 1974 was the final year of struggle.[1] At times their clairvoyant prediction was presented with occult implications, as if the inner circles in SWAPO were privy to a new master strategy. The predictions mystified and troubled the newspapers; the police made energetic attempts in their raids to uncover suspected conspiracies.

While the ideological hustlers in the SYL may, with all their enigmatic predictions, have given the White administration pause, they on the other hand delighted and cheered their audiences with promises of imminent messiah – like liberation. The independence they promised seemed real enough, sufficiently viable and internationally warranted; in the same breath they rejected Mr. Vorster's promise of independence for Namibia in ten years time. Who wanted to wait ten years? And even then what independence would Mr. Vorster give? Freedom was for now, not something ephemeral, in some indeterminate future time, or a bag of fragmented phoney States called Bantustans, the desert satellites of the White man's kingdom.

Most of their meetings in Ovamboland – held without the consent of the Chiefs – were technically illegal; as we have seen the outcome was violent intervention and prosecution. The meeting at Ongandjero was attacked with ferocity and their loudspeaker was smashed. In protection of a later meeting at Engela in July 1973 SYL leaders issued a press statement that warned of a general strike as a reprisal for any police intervention.[2] In the Republic such political intimidation would have led to an immediate prophylactic swoop under the Security laws; it was perhaps the very vehemence of Youth League protest, concentrating so much national and international attention onto Engela, that secured for them temporary protection. The meeting took place, but when it was all over, and the crowds had dispersed and tension in the Territory had subsided, the police acted, caught and arrested Komati and Nangutuuala and prosecuted them. This time the gaol sentence was one year.

It was now over to the Windhoek Executive members to arrange a mass meeting in Katutura, the heart of overt political life in Namibia. Their loudspeaker in pieces, they asked Meroro for a loan of the SWAPO apparatus. Meroro was not enthusiastic; fearing a militant energy that had already attracted serious retribution in Walvis Bay, in the form of compulsory repatriations, he made excuses. (An expulsion order from Windhoek could be catastrophic for those SWAPO members who had no permanent right to be there.) Meroro imposed a condition that speakers should first be checked out by the SWAPO Executive; this was turned down. After some squabbling the Youth Leaguers got their way and the machine, but the dispute did add to the tactical tension between SWAPO and the Youth League and the suspicion that Meroro, principally because he had never been arrested, was not to be trusted. This same tension surfaced in a later statement issued by SWAPO, implicitly disassociating itself from the florid militancy of SYL speeches that had led to charges under the Sabotage Act. According to their leaflet they were against violence or sabotage, had no part in racial hatred and had never planned agitation or demonstrations which could result in tension. 'We too have decent politicians who are asking in a decent manner for rights for their people. The purpose of speeches is to make people politically conscious' they explained. A footnote informed the reader that it had been issued by SWAPO 'not the Youth League'.

Throughout 1974 SWAPO, in conjunction with the National Convention, organised public meetings in Katutura attended by thousands of Blacks from the township and the compound. Meroro usually represented SWAPO; Gerson Veii led the SWANU team; Clemens Kapuuo spoke for the Herero organisation NUDO.[3] There was little of the SYL's exuberance; their speeches were imbued with restraint, their metaphor sufficiently prosaic to

78

appease the law. They made appeals for dedication and unspecified sacrifice and warned emphatically against division and fragmentation in anti-apartheid ranks. Kapuuo, an able orator, moved thousands with his sincerity. (No one could have foreseen that he would, within one year, spearhead demands for the separation of Ovamboland from the Namibian body politic.) There were also Black Consciousness themes: Blacks, they elucidated, were to be defined in terms of their political social and economic oppression; Blacks were exhorted to show courage and initiative and slough off their sense of guilt and inferiority; they were henceforth to refuse 'non-whiteness'; Black was to be their inspiration; Black was beautiful. The 'non-white' collaborators on the Prime Minister's Advisory Council were mocked and told to make off with their white masters to Kakamas – a town in the Cape symbolising squalid racism-words which seldom failed to produce ovations and laughter.

The SYL meeting on 12th August 1973 marks the apogee of its political campaigning. An audience of more than two thousand five hundred spectators massed around a makeshift platform in an open field and the Namibian flag was hoisted. A squad of over twenty youths was introduced to the audience as Namibian 'policemen' appointed to keep order. The meeting was enthusiastic and tolerant of the ritual presence of the Security Police who took notes and recordings of the orators at work.

The meeting opened with a prayer. Altogether eleven speakers spoke of their grievances, their struggle and their dream of freedom. Between harangues, young girls danced while a SYL official conducted a choir which sang freedom songs with energetic signals from his baton. The multitude was urged, in different ways, with different images and much passion to free itself from passivity and servile acceptance: freedom was in their own hands and would not fall from heaven nor the United Nations; the ancestral struggle and past heroes were recalled and Martin Kapewasha, in an extended hagiography, honoured the names of heroes and martyrs. There was much vituperation about the 'Boers', a well-used epithet prudently defined as a synonym for racist Whites. Joseph Kashea, twenty-one years old, gave his first public address: the Chiefs he said were the real oppressors of Namibia and should go off with the Boers to Kakamas for they had broken the SYL loudspeaker. 'The gun of the SWAPO Youth League,' he said 'they destroyed it.'

It was evening when the meeting came to an end with song and prayer. Groups of youths left singing, and danced their way into Katutura. No one was threatened; the Security Police officers, a most provocative presence, packed up their equipment and left. (In all the reams of evidence given in later trials, no policeman ventured to suggest that they had been threatened or molested.) The crowds disappeared with the SYL members who went home satisfied with a good day's work. Later that evening numbers of young people sang their way into the compound; on their way out they found the gates had been locked; the municipal guards had disappeared presumably to fetch reinforcements from the police station. The very existence of the gate had been a source of chronic irritation; the sudden fastening was now an inexplicable provocation. Anger flared, Ovambo workers attacked, and made short shrift of the locks; before the police returned the gates were broken down and the singers had vanished.

The following morning the Youth Leaguers were appalled by the storm unleashed upon them by the Windhoek press. The SYL speakers were accused of calling for blood, violence and the extermination of the white man and his supporters. The *Windhoek Advertiser* was later to refer to it as 'Bloody Sunday' marked with calls for blood and revolution.[4] There were lurid descriptions of incitement, of frenzied mobs, of a human tide which swept destructively into Katutura and violence which culminated in the destruction of the compound gates. The Press declared that the Youth League had inflamed political anger, set fire to Namibia and brought Blacks to the brink of a general strike and open resistance to law and order. (*The Windhoek Advertiser* obliquely fostered the notion that SWAPO could be banned.[5])

There were calls in the White community for draconian counter measures and reprisals in the midst of endemical anxiety.[6] The police launched a man hunt for the Youth League speakers, soon netted six including Jerry Ekandjo, and spread a dragnet across the Territory for the remaining five who were on the run or who had gone underground. The entire city of Windhoek was purged in a house to house search for the young fugitives; none was caught but the police took the opportunity to 'clean up' the city and arrested eighteen individuals who had contravened the pass laws. On the request of the Administrator the Chief Magistrate prohibited all meetings; the police followed up the prohibition, intervened and dispersed gatherings, and within a few days made over sixty political arrests, with a hunt afoot for more.

Dismayed and angered, put out, but undeterred by the venemous press campaign, SYL leaders still at large met in secret in Katutura, decided on action rather than retreat and made plans to deliver their counter attack at a further public meeting now scheduled for Sunday 19th August 1973. Foreign correspondents and reporters from Johannesburg, who they presumed would report honestly, would be invited and would witness the discharge of their thunderbolts against the local press and the clarification of their peaceable intentions. (In preparation for that meeting Ezreel Taaipopi, soon to become the acting SYL chairman, made rough notes for his speech. These were later seized by the police and put in by the defence at his trial as 'unprepared evidence' of the SYL state of mind.) But it soon dawned upon them that a further meeting was unthinkable: the police would act aggressively, seize would-be speakers at the meeting and ignite anger and public violence for which the Youth League would be blamed. The remnants of the Executive Committee refused to be check-mated, took their courage in their hands, made the momentous decision to call for a general strike on Monday the 20th, and promptly formulated, printed and issued their strike leaflet. It commenced with a prayer to God by the 'oppressed people of Namibia' and an urgent appeal to the world for help. 'Terror and murder on the people of Namibia' had led to an intolerable situation, they averred: they fulminated against the Government – that 'huge liar' – called for the release of political prisoners, an end to apartheid and an end to Government attacks on the Church. In that hour of crisis the authors saw fit to include a protest against the Government's hostility to the evangelical mission of the Churches.

On the night of the 16th the security police carried out a raid upon a house in Katutura where Executive members were in session and attempted to seize books and documents. The Youth Leaguers would part with nothing; there was an argument; in the ensuing mêlée a policeman shot a young supporter, Benjamin Phineas, who managed to crawl away, haemorrhaging, until death overtook him in a neighbouring garden. Youth Leaguers who saw the incident condemned the killing as an act of murder; news of the raid spread hastily through the townships. The sleeping quarters of the municipal police in the compound were attacked and set alight; the steel gates of the compound were ripped down while workers stoned and repulsed municipal police reinforcements. By dawn the entire compound was cordoned off; there were baton charges and over two hundred were arrested; men were searched by armed policemen in the shadow of armoured vehicles. In the ensuing days concentrations of police gathered at the compound to act against 'agitators' and 'encourage' workers to return to work.

On Monday the 20th Katutura stayed home. To thwart the call for the strike hundreds of policemen surrounded the township before entering with weapons and dogs in a house to house search. According to householders, men and women, who had not gone out to work, were assaulted and driven out of the township; there were complaints that many were bitten by dogs. Katutura smouldered helplessly. A wave of frustration spread beyond Katutura: fifty per cent of the students walked out of the Augustineum College;[7] schools were restive; protest meetings were held at Walvis Bay and other centres. More than a hundred people were arrested. That day and in the days that followed the police remained in the township to maintain the pressure; their methods worked. By Thursday the police had broken the back of the strike.

The Windhoek press kept up its campaign against the SYL and branded it as the whole cause of the trouble. The widening spiral of police provocation and violence was represented in the press as causally related to Youth League incitement, the entire chain of events, the burning, the stoning and the killing of Benjamin Phineas attributable to the spirit of frenzy kindled on the afternoon of the 12th.

From the commencement of the man-hunt the chairman of the SYL Jacob Shindika went into hiding from where he issued peremptory demands for the release of Jerry Ekandjo and 'all other political prisoners'.[8] His next call was coupled with a threat that 'serious trouble' would erupt unless the detained Youth League leaders together with Herman ja Toivo and other Namibian prisoners on Robben Island were released.[9] His lone thunder went unnoticed and yet the lesson of the Engela meeting where the Young League had apparently managed to ward off official attack by their threat to call a general strike was not so easily unlearnt. Now Jacob Shindika and Taaipopi, on the verge of fleeing the country, delivered a press statement once again threatening to call a general strike. This time their ultimation was embellished with an appeal to Namibians to rise up in 'revolution' and do battle; 'The SWAPO Youth League', Taaipopi wrote, hoping that the new cocktail of threats would reduce the authorities into submission, 'calls upon all Namibians to use every force necessary to overthrow and free themselves from the Boer's Government. Do not look to the outside world for aid. It is now the time to let the Boers feel rather than hear. It is now the time to remember our holy blood that has been shed and to take revenge. Now there are only two options: to overcome our oppressors and destroy them or perish.' His valedictory homily: 'The Boers must remember they can't get away with it because evil is self-destructive.'

On the 31st August as a parting shot Taaipopi and Shindika issued yet another ultimatum in the name of the SYL: 'The Youth League repeats once more that we will be content with nothing less than Black majority rule in Namibia. The Boer's Government had to leave Namibia or face a war to defeat, or the Namibians had to thank God because this is the last year for them to be under Boer's Government.' This unabashed *pronunciamento*, tantamount to a declaration of war, tailed off on a somewhat banal note: 'In conclusion SWAPO Youth League wants to say that our urge to freedom is a long and hard one. But remember fellow Namibians that we are no longer on that same road if we allow ourselves to be divided by the Boer's Government. Long recognition of the dignity of man.'

Months later in his trial Taaipopi characterised this declaration as a dangerous individual frolic which could have had serious consequences to the Youth League.

With the majority of the SYL leadership safely in detention by the end of August, the rest in full flight, their futile – and unauthorised – appeals for action unheeded by their supporters, the SYL organisational apparatus, like its loudspeaker, was in pieces. Namibian whites could breathe once again. The havoc had been accomplished in less than three weeks after the fictional 'Bloody Sunday', with Jerry Ekandjo, David Shikomba, Martin Kapewasha and Jacob Ngidinua imprisoned and indicted under the Sabotage Act. How was this smothering of an overt legal political organisation accomplished and on what basis? What was it in the South African system which made it so easy?

Because of Namibia's international status, the South African Government has shown episodic reticence in the launching of political prosecutions there. It has also been reluctant to declare SWAPO an unlawful organisation as this could have the effect of driving SWAPO militants underground as well as undermining rearguard action against the UN and diplomatic pressures. The South Africans have instead made liberal use of their powers to detain individuals indefinitely – without reasons given – in solitary confinement. When the South Africans did choose to prosecute they had a formidable array of security laws at their disposal including the Sabotage Act under which Jerry Ekandjo and his co-accused were charged.[10]

The Sabotage Act has taken the precaution of equating utterances with acts of sabotage. Its definitions, structured on wide-ranging generalities and its transferred onus of proof, present as a nightmare to defendants and their counsel. In the case of *The State v. Jerry Ekandjo & Others* the prosecution had no difficulty in charging the 'Bloody Sunday' speeches as acts of sabotage.

In retrospect it can be seen that the overwhelming body of rhetoric directed at the meeting on August the 12th amounted to a vehement denunciation of the Administration, its policies, and its collaborators. This was interspersed with arguments which hammered home the SWAPO programme and the freedoms which it envisaged. This was all spewed forth in the ambit of daily political declamation. The SYL, like any other political organisation plunging into the hurley-burley of the hustings – or its fringes – set out to sweep the country with its oratory. When their orators spoke of their loudspeaker – and they were put out indeed by its destruction – they referred to it as their 'gun'. Embedded in the amorphous mass of exhortation, homily and explanation, some speakers borrowed liberally from the imagery of vernacular speech. This was immediately fixed upon by the police to justify far-reaching criminal accusations.

The *leitmotiv* was the importance of the political struggle, the need to organise and join together in a process of national unification. The cry was for political action, not for the white man's blood. It was for political action fructifying in freedom even if it meant the old familiar road of arrest, beatings, shooting and death; even if it meant spilling Black man's blood, 'this blood'; and when Kashea called for 'hot water' to be thrown on their enemies and incited the Youth to get busy with 'brooms' to sweep Namibia clean he could hardly be taken literally, nor did his auditors do so. After his speech there was laughter and singing – not a wake of anger, furtiveness, and fear.

Martin Kapewasha borrowed from the same linguistic pot: 'You the Boer must know that before you carry out the instructions which have been given to you that SWAPO has now taken *iikilumbwati* (sticks), that is the weapon that he can use and is in a position to use as he wishes. He asks for the blood which you have spilled in Namibia.' Then, referring to martyrs of the struggle, he said: 'Boer you are now asked about the blood that you spilled on 10th and 12th of December in the Old Location (referring to the 1959 shooting in Katutura) . . . those people were killed because of the truth which they had proclaimed. We must ask for them. . . . You the youth of Namibia you must all unite to fight for your freedom.' For the prosecutors and the police these rhetorical allusions to the blood of heroes were a cry for vengeful carnage, an interpretation that ignored the fact that sticks do not belong to the Ovambo armoury; it also chooses to ignore the idiomatic function of language. The expression was a call to adopt a resolute stance, not to make off to war with sticks, bows and arrows, or more fashionable weaponry. As for the repeated reference to blood, was it not an obvious reminder to listeners and Government that theirs was a nation with a proud tradition whose martyrs and heroes would, in the future as in the past, have to be reckoned with? This form of eloquence belonged naturally in the style of contemporary liberatory politics in Southern Africa and recalls, for example, the panegyrical evocation of Black martyrs in the annual celebration of 'Heroes Day' by SASO (South African Students Organisation) students in the Republic.

Taaipopi and Shindika, like most of their brethren on the Executive Committee, did not get away. They were arrested and detained until October 1973. For reasons best known to Government officials, no prosecutions were instituted against them under the Sabotage or the Terrorism Acts for their part in the 'call' for revolution and general strike. Taaipopi was taken to the magistrate's court on a humdrum charge of resisting a police search at his home. On the evidence of a police sergeant, the search was justified because he suspected that Taaipopi's identity documents had been forged. In the face of Taaipopi's reputation this was too much for the magistrate who decided to throw out the case.[11] Taaipopi walked out of court a free man and again took up the threads of political activism and, as more colleagues were released, regrouped and early in October 1973 assembled with them as an Executive.

The many body blows to the organisation had done little to dampen their zest for action; they determined on a massive revival of political campaigning with meetings in all centres of Namibia, coupled with the publication and dissemination of a newspaper and pamphlets; they once again reacted to Press hostility and warned the *Windhoek Advertiser* that it was trying to sow emnity between Namibians.[12] Looking beyond the Territory's horizons they took the unprecedented decision to send a delegation to a meeting of the OAU in May of 1974. In an Executive meeting presided over by Taaipopi, their newly appointed Chairman, they wrote a letter to the UN requesting that it end dialogue with the South Africans and order them to get out of Namibia. 'We are suffering', they wrote 'under the Boers' inhuman oppression, therefore we want to know the day of the Namibian issue.'

Overt activity was paralysed; the first meeting following the August disturbances took place in Katutura only in November. Conscious that the security police would not hesitate to pounce on them again, they trimmed their language of menace and ambiguous metaphor, explicitly announced that their struggle was non-violent and that on their accession to freedom there would be no reprisals. 'Our weapon is the loudspeaker not the gun. We are here in peace. We must forget about the past and think of the future. Whites and Blacks can live in peace.'

The speed of their resurrection as a potent force in Namibian political life is a significant indicator of the fundamental structures of SWAPO support; this was a process which was to be repeated in years to come when the political field became emptied of leaders and activists after waves of police activity. The newspapers would announce the death of SWAPO only to witness – with unpublished disappointment – its miraculous resuscitation. What the papers and their editors did not realise was that the strength of SWAPO lay not in any bureaucratic cohesion nor in the charisma of prevailing leaders; it was rather that the grievances and grief, and a nation's aspiration, were mirrored in the language and action of SWAPO's leadership.

13

The New Defendents

After close on three months of solitary confinement SYL Chairman Jeremiah Ekandjo, twenty-six years, Martin Kapewasha, twenty-three years, and Jacob Ngidinua the Vice Chairman, twenty-four years, were indicted in the Supreme Court at Swakopmund, a fishing port on the fringe of the Namib Desert, on a charge, under the Sabotage Act, of encouraging Namibians to kill or injure those 'standing in their way' and to take up arms against the whites of Namibia: this incitement, it was alleged, endangered public safety and the maintenance of law and order.

Swakopmund, with its picturesque German colonial architecture, its steep iron roofs and bulging fenestration, lies two hundred and fifty miles by road from Windhoek. The accused, witnesses, policemen, court staff and the Judge were compelled to make their way through the stark hot countryside from Windhoek, even though the Supreme Court in Windhoek was the obvious court to exercise jurisdiction. The inconvenience of the shift to Swakopmund was justified in the name of security. Only one other political trial had been held at Swakopmund before, when in 1967 Gerson Veii was convicted of sabotage and sentenced to five years' imprisonment.

The pattern of holding political trials in areas remote from the accused's political support base had been established in the Republic; political detainees from Johannesburg would be held and tried in Pretoria; those from Durban would be dealt with in the inland town of Pietermaritzburg, those from Port Elizabeth in Grahamstown. The hearings were held in relatively small towns where the accused, alienated from the great reservoirs of township solidarity, would often face prolonged trials with little more than symbolic support from family and comrades. Supporters would be discouraged by the distances, the cost of transport, the risk of interception, and their exposure to police scrutiny and identification. Spectators have been subjected to search and questioning, and on one occasion in Pretoria, in a trial under the Terrorism Act against nine SASO leaders, the entire audience was locked in court while the police took down names. Even so when the Ekandjo trial opened the courtroom was packed with SWAPO supporters. Many vainly attempted to follow the evidence through the open windows.

The New Defendents

The Ekandjo trial marks a watershed in the history of political trials in South Africa and Namibia. Hitherto political accused went along with the style of dignified respectfulness if not craven submission fostered by court tradition, where answers to judges or magistrates were rounded off with 'Your Lordship' or 'Your Worship'. Every defendant is of course aware of the judicial punitive powers confronting him. The vision of the courthouse is forbidding to most Blacks. For many it is a place of conditioned fear where juveniles, convicted of minor or serious offences, are subjected to corporal punishment in the courthouse itself or its basement. The screaming of young children is a daily accompaniment of the judicial processes. In the smaller courthouses the court is cleared at lunch, boys are stripped and held over a bench in the courthouse and caned.

Judge President Badenhorst presided. The Attorney General appeared personally as prosecutor: his conspicuous intervention added to the gravity of the proceedings. But from the outset the accused trio brushed aside what they perceived to be the fustian style and intimidating mummery of judicial procedure. For a start they laughingly tore up their indictments; there were delays while court officials rushed to Walvis Bay to prepare copies. They dismissed Judge Badenhorst's offer to provide *pro deo* defence advocates; the Judge's reassurance that these advocates would be paid by the State, far from comforting them, was greeted with alarm. They would have nothing to do with such advocates and, if they were to get a free defence, they would only accept lawyers appointed by the United Nations;[1] Government lawyers were objectionable because, they said, the Government is a 'Boer Government' and is 'nailing the Namibians'.[2] The only request they had for the Judge was that 'all Namibians should be present'.

Judge Badenhorst, in the crimson robe that marked the exercise of criminal jurisdiction, sat flanked by two assessors, an unhappy sign that the death penalty was feasible. Outside and inside the court, police were armed with automatic weapons; the Security Branch was very much in evidence. Ekandjo and his co-accused in casual attire and without ties chatted nonchalantly in the accused's dock bestowing a variable interest in the proceedings. They showed a reluctance to take the oath in the form prescribed; Jacob Ngidinua, to the consternation of the Judge, swore to tell the truth in the name of Heaven, the UN and SWAPO.

From the start the Judge showed displeasure and warned that his patience was coming to an end; Kapewasha and Ekandjo laughed; the Judge ordered them with a schoolmaster's testiness to stand up. Black Sergeant Karel Atshivuze went onto the witness stand to provide formal proof that he had assisted the security police in making translations of the tape-recordings. Ekandjo turned on him abruptly shouting 'You have come into the witness box in order to nail your fellow Namibians. You too are a Namibian, you must quit your dirty work.' Invited to cross-examine they turned defence into accusation. Their questioning became confrontation and counter-attack; like ja Toivo they mingled their political credo with fundamentalist themes: they were there as representatives of the innocent people; they had the armour of God's protection; whatever sentence the court might impose the prison gates would open and they would be back the following year to join in the reconstruction of a new society; all those implicated in oppression and the implementation of their trial and imprisonment in Swakopmund would themselves be tried.

Startled Black spectators, compacted in heat and perspiration onto every inch of seating, relished their declaiming, but feared the outcome of such unprecedented audacity. Never had a Namibian Judge found himself face to face with such defiance. Atshivuze was told 'Judas Iscariot betrayed Christ and then hanged himself. God help you for you know not what you do'. The witness feebly protested that he was a 'South Wester' not a Namibian, and only doing his duty; he had heard of 'Namibians' but did not know them and only heard that they lived 'around'. 'God must forgive him for the work that he has done' Ngidinua interjected with indignation. 'He must lay off this work'. The Attorney General sprang up with objections.

The Judge: 'Are you intimidating the witness?'

Ngidinua with blank indifference to the excitement he was generating: 'He must lay off this work because he is one of our nation.'

Kapewasha now joined in. Atshivuze he said should throw away the money he was earning and, like Judas Iscariot, hang himself. 'The witness is the king of our nation and he can leave the witness box. He is a traitor.'

Ekandjo's cross-examination of Captain Nel on the decision of the International Court of Justice in 1971 was cut short. The Judge ruled that the issue had no legal relevance. A startled Ekandjo replied that nothing could be more to the point; for him South Africans were an illegal occupation force without moral right to control or try Namibians; their occupation had been condemned by the world, by the Churches and the world's highest judicial body as illegal; the trial should not be allowed to proceed. The Judge stopped him. Ekandjo recoiled, then hit out: it was significant, he emphasised, that they were being tried by a court that had no right to hear the case; it would be different if the court had that right, but the Judge had nothing to do with them. He was furious, gesticulating and impassioned, and brushed aside the Judge's instruction that he accept the court as it was 'and don't show your fist at the bench or to the witness. I will not allow anyone to address the court like that and don't make political speeches!'[3] Undeflected Ekandjo answered excitedly: 'Has this court perhaps obtained permission from the UN to try us?' On the 21st of June, he lectured the Judge, the World Court decided that South Africa was illegally in Namibia and had to get out; the UN alone was responsible for them. 'We refuse' he proclaimed 'to be tried by this court.'

Ngidinua: 'This court is nothing but a hole in the ground. We will not recognise the sentences which this court will impose on us.'

They viewed their innocence with crystalline simplicity. For men accused of much irrelevance, their cross-examination had elements of penetrating lucidity. What mention they asked had they made of firearms, assegaais and weapons in the meeting? What weapons did they have at the meeting? Did they not say the amplifier was their weapon? And what if they spoke of history and its Herero and Ovambo leaders who had died in the struggle? What they had said at the meeting was not humbug; it was the truth. No one wanted to fight; it was the police who arrived with weapons in the township. Who after all did the killing if not the police? When they said that schoolchildren at Walvis Bay were already fighting could they have meant fighting with real weapons?

Ngidinua summed up: 'We have sabotaged nothing. We are oppressed. The people in Namibia who do sabotage are the Whites of South Africa. This court is here illegally and terrorises us in our own land. Only the United Nations may hear us. We do not recognise this court and we will be back.'

Addressing the Judge *in mitigation of* sentence Ekandjo branded the Court as the 'temple of the devils where Namibians are being crucified'.[4]

They were each sentenced to eight years imprisonment.

14

Legal Reprisal

Towards the end of 1974 the revived SYL offensive became seriously under-mined by the perennial problem of finances; their ambitious project to estab-lish an independent newspaper, to saturate Namibia with leaflets and to establish a fleet of vehicles for campaigning around the country had come to nought. A fund-raising scheme in the deprived Black communities of Namibia necessarily brought in lean returns; Black shopkeepers, white-col-lar workers and teachers helped out but they too had limited means. In the White community few were prepared to make handouts. Beyond the bor-ders it was different: if only they could reach Sam Nujoma, whom they had never met, and the external wing with all its international connections. A letter previously sent to SWAPO officials in Dar-es-Salaam remained unanswered.

The fateful decision to write a letter to Nujoma was taken at an Executive meeting held in the Katutura workers compound in December. Taaipopi commenced the meeting with a prayer: 'We have faith, we believe in the pos-sibility that Christ will bring us freedom by June 1974'. Prior to the meeting in a handwritten draft note of the agenda Taaipopi wrote. 'A letter to the foreign wing of SWAPO if necessary'.

Addressed to 'The Honourable President Sam Nujoma' the letter launched into a description of police aggression, coupled with a blunt remin-der that earlier letters were unanswered. They wrote:

'We must know or bear in mind that the Struggle for our Freedom is a matter that needs seriousness and therefore we must not play with it.

1974 must be a year of sacrifice for Freedom and a year of the Realisation of the *Power* of SWAPO, not only abroad, but also inside Namibia. We must not wait on the UNO to bring us *Freedom* on a *plate*. We must rely on the Power we wield in Solidarity with our Brothers of Independent African states.

The Youth League would like to send a delegation to the meeting during May this year, but the problem is money. We are going to publish a monthly newspaper inside Namibia and we shall welcome information from the SWAPO offices abroad.

Our Comrades, Jerry Ikandjo, Jacob Shidika and Martin Kapewasha are kept in jail for fun and we would like to suggest that you must use your influence abroad so that these Comrades can be released because S.A.'s Mandate over Namibia is already ter-minated and she has thus no right to prosecute any politician in Namibia.

We hope and trust that you will do this immediately. S.A. is now jailing innocent people since 1974 because we mentioned at our last meeting that this year we are to bring the Boers' regime to a fall. Bring this to the attention of the United Nations and Organisation of African Unity.

We are pleased because our Arab Brother had boycotted S.A. with oil. We, the Namibians are not suffering because of the embargo and therefore we call for a total oil boycott against S.A. The Boers are feeling the Oil Boycott, it is why they are propagating that it is the Blacks who are suffering. Arabia must not waste his oil by giving it to S.A.

We must now awake out our sleep and free Namibia in 5 month's time. We must pull up our sockies before it is too late.

June, this year must be the month of Namibia's freedom. Until when are you waiting for somebody to free us. SWAPO's liberation Army must now fight the Boers and free Namibia before June. We promised the people that Namibia is to be free this year and now they are waiting for this freedom to come. Don't make us liars all in any possible way.

Yours faithfully, 1 Nashilongo E. Taapopi (Chairman)
2 Joseph Kashea (Acting Secretary)
3 Shihepo Iimbili (Treasurer)

The letter was addressed to the Administrative Secretary in Dar-es-Salaam. Intercepted by the postal services it was in the hands of the security police before the end of the day. Taaipopi, Kashea and Iimbili were arrested and indicted for incitement to murder, public violence and arson.

Determined to prevent a renewal of SWAPO's domination of the political atmosphere, all police in Namibia were, from November 1973, constantly on stand-by;[1] the municipal police force was strengthened and arrangements were made for joint action in cases of emergency. Arrests were carried out on token legal grounds. Early in January 1974 members of the SYL and David Meroro were arrested on their way to a meeting at Rehoboth. An entire convoy of vehicles, festooned with SWAPO flags and supporters singing freedom songs, was stopped by armed police and dogs at a road blocked outside of Rehoboth. A hundred and twenty men and seven women were taken from their vehicles, arrested and detained on the pretext that they had failed to show their identity documents.[2] By the time they got to court the next morning a further count of leaving Windhoek without travel documents was added to the indictment. There were assaults by the police; when the defendants appeared before a magistrate the following morning some spoke out, complained of assault and inhuman treatment and asked for the court's help. Their bid for protection was dismissed. 'I have no power to intervene with the police' said the magistrate.[3]

David Meroro was released only to be rearrested early in February together with nine other SWAPO leaders including Axel Johannes and Thomas Komati. Once again the press announced the effective end of SWAPO leadership. There were mass arrests in Katutura and in the compound; in one raid a hundred and forty-one men and forty-five women were detained bringing the total of arrests for one week to three hundred and thirteen;[4] there were door-to-door searches by the riot police. An embargo was placed on liaison between the police and press reporters – as if the legal strictures on publication were not sufficient.[5] Information on arrests and police behaviour could henceforth only be released through the Administrator. Political activists were removed from Windhoek and sent back to Ovamboland, and some private firms and Government bodies including the SABC dismissed employees on account of their adherence to SWAPO.

Meroro, Johannes, Komati and their comrades were detained incommunicado and in isolation under Section 6 of the Terrorism Act; the police implied that there was an investigation into a serious violent conspiracy. The wave of arrests was followed by demands for release from foreign human rights groups and the International Commission of Jurists; in April the US Government requested details of the arrests from the South African Government and expressed disquiet over the detentions which were 'disturbing' the relationship between the two countries. Neither pressures nor adverse publicity moved the South African Government, even though in retrospect, it is clear that the police had no basis for preferring criminal charges against the SWAPO leadership. After his eventual release from solitary confinement Meroro was charged with the possession of banned literature; he received a suspended sentence. Taaipopi and Kashea were prosecuted for their hand in the letter to Sam Nujoma.

The Trial against Taaipopi and Kashea opened before the Judge President in Windhoek on 10th June 1974.

Born at Uukwaludi in Ovamboland in 1954 Taaipopi and his family moved to Windhoek when he was nine years old. His father worked as a translator for an Afrikaans publishing organisation, the Taalburo. After passing Standard 8 at the Augustineum College, Taaipopi left school in 1973, joined the SYL and distinguished himself by an agile intelligence and an exceptional talent for public speaking. He was appointed to the Executive Committee a few months after joining the organisation. (The periodic police swoops created a regular need for new blood.) He took up employment as a clerk with builders in Windhoek; this job lasted one month. His writing and oratory reflected the influences of Black theology. He wrote 'Whatever difficulties we are to encounter in our work we must pray to God to send us our liberator, the Black Messiah'. At his Trial, Taaipopi formulated the quintessence of his belief: the Black Messiah was committed to freeing the Black man from slavery so that he too should appear as a person created by God.

Two weeks before trial I consulted them in the Windhoek prison. Although Taaipopi spoke English and Afrikaans fluently problems of communication arose immediately. Their answers were rambling, their memory fuzzy; it then emerged that they had been through five months of solitary confinement, hallucination and depression. They had come close to suicide.

It was hopeless. A proper defence could not be prepared on a foundation of defective memory and incoherent explanation. The defence needed time to muster its facts. The defendants needed time to heal. An application for a postponement was moved. The Judge was not spared details: their isolation (each in a cell no larger than the accused's dock), their hallucinations, disintegration and sadness, and the chaos in the defence camp.

The court was in no mood for delays. Instead of showing concern for the accused – who were presumed innocent until found guilty – the Judge, moving on from the disturbing sequence of facts, turned upon the defence lawyers, exhibiting a marked preference for probing details of their industriousness rather than the police penchant for locking up awaiting-trial prisoners in solitary confinement.

I protested that the Judge was one-sidedly critical of the defence. 'You don't ask the State why they (meaning the police) held the accused for so long . . . ' Judge Badenhorst misheard, and accused me of breaching court decorum by using the words 'why the hell the accused . . . ' The tapes were replayed until the misunderstanding was cleared up. Even then his public accusation was not struck out by a public exoneration. Numbers of police guarded the courtroom. The atmosphere was loaded with hostility to the defence, as if the accused, their lawyers and their advocates were a prime source of social evil. This was not unusual in political cases.

The defence predicament was also not unusual. The defendants had been kept in the cells for five months prior to the trial. What was the point of the delay? No complicated investigation was required; no witnesses needed to be traced; the prosecution case rested on one undisputed document and the evidence of Sam Iimbili; it is difficult to believe that the trial could not have commenced one month after arrest.

The accused pair could not complain that they had been singled out. Prolonged solitary confinement of political prisoners is in South Africa an integral part of the process leading to trial. After months in confinement the prisoner is one day taken up the steps from the courthouse cells into the unfamiliar perilous world of the courtroom; the prisoner has grown accustomed to close confinement, immobility and silence. The abrupt removal into streets, corridors and the courthouse produces bewilderment and disarray. Prisoners may be brought to court without their families being told; an early trial date is set and then only begins the struggle to contact family, lawyers, friends and witnesses. To do this the prisoners are always dependent on help. Many political trials are lengthy so it is hard to find lawyers with the indispensable attributes of competence, willingness and availability. Suffering from defective memory, disorientation and depression, the defendants may themselves not be aware of their true disablement; solicitors and counsel can easily mistake a fumbling account for blunt intelligence rather than illness; this is all too easy when lawyers and clients meet as strangers needing to create a rapport across the opaque barriers of linguistic, cultural, and racial estrangement.

Taaipopi was kept in isolation, sealed in a cell for one and a half months; he saw the sun not once and was not allowed out for exercises. A flush toilet in his cell sighed and whistled day and night; he thought he would go mad with the noise. There were troughs of suffocating depression alternating with fury. His sanity slipped. He started to speak to himself; during hallucinations he saw David Shikomba enter his cell. 'I spoke to him but he never answered.' Apart from very brief mechanical exchanges with the magistrate nobody visited him. 'I began to feel as though somebody was pressing my brain together.' To the magistrate he pleaded for a change, for company, for an end to the repetitious diet; he needed newspapers and something to read. The complaints were duly noted. Nothing changed. Later as the trial drew near and some rehabilitation became imperative he was allowed the New Testament and newspapers.

The trial started after a short postponement. Attorney General Advocate C. Rees S.C., a specialist in political trials who had been flown to Windhoek for the trial, represented the State.

The Trial went well at first. The most important State witness, Sam Iimbili, a youth who had himself been through the processes of arrest and detention and interrogation, refused to compromise. The letter he said had been sent to Nujoma to persuade him to activate the United Nations, not to start war. His words 'The style which SWAPO had taught us is to fight with our mouths, not with sticks or anything like that' were pivotal, as evidence of the Defendants' state of mind was at the heart of the prosecution case. The defence in turn set out to show the history behind the letter; the organisation's impecunious state, its financial woes and its ambitions to buy vehicles and start a press rather than an insurrection. Sam Shivute, a leading member of the SYL executive, and the defendants presented a panoramic account of their activities, their vision of Namibia and their belief in the UN. They pointed to the absurdity of suggesting that a letter, supposedly bent on military invasion, should have been sent on an SYL letterhead through the ordinary post. In the cut and thrust of cross-examination Taaipopi aroused the atmosphere of the court with his forcefulness, with his answers driven at the prosecutor with a mathematician's certainty. He was in turn corroborated by Kashea and another committee member. Iambo Nashilundo. Cross-examination dragged on through the minutiae of SYL history and its documentation; after wearying pedantic hours on the witness stand Taaipopi's evidence survived consistent and intact. With Kashea it was a different story: he battled vainly against the prosecutor's skill until allowed to flee the witness stand.

As a further blow to the prosecutor's arguments the defence produced a draft agenda for the Executive meeting in Taaipopi's handwriting. This document had been seized by the police; its authenticity undisputed, it provided an invaluable form of uncontaminated evidence. It read:

'1. Rehoboth meeting,

2. Passes,
3. Article in the Advertiser,
4. Newspaper. News must be collected for our newspaper and the National Executive Committee of SWAPO must be notified about this issue.
5. A letter to the foreign wing of SWAPO if necessary.
6. News.'

The argument was ineluctable. No one in his ordinary senses, intending to move a treasonable resolution to call upon Nujoma to invade Namibia, could have written of a letter to the foreign wing 'if necessary'. But that was not all. Other documents in Taaipopi's handwriting were handed in, one with the words: 'It is our last hope that the Security Council will . . . ' and another: 'But the question is what kind of action? We must simply stand up and demand our freedom by means of placards and street demonstrations'. As Taaipopi explained: all that was meant was that SWAPO abroad should act immediately; their duty was to jolt the Security Council into session before June in order to expel South Africa from Namibia. After all those promises of freedom in 1974 this was the very least which could be done.

The defence arguments and evidence were rejected; both defendants were convicted. Imbili's evidence implicating the Accused was accepted; that part of his testimony which supported the defence was discarded. Both defendants were sentenced to five years' imprisonment three years of which were conditionally suspended. This meant two years on Robben Island. Referring to their solitary confinement the Judge declared himself to be convinced that the circumstances were not as bad as they had claimed. Since no evidence had been led to contradict Taaipopi and Kashea on this issue it is difficult to understand how the Judge managed to arrive at such a palliating conclusion.

They were led to the cells. Taaipopi was glowing. 'I am off to college' he exclaimed eagerly. 'There I will meet our head boy Ja Toivo.' Outside the courthouse a cluster of Blacks demonstrated amongst the spectators with posters 'One Namibia One People,' 'Release all political prisoners,' 'Long live all freedom fighters'. From all sides there were clenched fists raised in salute, and songs of sadness and hope.

15

The Slow Poison of Madness

The process of mental disintegration in solitary confinement figured briefly in the Taaipopi hearing when the defence applied for a postponement. In the trial of SWAPO leader Thomas Komati the defence was driven to investigate, analyse and prove the phenomenon. The appalling claims to suffering made by detainees are not readily understood; the imagination is easily foiled, as the anguish – elusive, subjective and intangible – cannot, in the absence of a novelist's skill, be forcefully transfigured into a felt reality. In Komati's case a psychologist was brought to the witness stand to describe the dynamics and the symptomatology of a paradoxical process where a seemingly normal human being drifts imperceptibly into psychosis.

At the end of 1973 Komati was appointed to the SYL executive as a public relations officers. He was a careful speaker with eyes that radiated an impish confidence; despite his youth and boyish face he was sent as an SYL delegate to a Black People's Convention conference at Hammanskraal in the Republic. His harsh eloquence in Walvis Bay prompted the authorities to repatriate him to Ovamboland where, indefatigable, he continued to organise and address meetings. On 12th October 1973 he was arrested by members of the Security Police and locked in police cells. A month later he was handed over to the Tribal Authorities, 'tried', sentenced and flogged.

This was for him and his comrades in SWAPO an overwhelming vengeance. What the police and headmen did not foresee was that he and his colleagues would emerge fire-hardened from punishment. It was none other than Komati, still bruised and bleeding, who in the name of SWAPO brought a joint application for an injunction with Wood and Auala.

After his punishment he once again returned to the political fray until seized by police officers on the 31st January 1974 under the Terrorism Act.[1] There were no accusations – merely a laborious enquiry into his SWAPO activities which were in any event public knowledge. The interrogation was over in a few days; from then he was detained alone in a cell, within the banality of four walls covered with graffiti, cut off from the outside world and human contact. It was to be an experience of isolation concentrated interminably in himself. The bare bulb remained on at night; even sleep became a difficult rearguard action. His life in ensuing months was a gross inventory of negatives: there were no visitors, no reading matter, no Bible, no meat, no fish, no milk, no tea, and no coffee. His diet was bread, brought to him by silent uncommunicative constables; cleanliness was not at a premium – there was no soap. The surrealist simplicity of the cell was undisturbed by a chair or a bed or a bench.

The Security Branch had warned him that the 'case' was a very serious one. He was at first not bothered.

'I was unconcerned as I had committed no offence. After breakfast I would sit on my mat; I systematically attempted to organise my thinking. I would set out to review in my mind my studies when I tried for example to remember science experiments and poems.'

But as time slipped by his self-discipline deteriorated; his memory gave way. Morale and militancy, optimism and faith, faded as listlessness and depression encroached. 'I began to feel affected by sadness which at moments I found hard to bear. At times I thought of my family and of my friends in the SWAPO organisation. This brought on a deep sense of longing and despair.'

Then one day the immobility and gloom broke. He was taken out of his cell without explanations, booked out, driven through the Namibian scrub to Dordabis Police Station. There he was put in a cell where he could see the 'glory of the sky'. There was a tap on the wall and a voice which slipped through his cell window. He was astonished. It was his good friend Benjamin Namalambo, as recklessly thirsting for communication as he. They talked compulsively. 'I am unable to express the joy that I felt in speaking to him. We spoke at length, with obvious pleasure, and my sadness became lightened. . . . I felt like crying but I did not do so. I no longer felt lonely and in the daytime I sang and did my exercises.'

The bliss of incontinent dialogue lasted four days. During that time they spoke for long hours into the night as if with some premonition that this could not last; on the fourth night they were overheard by a policeman. The very next day the windows were closed up and tight wire mesh was fastened on the outside. It was now harder than it had been ever. Komati felt an overmastering loneliness and despaired. He was never to speak to Namalambo again in prison. The cell was now dimmer; he felt at times that he was suffocating.

His only food at Dordabis was porridge. His water supply for drinking and washing came in a bucket replenished every four or five days; to conserve the supply he used it mainly for drinking. His ability to organise his thoughts was steadily failing him.

He found memories of past events eluding him. It came to him that large segments of his past had vanished in his memory. When he tried to exercise he tired rapidly; it had become an insurmountable effort. He lost his appetite, started to cough and suffered from sleeplessness, woke at night and found himself unable to return to sleep. The greyness seemed unending; it was at this time that he began to feel frightened. In the beginning of his detention he had laughed off the mysterious suggestion that he had committed some great crime. Now in Dordabis he began to believe that he was doomed to many years imprisonment, that the charge against him was grave and that he might never see his family and friends again. His thoughts became uncontrollable, ideas repeated themselves and slogans borrowed from the political struggle such as 'peace', 'justice', 'freedom', chased around in his mind with strange insistence. 'It was as if I was hearing a cracked record at times and the repetition became harder and harder to endure and I held my head and my ears as if this could keep out the sound.'

He was prey to unconnected and scattered thoughts. In April he was shaken by his first hallucination. He was awake, staring dispiritedly at his cell walls when he found himself 'talking amongst some of my friends who were in the cell with me. In particular I remember conversing with Kashea and Namoloho. We were in the cell together talking about political matters. I spoke to them and I could hear their voices. I could see them. I am unable to say how long this experience lasted but the next thing I knew was that I was alone in the cell. I was still awake.' This initiatory hallucination was the forerunner of successive illusions; afterwards he found himself in dialogue with his brothers. Later Kashea and Namoloho, now joined by other Youth League friends, irrupted and jostled for a place to sit down next to him. It was life revisited; they gesticulated, laughed and argued until they evaporated through the brickwork abandoning him to face his desolation. 'At times when I spoke to my companions I spoke to them about our political struggle and I repeated to them the words "peace" "justice" and "freedom".' Then one morning, cheered on by his loyal phantoms, he took a spoon and in front of them knelt down and etched into the wall 'One Namibia One Nation'. 'I cannot explain why I did it and I have no recollection of any fear of contravening law or any knowledge of doing anything wrong. I simply felt that I had to do it . . . '

After Dordabis he was taken to the cells at Swakopmund; not long before his release he was given lecture notes and a Bible. Though impregnated with religious faith and accustomed to daily readings of the Bible, he was unable to overcome his listlessness and abandoned its study after a few days. By now he had given up all exercise and reading, would sit or lie in his cell day and night doing nothing, singing occasionally, or stare with animal-like blankness at his fingers or his blanket.

It came to an end as it started: abruptly and unannounced. His cell door was opened without explanation. He was taken in a police truck to Okahandja where a policeman gave the news that he was to be prosecuted for having scratched 'One Namibia One Nation' onto the wall of the cell. A sergeants said it was malicious damage to property; his sentence would be two or three months' imprisonment. The policemen were astonished.

Komati was radiant. Ravenous for human contact he could only think of imprisonment with other people and the delicious prospect that he could talk to them and labour with them as a convict in the prison grounds. 'From that moment I could think of only one thing and that was being sentenced to imprisonment and finding myself with people whom I could talk to. . . . It never occurred to me that I could or should defend myself . . . I desperately wished to avoid being returned to Dordabis where I might be kept alone so I told the policeman I would plead guilty immediately.'

In his Affidavit he contrasted his loneliness with the thrashing in Ovamboland. 'I had received an illegal flogging of thirty-one strokes. . . The punishment was at the time for me savage and unbearable. But I now say that the seemingly unending misery and despair which affected me in my loneliness in detention was by contrast with my flogging a terrifying experience. I say that the horror of uncontrolled thoughts and fears over months and months was for me a worse punishment sensed not only as unendurable pain but as the slow destruction of myself as a human being.'

True to his word he pleaded guilty when brought before the magistrate in Windhoek; the case was then adjourned for the prosecutor to obtain his police record from headquarters in Pretoria. In the meantime he was to be allowed out on bail.

At last out of captivity! Now that he was restored to life and the miraculous bombardment of human speech and touch he thought differently about further time in jail. Legal defence was arranged through Bishop Wood. Attorney Tim Owen and I were asked to represent him.

When the case was called the defence moved for the setting aside of Komati's plea of guilty on the ground that his engraving 'One Namibia One Nation' was the product of hallucination. His action was involuntary, went the argument; he was unaware of the nature of his deed; the legal formula for the defence of insanity was fulfilled.

Expert psychological evidence was led through Alma Hannon, senior lecturer in psychology and specialist researcher in the study of sensory deprivation, from the University of the Witwatersrand. She supported her diagnosis on the basis of extensive documented research, experimental studies and anecdotal reports given by explorers, pilots on high altitude missions and prisoners. Komati's creeping apathy, inability to concentrate and melancholy closely paralleled the behaviour of volunteers who after a few hours (sic) of sensory deprivation produced a consistent syndrome: their efforts in problem solving and concentration tended to be abortive, their thinking was sterile, garbled and confused, they hallucinated with vividness. Volunteers soon found themselves unhinged and asked to be replaced; many said it was terrifying. The constellation of symptoms was well established but belonged to an esoteric part of psychiatric research; what was important for the case she reasoned was that Komati, with an uncompleted education, could not have concocted his symptoms.

The magistrate listened with scepticism, puzzled because the policemen and magistrate who saw Komati in detention had not noticed signs of derangement. Hannon explained that the damage to mind and personality was as subtle as it was devastating; doctors, lawyers and policemen could not easily divine the symptoms. American prisoners returning from Korea in the aftermath of the war, though suffering from symptoms that bordered on psychosis, were not taken seriously; it was then that psychiatric investigation uncovered a clear psychological pattern.

The magistrate was not persuaded; after patiently listening to evidence and argument he rejected the defence application. Komati was convicted but not returned to the all too familiar cells. After payment of a fine he was freed.

It is difficult to comprehend the latent fury in a society whose legal system could prosecute a detainee, driven to the fringes of insanity, for the crime of recording – in the welter of sordid or rebellious graffiti on cell walls – his innocuous axiom of political hope. In the rhadamanthine stare of criminal justice solitary confinement has traditionally figured as an extreme and dangerous punishment. Under the prison regulations its infliction is meticulously controlled and limited. Why then the double standard? Why such tenderness for convicts and common law criminals while politically minded suspects are made slowly to absorb the bitter poison of dementia? And what rank offence was Komati's that his captors should act to seal up windows that had served generations of offenders from every criminal quarter of society as some access to Namibian skies and to one another? Mercy may of course not thrive amongst prison and police officials and prosecutors in on-going conflict with criminality but what of the judges and magistrates? Were the thousands of Whites who read extracts of Komati's evidence in the Press moved to some comprehension? The answer of course is locked up in their inner selves. What does emerge is that the architecture of interrogational and detention processes remains intact and that at every moment, within the space of White society's consenting silence, scores of men and women reflecting on their disintegration and suicide relive Komati's ordeal.

16

Meroro's Blood

The wave of arrests and detentions in 1973 and 1974 led to a medley of protests from the UN, the US and human rights bodies. Amongst the host of foreign voices there were calls for the release of detainees and dialogue with their leaders. It was broadly acknowledged that the great majority of SWAPO supporters – some ventured a guess of 90% – were practising Christians, orientated towards democracy and indifferent to dogma; there was therefore room for manoeuvre and negotiation with leaders who were not intractable Jacobins; communication and dialogue could only be salutary. But South Africa had its own ideas for political solutions and as we shall see later, was moving towards an all-embracing solution through a rival political movement headed by Black collaborators who were later to take part in the Turnhalle Conference in 1975. Whatever the real motivations might have been, SWAPO vice-president David Meroro was not invited.

After many years at the helm David Meroro was something of a grand old man in Namibian politics. Aged fifty-seven, father of thirteen children, he had led the organisation through difficult and dangerous years; he had stayed on and had not fallen for the questionable seductiveness of life in exile. His daily routine in Windhoek was devoted to running the organisation and his two shops. His businesses, his Mercedes Benz saloon and his cattle established him as one of the wealthier more influential Blacks in Namibia, a reputation calculated to compound political hostility and individual jealousy. Dapper, cautious, with anxious eyes, his awkward manner mingled with stubborn militancy and all the risks to life and property that it entailed. This is not to say that his leadership went unquestioned; with the passage of time the younger spirits lost their diffidence and came to harbour suspicion. In contrast to the SYL cadres Meroro seemed shielded from detention and its attendant hazards. His reluctance to part with the loudspeakers was interpreted as a grim confirmation of their fears. In letters from prison warnings were sounded that he was not to be trusted, for it was he who had never been imprisoned; it was he who had 'surrendered the SWAPO flag to the detectives at Security Branch offices where we are beaten while we lie on the flag'.

Their suspecting scowls vanished with Meroro's arrest on 7th February 1974. In a surprise nocturnal raid a squad of security men encircled his home and business premises. They searched toothpaste tubes, teapots, furniture and stock, laboriously and suspiciously. After hours of toil the raiders came away with unmomentous scraps and magazines. Apart from letters to members of SWAPO abroad and a number of telegrams from Peter Katjavivi the SWAPO secretary for information – officially delivered by the Post Office – the police found copies of the *African Communist*, a banned publication in Namibia. One letter from Meroro to Katjavivi summarised Meroro's public speeches; another to Peter Nanyemba in Dar es Salaam dealt with the plight of refugees. As it later turned out, after five months of detention in isolation the authorities restricted their legal attack to the possession of antiquated copies of the *African Communist*. The offence of supplying information to the external wing of SWAPO – deemed by South African law to be terrorist – was ignored for reasons which are not easy to establish. The communications seemed perhaps too incidental and it would be awkward to recast as terrorism correspondence over the plight of refugees. On the other hand, if SWAPO were given more rope for communication with the guerilla wing, the accumulated evidence might be enough to put the entire leadership on Robben Island and justify the organisation's definitive burial by banning.

From Katutura to the third floor of the Security Branch headquarters in Windhoek was no more than a ten minute drive. The offices, in a modest modern building standing aloof from the road, had one distinguishing feature – the presence of blinds throughout. There Meroro met Security Officers specifically imported, so it was explained to him, to 'fix' SWAPO *domomufitu* (maquisards – literally men in the bush).

The Security officers compose an elite with their own style of arrangements. In buildings occupied by them a particular floor is singled out for isolation behind an iron grille protected by an armed guard. The windows are barred, equipped with blinds throughout, including the southern flank unaffected by the sun. Interrogation designed to extract information from detainees requires no special installation; the investigation teams are usually composed of pragmatically minded men requiring little more than an ordinary office, and for those who preferred to apply 'third degree' treatment, immunity against unwelcome visitors. In Windhoek it was no different. What happened to Meroro took place in an anonymous room with tables and chairs and writing equipment, curtains, and lamps. Without the *dramatis personae* it presented with banality, like hundreds of other little offices in the city – an improbable milieu for brutality.

The interrogation according to Meroro's evidence started off with questions which followed in disorder, loudly and confusingly; it was not easy at two in the morning. Captain M[1] and Captain L kept on repeating the same questions; sun darkened in a safari suit, Captain L had the stoop of a hunter. Meroro was frightened, though mostly of Captain M's face, floating, soft spoken over L and another officer, Lt. H What number had he mentioned to the German woman on the telephone? Was it a code? And how did the *African Communists* come to be delivered to him and why? No he had to stand! No sitting was allowed: that was the rule. L's voice became loud and hectoring. Lt. H gave a push – a turning point of aggression. The next time it was a punch into the stomach; they ranted, bullied, pushed and pleaded; he was not allowed to go to the toilet; he was rather to mess in his trousers was L's advice. The hours of standing, exhaustion, abuse and menace went on till morning. The sun emerged. They breakfasted; for Meroro no food, nor water, nor tablets for a headache which cleaved his skull; only an exacerbating stream of questions and anger. He was mocked for being short, a little 'piece of shit' that had better open its heart and speak the truth or else. He was to remember that many had never left those offices alive.

It was at last evening, but their day's labour had brought no harvest of information. They paused. Lt. H approached him and removed the spectacles from his weary eyes with ceremony. The time had arrived at last to utter the truth: they were sick of his 'cheekiness.' Lt. H struck suddenly over his face with such violence that he almost fell. More blows: one on the cheek, another on the ear. The others joined in now, and beat him on his eyes and neck. He feared he was going to die – that was the worst part of it. They became exhausted and frustrated, bereft of the humblest prize which they could hand on. Then as if on a signal they stopped. It was time growled Lt. H to load on 'eggs'.

Capt. M and Lt. H went out leaving the hapless Meroro in L's custody; a young officer warned him with peremptory blows that he would have to 'talk' when M returned. L in the meantime pursued his own initiative hoping perhaps to surprise his seniors on their return. He brought in a rope, put one end outside the window and turning to Meroro said 'You must listen because now you are going to hear a ghost speak through this rope,' an enigmatic threat that might have been useful for frightening the illiterate and the superstitious. L saw Meroro's bewilderment and realised that his solo effort was not working. He produced a bottle of whisky and to Meroro's alarm drank purposefully. Was L also loading on 'eggs'? Was it that he and M and H needed an infiltration of alcohol to generate sufficient pious anger for the next attack? L sat down next to him and seized his jacket. 'Now you are going to shit . . . ' Capt. M and the Lt. returned and wasted no time. He was attacked from all sides. They pursued him round the office enraged, shouting like madmen that this was going to be his death. Meroro could smell the alcohol. M hit him on the nose; it began to bleed copiously. Meroro tried to protect himself, his eyes, and then his solar plexus when they hit him in the stomach, and back to his eyes again as they changed targets. He cried, whimpered and begged for mercy, only to be told it was pointless to plead that he had already told the truth. They had power to kill him, then take his body by helicopter and drop it to the crocodiles in the Caprivi. One of his attackers pursued him with a newspaper. He was ordered to bleed onto it and not mess up the floor. As far as Meroro could remember the blows went on for over twenty minutes. He lay in a heap, swollen, blood-stained and in pain though unbroken by the storm of crude violence. L took a SWAPO flag and draped it over him. His jacket, sticky with bloody, was put into a basin of cold water.

The last attempt to 'open him' had the deliberateness of an inquisitional procedure. First his wrists were handcuffed behind him; a rope was then attached, its other end thrown over the iron bars above the windows. The officers hauled at the rope, pulled his arms upwards, twisted, contorted unnaturally above his head. In a state of semi-suspension his shoulders seemed ready to be wrenched apart. He was yelling, unable to offer resistance. After some minutes his interrogators let him down to find out what he had to offer. The procedure was repeated; once again the operation proved futile.

He was left alone at last, swollen and bloodstained, his shirt ripped, his thirst unquenched and his vision troubled. Capt M ordered his shirt to be removed; it was replaced by one which did not fit. Afterwards he was given water but no food. That afternoon of the 9th he was removed from Windhoek and taken to the cells at Windhoek Airport.

He was examined in the cells of Windhoek's J.G. Strydom Airport within earshot of the great passenger jets. According to Meroro he made a complaint of assault – later denied by the doctor in court – headache, swollen painful eyes and painful shoulders from the hoisting. Doctor Y^2 and his partner Doctor W found him quivering, anxious, breathing rapidly and shallowly; in medico legal jargon he was hyper-ventilating.

The next five months were an unbroken experience of emptiness. He had no one to speak to except the magistrate who made a formal enquiry every fortnight, and the doctors during cursory visits. Unable to sleep he found sleeping pills unhelpful; silence dominated; police officers who brought him food refused to talk to him. Plans were made to intensify the monotony and immobility of his cell: special instructions were issued by high-ranking officers prohibiting his removal from the cell for exercise. At first he had magazines but these were removed. Was this also done on special instructions? He suffered chronic pain and cold in his feet; his chest in the area of his heart hurt him; he was haunted by fears of dying from a heart attack. He found his memory deteriorating; his letters to his family had symptoms of decreasing coherence.

It was towards evening in his third month of detention when he was overwhelmed by the vision of a rhinoceros rushing at him. Fully awake at the time he was quite unprepared for the terrifying immediacy of the beast; in days which followed he started to talk to himself uncontrollably; he had conversations with his wife who entered his cell wraithlike, laughingly, to tell him about the children and then to disappear leaving an insupportable encirclement of stone and iron. In another twilight hour apparitions entered his cell, aggressors wanting to beat and kill him; friends appeared and he yelled in frenzy for help. On another occasion, lying under his blanket he saw a black mamba, a deadly African snake, appear through the iron door; he started, petrified and threw the blanket in front of him. The snake disappeared but his secret certainty of sinking into insanity grew stronger. The suspicion that he was to spend the rest of his days in the *malkamp* (mental asylum) seemed a new form of hallucination. He could speak to the police doctors about his painful shoulders, his insomnia, his headache, but in his own mind dared not allude to the new invaders in his life.

It was in this state that I found Meroro at the time of defence preparations in the Taaipopi case. As SWAPO policy was to figure as a major issue in the trial, Meroro was the obvious candidate to give expert evidence on SWAPO history and policy. Taaipopi's lawyers had of course no right to consult him as he was detained under Section 6 but there were valid practical reasons why we should do so: without the benefit of Merero's help the trial against Taaipopi could be forced into a prolonged postponement until Merero emerged from the limbo of confinement. The police reluctantly agreed to my interviewing Merero together with attorney B. Maritz in the cells at the Windhoek Police Station.

He was seated at a police officer's desk; his face had a grey dust palor; he was fumbling with his scarf. Beyond the 'hello' his speech was curiously scattered, at times incomprehensible. He found difficulties in answering the simplest questions on SWAPO principles. There were outbreaks of stuttering and long pauses. He answered questions which were not asked and mumbled replies which were not understood. The great events of August 1973 flickered confusedly in his mind; Meroro, a considerable profile in Namibian history, had been reduced to this rambling creature struggling against his own bodily shivering and disarray. His removal from isolation was imperative if he was to be salvaged as a witness. A letter of request was sent off to the Chief of Police describing Meroro's disability, confusion and impaired thought processes.

The police did act but not to stop the ordeal. Anticipating public exposure, they, unknown to the defence, asked a psychiatrist to pronounce on Meroro's normality.

For a detainee the experience of loneliness unfolds in a world of unrelieved hostility. The policeman's frigidity belongs to the system, while prosecutors are committed to protecting the *status quo*. But what of the magistrates and the doctors? The former make visits like clockwork (but they are dependent on the police so that the clock often only starts after the breakthrough interrogation); their duty is to take details and to report; the circumstances usually remain immutable. Then there are the doctors called in at the behest of security officers. The detainee does not feel that his communications to a doctor will be treated with confidence; on the contrary some have had the impression that the doctors are aware of the quality of the interrogation.

It was common cause at Meroro's trial that when he was released from detention in terms of Section 6 he made an oral statement to Captain Tomasse about his possession of the banned literature. It was the defence case that at that time Meroro, terrified of the police and suffering from the effects of sensory deprivation, was not in his 'sound senses'. If so the statement would be inadmissable. This came up early in the cross-examination of one of the doctors. The magistrate interrupted when he saw the line. If this went on he warned he would send Meroro for medical observation. This he had the power to do; a committal to a psychiatric institution always carried the risk that a defendant might be certified insane. We replied that no basis existed for such an order as Meroro was perfectly lucid. Our case was simply that after five months in solitary confinement he was suffering from an impaired ability to reason *at the time* when he gave his statement to Captain Tomasse. The magistrate was not wholly appeased. 'Carry on but please keep in mind what I mentioned to you.'

David Meroro, as reflected in the mirror of Dr. W's evidence, turned out to have had minor complaints: sleeplessness, coldness in the feet and if he, Dr. W, 'remembers properly' headache. There were no physical signs of injury. Dr. W resisted the argument that Meroro was showing symptoms of sensory deprivation. The symptoms of sleeplessness, cold feet, listlessness and hallucination he contended were perhaps due to mild anxiety; in any event these symptoms could be found in people outside of confinement. Meroro he said had not told him of any assault. He had prescribed tablets for insomnia, analgesics for headaches, and tablets for the peripheral circulation. This evidence was a blow to Meroro's claims to eye injury and a strained shoulder.

In the meantime the defence had managed to track down a copy of a prescription for Meroro made out anonymously in the name of 'Detainee care of Major Myburg Security Department S.A.P. Windhoek.' What Dr. W had failed to mention was that Tanderil (used to reduce swelling) had been prescribed. After this prescription was produced, the doctor conceded the ugly portrayal of Meroro blighted with bloodshot pussy swollen eyes, restlessness, jitters, nervous tension, sleeplessness, palpitations, painfully cold feet and painful shoulders.

Dr. W and his colleague, having first dismissed his symptoms as attributable to mild anxiety, conceded under cross-examination that the entire constellation proved sensory deprivation and nothing else.

The police were next in the order of witnesses. They denied every accusation of assault and mistreatment. One of them had noticed that his eyes were swollen: this he thought had been due to lack of sleep: they had treated Meroro with courtesy throughout. No one had assaulted or threatened him.

With all the medical concessions reinforcing the defence evidence the argument for Meroro seemed powerful indeed. The magistrate did not agree however. In his judgment he rejected Meroro's evidence and found for a verdict of guilty. Meroro was sentenced to imprisonment for two months. The whole sentence was suspended on certain conditions.

Like Komati, Meroro went home to prepare for the next instalment in the struggle.

17

Exodus

The years 1972-1974, from the initial convulsion of the general strike through the flogging campaign to the great exodus, marked a crystallizing epoch in the political development of Namibia. Encouraged by Waldheim's visit and prompted by Vorster's promises to the belief that the way was open for political development in terms of meetings, arguments, campaigning, debate and persuasion, SWAPO members, and in particular Youth League leaders, plunged into campaigning and, as we have seen, scores of meetings were held across the country by the SYL as well as by SWAPO and the National Convention. Political argument was not always of the most delicate kind; undoubtedly there were excesses of enthusiasm but their logomachy hardly transcended an established culture of ideas and vocabularly already well entrenched amongst Black students and intellectuals in the Republic. Far from parleying with young Black crusaders – an indispensable process for an Administration burdened with a sacred trust and seeking to coach its wards towards self-government – the Administration struck at them with a ferocious energy more characteristic of governmental responses to the clash of arms than to the thunder of voices. Hopes faded as more and more Blacks perceived the obdurate intentions of the Administration.

The centrifugal forces of repression and disintegration joined together as Portuguese imperial power crumbled and the northern boundaries were opened. Angola now freed from the iron grip of Portuguese control beckoned in a brotherly manner. Beyond Angola there was the whole world, officially favourable to their cause, now presenting a store house of opportunities undreamt of in the status quo: education, homes, hospitals, dignity and above all an end to violence.

And so the great exodus began; from all parts of Namibia men, women and children turned their backs on their families, friends and possessions and made for the northern border to cross over on foot into Angola under cover of night. No one could take the risk of approaching the borders carrying the paraphernalia of a would-be immigrant; walking through the night they entered into an unknown future empty-handed. They saw little future for themselves in the Namibian impasse; many were students, teachers, and nurses whose skills were dearly needed in the Namibian community. After the Portuguese coup in April 1974 more than six thousand souls joined the exodus; once in Angola they then started the awesome trek through southern Angola to the Benguela railway line and then on to Zambia. By the end of 1974 most of those SWAPO activists who had been through the ordeal of flogging, detention or interrogation were in jail or had fled. Many who were released disappeared one after another across the border.

Their disappearance was an equivocal blessing for the Government and the Tribal Authorities. The departure of militant cadres could in the short run lighten the burden; but sooner or later would not the Thomas Komatis and the Andreas Nuukwawos return with hundreds of followers to destroy them? The human drain represented a great malaise in the whole of Namibia; the exodus from the South[1] as well as from Ovamboland revealed the chasm between Namibians and their rulers; the alienation of the Chiefs and Government was made visible for all the world to see. It did not require much vision to understand that the ranks of guerrillas beyond the borders would be swelled by thousands of supporters, that they would be harboured, and encouraged by their Black brethren in Angola and Africa to return and descend like armed locusts onto the homes and kraals of Chiefs and Headmen and their supporters.

Head Minister Philemon Elifas accused SWAPO of enticing people to cross the border with false promises of educational advancement. He put out obscure calls discouraging the emigration by saying 'Your mother remains your mother even if she is ugly and weak. You should not sire the mother of some other man.' Chief Jeffa Mukundi warned of imprisonment for those trying to leave without a passport and death for those helping others to go for military training. Rewards were offered for information leading to the arrest of anyone who encouraged the emigrants.

In this dilemma the Government and Chiefs made overtures to the one institution which could effectively staunch the flow into Angola: the Churches. Ovambo ministers contacted the Lutheran Churches and implored them to act. The Churches agreed. Word went out to the network of Churches in Namibia urging their congregants to remain in the community. The Ovambo cabinet in its attempt to ameliorate its image and move towards a *rapprochement* with the Lutherans held meetings with Church leaders. Jannie de Wet, concerned with the rate of emigration from the southern part of Namibia as well as Ovamboland, requested the Lutheran, Anglican, Roman Catholic, Congregational and Baptist Churches to mount an enquiry into the cause of the exodus.[2] To some critics this seemed an exercise in naiveté as De Wet should have had some prevision of the reasons that were to appear.[3]

The Church document, listing seventeen points, turned out to be an unpalatable litany of grievances: the failure to give independence, the spirit of the Odendaal Plan, apartheid, flogging, torture by electric shock, prolonged detention, the indiscriminate use of informers, the inadequacy of wages and the unacceptability of the programme of Bantu education. They pointed to 'the immense hatred and frustration' amongst the Blacks, their despair at the possibility of better human relations, the urge for freedom and human dignity, and the loss of trust in the Government because of its 'inhuman actions and empty promises.'[4]

In September 1974 the reasons for the exodus came up for analysis in an application made to Judge Hart for the release of Taaipopi and Kashea on bail pending the outcome of their appeal to the Appellate Division. The police opposed it on the grounds that the exodus had taken place on the instigation of SWAPO, and that Taaipopi and Kashea were also likely to join in and not face the outcome of their appeal. In a sworn affidavit Merero denied SWAPO's responsibility for the flight across the border. SWAPO he claimed was in fact distressed and had tried to discourage the flight. He defined some of the reasons.

'Many who fled were teachers, nurses and persons with secondary school education who had been compelled to give up their employment as a sequel to the intervention of the Security Police. Dismissal from employment usually ensued after members had taken part in SWAPO activities. Johnny Otto a leader of the organisation was a qualified teacher forced to resign from his post at Oluno in 1973 and had thereafter been compelled to live in Owamboland where he was unable to take up any employment. He became wholly dependent on the charity of friends, family and members of the organisation and I am personally aware of the fact that he found this fate to be unbearably frustrating. SWAPO members have been systematically persecuted in Owamboland and have been refused employment by the Bantu Investment Corporation or with hospitals or Government controlled bodies. This policy of victimisation has reduced numerous SWAPO supporters to a state of penury and desperation.'

Meroro's affidavit provided a crisp analysis of the exodus but did little for the prevailing sightlessness. It was also of little avail in court. Judge Hart after reading the affidavit characterised it as 'propaganda'. Bail was refused. No appeal to the Appellate Division was allowed. Taaipopi and his colleague were taken to Capetown and put on the ferry boat to Robben Island prison where they spent the next two years.

So the exodus took place, draining Namibia of some of its most talented souls. In the theatre of Namibian history it marked an *entr'acte* where the decor of public platforms, orators, leaflets, and the tumult of debate was to be steadily replaced by a backdrop of war, bombardment and death. From this point SWAPO in Namibia struggled to survive as a legal political force, whilst in the North the guerrillas with new reinforcements and new opportunities came to assert themselves along what was for them the only remaining meaningful path.

Exodus

Thenceforth all eyes looked North, to Angola and to the bands of SWAPO guerrillas who were more than ever to incarnate the aspirations of a subject people. The South Africans had taught them about power, its uses and abuses, a bitter lesson in which the Namibians were to show themselves adept students.

18

Of Metamorphosis and Men

After many months of rumour, innuendo and constitutional speculation, the National Party of South West Africa declared its intention in September 1974 to call a Conference – later known as the Turnhalle Conference – where the representatives of ethnic groups in the Territory would gather and collectively work out the constitutional salvation of Namibia.[1]

Anxiety flared up amongst Whites; many feared that the South African Government might, in order to make its peace with the international community, capitulate to the egalitarian demands of the UN. The bitter-sweet scent of major change was in the air. Prime Minister John Vorster had mounted an intense campaign of detente to win the support of several Black states in Africa; he had put out a dramatic appeal to be allowed six months in which to accomplish great changes; the people of Namibia were to be permitted to work out their own destiny and he had invited the OAU to send representatives to familiarise themselves directly with the conditions in the Territory.

In the Black community there were inchoate fears that the Constitutional Conference might lead to some form of unilateral and internal declaration of independence – probably in the form of a federation of Bantustans dominated by the White community. Blacks had not forgotten Vorster's vow never to surrender Namibia to Sam Nujoma, nor his stubborn hostility to SWAPO, nor the Development of Self Government for Native Nations in SWA Act, paving the way for Homelands independence, nor the uninterrupted constitutional construction work going on in the Homelands. And yet the prevalence of White fear, the wild rumours, the economic recession – immovable property was unsaleable[2] – the persistent reports that Robben Island leaders were to be released and Mudge's call on the Whites to surrender some of their luxury[3] for the sake of accommodation, to stay and not to sell, were comforting indicators of a new season of political thinking in establishment circles.

Dirk Mudge, the deputy leader of the N.P. in Namibia and Billy Marais, the Prime Minister's personal representative in Namibia, criss-crossed the Territory, cajoled argued and spread temptation in search of collaborators for a new constitutional programme. In this venture they were not unsuccessful in winning over some Black support. Their most significant prize was to be Clemens Kapuuo.

It was, in short, a time of confusion and uncertainty and bold predictions by Axel Johannes that Namibia would be independent within a few months were not successful in masking SWAPO's misgivings.

From 1973 onwards the cracks had widened in the alliance between SWAPO, SWANU and Kapuuo. A process of metamorphosis had overtaken the militant Kapuuo who abandoned his parochial life style in Katutura, became a frequent visitor to the great capitals of the West, adopted a statesman's ponderousness, and issued carefully composed declarations presumed to be the work of paid assistants. Though ignorant of the details SWAPO comprehended that important subterranean developments had taken place: Kapuuo's roots were now nourished in a different political and financial soil; Kapuuo now enjoyed financial backing from his not too altruistic friend and collaborator, the businessman James Endycott,[4] or big business in the Republic or the South African Government itself.

At the UN Kapuuo supported by Gerson Veii struggled to win recognition for the Convention – to the exclusion of SWAPO – as the sole authentic representative of the Namibian people. With the approach of the Turnhalle Conference, Kapuuo's attacks on SWAPO leaders became direct and mordant: they were not the sole authentic representatives of the Namibian people; they were imbued with Ovambo tribalistic chauvinism; the Ovambos had kept away from the bloody struggle against German Imperialism and would now, their overwhelming numbers unaffected by the Reich's essays in genocide, wield dictatorial authority over other ethnic groups in any new unitary dispensation. It was with this reasoning that Kapuuo prepared the ground for the final leap in a political syllogism that culminated in his call for the excision of Ovamboland from the body politic of Namibia. The Ovambos and SWAPO now had to go it alone and work out their own separate destiny. This theme, we shall see, fitted deftly with Chief Elifas's demand for the accession of Ovamboland to separate independence.[5] This demand, inspired and eagerly supported by Jannie de Wet, went far in the early fragile stage of constitutional debate to palliate the very notion of change in the White electorate.

Kapuuo's programme for a separate Ovamboland struck at the heart of the Convention programme – the establishment of a unitary state. His call would facilitate the Government search for a constitutional settlement and provide it with some legitimacy. It was also an extreme provocation, compounded by a readiness on Kapuuo's part to inflame fears of Ovambo hegemony.

Kapuuo was branded as a 'sell out'. If this accusation were true, Kapuuo's actions represented a reversal of a lifetime of struggle. As successor to Chief Hosea Kutako, Kapuuo, the proud inheritor of the Herero tradition of resistance had acted out a determined and pioneering role in the early days of struggle, collaborated with the Rev. Michael Scott, submitted petitions to the UN, reported grievances in Namibia and resisted the Odendaal Plan and Verwoerd's master plan for Bantu education. White politicians and officials referred to him as the 'little Katutura shopkeeper' and the 'little kaffir'[6] and characterised him as radical and dangerous.

The internecine turmoil in the Convention left it paralysed; it was rent by differences between conservative and more militant elements, lacked political direction and, at a time when anti-apartheid Blacks most needed solidarity, a common front to oppose new Government–nurtured alliances. In December 1974 SWAPO conferred, assessed the contagion of disaccord and at a Press Conference in the Grand Hotel, announced their break with the Convention. The Convention was dead, they declared;[7] it had been incapable of living up to expectations, its unity had crumbled and it had become infiltrated by Boss agents (an oblique reference to Kapuuo and his connections).[8] The SWAPO rebellion was soon followed by SWANU, the Rehoboth Volks Party and a small group with the large title of Namibia African People's Democratic Organisation (NAPDO). This left a motley rump of minor figures, organisations and chiefs: the Herero and Nama chiefs' councils, the National Independence Party (NIP), a Coloured organisation led by Charlie Hartung, the Damara United Front (DUF), a splinter group of Damaras led by E.H. Christy and the Rehoboth Liberation Movement, a minority party in the Rehoboth community. By the end of the year these organisations had opted for participation in the Constitutional talks popularly referred to as the Turnhalle Conference or simply Turnhalle.

The cleavage in the Convention coupled with the defection of SWANU the SWAPO camp came as a major political upset to Kapuuo. The triumphant rebels constituted themselves under the banner Namibia National Convention (NNC) appointed Albertus Kangueehi Chairman, with Japhta Tjozongoro a powerful SWANU leader, as new President. Martha Ford of the Rehoboth Volks Party became the vice-President. In its first Press Conference the NNC called on the South African Government – but explicitly not the Whites – to quit. The birth pains of the new organisation were accompanied by fears of an immediate banning.

As 1974 drew to a close the Ovambo election, fixed for the 13th January 1975 loomed ominously; now that Elifas and the Ovambo Government were officially calling for independence and the incorporation of fellow tribesmen on the Angolan side of the border, the percentage votes to be polled had acquired a strategic political importance, for the entire solution to the Namibian impasse was not feasible unless the Ovambo Government could claim legitimacy through credible democratic elections. The alternative solution – an Ovambo Government endorsement of an internal constitutional settlement – also required credibility. With this in mind the constitutional structure of the Ovambo legislative assembly was amended to allow for a majority of elected members in the chamber. The elected members were increased from twenty-one to forty-two. The appointed members remained thirty-five.

Much had happened since SWAPO's destructive boycott in 1973 when only 2.5% of the voters went to the polls. In the intervening period the administration had analysed the roots of the 1973 debacle, made its diagnosis and formulated its remedies. A comprehensive scenario was quietly prepared; a system of new persuasive techniques was to be applied: the skies would be crowded with aircraft and helicopters; the Army and police force would overrun Ovamboland; an all-embracing grip on Ovambo peasants through a pyramidal structure of power made up of chiefs and headmen would be applied to extract votes. The choice would be simple but critical: if they did not vote they would not be permitted to plough, nor take up employment nor receive medical services and pensions. Teachers, clerks or nurses in the employ of Government bodies would lose their jobs; shopkeepers would be faced with closure and insolvency. To allow the persuasion to soak in, the election would this time extend over five days, not two; the quasi emergency regulations under Proclamation R17 were to be tightly enforced under the surveillance of security police, soldiers, Government officials, and tribal policemen.

SWAPO moved into action but the exodus had taken its toll in its ranks with the flight of six thousand into exile. Large meetings of contract workers and township dwellers were held in the south; thousands of leaflets were distributed; but in the north, where it mattered most, SWAPO meetings were banned.[9] When SWAPOmembers started to distribute pamphlets calling on the Ovambo people to boycott the election they were called 'nocturnal jackals' by leaders of the Ovamboland Independence Party. An attempt to defy the ban by holding a meeting at Oluno on the 5th January precipitated an attack by tribal policemen armed with .303 rifles, rubber truncheons and swords; they stormed without a warning to disperse, attacked onlookers, beat one spectator senseless and injured others. At Ondongua tribal police used clubs to break up a gathering. Ovambo radio warned listeners not to attend. At this point Bishop Wood intervened and issued a public call upon Ovambos to keep out of the voting booths.

On Monday the 13th January the elections opened; a trickle of voters appeared at the polls. It was the same on Tuesday; the boycotters appeared to triumph once more.[10] It was then that remedial plans which we shall examine later were successfully put into operation.

In the end fifty-five per cent voted;[11] this presented a resounding vindication of Governmental effort and planning. SWAPO the NNC and Church leaders cried 'foul' with accusations of generalised and selective intimidation and fraud. Peter Katjavivi, the United Kingdom and Western Europe representative for SWAPO, dismissed the election as Pretoria's 'greatest joke', as devoid of all truth, as an exercise in 'fixing' in an overall strategy to perpetuate South African occupation of Namibia.

In response to the clamour from Ovambo citizens Auala and Wood briefed me and Attorney Colin du Preez of Windhoek in the hope that the election might be set aside through Court action. Though some witnesses were available in Windhoek no election petition could be prepared without extensive research and consultation amongst voters in the north. Permission to enter Ovambo was delayed by the authorities who wanted details of the expedition and the identity of our witnesses. Our purposes had to be revealed thus depriving the applicants-to-be of the advantage of surprise; fearing further intimidation we refused to pass on the names of our witnesses. Armed eventually with entry permits we flew to Ondongua together with Mr. B. Mautschke, an articled clerk in the legal firm, and a secretary. It was on our arrival that an official conveyed the Administration's ruling that consultations could only be allowed in the courtroom at Ondongua. This building stood at the centre of an administrative and army complex and had been the scene of a savage baton charge on spectators at the trial of Johnny Otto in 1973. A number of witnesses waiting at the Finnish Mission Station five miles away refused to come. Auala himself turned up, a large, simply clad figure in a safari tunic, with a brief message: any attempt to arrange consultations in that courtroom was a total waste of time. We explained the problem with frankness to the officials: since the purpose of our expedition was to accumulate evidence of the intimidation that had emanated from Government officials, policemen, soldiers, and headmen, it would be absurd to expect witnesses openly to make their way to a courtroom in the centre of an administrative enclave that teemed with those very officials. The Administration remained impervious to our complaints: no consultations could be allowed at the Mission Station. There was nothing left to do but for the lawyers to pack their equipment and their bags and fly back to Windhoek.

The Administration remained adamant despite renewed requests for permission and much ascerbic comment and protests from the Churches and SWAPO. Once again the South Africans had scored: henceforth they could trumpet abroad the legitimacy of the Ovambo Government and the decline of SWAPO – invaluable propositions for the South Africa propaganda machine operated by the Department of Information under Dr. Eshel Rhoodie. (Both were later exposed in the 'information scandal' in South Africa.) The final statistic would henceforth sound sweetly in the ears of those who felt solidarity with the regime. For those who felt otherwise there was comfort in the denunciation put out by Wood and Auala. A prima facie case of intimidation at all levels 'from the highest official in the area to the lowliest tribal policeman' could be deduced from affidavits they declared. Their press release read:

'A powerful claim for the voiding of the election could undoubtedly be made.

'This, however, would require free and unrestricted movement of the legal team with the right to consult with anyone in any place. The eyes of the world were on the Ovamboland election. The results have been widely used in propaganda to support the Government claim that the homeland policy is now the will of the Ovambo people.

'It is desired to test this claim in the courts of the land.

'Threats of dismissal, the loss of pensions, refusal of ploughing rights, fines and other reprisals are alleged.

'Acts of violence by Tribal authorities are again being committed.

'If a reputable advocate and legal team of the highest repute are refused the necessary freedom to complete their investigations, the belief that the allegations of grave and extensive irregularities during the elections are true, will be unavoidable.

'At a critical time in the political development of Namibia it is most essential that the true will of the people in Ovamboland should be clearly before us and the eyes of the world.

'An acceptable failure cannot be built on deception and coercion and no Government should be prepared to live a lie.'

With the approach of the Constitutional Conference, SWAPO and the NNC – with an eye to the internal and international implications – made strenuous efforts to muster the maximum visible mass support. At a mass meeting of over two thousand spectators in Katutura in February 1975, the dominating theme was SWAPO's goal of justice for all. Not surprisingly the Ovambo elections were the target for intense vituperation: it was an 'inflated balloon' liable to vanish with a pinprick. Axel Johannes, during a rare period out of detention, commenced: 'This is the voice of SWAPO.' Thousands of voices roared approval. He branded the election as illegal and the ubiquitous police presence as an intimidating pestilence, in a speech whose theme was the cry 'We promise fraternity'. This was later elaborated in a press release by SWAPO Treasurer Aaron Mushimba who tersely rejected Vorster's assertion in the South African House of Assembly that SWAPO had a policy of confiscation.[12] This, wrote Mushimba, was untrue and the repetition of untruth did not make it truer; all Namibians irrespective of race would be entitled to their basic human rights including the right to own and enjoy property under the protection of comprehensive anti-discrimination provisions in the future constitution of a state.

In a series of Press Conferences Dan Tjongarero, bearded Nujoma-style, emphatically underscored SWAPO's non-violent legal orientation, its non-Communist quality and its determination to encourage, not to eliminate, whites. The Churches joined in the choir of reconciliation, pointed to the religious discipline and peace-loving aspirations of their followers. Inevitably the Church leaders were filled with hope, but they were not deceived by the sibylline promises of great change. Frustrated by Government policy the Churches, for the first time in Namibian history, entered into a direct formal dialogue with political parties. They were tired of the Government's traditional policy of divide and rule, hence their determination to foster a grand *rapprochement* of anti-apartheid organisations. The Churches noted with gloom the steady enlargement of the South African military presence in the Territory, the investment of millions of rands in the construction of military roads, installations, outposts and airstrips and – in contradiction of confident predictions that the South Africans would soon pull out – pointed out that the Army and the Administration were as busy as ever on a 'business as usual' basis.

Their pessimism was darkened by knowledge of the dichotomy between reality and pretensions to a 'new deal'. It was the immobility of structures which haunted the thinking of Church leaders; Namibia remained the same and no 'new deal' found its way to workers who received the same insufficient wages, lived in sordid conditions and learned to carry on living under the yoke of apartheid. The sense of disenchantment was unexpectedly confirmed by the shooting down of Ovambo workers in the Katutura compound on Wednesday the 23rd April. According to the newspapers thirty-two policemen and the compound manager were stormed by massed Ovambo workers during an inspection of identity papers at the compound gates; when officials took refuge in an office they were attacked by a violent stone throwing mob; only their weapons stood between them and certain death so they opened fire killing one man outright injuring three others seriously whilst seven men sustained 'light wounds'. The attackers fled, reinforcements were summoned, the compound was encircled and two hundred and ninety-five Blacks were detained, of whom a hundred and twenty-seven were identified as attackers. The newspapers conveyed an overall impression of unruly, senselessly aggressive Black mobs on the rampage.[13] In vain David Meroro and leaders in the NNC wrote letters of protest describing the hostel as a 'slave labour camp' and the dead as martyrs of a system of viciousness.

Of the hundred and twenty-seven originally identified as stone-throwers, only eighty were brought to court. Bishop Wood arranged legal defence. Colin du Preez and I were briefed. We immediately demanded permission to see the injured victims who until then were kept isolated in a hospital ward. The members of staff were under police orders to release no information. Our request to see the victims was refused until we threatened an urgent application to court. We were then allowed in to the ward and took statements. The emergent facts pointed less to a riot than to an exercise in unlawful killing.

Matheus Leonard, a twenty-five year old worker at the municipal power station, was allowed through the gates that morning of the 23rd after producing his documentation. He was by then in a privileged position to follow the fatal sequence of events. This is what he saw:

'Outside the compound gates a crowd of men stood waiting for their transport. I also stood around waiting for the power station truck to fetch me.

A vehicle went through the main gate. One of the compound inmates with a bicycle attempted to emerge from that gate. This man was pushed back by a municipal policeman whose name I do not know. He beat this person with a rubber truncheon, and then threw a stone at him. The same municipal policeman then threw a stone into the crowd outside the gate, saying that the men should get away from the gate

118

and go and stand behind the row of cars. Some people in the crowd immediately responded by throwing stones at the municipal policeman and he and other policemen then ran to the office near the gate. The stone-throwing then stopped.

A short time thereafter, approximately 2 or 3 black municipal policemen again ordered the crowd to move further away and in order to hurry the crowd they threw stones into the crowd. The crowd was now bigger than before. And again persons in the crowd immediately replied by throwing stones at the municipal policemen. These ran to an office for shelter. Members of the South Africa Police who were in the vicinity also went in that office. Thereafter members of the crowd opened the main gate and a number of persons then came out. Shots were suddenly fired without warning at the men coming out of the gate. I noticed one man shot down and fall on the ground.

The persons who ran out of the gate were hurrying to leave the compound to go to work. No one attempted to attack any of the municipal or South African Police who were there. Those who ran out of the gate were shot by the police either from the side or behind. At no stage prior to the shooting was any order given to our people telling them to stop running.'

Matheus Leonard might have had a privileged insight, but the hundreds of workers crowding to get out were unable to see what was going on. The police check had delayed them for hours; their main concern was to get out and make their way to work. When the gates were opened eventually – few had any notion as to how that had come about – the crowds of workers poured out while the rest followed; it was only then that shots suddenly rang out and there was bewilderment, death and cries of pain around them.

The affidavits were later used in an application for bail before the magistrate of Windhoek. The police witnesses were there in force, ready to defy the counter evidence of hundreds of workers. They adhered to their story of mass attack; it was a matter of shoot or die. At the end of the trial the magistrate would be asked to reject the evidence of eighty accused and their witnesses in favour of the prosecution version. The trial might well have ended in mass convictions but for the circumstantial evidence which the defence had revealed. It was in the power of the prosecutor to argue away the evidence of the defence but not the eloquent testimony of bullet wounds: Shetuneyinga had been shot in the back; a bullet had penetrated Tolinane's left hip from the side; Ita was penetrated by a bullet shot from the side; Petrus was injured by a bullet which had grazed him behind.

With hindsight the attempt to isolate the injured from journalists and lawyers in the hospital ward is understood.

The magistrate granted bail: three hundred rand for each man – an unrealisable sum of money tantamount to no bail.

Finally on the 29th May 1975 the defence triumphed without battle: the case of the hundred and twenty-six 'positively identified stone-throwers' came to an end with the prosecutor's withdrawal of all charges.

The Commission of Enquiry which SWAPO had demanded was never established; there was no outcry in the Press, nor in the Legislative Assembly. No truthful reconstruction of the tragedy appeared in the Press other than in the *Sunday Express*.[14] The *Windhoek Advertiser* confined itself to an unobtrusive article entitled 'Unhappy chapter closes'.[15]

The world was deceived but Katutura knew better; the incident had no novelty; the inhabitants had seen their own kind killed or beaten before. With or without the circumstantial evidence they believed the victims to be blameless; by the same token they knew that Katutura would be misunderstood or blamed and that for the police there would be neither rebuke nor retribution. It was yet another event which, for Katutura, cut through the tenuous barriers of ideology and tribalism and helped forge an imperishable bond in their own community and with those who were prepared to stand up and do battle.

19

'Ethnicity Stinks . . . '

If the architects of the Constitutional Conference drew up their blueprint with a view to excluding SWAPO and its companions in the NNC, they could not have engineered a more effective mechanism. From the outset the constitutional process was to germinate and flourish under the protective vaulting of ethnicity; only those leaders or organisations that had proved themselves to be truly representative of an ethnic group by performance in ethnic elections could gain access to the conference table – so went the formula.

For anti-apartheid Blacks whose struggle was directed against racism the constitutional formula was anathema, an arrangement blighted by the irremediable curse of ethnicity. But the evolution of the constitutional talks was stumbling and painful, and it inspired, at least in the initial months, frail hopes of a drastic revision of the Conference structure. Skinny Hilundua, SWAPO chairman in the north, foreshadowed SWAPO's participation once the South Africans had withdrawn their presence, lifted Proclamation R17 and realeased political prisoners.'[1]

Despite their protest 'Ethnicity stinks in our nostrils', SWAPO opted for a nuanced approach, and at a Press Conference in January 1975 posited the fulfilment of four non-negotiable conditions as a prerequisite to its entry to the talks: the recognition of the right of Namibians to independence and sovereignty; recognition of the territorial integrity of the whole of Namibia; withdrawal of South African troops and police and the repeal of Proclamation R17. The fourth demand – the unconditional acceptance of the 'historic' and 'universally acknowledged' fact that SWAPO was the sole authentic representative of the Namibian people – also served as a warning to Vorster that SWAPO would match his *kragdaadigheid* (forcefulness). Three months later SWAPO introduced a more flexible stance: from outright denunciation the organisation moved to expressed willingness to discuss Constitutional issues with any representative of the South African Government; SWAPO was now prepared to sit down at a Conference Table with other authentic leaders in the community, in the ambit of a UN supervised Conference with the ultimate aim of full and free elections under UN supervision and control.[2] The proud demand for unique recognition was quietly dropped, and in June 1975 SWAPO released a discussion paper on its Constitutional plans for the future. The entire tone was that of judicious accommodation: Namibia would be a republic with English as the official language; a President would head the Executive in a Constitutional structure which envisaged a single chamber Legislature, though a second chamber in the form of a house of chiefs with no legislative power was foreshadowed. People's representatives would be elected by simple majority in a hundred constituencies; an independent judiciary would be guaranteed; the judges of the Constitutional Court would be entrenched in their independence in a period of tenure of not less than ten years; a Bill of Rights would include comprehensive anti-discrimination provisions. The determination of the economic structure, and its components of free enterprise, socialism or a mixed economy was to be left to the sovereign discretion of the nation's representatives.

SWAPO's moderation was not reciprocated; if anything, political life had become more difficult, more hazardous. Prohibitions of meetings, arrests, assaults, detention and threats of banning, remained part of the ongoing political experience. In February thirty-nine SWAPO members were arrested and imprisoned for the technical offence of failing to produce their Passes after an attempt to hold a meeting at Outjo. (They only got as far as announcing their meeting with a mobile loudspeaker.) At Rehoboth, members of the Executive were arrested, detained in a lock-up and prosecuted for being there without a permit.[3] Requests to hold meetings in Gibeon, Otjiwarongo and Berseba met with outright refusals. In June the NNC gave notice of a peaceful three-thousand man procession through the streets of Windhoek to protest against the South African 'occupation'. 'The march will go on' answered Tjongarero in defiance when permission was refused. This set off a war of nerves; within hours the Minister of Justice intervened and ordered the Chief Magistrate to ban all meetings;[4] police and army commanders conferred in closed conferences while police reinforcements were rushed to the capital. Tjongarero responded by publicising details of the demonstration: it would go on as planned, the marchers would line up four abreast accompanied by NNC 'peace officers' to enforce discipline and ward off *agents provocateurs*; no one would be armed, no one would break ranks. 'I will be marching up in front' remarked Tjongarero to a conference of reporters, heedless of the blanched faces surrounding him.[5]

Journalistic predictions of baton charges and bloodshed in Kaiser Street, the main street of Windhoek, were not fulfilled. Against the phalanxes of riot policemen, machine pistols, riot sticks and shields, dogs and tear-gas equipment, prudence decreed the cancellation of the march, though the day did not pass without some excitement in the form of a 'spontaneous' demonstration of NNC members led by Martha Ford outside a Government office in the centre of Windhoek. Eighteen demonstrators including Martha

Ford arrived with posters upon which were emblazoned 'Martyrs of Liberation' 'Get out of Namibia' 'Vorster shoots – we resist peacefully'. In the presence of some Church officials and Cathy Wood, Martha Ford and seventeen demonstrators were unceremoniously arrested, put in waiting police vehicles and taken to the cells.[6] (Unbeknown to the demonstrators and the police the arrests were illegal. A subsequent court action for damages led to a windfall for the demonstrators in the form of a tax-free gain of four thousand rand.)

It was now the SYL's turn to press for permission for a protest meeting in the centre of Windhoek outside the French Bank Centre. The application to the City Council was served with a curt note requesting 'the White Community and illegal authorities in our holy land Namibia' not to commit suicide by standing in their way as the meeting would willy-nilly take place.[7] These were brave words; like Tjongarero's they came to nothing. The White papers scoffed: Tjongarero had tried a bluff; the SYL ultimatum was farcical. Perhaps. But all the bold talk was something of a revelation for Whites who lived in ignorance of the co-existence of Black political voices and social aspirations. The march did not take place but the precise vision of Blacks on the march, so swaggeringly laid on by Tjongarero, brought home to them the reality of an awakened Katutura wishing to explain itself, communicate and take up its rightful place in the heart of the capital.

The new strategy was to break out of the ghetto, to proclaim the SWAPO/ NNC vision in the streets and squares of the city, to clamber on a central common stage of history and reveal to the world their challenge to the South African Government and Turnhalle. But with their meetings prohibited, their organisers speakers and followers arrested detained and prosecuted, their leaflets distributors turned back, SWAPO and the NNC (bereft of their own press and deprived of access to the mass media and radio), found their paths blocked and saw their strategy founder. And yet if they could not enter Windhoek in peaceful formations they could do so singly as individuals, and in the deserted streets at night time provide evidence of their force with immense slogans written across road surfaces and the solemn faces of Government buildings. Throughout Namibia young men and women crept out at night armed with brushes, paint and spray-cans; a creeping rash of giant graffiti glowing in lurid orange or sky blue started to spread across the face of Namibia. On the highways 'SWAPO' and 'Namibia' proliferated in competition with 'Stop' and 'Slow'; the country abounded with 'Namibia', 'One Namibia One Nation', 'Boers go home', 'Black Boers – Kakamas is waiting', 'The time is now', and for the benefit of the smug, the laconic instruction 'Think!'. In Katutura there was even less restraint: 'Namibians don't be afraid of the bloody Boers', 'God save us from the white bloodsuckers' and 'There is no apartheid in heaven'. On a lavatory door at the Katutura stadium: 'Blacks only – sorry Boss'. In Ovamboland Elifas broadcasted stern promises of punishment and the police were put on the alert.[8] Most got

123

away, but not all. Two young men and a girl, equipped with a bicycle, brushes and paint, were surprised by an Army patrol at night and fled; soldiers opened fire with machine guns and killed the girl. Her companions were taken to hospital with bullet wounds.[9] Ruben Hauwanga, suspected of organising the slogan writers, was arrested by the security police, held for interrogation and later released. In Pretoria the Minister of Economic Affairs, Chris Heunis, announced in the Government Gazette that SWAPO's emblems were to be proscribed under the Trade Marks Act; the Youth Leaguers riposted tartly that they would disobey the new law, and reminded the Government that it was dealing with the Youth League not the Afrikaanse Studentebond (Afrikaans Student Society).[10]

SWAPO and NNC leaders, reviewing their struggle, might at this point in time have felt burdened with more than their due of predictable adversity. They had survived, but for how long? In the background the Ovambo Government kept up a steady drone of agitation for the banning of SWAPO. To the pessimists the immediate future gave promise of little other than danger; even so no one could have foretold that most of their leaders would be behind bars or find themselves in the Namibian diaspora by the end of August and that a remote agricultural college at Ogongo, converted to the purposes of specialist interrogation, would be waiting for those who did not get away.

20

The Prophetic Vision

On the 16th June 1975 security policemen surrounded Bishop's House, the official Anglican Bishop's residence built onto a rocky eminence that dominated Windhoek in the valley below. Boxes and piles of letters, documents, tapes and posters were assembled during a meticulous search through the private possessions, clothings, bric-a-brac and children's toys of the Wood family. After the search a notice of deportation[1] was served upon Wood; identical orders were later handed to his American wife Cathy and to Rolfe Friede, the Director of the Christian Centre in Windhoek. The notices of expulsion were categorical; no reasons were given; each was to be out of the Territory within seven days. For a Bishop whose diocese exceeded the dimensions of England and France, this posed perplexing practical problems. The authorities allowed no respite: there were no rights of appeal.

News of the deportation orders led to surprise, indignation and protest, and in Katutura a prevailing sense of restlessness. Many in the township had learned to recognise Wood's firm, amenable profile, an ever present supportive figure at political trials, whose home, open at all hours – the front door was never locked – had become a clinic, a hotel or a club for those in need of comfort, advice, money, legal assistance or spiritual aid. It was a home that accorded moments of protective release not easily attained in Black townships, with its posters breathing silent defiance: 'This house is bugged' and 'The God we believe in intervenes in history to break down the structures of injustice.'

The day preceding Wood's deadline, Katutura had its say. Hundreds of marchers moved in procession headed by Wood and Friede with Namibian flags, the Anglican processional standard and SWAPO flags held aloft. They sang freedom songs and cried 'Power' through the dusty streets on the way to the Lutheran Church. The valedictory service was surrounded by crowds of sympathisers who, unable to squeeze themselves into the Church, joined in with a throaty contribution to the song. Inside the Church there were prayers and an antiphony of praise for the exiles to be, and words of bitterness and reminders that neither death nor repression could snuff out a people's will.

Wood had no intention of quitting. When he finally drove off to the border, it was – unknown to the police – in a Land Rover equipped for a venture into the interior; his plan was to drive through Botswana to Lusaka and then westwards to Angola's border with Ovamboland. There in sight of the border he would establish his mission.

As Wood made his way through Botswana, Edward Morrow – destined to take command of Bishop's House in the role of Vicar-General – awaited his ordination in England as a prelude to enacting the political resurrection of Wood's spirit in Windhoek. Theatre-like the voice of the new inheritor to the hot seat in Windhoek was heard as Wood made his way through the barren heat of southern African plains. From England came the words of Morrow's attack: expelled or not, Wood would remain Suffragan Bishop, recognised as such by the overwhelming majority of his people, many of whom had streamed to meet him in their thousands during his last visit to the Angolan border; the South Africans had acted with cynicism and had turned Bishop-baiting into a national sport with no purpose but to destroy the will of a nation kept in drudgery.

Cathy Wood's American citizenship made her vulnerable to expulsion yet she refused to move. The daughter of a U.S. Army officer, she had gone out to Namibia as a swimming instructress where she had met her husband.

For two days she remained on in possession of the manse, a one woman defiance campaign encouraged by friends – mainly Black – in a commune of loyalty, laughter and reminiscence around the log fire. Her motives were simple: with the passing years she had watched friends driven out of the Territory by expulsion orders and had vowed that when her turn came she would not go voluntarily. Many visitors called to show solidarity and bid her farewell. Finally the detectives came: arrest was followed by immediate removal in a police car to the airport where an aircraft stood waiting on the apron ready to depart. There were no familiar faces to comfort her and her daughter, Rachel, before their definitive take-off from Windhoek Airport.

In Windhoek the relief was not without some ambiguity for Cathy's tall spare figure, lank flaxen hair and childlike fearlessness, conformed to white Windhoek's standards of Aryan beauty; if only she had not been so irritatingly informal and filled with laughter at officialdom and unbearably affectionate to Black friends whom she accompanied through the streets of Windhoek barefooted.

The indignation which followed in the wake of Wood's banishment was perhaps justified – not so the surprise. The rebellious clamour in the Lutheran and Anglican Churches had irked the Government and tried its patience too far. Under Wood, Bishop's House had become an automatic halt on the path of fact-finding missions, journalists, Namibia watchers, politicians and diplomats who came for a 'computer print-out' of contemporary analysis, stayed for dinner and departed firm friends. It had the force of an embassy that represented some immense and inimical Power, a little chaotic, very informal, but rudely undermining of South Africa's troubled diplomacy.

As for Wood he had acted too vigorously, spoken too forcefully on every issue between Church and Government for his office to remain undisturbed. His call for a boycott during the Ovambo elections was a profoundly political intervention at a moment of pivotal importance; after the elections he was at the centre of preparations for legal counter-attack. With Auala in the remote north, the task of conceiving and initiating legal moves, organising funds and planning forensic strategy with attorneys and counsel fell in the practical situation to him. The thwarting of the petition to set aside the election was a defeat converted to solid gain by the Church exposure of the Administration's game. Then there was his voice on the BBC World Service, nonchalant, incessant and credible, spreading its acrid understanding over South Africa's diplomatic and propaganda efforts.

Less than three weeks before deportation the newspapers carried Wood's call for a South African withdrawal from the Territory. (He did tend to speak of the Government as an occupying Power.) Wood added: the South African presence was baleful,[2] there had been fifty years of misrule, the current initiatives were false solutions, Blacks did not care for reform and above all wanted the South African presence to vanish. This tirade coincided with the Security Council debate on Namibia. He also had an unsettling talent for unorthodox manoeuvres which could not be legally faulted. After the installation of a new Government in Angola, Wood side-stepped the Government's determination to keep Anglican Bishops out of Ovambo by simply requesting a transit visa to the Angolan border. This was not a ruse: the visa entitled him to travel through Ovamboland without stopping; but from the safety of the Angolan side of the border he could minister to his people. On a second occasion he and Colin Winter held Church services under the shadow of South African border guns; over a thousand attended; South African soldiers fired futilely into the air, but frightened no one away. On their return Wood and Winter spoke of a new generation of Namibians now talking of an armed struggle. Their exposure was ruthless. Vorster, said Winter, was building policies of self-delusion and the end of that road was a Vietnam in Namibia; the Ovambo elections were a national forgery and the pro-Pretoria collaborators working on so-called constitutional reform were without relevance. 'The thief has no say in the reallocation of stolen property. He has one function only – to restore that stolen property.'[3]

Theirs were voices whose candour if not insolence could only radicalise the venturesome cadres in the Church, and bear witness to struggle which the Government preferred to characterise as contemptible and terrorist. It was in a climate of such daring that Lukas de Vries, without the help of Aesopian cover, could speak openly of Christian participation in armed struggle against South American dictatorships, and propound the principle that violence as a means of political action was admissible;[4] that though reconciliation was nearer to God there was a distinction between cowardice and Christian passiveness. In Government eyes this was yet another apology for

SWAPO – this time the external wing; and once again Namibian Christians, braving the scorched edges of the Terrorism Act, proclaimed what others had dared not venture to whisper.

The Church leaders and workers did not confine their innovative ideas to secluded seminaries; they reached out into the community at large. In December 1974 Dan Tjongarero and Pastor Zephania Kameeta, later appointed Principal of the Paulinum Theological College, organised a Black Consciousness Conference at Okahandja. There they pressed for a new vision untinged with a sense of inferiority, a Black theology and a new indissoluble fraternal bond. The impetus from this Conference shaped fresh attitudes and contributed towards a *rapprochement* of rival groups, the defection of SWANU from the NC and the establishment of the NNC. The metaphor and texts of Black theology became the exegetical prism of their new liberatory praxis. They set out to solve the problems inherent in the Christian ethic whose theology cast out the God of the oppressed and reshape the racial configuration of God's countenance. They excoriated the South African Government for its pagan brutality; its very presence was described as a threat to the Gospel. Pastor Kameeta:

'Thus I see it as the task of every Christian to work for the knocking down of this Government. In this country which claims to be Christian you can be a Christian ten thousand times over, but if you are not white you are treated like a dog. . . . in Windhoek this Government is committing the greatest political deceit of the century! While they are busy removing the apartheid signs from the buildings (but not from their hearts!) high officials are still fighting for the superiority and dictatorship of the so-called whiteman.'[5]

Church leaders were henceforth to examine political and social issues in the context of the Christian confession. Henceforth Jahweh was profiled as a God who shared with the oppressed and cared for them in their alienation. The Bible became the Magna Carta for a new humanity and quotations such as 'For freedom Christ has set us free; stand fast therefore and do not submit again to a yoke of slavery' became the textual root of a simplifying unshakeable faith. His new attributes were compassion rather than wrathfulness; He suffered with the suffering in exile and in the ghettos. Since God by definition was free how could His Word be anything but a message of liberation.[6]

Kameeta's message merged with a clear apology for the armed struggle:

'All this is proclaimed with the "help" of the Bible and in the name of Christianity as the holy will of God. And to make this a reality, force is used. The one who dares oppose this "Divine" commission of the "Europeans" is tortured or thrown in jail or restricted or banned or deported. Those who on the other side of the borders of this country try to find an answer for this violence, are seen as faithless cold-blooded murderers, and daily prayers are made to the Lord against them.'[7]

In the north the Churches fulfilled their Christian duty of bearing witness. Their evidence of the unfolding war developed into an embarrassing exercise in exposure. Pastor L. Haukongo, an Archdeacon under Wood, spoke of the unremitting disquiet in the north where children raised their fists at passing soldiers calling out 'Power – One Namibia One Nation'. Church leaders spoke of the rapidly deteriorating situation in the north which they attributed to the 'terror practices' of the tribal police and the soldiery; of a dangerous South African created impasse of antagonistic groups, the one of pro-South African headmen, the other an unwilling population under the yoke of alien occupiers. They described the South African Broadcasting Corporation as an instrument of obnoxious propaganda; they brushed aside the political nostrums in the constitutional process and called for genuine reconciliation and genuine sharing on the basis of Black initiative. Above all the Churches sought reconciliation, but repentance they insisted must be coupled with a readiness on the part of Whites to restore. In the eyes of Jannie de Wet these sentiments were dangerously on the road to Communism.

Auala, de Vries, Dumeni, Kameeta, were all Namibian born. They were undeportable. Colin Winter had been dealt with. It was otherwise with Richard Wood. He had to go.

Before the deportation order came through there were already signs presaging the approach of the expelling season. Rumours drifted through Windhoek: Wood was an agitator in the pay of SWAPO, trained to write their speeches and give directions.[8] The police accused him of helping organise the abortive march on Windhoek. In Windhoek's white legislative assembly he was denounced as the author of SWAPO statements. The journalists also tried to play their part. After Wood's call for an Ovamboland election boycott journalists put questions which he immediately rejected as loaded and unobjective.[9] There were threatening telephone calls and graffiti. After the order was served the words 'SWAPO headquarters' were sprayed vividly upon the Anglican cathedral. In the garage at Bishop's House 'SWAPO' and '*SWAPO se moer*' – an expression of banal crudity implying female sexuality – were daubed across the cars and on the walls.

Wood crossed the border into Botswana shortly before the deadline. After motoring to Lusaka he found his plans blocked by the course of civil war in the south of Angola. On Winter's suggestion he flew overseas and addressed gatherings and conferences in Europe, England, and in America. At last he could be explicit and so lost no time in explaining the paradox of Christian faith and armed struggle.

He expounded the view that all states have armies and that military gestures are often, however regrettably, a culmination of interstate dialogue. There were millions of Christians in the armies of the world. There could on a question of fundamental principle accordingly be no basis for distinguishing the morality of national struggle for independence through guerrilla means and the onslaught of standard armies acting with the benediction of bishops and priests. He too was prepared to stand with the oppressed and take up arms if vital change were not granted.

21

The Assassination of Elifas

On the evening of the 16th August 1975 Chief Filemon Elifas, emerging from the bar of the Onamagongwa Bottle Store, of which he was a habitué, was shot down by an unhurried burst of firing from four Tokarev machine pistols. Nineteen shots were fired – three entered his body; he died a few minutes later from a fatal penetration of the liver. His assassins, anonymous unidentified shadows, disappeared into the night leaving no traces other than nineteen spent shells. No one knew where the attackers had come from, nor their identity, nor their destination. The Chief Minister had spent his last thirty minutes with friends drinking whisky and conversing haphazardly. Nothing eventful had happened till then except that the Bar owner, Phillipus Thomas, had words with a young man called Hendrik Shikongo, a distant relative of the Chief, over the way Shikongo had driven off the day before scattering dust onto the steps of the Store. The argument was not particularly acrimonious and the SWAPO badge sported on Shikongo's lapel passed without comment. Shikongo left, walked to his car and drove off. Five minutes later Elifas heaved himself to his feet, went out and closed the door behind him as the immediate prelude to a deafening and deadly fusillade.

In Ovamboland there was rejoicing; in Windhoek and other white towns a hard reaction congealed against SWAPO which was instantly suspected and accused. The anger in high places was particularly intense as the entire hierarchy of Bantustan friends and collaborators would henceforth feel vulnerable. The assassins had got away unpunished; the internal wing of SWAPO, still enjoying a threadbare legality, applauded secretly.

The Security Police struck immediately, with efficiency, though little discrimination. The following morning Hendrik Shikongo, a chief-clerk in a wholesale firm at Ondongua, was the first to be seized. He was not a SWAPO official; his support had over the years been expressed more through music than political activism and in 1972 he founded his own choir at Okhenea with a repertoire of SWAPO songs and hymns. Two Black sergeants woke him at his house at 8.30 and searched unsuccessfully for his SWAPO badge in the house and grounds. 'Come along with us and you will see for yourself how you are going to get hurt.' He was taken in the back of a Police pick-up van enclosed with wire mesh and a locked iron door, to the Ongonua Police Station. An Investigating Officer, Lieutenant B[1] was waiting. 'Where is the gun you used to kill Elifas?' B asked without preamble. Shikongo replied that he knew nothing about the shooting; he then saw the anger in B's face and grew afraid.

A little later that morning SWAPO secretary in the north Sam Shivute, and Ruben Hauwanga, driving to the latter's house to listen to music, were arrested by security officers on the main road near to Oshakati. They were ordered out of the car and taken to Oshikongo where Shivute was put into a cell filled with an intolerable stench from a blocked lavatory; there were also rats in the cell. He complained to a white policeman who laughed: 'It's your own business. You shit too much.' Shortly after noon a tall lumbering policeman, Warrant Officer P ordered him from the cell with a laconic 'get out', took him to an adjoining room and with the help of a long limbed blond constable kicked away Shivute's feet from under him, then trampled on him where he lay, shouting 'Who killed Chief Elifas?' Through an open door armed soldiers peered in with curiosity; Shivute, protesting and unprepared, thought he was going to be killed, not realising that their attack was but a brief prologue to an interrogational nightmare in which his delicate health and title of General Secretary would seem to figure more as a provocation than protection.

Ruben Hauwanga had the incalculable misfortune to be arrested only three days before his intended departure for the United States where he was to study medicine. Once in the police vehicle he had an immediate foretaste of what was to come; Lt P moved so swiftly that the unsuspecting Hauwanga never saw the first blow onto his mouth which started to bleed immediately. 'You Kaffir, you will really shit today' thundered P's voice on the journey to Oshikongo; there were other threats garnished with imprecations and 'Who killed Elifas?' At Oshikongo he was taken to an anonymous iron-doored white house occupied by the Security Police where his ankles were shackled and his left wrist handcuffed to a window frame. It was not long before Lt. E appeared. 'I won't have any lies from a *swartgat* (black anus)' he bawled, striking him on the head with unprovoked fury. The handcuff, chained above him to the top of the window frame, bit into his wrist; after fifteen minutes he felt trapped by the painful traction. A Senior Officer appeared and in an aside warned him about E – it was better to cooperate as the man could be very dangerous.

While the apparatus of State Security hunted detainees throughout Namibia, in Windhoek Kapuuo unleashed angry followers. SWAPO and SWANU supporters were seized in the streets by his vigilantes who, enjoying official connivance, turned Kapuuo's house into an *ad hoc* 'interrogation' centre. They caught and pulled Gerson Kangueehi, a leading member of SWANU, through the streets, ejected Samuel Tjahere from his car, kicked and struck at it and smashed its windows. In Kapuuo's house self-appointed interrogators clouted and pommelled them and threatened to cut off their testicles. Another group, with faces masked in stockings, brandishing an improvised weaponry of sticks, rods and wire, fell upon Axel Johannes and Aaron Mushimba, marched them to Kapuuo's home where they were interrogated, abused and beaten on their heads. A Black member of the police force sat in the room eyeing the treatment with interest; in an adjoining room – the door was ajar – Kapuuo brooded and watched without intervening. The captured pair was later handed over to the Security Police at Windhoek from where they were driven as hand-cuffed prisoners in the rear of a police car to the white house at Oshikongo. Lt E was there; he stared silently at Johannes, then struck him across the left cheek with the butt of his gun and put iron shackles tightly around his ankles. Later on the limbs became swollen and the skin broke under the grip of the iron, causing permanent scarring.

Over two hundred men and women were caught and detained incommunicado in the wake of Elifas's death. Other SWAPO executives included Skinny Hilundwa, Othniel Kaakunga, Elifas Munjaro, Johannes Nakawa and Alpheus Naruseb. David Meroro managed to evade a raiding party sent out by Kapuuo and successfully escaped to Angola. Even the shadows of past history were pursued: Lamek Iithete, arrested but not prosecuted at the time of the Ja Toivo trial in 1969, was now seized by soldiers who cooperated in the nation wide cleansing operation and taken to the military camp at Oshakati. Issak Shoome had also been arrested in 1969 but not prosecuted; since then he had farmed in remote isolation at Okuwale until arrested in the swoop. Seven churchmen were apprehended, six of them were pastors including Pastor Kameeta, Principal of the Paulinum Lutheran Seminary, who was arrested at Katutura during a rally of the NNC. Pastor Titus Ngula was taken to the white house at Oshikongo, handcuffed and kept awake for three days and nights. Lt E mocked the Church and said he was sure that the Pastor understood the South African Police; 'If you sleep you get electric shock.' Pastor Josefat Shanghala was shackled and handcuffed and warned by an officer with a goatee to 'write facts otherwise we are going to fight with you'; if he did not speak there would 'really' be trouble: he would be hung up with a rope and get a dose of electricity. There was an electrical apparatus in the corner. (Because of the practice of blindfolding detainees, Pastor Shanghala was one of the few to see a machine which could have served as a generator.) From the Engela Mission Hospital in Ovamboland six nurses were arrested and kept under Section 6 of the Terrorism Act.

Section 6 of Act 83 of 1967 (the Terrorism Act) empowered any commissioned officer of or above the rank of Lieutenant-Colonel to arrest a person without a warrant and to detain him at any place if he has reason to believe that such person is a terrorist or is withholding from the South African Police any information relating to terrorists or to offences under the Terrorism Act. 'The detention shall continue until the Commissioner orders his release when satisfied that he has satisfactorily replied to all questions under inter-rogation or that no useful purpose will be served by further detention.' In practice the Commissioner acts on the advice of security officers. The isola-tion is spelt out: No one 'shall have access to any detainee or shall be entitled to any official information relating to or obtained from any detainee.' Inter-fering lawyers and judges are kept out: 'No court of law shall pronounce upon the validity of any action taken under this Section or order the release of any detainee.'

The prisoner has few rights. He has no right of communication with the outside world, neither with his family, nor his lawyers nor friends. He has no right to be seen by his own medical practitioner, nor to buy his own food or toilet requirements though in practice this might be allowed as an induce-ment to cooperation.

The Section is silent on the detainee's right to receive reading matter but the Appellate Division – in a disquieting decision where tedium was equated with the horror of isolation – found that it was not the intention of Parlia-ment that 'detainees should as of right be permitted to relieve the tedium of their detention with reading matter or writing materials;' detention should be maximally effective in inducing detainees to speak. In human rights terms this was a disastrous judgment, for the Judges had the opportunity to protect the individual prisoner rather than help tighten the screws. Against the exigencies of State Security they could have weighed a traditional and golden principle of legal interpretation: that the courts should protect indi-viduals from executive inroads into liberty by placing a restrictive interpreta-tion on Draconian legislation. Regrettably their judgment reflected a foren-sic wisdom prepared to tolerate rather than ward off authoritarian mechanisms.[2]

The Lutherans, shaken by the wave of arrests and fearing for Kameeta's fragile health, cherished no comforting doubts that one purpose was to strike at the Churches' outspokenly 'prophetic' stance against apartheid; it was an opportunistic abuse of power and ambiguity, to exploit Section 6 on an unprecedented scale. This was no longer 1974 when the arrests of David Merero and others – a transparent misuse of legal mechanisms – led to national and international protest. Now real assassins had struck; the death of Elifas could not be argued away; fear and suspicion was rampant and everything seemed possible. The security officers understood and seized their opportunity.

Doctor Carl H. Mau, the General Secretary of the Lutheran World Federa-tion (LWF) wrote to Prime Minister Vorster:

'By continuing to press a policy of Separate Development there, the unity of the Church which is seeking to unite all peoples in that country is being hampered. By rejecting applications for residence permits, or their renewal, for church workers from outside the country, invited to assist in the ministry of these churches, the ser-vice and work of our churches are being hindered. By arrests which include a number of pastors and teachers and many members of our churches as well as other Christian churches, and by the expulsion of pastors and leaders of Christian churches of the area, we can only conclude that the South African government is engaging in a systematic attack upon the Christian churches in Namibia of a kind that is intolerable and an offense to the world community of Lutheran churches.'

Anxiety over the safety of their brethren and the other detainees prompted the Lutherans to invite Erwin N. Griswold, former Solicitor-General of the United States and Dean of Harvard Law School, to intervene. Griswold was a man of international eminence; he had been to South Africa as an observer in a previous trial, was known to the authorities and was more likely than anyone else to be granted the privilege of penetrating the inaccessible world of Section 6 detainees. Griswold applied for a visa; the South Africans did not refuse but it was only granted after inexplicable delays on November 15th. He was then only allowed to see six prisoners awaiting trial under the Terrorism Act and on condition that a security officer be present throughout the interview.

Police cells throughout the north were overcrowded with prisoners after the ambitious swoop; the security police were also hampered by a lack of facilities at Oshakati where their offices were too confined and too inelastic to allow for multiple parallel round the clock interrogation. The white house at Oshikongo to which Shivute and Hauwanga were taken, was far from spacious and stood exposed to all eyes near the Post Office in the centre of the village. The prevailing atmosphere was one of anxious preparation and uncertainty; an interrogation centre would arouse the interest of armed SWAPO guerrillas a few kilometres away on the Angolan side of the fence.

The Agricultural College at Ogongo, tucked away in the Ovambo bush, had more promise as a haven for interrogation.

The College complex itself provided some flimsy camouflage and the protective presence of soldiers on Government property – and they were active throughout Ovamboland – would arouse slight attention. The security police themselves sedulously cultivated a surface ambiguity: they wore no uniforms, drove ordinary cars and gave no public sign betraying the concentrated activity of an elite officer corps in the area. The problem of cell accommodation was solved at Ogongo by the simple expediency of confining the detainees, whether they were pastors, teachers, students or the genuine article under the Terrorism Act, in police vans which served as mobile cages. The system of rules intended to regulate the detention and protection of prisoners was ignored with pragmatic phlegm. Blankets and mats became beds, handcuffs were used instead of padlocks to lock the doors of the vans, and risk of escape was reduced to a minimum by a liberal use of shackles and handcuffs. In Ovamboland temperatures in the shade often approached 40°C in summer. The heat in the vehicles might not add to the detainees' comfort though it could encourage cooperation. The security officers brought in stretchers and helped themselves to the furniture in the two houses. For those officers who opted for violence, the interrogational process itself required minimum equipment. The food for the prisoners was cooked by Black detectives; it was usually over-salted and unpalatable. A white adjutant officer was in charge of culinary operations for white staff. Detainees who had been won over – an interrogator's euphemism for 'broken' – sometimes shared the tinned fish or meat and mealie porridge diet of the Black detectives. Most of the police officers were drawn from different centres in Namibia and the Republic and showed a ready adaptability and preparedness to spend weeks in the bush, sleeping on stretchers and performing duty at all hours away from the routine and comfort of their offices and homes. In accordance with established practices the interrogation was left exclusively to White officers who had mastered the art.

Some of the White soldiers and uniformed policemen guarding prisoners and the establishment shared the aims of those less scrupulous interrogators. Some it seemed even enjoyed the spectacle of duress and were on occasions allowed to lend a helping hand by way of a slap or a punch.

Such was the quality of White solidarity.

22

Ordeal at Ogongo

On the morning of the 15th September 1975 Victor Nkandi, SWAPO Secretary for Transport, was arrested while supervising the construction of his shop at Oshipanda. A little earlier that morning shopkeeper David Sheehama had driven past to warn him that SWAPO leaders were being rounded up but this was no news as reports of police activity had spread across Ovamboland well before then. An hour later Sheehama returned, this time as a handcuffed prisoner with a dazed expression on his face at the back of a police pick-up driven by two Black security officers, H and K. They searched Nkandi's temporary quarters, found nothing, gave no explanations, handcuffed him and drove him and the hapless Sheehama to a secluded corner in the grounds of the Ogongo Agricultural College. There they stopped outside two houses, concealed by high ostrich grass, occupied by Black and White officers of the Security Police. Sergeant N was the first to approach the van to inspect the two prisoners in their cage. 'Here we have another terrorist' he observed. A squad of officers assembled and drove off with Nkandi to his father's home at Oshitundu. Armed with rifles the police surrounded the home, ordered the aged Stephanus Nkandi with his children and grandchildren to collect together in a group in the yard. While the officers were searching Mrs. Nkandi started to cry. 'Your child kills off people and he tells you nothing' said one of the Black detectives. The father was in tears. 'Is it true Victor did you kill someone?' 'No father I don't know what this man is talking about.'

It was only on the way back to Ogongo that Nkandi was given a first inkling of their purpose. Sergeant H: 'Were there not guests at your father's house, I mean your friends from the bush who came to stay with you?' Nkandi replied 'I don't know what you are talking about.' It was an answer given with naive immediacy, an answer that he was to repeat in the weeks to come with extremely painful consequences. If at that point Nkandi felt fear he had every reason to do so; he was perhaps bewildered but what he could not have predicted was that there would one day be a trial and that his life would depend on an inquiry into the detailed history of his sojourn at Ogongo.

Ordeal at Ogongo

Clad in a white shirt and neatly pressed trousers Nkandi did not look a likely terrorist. Early poverty had taken him out of Primary School – his formal education went to Standard 3 – but he pursued informal studies reading what he could and seeking explanations. Once he had overcome the problem of literacy he passed a driving test and became a truck driver; with his earnings he bought a battered delivery van, learned the hard way how to keep it going and so eke out a living through 'pirate taxi' work. But a lack of business confidence had brought on recession and he was put on indeterminate leave. It was then that he decided to build a shop for himself at Oshipanda, with plans to move with his wife and child from Katutura and settle down in fields familiar to him since childhood. He was a self-made man; he had by dint of effort developed a striking command of the Afrikaans language; later in prison – facing the death sentence – he studied English and achieved a remarkable mastery of a language which in the Namibian context was rarely heard and even more rarely spoken. Politically conscious but unambitious he had never addressed a SWAPO meeting, though he was often there to lead the singing. On the tenuous basis of his taxi-business success, the SWAPO Executive held his appointment as Secretary of Transport adequately justified. He had an immense quiet certainty which inspired confidence; beneath calm semitic features and a prophet's beard lurked a smile ready to surface under the most testing conditions.

The Agricultural College lies not far from the village of Ogongo near to the main road between Oshakati and Ruacana, surrounded by the flat plains of Ovamboland with its balanced adornment of high palm trees, thorn bushes and long yellow tangled grass. At the time of Nkandi's arrival the wooden boom across the entrance to the college was manned by soldiers; a narrow canal flanking the college fence provided symbolic rather than real protection. From the boom the police cars travelled along a gravel road past a high reservoir and a screen of ostrich grass to stop in front of two contiguous low brick houses. These had served the college at some time; there was now no sign of staff or students – only security officers, uniformed policemen and soldiers. A surface serenity prevailed with little to betray their purposes except the presence of numerous police vans covered with wire mesh serving as cages for silent Black men and women locked singly inside them.

One of the officers who had been at Oshitundu, whom he later found out to be Warrant Officer O propelled him towards one of the houses. It would be some time before Nkandi became practised in moving around with his shackles; walking was particularly difficult as the chain between the shackles was very short. O pushed him. 'Move on terrorist, move on, we haven't got the time.' Another push from O this time accompanied with a kick and Nkandi fell to the ground, picked himself up and clanked waveringly into the house. None of the usual police procedures was carried out: no PPR (Prisoners' Property Receipt) was issued, for nothing was taken from him; he was not searched nor was he 'booked in' in terms of mandatory police

137

regulations. In one of the many rooms, on the sprawling complex, unfurnished but for the presence of chairs, he was ordered to stand in a corner, to look at the wall, not to look around and never to sleep 'even if its a month before you tell us what sort of terrorist you are.' O pointed to a soldier with a rifle. 'This man here, he is here to watch that you don't sleep. You don't look round, you don't sit down – if you try anything this man will *donder* (thrash) you with his rifle.' Nkandi was accused of nothing specific. 'We want to know everything you know and we have plenty of time' was some indication that as late as the 15th of September the Security Police Intelligence had as yet no significant leads. Nkandi remained in the corner facing smudged walls for four days and nights. Under the unrelenting weight of his tall spare frame his feet and legs became bloated; he could no longer feel his legs as an extension of his body – only pain, and gathering discomfort in his bladder. One visit to the toilet was allowed each day and that had to be hurried and watched; he was not to be 'sly' and help himself to a rest. Warrant Officer O and Warrant Officer T, an officer with bruised hands took turns to interrogate – another word for an unremitting, frightening, hectoring pressure, on occasions reinforced with assaults. Others occasionally joined in with slaps. Strange faces passed him as policemen and soldiers came and went; some paused to clout him across the face, make faces at him and tug his beard and ears with the words 'You terrorist', 'Now you are going to shit' and 'Die you shall.'

By the third day he felt lost; it was the fatigue; there were moments when his identity faded; time seemed incomprehensible; he forgot where he was and the walls wavered. He was standing with his eyes open when – 'it was as if my heart had stopped' – he dropped to the floor. The soldier yelled, sprang from his chair and swung the rifle against his mouth. His lips and tongue were already bruised and swollen. From then on speech was difficult as if something were jamming his mouth, his answers as far as possible simply 'Yes' and 'No'.

That same afternoon, when his resources were at their lowest, T perhaps sensing the fragility of his morale, became most violent. It came about without warning; the officer pulled him round and in a loud voice said 'Terrorist you have got to talk. Now it is my turn to make you.'

Nkandi mumbled something about not knowing what he had to say.

'Then I will choke you' he shouted. 'Now you are going to shit'.

As large bruised fingers compressed his throat Nkandi was unable to fight or flee, or struggle; the scream died in his throat as his breath was sealed in; in a state of collapse he remained upright, pinned by his throat against the wall. When he lost consciousness, the soldier was chortling gleefully; when he woke, the soldier was shouting 'Get up, Get up'. Wary of the rifle butt he raised himself as best he could. T's fists came again, over the face, under the jaw and into his stomach; the blood tasted salty in his mouth. 'Who killed Elifas?', T roared 'Tell us or you will not leave here alive.'

T finally let him be. What seemed like a bad dream was over till that evening, when Warrant Officer N appeared wielding a knife. (In retrospect Nkandi understood the planned strategy and careful timing underlying the storms of wild seemingly spontaneous animal violence.) N came towards him in a savage mood; his voice was hoarse, overcome it seemed with rage, more frightening than T's bellowing efforts.

Clutching Nkandi's hair he pulled his head right back, chin high up, like an animal's ready for slaughter. Nkandi jumped backwards in his shackles, a desperate froglike leap and fell over.

'Jou Swapo *moer*[1] – life is sweet.' N made a quick throwing movement. Nkandi dodged as the knife came at him and then struck the wall.

'I can see that you have been trained to duck knives in Russia' commented N. At that moment someone roared with pain in a neighbouring room.

N: 'That is a Swapo *moer* – shitting himself – your turn is still to come.' Screams became an unbroken wail. 'Do you hear?' asked N. 'Here we don't play with Swapo *moere*.' He again launched the knife with a knifethrower's dexterity; it flew past Nkandi's shirt and richochetted off the wall.

Nkandi's nerve snapped at that moment: he screamed and cried, recklessly and uncontrollably like a child while his captors looked on with mirth.

'You know Axel and David Merero and Aaron Mushimba?' enquired N 'We had them here but they are now dead because they wouldn't talk.' Somewhat contradictorily he added, 'They said that they planned to kill Elifas and that you must have run away to Angola.' Nkandi stopped weeping; next door the screaming had stopped – only the scraping of chains. He was beginning to believe N.

Nkandi: 'I will talk what I know.'

N immediately brought paper and pen: 'Now write and just don't write shit'. A table was brought to him, the handcuffs were removed; he was left to himself under the uncommunicative stare of the soldier; for long hours he tried to comply and wrote about himself, David Merero and SWAPO. When that was over N ordered him to stand and disappeared with the papers. Not long after, N returned with a white man whose face was ravaged by the sun, freckled, in part pigmentless. The stranger came up to him; inches separated them. 'You think we believe all your nonsense? That we are children?' he barked. The newcomer was another investigating officer. His name was E.

During the building of his shop Nkandi made many trips to and fro between Windhoek and Ovamboland. Small wonder that his friends and David Merero used him as a courier. On behalf of SWAPO he had taken cash money for a shopkeeper Usko Nambinga. He had also driven a second-hand Land Rover which Meroro had bought for the Oshikongo Branch. Unfortunately the Security Branch had a different notion of his history. Some of their questions struck him as comic – if only he were able to laugh. Had he and Axel and Aaron not flown from Angola to Lusaka to arrange Elifas's death?

Had he not brought up the Land Rover for the use of terrorists? Had he and Meroro not gone visiting terrorists? E tried out these and other desperate inventions – perhaps concocted by despairing prisoners – searching for corroboration. Again the fateful answer 'I don't know what you're talking about.' New names popped up. What had happened between him and Usko? What had he and Nicodemus Mwahi – to whom he had handed over the Land Rover – been up to? But none of the facts, no matter how detailed, no matter how hard he thought, approached the ambitious sagas which E tried out. E cautioned him: he knew much more than he pretended. 'I treat you like a gentleman and you bullshit me' was his summing up. Now he was asked to tell them all about his dealings with Hendrik Shikongo. This was the first time the name was mentioned. Nkandi shook his head; he simply did not know.

'Get up and stand terrorist' commanded P 'Your time has now come.' In an attack of insane and inexhaustable energy the fists slogged at his head, in his eyes, in his stomach and over the body. With one blow he slammed Nkandi's head against the wall. Something seemed to crack. Nkandi fell into the corner unconscious. When he woke he found himself surrounded by white faces. Someone was throwing water on him; there was blood in his mouth and in his nose and blood stains on his shirt and on the walls. P had vanished leaving a soldier in possession. The soldier looked down at Nkandi teasingly. 'I do feel sorry for you because that's just the beginning of the fun.' At that moment Nkandi gave no thought to this threat; in the back of his skull there were alarming flashes, like momentary flares. This he thought was the beginning of madness.

Later that evening there was a party in the adjoining house. The sounds of boisterous carousal, singing and the frenetic strumming of a guitarist playing *boeremusiek* drifted across to where Nkandi stood, immobile in his corner. He listened and heard SWAPO songs being played from confiscated cassettes. Afterwards the officers sang the songs themselves and inverted the meaning. Sturdy voices sang 'Vorster shall never be defeated by SWAPO', and 'We shall overcome' to the accompaniment of the cassettes. They ended off adding their own meaningless crudity to the repetoire with *'Terroriste se ma se moer* Sam Nuyoma.'

As the party died down a number of officers moved over to inspect the detainees. Nkandi was surrounded by policemen; some of them were unfamiliar faces. An anonymous squat white man directed an incomprehensible farrago – which Nkandi thought might be *Fanakalo*[2] – at him and then pushed a burning cigarette stump onto his chest near the nipple when he refused to answer. Too exhausted, and too afraid to cry out, he clenched his teeth till the pain subsided. Someone extinguished a second cigarette above his stomach intoning appreciatively, 'This *moer* is tough eh? You should have seen Aaron when I cut his penis open, God how he screamed like a pig.' The men around him seemed equally ready for amusement and cruelty. One of them hit him with a fist, another pinched him, and yet another pulled his beard offering to slice his testicles.

After the group left him to continue this inspection of 'terrorist specimens' in the establishment, N brought in toilet paper and made him clean up the blood. When that was done he was ordered back into the corner. If he now no longer feared death he was also not far from caring for it. His arms were weak, his lips were swollen, his left eye was closed and was oozing pus. When he heard himself talking to himself without thinking he thought he was no longer normal. A guard shouted 'Keep quiet'. The prospect of madness frightened him and he kept silent. A little later he fell asleep standing up, tripped over his chains and nearly fell onto his guard. The man jumped up in fright, threw away the book that he had been reading and struck him on the right cheek with a rifle butt. 'Try that once more and I'll shoot you.'

The next morning E brought Captain F along. The Captain smiled enigmatically and enquired where the blood on his shirt had come from. Ignoring Nkandi's silence he ordered a chair and offered an affable invitation to Nkandi to be seated. There were many questions on his mind but what he wanted most of all was confirmation of a conspiracy to kidnap Elifas and use him for propaganda purposes on Radio Zambia. The Captain did not make much progress, neither on this nor on other theories.

'I don't know. I don't know about all that' Nkandi replied uneasily.

F stood up; he towered ominously, his face clenched, over Nkandi.

It was a critical moment. Nkandi ventured that he would try again. N brought paper and wrote as Nkandi's hands were swollen. Reading from interminable statements written laboriously in someone's handwriting N put a number of propositions to him. Nkandi replied affirmatively to questions such as 'Did you and Meroro go and visit SWAPO soldiers?' Half asleep, half terrified and yet grateful for a miraculous moment of rest, he doled out the 'Yeses'. E entered and produced a passport. 'Do you know this man?'

'Yes.'

Not having the remotest idea of the photograph's identity he did not embellish.

'This is Dimo' explained E 'He is the big shot. You and Meroro must have spoken to him.'

Nkandi: 'Yes I know him.'

He confirmed an entire epic how he and Meroro had made plans to help SWAPO soldiers, supply them with clothes, blankets and food and finally hatched a plot to assassinate Elifas.

E stopped scowling; confident and satisfied, his mission accomplished, he went off with the handwritten statement without noticing Nkandi's face puckered with uncertainty. For the moment at least the ordeal was at an end; a Black security officer turned up and led him to a small pantry to sleep. Constable W threw down some blankets and a warning to work well with the *base* (bosses) as many prisoners who had spoken the truth had been released.

Nkandi: 'Are Axel and Aaron and Merero really dead?'

'It's possible. I don't know.'

Fatigue overcame him; too tired to bother about his handcuffs he put his head down and slipped swiftly into oblivion.

When he woke he had no sense of time and could not guess how long he had slept. Constable W pushed mealie meal and tinned fish into the pantry; he ate eagerly though with hesitancy as his mouth was still raw and swollen. He could not remember when he had last eaten. N appeared, summoned him to a table and rewrote parts of the statement, nibbling for elaboration; someone's fantasy of a secret air journey to Zambia interested him most of all. Nkandi embroidered anxiously wondering when his crude fiction would be discovered – terrified of the possible consequences. After that the was allowed to sleep undisturbed. W brought his food periodically and allowed him to relieve himself when necessary. It was a week of repose and growing worry. When a policeman carrying a rifle woke him from his sleep one night and pulled him out of the pantry Nkandi concluded that N had seen through the fantasies and decided on his liquidation. He was instead given a bucket of water and told to clean the floors where two officers engaged in horseplay had scattered a white medicinal fluid on the floors and walls of a corridor. He cleaned up while the guards played at darts. At the end of the corridor he found a door to the garage standing ajar; he peeped through and saw someone whom he thought he recognised as Johannes Nakawa hanging arms outstretched from chains in a crucifixional pose, his toes just touching a little table. Below him a policeman cradling a machine gun kept watch with a parrot next to him for companionship. The following day Nkandi was ordered to clean out the garage; Nakawa had disappeared leaving the guard behind; the parrot was also there and kept muttering, perched upon a branch tied up against the wall. The guard instructed him not to disturb the bird. In the corner of the garage there were rags which looked like the remains of Aaron Mushimba's Afro-style shirt. In his dread he decided that Mushimba had been murdered.

Nkandi's status now embraced the role of domestic servant. He was made to clean out the houses, rake and weed the property, and help with the cooking; in this time anxiety festered in his thoughts. Each day after he had performed his duties he was returned to the pantry. On one occasion he found the opaque glass window of the pantry had been left open; he peered through and rejoiced; outside sat Aaron Mushimba with shackled ankles, almost unrecognisable behind swollen eyes and cheeks. A corpulent white officer wearing a wig was guarding him armed with a rifle. There were other familiar faces; there was Nakawa, Festus Shaanika, Taleni Hamukoto and a nurse from the Engela Mission Hospital, Rauna Nambinga.

Finally the storm burst. E appeared abruptly at the door of the pantry, crimson, enraged and cursing; Nkandi looked up into homicidal eyes. E flew at him, struck him on the face and broke lips which were slowly beginning to heal, snarling at Nkandi for all the nonsense he had spoken, the 'shit' that he had made them write down, the inventions he had sucked out of his thumb 'saying Meroro says this and Dimo says that'. He had him on the floor, kicked his head and then his stomach; Nkandi felt the heel of his shoe driving towards his groin. E launched himself; Nkandi felt him trampling on his body; a heel crushed his testicles; he screamed but could not turn away. There was still no respite from the fury; E now beserk, kicked and shouted until he was exhausted. E: 'Don't you every play with me again you whore's-child. You tell me who murdered Elifas else you shit. I am going to Oshakati to get the *waarheidsmasjien* (truth machine) – that will make you talk.'

After E had left K led him out of the house and locked him in a van. He felt ill: he was bleeding, swollen and bruised and there was blood in his urine: later on he noticed a discharge of pus and he thought it might be syphilis. That night the van was parked alongside long grass; innumerable mosquitoes attacked with relish. Later in the evening K came and stood at the back of the van and stared at him and then threw a lizard onto him. That night he hardly slept, troubled by elusive fears and thoughts that struggled vainly to shape in the imagination some image of the evil that lay in store for him.

A few days later shortly after sunrise a taciturn Black officer D guided a very bedraggled dispirited Nkandi to the garage of the house next door. There he tied a rope slung over the beams to Nkandi's wrists. Hoisted off the ground Nkandi hung from the rope, arms outstretched, totally suspended until D brought a small table which he placed under his feet. Not long after E came in. He entered with theatrical affability. Nkandi had long noticed that his interrogators enjoyed playing different roles, especially that of artless innocence.

'How is old Victor? Are you hanging here again?' enquired E.

Nkandi did not answer.

'Get him down and give him a chair. I want to talk to him.'

After sitting down Nkandi noticed that E had a SWAPO flag in his hand which he gave to D. Appearing to know what was required of him D then tied the flag around Nkandi's head blindfolding him. He then felt his one hand being tied up; twine or wire was tied to the small finger of the other hand; something was also attached to the little toe of his right foot. In an instant there was screaming in his head; his body writhed and shook. His muscles were powerless; when his body had stopped shaking he was on the floor. He could see nothing; his finger and the extremity of his foot were burning. Someone drenched him with water.

E: 'Who killed Elifas or would you like to dance once more?'

143

Before he could answer the current was turned on again; the electricity clawed inside him; he felt it tearing him apart. It shot pain which had an indefinable solidity through his limbs and head.

Nkandi was whimpering: 'Please don't do that again, I will talk.'

'Well let us hear, who were they?'

Nkandi thought frantically. 'One of them was Ahmed' – the name of an Arab that he had read about in an Afrikaans magazine in the pantry. 'The other was Kashalulu' – a name noticed at random in a photo album of suspects and corpses that the Police had showed him.

Once more E seemed satisfied and told D to untie him. All that remained was for Nkandi to embellish a description of the imaginary assassins.

When Captain F reappeared on the scene he exclaimed 'This man stinks terribly' and ordered D to take Nkandi for a shower. He had not washed since arrest; his shirt and trousers were bloodstained, creased and filthy; the disconcerting discharge was still there. After he had washed F sat down with him at a table and for four days – he slept at night in one of the vans – plodded through every detail of the facts and fantasies which passed for his statement.

F's conciliatory voice explained that he wanted Nkandi as a witness and not as an accused. He needed and had secured Nkandi's cooperation; once Nkandi had given evidence he would be free to go back into the world. 'The case' he said 'will be a warning to those who want to help terrorists.'

Then as an afterthought: 'You will also convince the court that both wings of SWAPO are part of the same body. I see that your statement is not altogether right but don't you worry.'

For some weeks after that he was kept on at Ogongo spending most of his days sitting outside under the vigilant scrutiny of Black officers, dreading to hear the sounds of interrogation and pain and yet curious to see what was happening and who had been caught. There were altogether twenty-five white and ten Black security policemen at work there. There was profuse cursing and swearing day and night. Sensing the latent panic in prisoners waiting to be processed, and himself so aware of the knacker's omnipotence vested in the interrogators, he came to think of Ogongo as a sort of abattoir. And yet parallel with the labour of interrogation and all that went with it the officers saw to it that they had a good time; those who were off duty lay in the sun, chattered, jogged and played tennis; there were picnics into the countryside and trips to Ruacana and much carousing at night under clear Ovambo skies.

The bizarre admixture of interrogation and recreation puzzled him and added to his confusion and sense of rankness; though life at Ogongo was not entirely stripped of elements of salvation. One evening Nkandi's mobile cage was parked outside somebody's bedroom window. Towards eleven o'clock the light went out. He heard a voice filtering through the window into the night; it was the voice of Captain F at prayer. Nkandi lifted his head and listened attentively and made out the words of the Lord's Prayer spoken solemnly in Afrikaans. He heard 'Thy will be done' and contrasted in his thoughts the humble image of the man at prayer while the prisoners reckoned with their grief in vans and corners.

The saga of Victor Nkandi's ordeal at Ogongo is qualitatively inseparable from many of the other seventy prisoners who passed through that institution. This was the tragedy of Ogongo. The microscopic threads of Nkandi's endured pain provide us with a necessary though harsh insight into his subjective journey through hell; it is through this that we can begin to identify the ordeal which other prisoners – were they teachers, shopkeepers, national heroes or unknown peasants – shared with him.

In the trial which followed, Nkandi's entire version was disputed by the police. No single detainee they asserted had been assaulted or maltreated.

After Kapuuo's 'storm-troopers' – as SWANU members preferred to characterise them – had handed over Mushimba to the police at Windhoek, he spent fourteen idle days in a cell. No questions were put to him and there was nothing to suggest that the police had any hope of connecting him with the assassination. According to Mushimba life changed abruptly when he came to Ogongo where Captain F welcomed him as the big 'Swapo fish'. There he was ordered to sit on a chair and describe the conspiracy which led to Elifas's assassination. Combining threat, violence and cold water, he was kept awake for eight days and nights. By the eighth night his mind was uncontrollable and disorientated – a scrap heap of recurring fear and irrelevance. Instead of writing about SWAPO he found himself writing a delirious fantasy about the capture of goats. In the ongoing state of limbo between encroaching sleep and dazed consciousness his interrogators plied him with excerpts – they seemed like bowdlerised regurgitated police accusations – from the statements of other detainees. When had he gone off in an aeroplane to Zambia? What did he say about Elizabeth Namunjebo's assertion that he had admitted that he and Axel Johannes had training as guerrillas? Mushimba withdrew crustacean-like into himself and held his ground. His captors then tried hoisting him, at intervals, during four days and burnt him with cigarette stubs and a cigarette lighter; in a fit of bad temper one of his questioners tore up his shirt, forced it into his mouth until he started to choke; he was beaten on his head and body – even over the stomach and legs which had ballooned.

The badgering questions, indifferent to the hour, were repeated tirelessly. What had he done in Zambia? Where had he imported rifles into Namibia? How many cars had he bought for the terrorists in Angola? Mushimba remained impregnable. On one occasion Captain F invited him to become a state witness. When this failed they dangled the privileged and lucrative role of informer in front of him. This too he refused, but the fatigue became overwhelming. He started babbling to himself in incoherent, incomprehensible, disjointed sentences, until at last F ordered that he be allowed to sleep 'be-

145

fore he goes mad'. F ordered him to be untied. By then his legs were so swollen that he had to be carried to the toilet. One of the Black detectives was told to give him pills and ointment – both were nameless – to rub onto his legs and stomach. Whatever accusations might be levelled at the security police no one could accuse them of lacking foresight.

In the white house at Oshikongo, Sam Shivute was given a clear insight into the interrogational methods which were in fashion. Handcuffed to a chair he was kept awake for seven days and nights. After a few days he found himself drowning in confusion. By the seventh day he was afflicted with amnesia and altogether forgot about an account of the Elifas assassination – yet again an effort in fiction – which he had given E a few days earlier. In his first hour at Ogongo an unknown policeman banged him on the head with a clenched fist. When he complained of the assault the policeman smiled and facetiously explained that he was merely hitting himself. Sgt. S saw his Bible and instantly confiscated it saying, 'The devil is not allowed to read this Bible'. Since he was SWAPO secretary in the north he had to know all about the killing of Elifas, they insisted. 'I know nothing' he answered, so they hoisted him in the garage. He begged them to let him down, promising that his story this time would be true, but his inventive capacity was not up to the requirements of his interrogators.

E turned up with a SWAPO flag and draped it over Shivute's shoulders where it hung like a proud mantle.

'You are a brave man, do you feel good? As a great SWAPO leader do you feel proud?'

Shivute pondered: 'Yes. I know I am proud to belong to SWAPO.'

E grunted, blindfolded him tightly with the flag and put a bag over his head.

'Do you know what is going to happen?'

No answer.

Something was attached to each of his little fingers and to his big toes. Without warning the current rushed through him flooding him with pain. 'It burnt right through my body. It threw me and it shook me. When I tried to scream I could not and all I could do was twitch. I couldn't help it and I fell on the floor.'

During all this there were voices mocking him. When it was over the laughter had died down.

'Haai what's going on here? Who's doing this to Sam?' came E's voice.

The flag was untied. E: 'Who tied the flag around his head?'

'It is you' answered Shivute.

E tried to sound offended: 'Haai Sam don't be funny! I wasn't here and I don't know why anyone would do such a thing to a good chap like you.'

Shivute was no stranger to violence. He had witnessed hideous floggings and their consequences; he himself had been set upon and battered by tribal policemen: but all that paled in comparison with what had now happened to him. His body trembled and felt as if it were on fire; he had bitten his tongue during a convulsion; he was let out to wash his mouth and found that he was spitting blood. Lieutenant E waited till he was finished, then accompanied him back to the garage.

E: 'Now tell us all you know about the death of Elifas.'

Reuben Hauwanga followed on the *via dolorosa* at Ogongo. Lieutenant E did not concern himself with him as he was not considered primary material. Even so this did not save him from suspension in the garage. Joseph Zacharias, a Windhoek businessman nicknamed 'Ice Cream', was suspended and shocked with electricity. He was shocked three times on one day. In the spirit of experimentation his interrogator tried the electrode against his hip, then his ears, then his tongue. From there he was taken to a military camp where he saw blindfolded detainees being taken into a tent, and heard the clamour of pain. It was at Ogongo that Pastor Josefat Shangala was handcuffed and threatened with suspension and electricity if he did not talk. From another room came the sounds of weeping. Jason Nangombe, a teacher at Ombalantu, after arrest by members of the SADF, spent three days of incarceration at Ogongo. He happened to be locked in a vehicle parked near the garage from where he heard the whimpering of someone in pain. For three days and nights he was allowed no sleep and all his written statements were torn up. Later he recognised the voice of an acquaintance whom he knew as Kamulu begging for mercy in the garage. Terrified by the atmosphere of the place he offered his immediate cooperation to his interrogators but they were unsatisfied. After tearing up his statements one of them threatened to choke him, but he was not assaulted. Johannes Nakawa was beaten, suspended, and kept awake; water was thrown on him whenever he seemed to be dozing off; smouldering cigarette ends were also deployed in the task of keeping him awake. Towards his seventh day he could not distinguish night from day. In a whirl of confusion he thought to himself that his mind 'had gone'.

On the 20 October 1975 Eva Muandingi, a nurse at the Engela Hospital, was brought to Ogongo after the hospital had been surrounded by security officers and soldiers. At Ogongo her interrogators became wrathful and demanded different answers. Finally E suspended her with a chain dangling from the ceiling; only her toes touched the ground. The handcuffs' pressure blocked off the circulation to her right hand which went black, and as late as 1977 her wrists bore the marks of injury. She was deprived of food and water, interrogated through the night and promised electric shock by E. Once she heard the screams of people 'undergoing torture' but saw none of the victims. Nurse Rauna Nambinga was also arrested at the Hospital. She was kept awake from Saturday, 20th September, till the following Tuesday. The investigation team had a wide range of questions. They wanted to know who killed Elifas and details of her contribution of money and sanitary towels to terrorists. When she started to doze she was prodded and cold water was thrown on her. Kept away from the lavatory she urinated into her slacks. On one occasion her head was pushed into a wall leaving a scar above her left eyebrow. Her body swelled; the puffy skin of her face closed in on her eyes and interfered with her vision. A threat to suspend her with a rope was not carried out. Rauna's colleague, Naimi Nombowa was interrogated and pushed vehemently into a wall against which she struck her ear. After Constable W had taken her to the chains she panicked and disgorged her information about nurses' meetings in the hospital. Another nurse, Anna Nghidhongjwa, was less fortunate; she hung without touching the ground for half an hour. Esther Shangano was threatened but not harmed. A white policeman put a centipede in her dress. His hand followed to extract the creature from between her breasts. Kaino Malua, destined to be a state witness, was from the same hospital. For some reason which she did not understand the detectives thought her impudent and hung her up in the garage with only the tips of her toes touching the ground from three o'clock in the afternoon until one o'clock the following morning.

Axel Johannes was transferred from Oshikongo early in September. Hemmed in by detectives for fourteen days and fourteen nights he was one of the few to answer aggression with aggression. He was kept awake with a variety of techniques: water was thrown in his eyes, his head was bumped against the wall, his elbows were burnt with cigarettes, he was compelled to sit in a crouching position with his hands outstretched like an immobilised gymnast, and K – the man had a penchant for harnassing reptiles and insects to the course of duty – put an *akkedis* (lizard) into his shirt. It crawled and tore and scratched his skin; when he tried to remove it K wrestled with him. With deepening fatigue Johannes fought back and struck at K. K was no sportsman; he had no hesitation in taking advantage of Johannes's vulnerability – he was shackled and handcuffed – struck him violently on the head, then kicked him in the ribs and in his spine when he was on the floor. Later on Johannes began to rave. His intellectual disintegration was so far gone and his equilibrium so affected that in the end he had little recollection of his own aggressiveness. Constable D afterwards told him that he had tried to butt them with his head, made frenzied charges at them with sulphurous eyes: it became a sport for the interrogators and their off-duty colleagues who joined in like picadors to help provoke him, side-stepped when he charged and tried to bite them, and laughed when he fell. They would crowd around when, breaking into the vernacular he launched into a tirade against invisible persons. Long after Axel Johannes had been 'processed' the interrogation team spoke of him with respect. (It was Victor Nkandi who overheard Warrant Officer G report on Johannes's feat of endurance, his 'record' of fourteen days and his stoic acceptance of cigarette burns. In that entire period he was not beaten when Captain F was around.)

Some time after the completion of his statement Nkandi was moved to the cells at Ondongua. The police dossiers – the accumulated harvest of months of interrogation – were transferred to the Attorney General. It was now over to the prosecution.

On the 25th November Nkandi was taken from the cells to the detectives' offices, where Lieutenant B put questions about Shikongo's delivery van. B noted his answers in the margin of a typed document without comment, scowled and had him returned to the cells. Soon after Lieutenant J told him in the cells that the prosecutor wanted to see him in the Grand Hotel in Windhoek; the prosecutor had decided to charge Mushimba and Shikongo and others – J did not specify who – under the Terrorism Act. A little later J and a Black constable drove with him through to Windhoek and on to his home in Katutura for a change of clothing. In the unfamiliar luxury of a private lounge of the Grand Hotel he met a tense bespectacled young man who was introduced to him as Advocate Jansen.

Jansen was immediately affable and predicted close cooperation with him.

Jansen: 'I value your cooperation. I wanted you here because you are an important guest.'

He poured out a beer for Nkandi and spoke persuasively of new Namibian prospects for multi-racial cooperation; he explained that Whites, Blacks and Coloureds were cooperating in Namibia where the future was being decided at the Turnhalle. He elaborated with simple allegorical allusions – he had perhaps misjudged Nkandi's intelligence – to a three-legged pot as an explanatory symbol of unity: just as it cannot stand with one leg missing, so the three racial groups in Namibia needed one another. Nkandi too should be at the Turnhalle, not wasting his time dangerously with leftist violent organisations like SWAPO; he should avoid the evil and Communism of a man like Meroro, which could only get him into trouble. He invited Nkandi to lunch with him and offered *carte blanche* on a menu which after months of dirt, illness, violence and privation seemed unimaginably sumptuous with soup, varieties of meat and fish, exotic cheese, desert and fruit. Jansen, made it convivial; they ate and drank wine at leisure while B made flattering comments to a waitress whom he thought to be French-speaking. Lieutenant B took her hand but she pulled it away. B and Jansen were like friends and when it came to the bill B imperiously instructed the waitress, 'Put it on the Security Police account'. While they waited J accompanied Nkandi to the toilet, and as they both adjusted themselves in the mirror observed that their very togetherness in the lavatory was proof that apartheid was dead.

Jansen took his leave and extended an invitation to hunt game with him once the case was over.

From the Grand Hotel he was taken back to his house to change into clothes more appropriate to the prison cell.

The prosecutor had tried with lavish diplomacy where violence had failed.

The return to Ovamboland was scheduled for the next day. At the Windhoek Police Station Lieutenant Q told his prisoner that Mushimba and Shikongo were in the cells there, and that he wanted him to carry out a mission.

Q explained: He was to be put in a cell with Mushimba and Shikongo. Once there he had to pretend that he was an accused, show concern about the defence, ask when their attorney was coming, and – this was vital according to the Lieutenant – find out everything about their defence.

Nkandi did not carry out his mission. What followed in the cell was a prolonged, heartfelt, anxiously whispered renewal of his friendship with Mushimba. The next day Q was incensed at his disobedience and refused to have anything further to do with him, called him a '*fokken* idiot' and walked off. A young policeman drove Nkandi back to his cell at Ondongua.

This, as we shall see later, was not the only attempt to monitor defence preparations. But when the full blown espionage operation in the attorneys' offices was later uncovered Nkandi was still in the cells, incapable of passing on vital evidence of this episode.

23

'Terror Trial' at Swakopmund

Of the scores of prisoners still in detention in November 1975 Dean Griswold was granted the privilege of seeing only seven persons whom the Attorney General – for reasons which were at first obscure – set out to prosecute jointly on charges under the Terrorism Act. Weeks had passed since they had last been interrogated; they had by then been brought out of isolation as part of the process of rehabilitation for trial and restored to a form of normality; the injuries and burns had healed. The Lutherans asked for permission to send a Bishop to accompany Griswold as he was a stranger to the defendants and there could be no certainty that they would talk to him. This was not allowed. On the morning of the 20th November Griswold was ushered into a room at the Windhoek jail where he met four of the accused, nurses from the Lutheran Hospital at Engela, by name Rauna Nambinga, Hendrina Shaketange, Anna Nghihondjwa and Naimi Nombowa. The security officer who remained present at the interview – in conformity with the previous arrangement – was none other than the head of Security. An interpreter stood by. The nurses were shy and rather reticent; though they accepted Griswold's bona fides they merely charged him with the task of conveying optimistic greetings to friends and family. The three male accused were waiting for Griswold at the Windhoek Police Station. They were Aaron Mushimba, nominated Accused No. 1 by the prosecution, more for his seniority in the SWAPO Executive than for any direct complicity in the assassination. The second accused was Andreas Nangolo, the third Hendrik Shikongo. In reply to Griswold, Nangolo complained that they had not been well treated: he explained somewhat enigmatically that they had no right to speak and that if they told the truth they might commit a crime. Their message was brief: if Griswold had really been sent by the LWF he should ask the Church to pray for them as they were not well treated. Mushimba said 'Look' and held up his hands to demonstrate the scarring, and said, 'Look how they beat me, look how they injured me'.

The six defendants were brought before Judge President Badenhorst in the Windhoek Supreme Court on the 1st December for formal remand. SWAPO members were out in force, demonstrated solidarity with the defendants, held up placards and sang songs; the moment the court doors were opened the demonstration broke up as everyone rushed in for an opportunity to see old faces.

For unexplained reasons the public was kept out of the loggia portion of the public gallery. All accessible space was crammed with spectators, newspapermen and policemen.

The defence represented by Advocate Hans Berker and Attorney Colin du Preez had already agreed that the trial – now much of a *cause célèbre*, referred to in the Press as 'the Terror Trial' – should start up on the 19th January. As the state prosecutor planned to call over thirty witnesses the defence considered the adjournment to afford insufficient time for preparations. The Judge President was not in agreement and, in order to 'assist' the prisoners who had been in jail for over three months, suggested that two and a half weeks should suffice.

Turning to the prisoners the Judge enquired about their health and treatment and whether they had been visited by a magistrate. Nangolo answered disconcertingly that their treatment had been 'terrible' and started to demonstrate how he had been suspended. The prosecutor objected. No further questions were asked.

The prosecutor advocate Jansen requested that the trial be held at Swakopmund; Berker's vigorous objections were dismissed and the trial was ordered to start in Swakopmund on the 16th February 1976.

The assassins were never caught. The only defendant directly implicated in the Elifas murder was Hendrik Shikongo accused of having driven three assassins to the scene of the murder. The charges against Mushimba were that he bought a Land Rover, gave it to Nkandi for delivery to terrorists, and sent on three hundred and eighty Rand, a radio and blankets; Nangolo was accused of purchasing a Land Rover for delivery to terrorists; Rauna Nambinga was indicted for collecting money for guerrillas and donating a dress, soap and sanitary towels to a woman who accompanied them; Nambinga's colleagues had allegedly committed the crime of terrorism by each giving ten Rand to help guerrillas.

From the outset the defence team, now led by Advocate Wilfred Cooper, S.C. Counsel from Capetown, was beset by the problems of untangling a multitude of facts – the lawyers were after all faced with six trials in one – analysing the evidence, gathering histories and finding defence witnesses. Only after many delays were they allowed into Ovamboland to track down and consult witnesses and inspect the scene of the assassination. They were there closely observed but not searched by the police; at Oniipa the police hovered nearby keeping them under constant surveillance – a dark augury for unwilling witnesses. An overnight stay in the Mission House was forbidden; this meant an extra flight to a hotel at Tsumeb, time wasted and increased costs. (The entire defence was realisable thanks only to the efforts of the Namibian Churches.) After the lawyers had departed the then assistant to the Bishop of ELOC, Kleopas Dumeni, was telephoned at his home. The hostile voice of Minister Cornelius Ndjoba levelled the accusation that the Church was cooperating with terrorists and helping the lawyers to mount a 'cover-up'. Members of the team later flew to London to interview David Meroro who – on the prosecution case – stood at the nub of the conspiracy. During their interview the lawyers formulated a code to facilitate an ongoing postal communication between London and the defence attorneys Lorentz & Bone in Windhoek. This seemed prudent in a country where mail could be officially intercepted and telephone calls monitored; the lawyers were after all under a duty to protect secret and legally privileged communication from the curious eyes of the Security Branch. On their return one copy of the code was stored in the strongroom at Lorentz & Bone.

When the trial finally opened on Monday February 16th 1976 the defence team had no idea that the security police were in possession of copies of the code and the entire defence documentation.

Swakopmund was tense the Sunday afternoon before the start of trial. On that day the NNC held a meeting in Swakopmund to show solidarity with the defendants; police blocks were set up on the main road from Windhoek and Black travellers were searched and checked. In the late afternoon near the main road in the Okahandja area a young farm couple was shot down with automatic weapons; the newspapers blamed guerillas; in white hearts there was rancour and apprehension. It was an ill-omened prelude to the trial.

On Monday morning more than two hundred SWAPO supporters and relatives of the defendants gathered at the courthouse, sang freedom songs and agitated placards reading 'South Africa the evil that men do lives on' and 'There is no struggle without many sacrifices'. When the trial started the crowd stood patiently outside as only a handful of spectator were able to gain access to the miniscule courtroom. Blacks were allowed into the courtroom only through the side door leading out to a sandy lot; they were searched upon entry; Whites were not. The indictment was formally read out to the defendants who tersely pleaded 'Not Guilty'. Lieutenant Dippenaar of the Security Police sat next to Jansen at the prosecution table; the defence team clustered separately. Judge Strydom presided without assessors. Barrister P. MacEntee, an Irish Senior Counsel on a Mission for the International Commission of Jurists, observed the opening of the trial, together with Church representatives and observers from the U.S. Embassy in Pretoria.

When the demonstrators resumed singing at lunchtime the police ordered their dispersal. The demonstrators moved away from the courthouse but not quickly enough, and many hung around to see the defendants brought out in the Black Maria. Policemen guarding the courthouse with alsation dogs turned on the crowd in a concerted movement and charged; Blacks fell in the ensuing pandemonium and police dogs mauled three people. A newspaper reporter, Eric Abraham, was assaulted by a policeman while taking photographs.

The prosecutor called a succession of disparate witnesses to the witness stand: a second-hand car salesman who sold vehicles to Mushimba and Nangola; the owner of the Onamagongwa bar; and policemen who were at the scene of the crime and carried out arrests. Many of the Black witnesses were detainees; they gave evidence warily as material contradictions with their police statements could lead to charges of perjury. (It is not unusual for the prosecution to remind them of this danger before they take the witness stand.) Sam Shivute implicated Shikongo: he had admitted to driving two unknown SWAPO men to the store shortly before the killing. Though challenged by the defence Shivute stood his ground, pausing often, answered thoughtfully with a dry resigned voice. He conceded interrogation and solitary confinement; on the theme of assault, enforced wakefulness, suspension and electric shock he chose to be silent. Kaino Malua was one of the state witnesses prepared to talk about her interrogation, the way 'they' had torn up her statements, kept her awake and hoisted her by the arm. There was no consternation in court; the evidence was duly recorded. After Malua left the witness stand Judge Strydom expressed the hope that the authorities would investigate the allegations.

It was Adjutant Officer Gabriel Dawid who, floundering in the witness box, let slip far-reaching facts. He admitted having interrogated Kaino Malua. He was then asked:

'Well she has made serious allegations here in court. Do you hear these allegations?' . . . 'Yes'

'You heard that she said that she was suspended by her right arm, that there was a chain on the arm, and that she stood in such a manner that her foot barely touched the ground?' . . . 'It is possible'.

'Is it sometimes done to witnesses who are interrogated?' . . . 'That depends on the Investigating Officer himself'.

'Oh you say that some Investigating Officers do it?' . . . 'Yes'.

Nkandi's entrance onto the witness stand was a crucial moment for the defence as all indications pointed to him as the linch pin of the supposed conspiracy. But much had happened since his unforgettable sojourn at Ogongo. Time and nature had healed his injuries and his morale had recovered from the ravages of pain, uncertainty and despair. By the time he was brought to the Grand Hotel he was already moving towards a firm resolution not to give evidence. After his refusal to act the nark in the cells at Windhoek Police Station the investigators should have noticed the danger signals of stubbornness and renunciation. It was paradoxically that very mission, designed to destroy his comrades' last threadbare hope of survival through legal defence, that moved Nkandi to exclude the possibility of any collaboration with the police. There was one other event which sealed his resolve.

At Ondongua, it turned out that a prisoner in the cell next to his was none other than Eva Muandingi. When they spoke she related her experience at Ogongo; she had been pregnant at the time. Somehow it had turned out that her pregnancy survived the gross physiological and anatomical strain of suspension in the interrogation room at Ogongo. At Ondongua she was kept alone in a cell, allowed no exercise and fed exclusively with over-salted, poorly cooked mealie porridge. Her complaints to the magistrate brought no relief and she miscarried in her cell. The constable on duty summarily ordered the foetus to be thrown into the cess pool. For days thereafter it remained on the surface, its putrifying surfaces covered with flies. It was Victor Nkandi's daily duty to return to that hideous mess in order to empty his slop bucket. It was the image of this foetus which brought home to him a sense of a failure of humanity, and the certainty of a pervasive depravity in official ranks. This ruled out collaboration no matter the cost.

Victor Nkandi's intelligence did not betray him; in long hours of lonely rumination he came to understand that the price of non-collaboration might be his own life.

Nkandi was duly brought to Swakopmund as a prized and protected major witness but it was not long before the Security Police became aware of his very clearly stated resolve to keep silent. Senior officers hastened to Swakopmund to find out what his reasons could be. They admonished Nkandi. One of them offered to arrange an interest-free loan of five thousand Rand with the Bantu Investment Corporation if he gave evidence: with this he could start a new business; with that amount of money it was urged Nkandi could buy a new delivery truck and do livestock business in Kaokoland. The answer remained 'no'.

For once it was the police who were helpless. There was nothing to be done but return their intractable charge to the cells.

The court was hushed while Nkandi was led to the witness stand. The Judge's registrar stood up to administer the oath.

Nkandi, gaunt and ashen faced, looked ahead of him with sightless eyes.

Nkandi: 'Before I take the oath: I stand here in this trial; if I am not here as an accused, then I will not be a witness.'

Strydom: 'What do you mean by that? . . . This does not make sense to me, could you explain?'

And so he tried. . . . 'As far as I'm concerned I do not know what the truth is and I do not know to what truths I should testify . . . I refuse to testify.'

Judge Strydom was at first patient – almost sympathetic. He crystallised the legal implications: the court could summarily sentence him to twelve months imprisonment.

Nkandi explained: he had been arrested and taken to Ogongo, beaten unconscious, made to stand for four days and nights, and threatened with a knife. He had been promised no mercy because he Nkandi was a terrorist. He then gave the statement 'as to how I should testify here today . . . I only

155

talked in order to be released. . . . I also heard people screaming . . . I made my statement only because I was afraid; because many words were said by the investigating officer as he stood; that he would suspend me if I refused to talk.'

' . . . I prefer to be regarded as an accused rather than a witness.'

There was an implacable determination behind a wall of diffidence. The more this became plain, the more the indulgent tones waned; the law's wrathful potency was once again vainly paraded before him; and still he refused.

The Judge sentenced him to the maximum of one year's imprisonment. Bearing in mind Nkandi's uncontradicted testimony of suffering and isolation, the punishment appeared harsh.

Axel Johannes, with a characteristic grey palor of prolonged incarceration, shuffled to the witness stand; his unsettled eyes darted around the court with a hunted defiant expression. While in jail Amnesty International had adopted him as a Prisoner of Conscience.

His refusal too was absolute; it was a refusal impregnated with scorn for, as Johannes explained confusedly, no civilized legal system could subject witnesses to such destructive punishment; that could only be reserved for heinous criminality.

Axel glared at the Judge: 'I just want to tell the court that I have already been detained for two hundred days, that I have broken the law (sic) of South West Africa. I was not arrested to come and testify. I just want to tell the honourable Judge that . . . I will not testify until I stand in the dock. I wish to stand in the dock.'

He declared that he was innocent of crime. 'If I am not guilty I would not have been detained for two hundred days.'

The Judge repeated the procedure. The law was explained; the possible aftermath of its breach was defined.

Axel was aloof, unyielding. After two hundred days of solitary confinement he was sent back into prison to serve one year as a convict. Once again the Judge opted for the maximum penalty.

From the outset of the trial SWAPO stood in the dock as an invisible first defendant.

The Prosecution strategy was patent. By lumping the accused together, the indictment implied that major SWAPO leaders – Mushimba was the National Treasurer – were implicated in the plot. An analysis of the case revealed that in reality the prosecution evidence against Mushimba was not directly relevant to the assassination. Nangola and the nurses were also not implicated, but the involvement of the nurses in the trial helped underline the accusation that SWAPO was a vast conspiracy bent on aiding guerilla activity. On the state evidence the nearest the security forces came to capturing the assassins was the arrest of their alleged chauffeur, Hendrik Shikongo.

The meagreness of this victory did not deter the prosecution from leading lengthy jaundiced evidence of the structure and physiology of the outside wing in the hope that the infiltration of these facts into a trial of members of a legal domestic organisation was bound to have a useful aggravating effect. And so Nelson Kavella – ex-guerilla fighter turned tame – was put on the witness stand to present extensive rambling testimony of his entire political history and guerilla training in Tanzania and Russia after his recruitment in 1962. He was followed by Petrus Ferreira, former captain in the security police, now self-styled expert on SWAPO. The court and a very avid South African press – listened to a monograph on the origin, history and development of SWAPO. He took care to explain – in conformity with official propaganda – that its sinful roots had been nourished by members of the Capetown Communist Party; the Ovambo strike was attributed to a malevolent SWAPO conspiracy; the thousands of strikers repatriated to Ovamboland figured as robbers, murderers and plunderers in his descriptions. David Meroro, Johnny Otto and Reuben Hauwanga had plotted and brought out the strikers. This was news for historians and for the defence team. When asked for his source of information he demurred: it was a 'delicate' matter; his under-cover oracular informer would be endangered if his identity were to be revealed. He did not want to reply, and sought the court's protection. This was given – correctly in law – on the grounds that no cross-examination is allowable to identify informers.

On May the 11th the Judge, after hearing argument, found all defendants guilty except for Nangolo and nurse Nombowa. A considerable part of the judgment was devoted to an analysis of the evidence on SWAPO, its history, documents, songs and weapons. The court remarked that the 1966 draft Constitution of the organisation contained no references or profession that God through his omnipotence guides and controls the destiny of man. Ferreira's and Kavella's evidence were accepted. Mushimba was found guilty.

Because the vehicle he had sent on with Nkandi was captured – some weeks later – from guerillas, the inference of his intention could be drawn from that result. Shikongo was described as an arrogant presumptuous, evasive and lying witness, who had knowingly driven Elifas's assassins on their mission. After the verdict Colonel Schoon in 'aggravation of sentence' testified to fifty-nine 'terrorist' incidents which had occured in Ovamboland since July 1975. As many of the episodes had never appeared in the Press, Schoon's evidence – if true – had interesting implications as to a system of censorship which allowed little other than a scant flickering insight into the progress of guerilla activity.

Rauna Nambinga was sentenced to seven years imprisonment. The other nurse was sentenced to the minimum term of imprisonment under the Terrorism Act: five years. Judge Strydom turned to Mushimba and Shikongo. They had given no evidence of remorse, nor had they severed themselves from SWAPO: their silence evidenced a sustained evil disposition. After the ceremonial 'Hear ye, hear ye, hear ye' Strydom pronounced: 'Accused No. 1 and No. 3 – the sentence of this court is that you will be taken to the place of custody and that you will be hanged by the neck until you are dead'.

Cries of consternation and wailing filled the courtroom. Mushimba and Shikongo faced the public and saluted, SWAPO-style with clenched fists, a gesture answered with near unanimity in the public gallery.

24

Kaiser Street Matahari

The death sentences were the culmination of a trial that had brought little cheer to the defence team. When postponements had been required, the Judge seemed reluctant to grant them. Their applications to hold an inspection *in loco* in Ovamboland to demonstrate to the Judge that the evidence of state witnesses could not be true were rejected; the interpretation of evidence in court left the defence uneasy: on the one occasion that the tapes were replayed the divergence was proved to be remarkable; defence objections to Kavella and Ferreira were overruled. Before the trial started the prosecution told the defence that they would not request the death sentence: in the event they did so. They were of course entitled to change their mind, though their intimation might have inspired a belief in the defence team that the court atmosphere was to be 'kept happy' – not vexed by a vigorous exposure of police methods. The defence team carried on doggedly, inhibited and isolated. Worse still, with the steady evolution of the trial, the defence was affected by a baneful paranoic suspicion that the prosecution had advance warnings of cross-examination strategy; witnesses seemed prepared; the state was seldom surprised; when it was the turn of defence witnesses to speak the prosecution seemed ready for immediate attack.

Committed to remote Swakopmund, a town more 'South Western' than 'Southwesters', more German than Germany, the defence team, lodged in an hotel, felt some alienation. Jansen and Lieutenant Dippenaar shared accommodation in police quarters. It was a small town where prosecution and defence might find themselves together in a lounge or restaurant. In the defence team Colin du Preez an attorney of the firm Lorentz & Bone was deeply immersed in defence preparation; he most of all felt monitored, encircled and therefore vulnerable. His disquiet became aggravated over drinks with Dippenaar who – whether in his cups or not – boasted that he knew everything about the defence; their files; the size of their fees and the names of their funders; and all the employees of the firm were on security police files he added.

Du Preez reported the conversation; the defence team conferred and decided that nothing could be done about it. Du Preez at first suspected that the leakage might be traceable to interpreters or prison staff, so he warned his counsel and clients to use discretion. But his suspicions were aroused, and he recalled how, while working on the application to set aside the Ovambo elections in 1974, the internal door at Lorentz & Bone had been broken open – though the front door evidenced no sign of tampering. On his return to Windhoek he called his staff together, declared that there had been a leakage and, appealing to their sense of loyalty and justice, asked for help. It was an appeal made out of a sense of duty though without hope; all avenues had to be explored. Though he had pontificated and fussed in front of the staff, he knew there were other explanations such as monitored telephones, secreted microphones, electronic eavesdropping in their homes and offices, or in cars, restaurants, cells and consulting rooms at the jail, and the ever-present danger of a slip on the part of their clients or members of the defence team.

And yet it worked. On May the 19th his secretary Mrs. de Beer asked to speak to him privately. It was only then that du Preez began to realise that tales of drama and espionage were not the unique preserve of fiction writers.

It was sometime in November that de Beer had been allocated the job of typing defence statements in the trial, a task which fell into the spectrum of her duties as typist. One afternoon at the precise moment when she was busy with defence statements, an anonymous caller asked her on the telephone whether she was a typist in the 'terror trial' and whether she was prepared to provide information. The request struck her as silly rather than sinister; she answered 'No' with energy and put the phone down. A week later she was approached by the telex and switchboard operator in the firm, Mrs. Ellis, a vivacious buoyant personality, later described as the Matahari of Kaiser Street, who confided that she had been approached by the security police to provide information. Mrs. de Beer, she said, was invited to join in; she herself had been 'operating' for a long time; de Beer could place absolute trust in the discretion of the security police. In any event what she had to do was passive – merely to leave the documents in the Mushimba case on du Preez's desk; the security police would take them at night and photograph them. At the time Ellis did not divulge the fact that there were other moles active in the firm. At first Mrs. de Beer hesitated. Her colleague was a senior trusted employee, had access to the office complex at any time of day or night and was possessed of a dominating personality: she could have made life difficult. de Beer declined apprehensively but Ellis persevered and, in the hope of embroiling her, confided that she had taken documents from time to time and handed them to the police; one of them was Hendrik Shikongo's statement. In the profusion of confidences which ensued, she admitted to removing tapes from the office and transcribing them herself for the police; from time to time she had passed on Telex messages and had handed a statement of David Meroro transmitted in code from London, to her contact in the security police, Captain Nel. Her practice was to arrange a rendezvous with him in the Public Lbirary at lunchtime. It was a barely resistable offer: everything fitted so neatly into place, it was cosy – almost romantic.

Unbeknown to de Beer one of the partners in the firm, Anton Smit, was a long standing agent of the security police. From time to time he appeared in de Beer's office and nonchalantly glanced at the trial documents. Not satisfied with two spies in the firm, the overzealous Captain Nel used his charm laced with chauvinist argumentation to win over an articled clerk in the firm, Mr. B. Mautschke, to spy on me at the time of the Ovambo election investigation when the security police – according to Nel's later evidence-developed interest in my movements in Ovamboland and the identity of witnesses I met. It was no coincidence that the day after Nel's approach Anton Smit called at Mautschke's office and enquired about his 'friend' from the security police. Smit gave Mautschke every encouragement. It was an open secret that Smit loathed SWAPO; they were 'the scum of the earth', yet another species of *untermensch*.

In the same month that Mautschke was approached unknown intruders broke through the internal door in the attorney's offices. This prompted John Kirkpatrick a senior partner to approach Colonel Myburg, the Chief of Security. He complained that he suspected that the security branch had been responsible. Myburg in turn rejected the complaint; he said that he could not comprehend why his men should be suspected; in any event he added jokingly it could have been the work of the Bureau of State Security (BOSS).

Mrs. de Beer's revelations left du Preez and Kirkpatrick in no doubt as to their duty. What they had to do was not easy. In Windhoek the firm's partners enjoyed an uneasy prestige: there were many who despised their taking up the forensic cudgels of behalf of SWAPO and the Churches. The legal partnership with Anton Smit was summarily dissolved – an inevitable drastic step not likely to endear them to the hearts of white Windhoekers. (Ellis required no dismissal: she vanished the day after de Beer upset her game.) The espionage had struck at the root of legal privilege: beyond justice, justice needed to be seen to be done; no matter what justification Captain Nel might have cherished for the invasion of legal secrecy he had precipitated an irretrievable irregularity fatal to the texture of trial procedure. If the facts were correct, the death sentences would have to be struck out and – in the eyes of white Windhoekers – callous terrorists would have to be freed. An application to set aside the death sentences would mean leading evidence of security branch espionage and Dippenaar's admissions. For many white Windhoekers the honour and efficiency of 'Security' was a matter of primordial concern. Du Preez and Kirkpatrick, to their enduring credit, harnassed themselves to preparations for an application to set aside the sentences on the grounds of irregularity. Their professional rectitude, in the best tradition of legal practice, allowed no evasion in spite of their awareness of the risks.

The application was brought by Issy Maisels QC, a leading advocate of the Johannesburg Bar. In terms of settled procedure the defence led its evidence. On behalf of the police Colonel Myburg denied any complicity in espionage; he did concede that the activities of Colin du Preez had been watched for some time but not – so he claimed – to procure privileged information. Captain Nel joined in the denial; he had, so he testified, been assigned since the beginning of 1975 to watch my activities in Windhoek: there was no question of attempting to extract defence secrets. As for Anton Smit he conceded he had played the spy – without passing on confidential matter; he was proud of his spying activities which he judged to be in the national interest. Witnesses on both sides were examined and cross-examined. As the surgery of cross-examination began to take effect the rancour smouldered deeply in the ranks of the security police. Passions were generated at the hearing and broke the customary public urbanity of the senior officers. When Captain Nel emerged from court he tried to avoid the camera of John Matisonn, a prominent South African journalist. He averted his face, lunged out at Matisonn in the presence of astounded members of the public, pulled him down by the neck, and confiscated his camera.

After lengthy argument before Judge Hart on tangled issues of law and fact, the court formally noted the irregularity and allowed an appeal to the Appellate Division. The appeal was heard in February in Bloemfontein: later in March, in a written judgment handed down by Chief Justice Rumpff, the court found that the grossness of the irregularity could 'scarcely be surpassed'. Jansen was exonerated; but the court did find that a channel had - unknown to Jansen – been created from the office of Lorentz & Bone to the prosecutor. The court ruled that the irregularity was fatal and vitiated the entire proceedings.

All convictions and sentences were set aside; Mushimba and Shikongo and the nurses were freed; in Katutura there was pandemonium, a wild elation with singing and dancing and, on the part of Youth Leaguers, an extravagent cavorting and violent embraces which posed a new though felicitous threat to the wellbeing of the long suffering defendants.

25

Oshakati

Nemesis in the shape of Lieutenant X[1] was waiting at the fortress-like door of Windhoek prison on the morning that Nkandi's prison sentence expired. As he and Johannes emerged into the unfamiliar brightness of daylight, they were arrested under Section 6 of the Terrorism Act, handcuffed and put into the back of a police vehicle that would take them to Oshakati.

Nkandi sensed vengeance in the air; he knew that X had not forgiven his 'betrayal'; it was now his turn to square up to an ominous destiny. The enormous cost of the Ogongo operation in energy, resources and time had ended with the release of the Swakopmund defendants – in a most ruinous débâcle. The security police had been very ambitious. He preferred not to think of their fury, now that they had been cheated of exemplary hangings.

All that was left to them was Victor Nkandi; they could at least, with his successful prosecution and execution, appease their exasperation and rehabilitate their soiled prestige.

Travelling northwards X offered Johannes a tin of beer. Without looking at Nkandi he said 'Victor – I am giving you nothing because you told you advocates that you drank with us on Swakop beach.'

Nkandi looked apprehensively out of the window without answering.

X: 'One thing you must understand very well – this time we are not going to spend time with you. We will pull out your teeth one by one until you have vomitted the full truth.'

The cells at Oshakati, unlighted, grimy, rectilineal corrugated iron boxes, concentrated the stifling heat of an unmerciful African sun; in the rainy season rainwater en revanche flooded through apertures which served as ventilation holes and seeped through the floor saturating the mats, blankets and clothes of prisoners who were impotent to do anything about it – other than to remain standing, sometimes through the night. Nkandi was convinced that his blankets were the very ones that had served him in 1975 – unwashed since then, stinking, mottled and flecked with blood and sputum and infested with wingless, sucking, huge-clawed red lice. His amenities: a bucket of water and a slop pail. His diet: the familiar starchy regime of over-salted, hard mealie porridge which hurt his throat; though he and Johannes both had money the police refused to allow them to request purchases of food.

After three days X summonsed him; this was the moment he had been dreading.

His statement was on X's desk. He had told the Judge at Swakopmund that his statement was not altogether true began X; if that were so Nkandi had to tell him exactly what was true and what was false.

This, thought Nkandi, as X went through his thirty-two page statement, sentence by sentence, sometimes word by word, was only the beginning; what had the Lieutenant in store for him now? In the margin X wrote against each disputed sentence: *'vals'* (false). The feared outburst did not materialise; X was restlessly passive and duly recorded his comments. After that Nkandi was put back in his iron hutch.

He and Axel were taken to a visiting magistrate together. Nkandi waited outside the office with the guard while Johannes entered. He could hear them speaking. The magistrate put the standard formula 'Have you any complaints?' Johannes answered that he wanted permission to buy his own food because the prison fare was inedible. The answer too was standard: the magistrate said that he would see what he could do; he would take it up with the police. After that Nkandi entered, objected to the food, lodged the same request and received an identical answer.

That evening Nkandi went to sleep without food or water; he could not understand why. His guard was sour; when he asked for food he was told: 'Go and ask the magistrate. You complained – now it is up to the magistrate to bring you food and water.'

The magistrate reappeared after that with regularity. 'Where had the magistrates been during those dark hours in the pantry?' mused Nkandi reflecting back to Ogongo days.

Their renewed requests were answered by the same meaningless recital of intention – he would see what he could do: the magistrate gave no explanations. Their resentment grew; he could at least have put an end to a trying charade by simply declaring his impotence.

On the fourth visit Johannes was inflamed: 'You don't come here because you care; you only pretend you are concerned; you don't solve problems. I don't want you to visit me any more, I don't want to see you again.'

The magistrate smiled awkwardly, rose and signalled him to leave.

The fifth visit. This time Johannes refused to leave his cell. Without a word the white constable pulled his jacket, then pushed him towards the office; Johannes fell, turned to flee, was grabbed once again and thrown violently into the room where the magistrate was waiting.

Johannes snarled and panted: 'What do you want?'

The magistrate's voice was gentle: 'Have you any complaints?'

Johannes: 'Why don't you people do what your own law orders. I am kept here under Section 6 and don't get the treatment which this law says I am entitled to. I have been under Section 6 very often, I now what it is about, bring the book if you don't believe me. You visit and visit and you do nothing.'

The magistrate's eyes were glistening. He paused, sighed and then answered softly: 'Yes I know. It wasn't my fault, its the police who decide. I'll see what I can do for you.'

The next day they were granted permission to buy food, though this privilege ws not extended to Thomas Asino, Frans Ithethe, Willem Dawid and other prisoners – not even Pastor Imene.

The days passed, time dragged on, and yet X did not return. The more Nkandi was left alone, the more he foresaw peril.

Most of the time he was alone, though there were occasions when he and co-prisoners were taken out to do some policeman's bidding – a form of compulsory labour which had the merit of breaking into his languishment. One duty was to unload unknown corpses from police and army trucks, and carry them through to the mortuary. On these occasions he took his opportunity to speak to the others.

He met Pastor Nabot Imene and Thomas Asino: their hands and wrists were cut and swollen; they said they had been tied and strung up. Asino's neck was swollen and had marks of chafing: a motor car tyre had been put around it and loaded with stones; this all took place in the *waarheidskamer* (truth room) adjacent to the Oshakati charge office. Not long afterwards Nkandi, together with Frans Ithethe and two others were taken to the very *waarheidskamer*, not for treatment but to help lug its furniture and equipment to the new security police offices. There were bars on the windows covered with black blankets; chairs, iron rods, a rope, and a motor car tyre that had been cut out in places. On the outside the door was adorned with a red cross.

This was the first time that Nkandi had heard about the *'waarheidskamer'*; it was a sinister sounding name which invoked thoughts of mediaeval inquisitional procedures. In this way the very vocabulary cultivated by the security police – detainees in Windhoek, Pretoria, Johannesburg, Durban, Port Elizabeth and other centres, unconnected with one another in time and place, had heard of the *waarheidskamer* – inspired fear in the hearts of prisoners.

From Frans Ithethe he understood the full implications: it was in the same room that the Pastor had been blindfolded, clamped around his ears and feet, and shocked till he fell down; afterwards his hands were tied behind his knees, iron bars were inserted between his knees and his arms, he was then lifted and suspended between two petrol drums: in the same room the tyre was put around the prisoner's head and loaded with stones; if the prisoner bent his neck he would be beaten. He himself, Frans, had been 'burnt' with electricity in that room. Johannes Kautwima had been there: he was shocked on his sex and in his anus. A Shimbundu[2], Adreano Paul had messed his trousers when the contraption was turned on.

165

Adreano Paul had been one of Nkandi's builders. He could not begin to understand why he should ever have been brought to the *waarheidskamer*. But there was worse news for Nkandi. Thomas Asino had been in the Oshakati Army Camp and had much to report. There he had seen an old man fastened to two poles between two Shimbundus. The three were shocked with electricity. 'They have no mercy for you there if you don't speak well' he reported. The old man he observed was an Nkandi – Stephanus Nkandi.

Victor Nkandi's father.

If there were any doubts they were soon dispelled by Thomas Asino. While he had been in the camp there were four women, Elise, Beata, Frederika and Helena.

Frederika was Nkandi's mother; Helena his sister – in captivity with a child at the breast. Frans had in fact taken the old man food where he stood, 'naked except for his underpants' fastened to two poles; for three days and nights the guards threw cold water over them when they grew drowsy. On one occasion Frans had heard raving at Frederika and Helena saying that they would '*kak*' (shit). Nkandi's heart was filled with vicarious suffering, guilt and self-accusation; but for him they would not have been dragged along a martyr's road.

Two days later Willem Dawid and Kanisius Hamuulu were taken away from the cells. On their return they reported having to bury three bodies – they did not know whether the dead were guerillas or 'ordinary people'. Before the bodies were put in a ditch, the captain of the police cut off the fingers. Dawid and Hamuulo were then taken back to the cells and told to keep silent.

Towards the end of March a Captain C sent for Nkandi; an altogether 'new statement' was required from him omitting the parts which he said were false. Once again Nkandi was taken through his statement, this time with punctilious care. The true facts were marshalled and recorded; the re-writing took up four days. Even if the police were in deadly earnest there was little, Nkandi felt, that he could do about it. He had no wish to return to Ogongo, nor say anything which could provoke the re-emergence of X on the scene. At the foot of the statement C had written 'I have made this statement voluntarily. I was not threatened or assaulted. I have my full understanding and I understand my rights.'

Nkandi signed, thus contradicting his earlier statements. The prosecution case was now ready.

The forensic pathway leading directly to the gallows now awaited him.

26

Ogongo On Trial

The trial opened before Judge President Badenhorst in the Supreme Court at Windhoek on the 24th October 1977. The main charge, formulated under the Terrorism Act, accused Nkandi of driving the assassins to their fatal rendezvous in front of the bar at Onamagongwa bearing the sign 'Atlantic Bottle Store.'

The defence was faced with an ominous inventory of evidence – the product of months of intensive preparation aimed at the judicial execution of Victor Nkandi. There were thirty-two witnesses on the official prosecution list: a ballistics expert, military experts, experts on SWAPO, medical witnesses, the Nkandis – Stephanus, Helena and Frederika; Elise, and Beata whom Asser had seen in the Army Camp at Oshakati, Elizabeth Queen Namundjebo, Nkandi's builders, five shopkeepers, and various detectives. Somewhat mysteriously the list did not embody the investigation team at Ogongo, nor Jansen, nor the magistrate who interviewed the defendant, nor Captain C. The state was armed with evidence of three statements made by Nkandi: his 'confession' at Ogongo, an oral 'confession' at Ogongo and his statement to Captain C.

The onus was on the prosecution to prove beyond reasonable doubt that the alleged confessions and admissions were made freely and voluntarily and without undue influence. With more than twenty senior officers waiting in the wings the prosecutor's confidence was understandable. Deputy Attorney General Jansen was held as a reserve witness to prove that Nkandi had – during their exchange at the Grand Hotel – cleared the police of brutality. Stephanus Nkandi and Frederika had been coerced into implicating their son; as they were cut off from contact in detention their evidence was an unknown quantity. Elise and Beata had also been in the camp. Their eventual evidence would be deadly – if accepted. From them the prosecutor would obtain evidence of Nkandi's supposed movements immediately before and after the assassination, his departure in the Land Rover with strange secretive men from Angola and his gratuitous – they were not friends – confessions to Beata and Elise of his participation in a conspiracy to murder Elifas.

The assessors were sworn in with the sombre foreknowledge that a verdict of guilty could lead to the defendant's death by hanging in Windhoek prison. Advocate Francois van Zyl prosecuted; I appeared for Nkandi assisted by Advocate Brian O'Linn of the Windhoek Bar with Colin du Preez as Instructing Attorney. The defendant pleaded not guilty.

Interrogational methodology was at the heart of the conflict between prosecution and defence. The major prosecution task was to prove an Ogongo cleansed of violence and threat; this task was not so formidable as might at first appear: there was no photographic or documentary proof to contend with – not even ordinary police registers of prisoners booked in or out – nor could the defence muster evidence beyond the say-so of its own witnesses and cross-examination. In the past the police had often been successful in court confrontations – the 'trial within a trial' over the voluntariness of confessions; many judges and magistrates had admitted confessions in spite of the probability that defendants do not voluntarily implicate themselves, nor confess, nor point out fatally incriminating evidence unless under the shadow of violence. And if there were proof of injury or death during interrogation – and injuries have a perverse capacity to leave traces – the police witnesses, seasoned warriors of evidential conflict, often have ready explanations; the prisoner ran and fell, or had attacked them, or – in the case of electrical burn – must have burnt himself cooking food, or – if he sustained cranial injury – slipped on soap while in the shower. Captain F's historical reconstruction of Ogongo came as no surprise to the defence: in the first place a major consideration for appropriating Ogongo was the comfort of the detainees themselves, as the ordinary cells were crowded; the atmosphere was peaceable – almost holidayish – and the prisoners' dietary regime was no different from that of the Black detectives. As Security Chief at Oshakati it was his duty to pursue the investigation of Elifas's death. After receiving a report that Nkandi had been brought in he hastened to Ogongo, for Nkandi was a very important witness. F's version of the way in which Nkandi unburdened himself of those fateful secrets of conspiracy and death was eminently simple: he initially explained to Nkandi that he had reason to believe that Nkandi could help them in the investigation. There was at first no answer, his head was lowered, giving F the impression that he was hesitating. He showed Nkandi a receipt for money that he had given to a SWAPO shopkeeper – in the course of his job as courier – murmuring that it had been found in the possession of guerrillas. Nkandi hesitated then answered: 'I'll tell everything'.

F alone asked the questions; he had instructed his officers to defer interrogation until his arrival; Nkandi was spontaneous, spoke naturally and fully; after an hour he was given pen and paper and left to write out his history in the pantry where, for his own comfort, he was allowed to sleep at night with mats and blankets; he enjoyed the same food as F and was permitted a bath every morning. Altogether seventy detainees had passed through Ogongo for interrogational purposes; F had throughout monitored the conduct of his team; threats, assaults, suspension and electric injury were unthinkable; if a detainee did stand during interrogation it could only have been by choice.

It was a plausible history of an investigation imbued with legality and consideration; it was testimony delivered with care, urbanity and boldness: the evidence of a score or more of former detainees testifying to episodes of brutality at Ogongo could only be based on perjured foundations.

Captain F's history was easily said but could its integrity survive cross-examination? The detainees at Ogongo were not common law criminals; most were dedicated SWAPO supporters imbued with Christian consciousness and convinced of the iniquity of the regime and its police protectors. What was the magic in the interrogational methods which persuaded many prisoners to yield up a statement or a confession? Nkandi too belonged to their *genre* – what had made him report his murderous involvement with a boy scout's readiness? Captain F parried with an explanation: Nkandi was 'one in a thousand' – though he tried to water down this answer. But what of those ideologues, Axel Johannes and Aaron Mushimba – both on the National Executive? They too had given statements and made admissions.

The Captain admitted that there was blood on Nkandi's shirt; he had asked about this, he said, and was told that Nkandi's nose had bled; whenever he visited Ogongo there were no signs of injuries, swellings, or abrasions; never blood on the floor or on the walls. He was left for four days and nights in the pantry as there was a shelf on which he could write; it would have been less comfortable in the police van. In the pantry he was guarded by three officers – they did not interrogate him. This led to intractable problems. Were the police resources not strained? How could a trinity of experienced officers waste time looking at him in a pantry? To see that he did not escape, tripping across the plains in his shackles? There were other problems. Captain F could not account for Nkandi's change of attitude, nor his stubbornness at Swakopmund, nor could he produce the investigation diary kept at Ogongo; his excuse that another officer had burnt it with other rubbish was more than embarrassing. In the ranks of elite investigators that does not happen so easily.

The evidence of the interrogators corroborated their chief's version; but it was also undermining. According to one Adjutant Officer, F called the interrogational team together to warn them that the case was one of international dimension and there should be no assault on detainees. In the ambit of police culture this appeared as a suspicious embellishment for was it not officially axiomatic that security officers do not assault or threaten? It further emerged that not only had the investigation diary been burnt but that the officers could not produce pocket books – which they were obliged to carry in terms of Standing Orders – because they had 'no use' for them. Some interrogators swore that the detainees simply slept where they had been interrogated during the day – a clumsy rearrangement of facts for an unnecessary number of guards would then be required; security could best be served by isolating prisoners in their cages. Behind the maladroit reconstruction of some interrogators one fact clung firmly: the prisoners remained frozen to one spot, day and night, during round the clock interrogation. Caught somewhat off guard one officer conceded that they had worked in shifts, then recollecting himself – or spotting some admonitory signal in court – he dithered, then slid into vagueness with 'maybe' and 'it could happen'.

'Were people interrogated at night?'

'That I can't say. I did not do the interrogating myself.'

None of the interrogators saw blood on Nkandi's shirt. The testimonial lily could not easily survive this sort of gilding.

The move to use Jansen – now Deputy Attorney General for the Transvaal – to seal Nkandi's fate was surprising as it is rare for prosecuting or defence counsel to enter into the arena. His potency as a witness was obvious – who would disbelieve the word of the Deputy Attorney General that Nkandi had exonerated the police over lunch at the Grand Hotel.

Forewarned by cross-examination in the Mushimba case, Adjutant Officer Gabriel Dawid held his cards a little closer to his chest. He was asked about Nurse Eva Muandingi's assertion that she had been suspended by a chain. 'Can that be so?' – 'It is possible because I wasn't at that interrogation.' The detectives, he said, did not beat their detainees because that made their heads hard; interrogators would relieve one another and he himself would interrogate day and night. By the time he admitted the possibility of an interrogation which lasted through to the evening of the second day he began to realise that he was giving the game away. In him the unconscious truth spoke all too often: asked whether he had seen any interrogation at Ogongo he answered 'With my eyes I saw that there were people *standing* there. They were being interrogated but I wasn't with them.'

Mrs. X was a potentially dangerous witness as she had not been directly involved at Ogongo, but under cross-examination her evidence became an embarrassment and bordered on comedy. The wife of an Adjutant Officer she had – so she claimed – been employed at Ogongo to care for women prisoners. She pretended to a total ignorance as to why she had been called to give evidence: she claimed that she had no prior consultation with the prosecutor – a proposition which the prosecutor properly refuted in open court. Mrs. X was the classic example of a witness who, fighting shy of dangerous themes, unintentionally sketches a negative image of truth. Even though the Mushimba and Nkandi cases had run over many months and had been reported widely in the press, she had never heard the slightest whisper of accusation against the officers at Ogongo; she had read the newspapers but they were very rare in Oshakati – she made it sound more like a village in the Sahara than an active administrative and army centre. Her concern had been with the women detainees and yet she never knew that Queen had been bleeding, nor had she seen her during interrogation; when she took her to the toilet Queen would be waiting at the garage door. She never entered offices when interrogation took place – not even to offer a sustaining cup of coffee; she could not explain why not. It was not necessary to bring Rauna any water because 'they were always getting cold water in the kitchen'. Since the jug's capacity was about four litres the interrogation process was for some unexplained reason rather thirsty work – unless someone was being drenched. Under cross-examination about the garage she answered that the steel door was always closed during interrogation; that was an unfortunate slip so she added that she was sure it was open and that in any event she never went out of the house – she was 'too busy' to step outside.

Soldiers know never to fire backwards in the firing line. So too policemen understand that they are never to admit to violence against detainees. But where their own witnesses have been victims, the facade becomes imperilled and that is what happened in the trial.

State witness Beata – girlishly timid yet sluggish – was at first reluctant to talk about her interrogation. She conceded that she had been taken to Oshakati military camp; at this point the prosecutor objected to an investigation of the camp, but he had, in law, to be overruled. (It was only in later weeks that we began to appreciate the full reasons for the army's sensitivity.) From the camp she was taken to the security police offices at Oshakati. 'What did they want from you?' She was puzzled, fidgeted, fingered her nose and wanted desperately to be out of it. She answered that she could not remember – an intellectual loss which squared badly with the detailed precision of her evidence against Nkandi. The defence was not put off so easily; as cross-examination persisted and probed and scratched at her evasion the awkward facts crept out. When the police were not satisfied with her answers they 'hit' her.

'What else did they do?' 'They just hit me.'
  'On your face or your body or where?' – 'On my head'.
  'Were you hit hard?' – 'Yes they hit hard because my ear was painful.'
  'Your ear or your eye?' – 'My ear yes.'
  'What had they done to Elise?' – 'They shocked her with electricity.'
  'On what part of her body?' – 'According to her it was here.'
  'On her breast?' – 'On her breast' . . . 'She said she had pain and she was taken to hospital.'
  'Were you threatened with electric shock?' – 'They said I must talk and if I don't talk they'll take me to the big camp.'
  'And what did they say will happen in the big camp?' – 'So that I must go and shit there.'

Great intelligence was not required to understand the aim of their interrogational cross-fire. Nkandi's complicity was an evidential linch pin – all that remained were the details: had Nkandi, and Nicodemus – her employer – made contact with the 'SWAPO soldiers', with what vehicle had they left at the critical hour, and when had they returned? And the next morning, Nkandi surely boasted of his exploits? The fact that Beata and Elise were not his friends, let alone confidantes, did not deter the interrogators. Beata's predicament was serious; she could not with the best will in the world tell them. 'I did not know about it.'

By the time she was brought to court she *did* know about 'it'. Her written statement, she admitted, had been read to her four times; her memory had been refreshed on a fifth occasion, and she was ordered to repeat it all in court.

Beata – and later her companion Elise – testified to Nkandi's confession to his exploits with a mechanical deliberateness. When asked to repeat the 'confession' in cross-examination it was plain that she had learnt her evidence by rote. A revealing weakness was her tendency to carry on with the recital of irrelevant portions of her statement. It was an exercise in pathos. Asked 'How is it that the smallest details of your evidence are the same as your evidence in chief?' she could only murmur 'It is something which was told to me, I did not tell it out of my own head.'

The defence's industry was paying off; after pursuing all realistic – and improbable – leads, the defence team – thanks to an indispensable Church honeycomb – managed to track down former prisoners from the Oshakati military camp who had spoken to Elise.

Initially Elise parried the question: throughout her stay in the camp she never spoke to any men prisoners. As an afterthought she admitted that she had spoken to Asser – but told him nothing of her treatment. (The defence was at that moment in possession of Asser's statement reflecting his discussions with Elise).

'But you did tell Beata (about her police treatment)?' – 'I only told Beata'.
  'What did you tell her?' – 'I said to her today at court that I had been burnt.'
  'On your breast?' – 'Yes.'
  'With electricity?' – 'Yes.'

The testimonial carapace was now broken and the facts poured out: it was on a Tuesday that it had happened. In the security police offices an interrogator had blindfolded her; she was unable to answer the questions – they said she was giving the wrong reply – so they shocked her. 'I couldn't remember well how to tell the facts in sequence.' This was a pitiful impasse for a witness lacking the memory and intellectual equipment to repeat coherently the admissions obtained during questioning. Without the necessary ability the less intelligent witness is constitutionally committed to repeated shock until the lesson has been learnt and acceptably expressed. Elise was shocked for about fifteen minutes.

'When you felt the shock did you go dizzy or what?' 'Describe how bad it was?' – 'Yes, I suffered severe pain and afterwards I did not know where I was.'
  'Did you lose consciousness?' – 'Perhaps, because I did not know where I was.'

'Did you find yourself on the floor at any stage during this process?' – 'I couldn't fall because I was tied up to iron bars as I stood there.'

Maladroit and shy she demonstrated, arms outstretched, raised to the level of her head. She had cried and begged for mercy; she got it – after fifteen minutes.

This is how she described the questioning:

'When you were interrogated were you at any point told that you must admit that Victor was with the men who killed Elifas?' – 'He asked me to tell if Mr. Victor was also there with those men and whether they went to Odibo.'

'Is that what he wanted to hear?' – 'Yes.'

There was awkwardness in her voice: experience had equipped her neither for the scores of faces focused upon her in court, nor the questions, which took her by storm and drove her from controlled recitation to revelations that she dared not make. Behind her stolid countenace lay her real strength as a witness – an absence of imagination and intellectual nimbleness. Her evidence against Nkandi and Nicodemus had been shredded and exposed as a tissue of untruth. By contrast her coherence in describing her experiences at Oshakati had the ring of truth.

Queen Namundjebo was another state witness to turn on the prosecution case – albeit unwittingly. She was cross-examined on the details of her depression during solitary confinement from August 1975 till February 1976. In court she described the encircling emptiness of her days in isolation and her sense of doom. As the memories flooded back cross-examination led her to Ogongo; there she was afflicted with illness; her legs and thighs were swollen; she was not taken to hospital.

This fragment of evidence allowed another defence breakthrough. 'And how did it come about that your thighs were swollen?' – 'There at Ogongo you don't sit, you only stand and that is why I got the swelling;'

'For how long did you stand?' – 'Eight days. Eight days and eight nights, day and night.'

She was bleeding – constantly and heavily; it was not her ordinary menstrual flow. The police knew of her illness; she had told them of her blood loss, her fear of death, her feeling of faintness and her incapacity to concentrate. 'They said I am not talking. But I in fact did not know the things that they wanted from me.'

'And you were not allowed to sleep?' – 'I just sat. I had no chance to sleep. If I wanted to sleep while sitting then water was thrown at me. If they didn't throw water at me then they would hit me'.

She had been hit hard, – not, as she saw it, the way a man should treat a woman.

'Sometimes you got documents and you had to write yourself and then in the night,

173

while you are drowsy, more questions were put to you and then the policeman writes himself because they change shifts . . . '

The defence allegations and the accusations of Beata, Elise and Queen were stoutly denied by the police. All the detainees had been properly treated they insisted.

The 'trial within a trial' came to an end in December, 1977 after twenty senior officers had given evidence under oath in defence of Ogongo; the transcript of testimony ran to more than fifteen hundred pages. The prosecutor had set out to demonstrate that Ogongo had the settled calm and legality of a sanitorium but the State's case had too often been breached and betrayed. When the prosecution weighed its gains against its losses, it might have been all too clear that the police witnesses were unacceptably vague, contradictory and self-contradictory; they had battled against a tide of improbability and had at times been close to achieving high comedy – who could observe the sketch of veteran interrogators, idly observing Nkandi in the pantry for four days and nights (for no other purpose than his comfort) without mirth? And to add to the dilemma there were the political implications of forging ahead: elections were foreshadowed, the Western Five were active and world-interest had been aroused; the Turnhalle delegates were laying the foundation for their election campaigns and were taking punishing criticism. If the trial went on defence witnesses would occupy the stage, command world attention and present evidence of their treatment with an organic coherence which only real victims can portray and sustain. Their tales of martyrdom would be understood and readily believed by Black Namibians; the security police, the protectors of the status quo and the Turnhalle, would emerge as the new *Gauleiters*.

On the 1st May 1978 the prosecutor formally withdrew the indictment and Victor Nkandi, at last free, could turn his back on the dreaded machinery of justice.

The trial was at an end; nothing was left to the Court but to acquit the defendant. Instead the Judge President set out to exonerate the police even though, on his own admission, he had not heard defence evidence. He delivered himself as follows:

'I do not think I exaggerate when I say that the picture which has been painted here is one of callousness on the part of the Police vis-á-vis detainees and although the Court does not have available the evidence of the Defence relating to the allegations of torture, I intend passing certain remarks, for were I to have the slightest suspicion that the Police assaulted persons, as has been alleged, then steps should be taken against the Police since – and I wish to emphasise this – assaults by the Police upon detainees will not be tolerated by this Court.'

While conceding that he had not heard the defence witnesses the Judge saw fit to present the police with a most flattering bouquet:

'Now I wish immediately to say that, considering the contradictions of which I have also made mention, there was not one single Police witness who did not make a favourable impression upon the Court and who I did not consider to be a reliable witness. It is of course so that the Defence did not place any evidence before the Court and that it is thinkable that such evidence may have been of such a nature that it may have cast suspicion upon this reliable evidence.'

The Judge also took it upon himself to stigmatise the accusers. Concerning Elizabeth Namundjebo:

'She alleges that she has been shocked with an appartus (she had in fact only testified to having been *threatened* with electric shock) had not been allowed to sleep et cetera. This witness made a very poor impression upon us – and I speak of the Court as constituted with the Assessors – and we consider her to be untruthful. It is clear that she lied either during the Swakopmund trial or in this Court in order to save her own skin. Beata Asino and Elise Kadela also testified that they had been assaulted by the Police. These two witnesses also are considered by us to be unreliable witnesses. . . . As regards the Accused it would seem to me highly unlikely that he was ever assaulted as was alleged.'

But in Nkandi's heart there were no thoughts for unsolicited pronouncements. The words which counted were: 'He is found Not Guilty and is discharged upon all the charges upon which he stands arraigned.' He was free again, left alone to fight his way with ineffable pleasure through crowds of uproariously welcoming humanity.

27

A Vitória é Certa

The Elifas assassination cleared the way for an attack on SWAPO and out-spoken Church leaders, and presented a matchless opportunity to cut down organised opposition to the constitutional talks due to open in the Turnhalle, a refurbished German gymnasium, in September 1975. The failure of the strike call in protest against the Turnhalle Conference was partly attributable to the decimation in SWAPO and NNC leadership ranks. The assassination also relieved the South Africans of some embarrassment; Elifas's worth as an obedient servant of Jannie de Wet had been offset by his incorrigible clumsiness, a zest for brutality and a notorious attachment to hard drinking.

The wave of arrests and its sequel brought home an unsettling knowledge of SWAPO's Hydra-headed flair for making good its amputations. Thousands of new supporters from different ethnic backgrounds in Namibia joined the organisation which, for many, had become the only unifying political voice; SWAPO had acquired an air of invincible potency. There were, however, other reasons for its success.

Through the months of preparation leading to the opening of the Turnhalle Conference, SWAPO kept up a steady stream of criticism. At the start of the Conference scores of SWAPO and NNC demonstrators confronted delegates in the streets, waving placards in their faces: 'No more Boer lies, away with Hitlerism', 'South Africa must quit' and 'Detente: Smith talks to the ANC and Mudge talks to Chiefs'. Their talk was tough and they looked tough; Dan Tjongarero, holding a message-bearing poster, patrolled the streets outside the Turnhalle, a bearded figure with a pugilist's jaw, radiating self-assurance. The demonstration was enthusiastic, slightly turbulent, and burst into singing 'We shall overcome'.

Though the official abuse against SWAPO did not falter, the atmosphere became pregnant with change, or so many people thought, with predictions that some or other form of compromise would be fashioned, culminating in old enemies settling down at a common table without loss of face. The intransigent John Vorster was prepared to tolerate SWAPO's participation in the talks; Sam Nujoma in turn was prepared to talk to South Africa and

Kissinger;[1] and even if Kissinger did not meet the SWAPO leadership during his southern tour this did not disprove the possibility of momentous shifts in attitudes. In Windhoek, NP leader Eben van Zijl – to the discomfort of Black participants in the Turnhalle – made unsuccessful attempts to confer with Tjongarero and spoke publicly of preparedness to meet the internal wing of SWAPO under certain conditions.[2] The United Party and the Progressive Federal Party were urging the Government to bring SWAPO into the Constitutional Conference. Reports of a visit to Ja Toivo, by Turnhalle spokesman Emile Appollus implied the possibility of a policy shift directed towards making a deal with the internal wing. In Stellenbosch, Afrikaans students invited Tjongarero to address them. This invitiation to the university campus, a historical sanctum of Afrikanerdom, seemed portentous even though, in the fuss which ensued, the organisers disclaimed knowledge of Tjongarero's connection with SWAPO. Tjongarero took up the invitation and with a mixture of the exotic – he wore a brightly coloured Afro-caftan – and plain speaking startled Afrikaans Academia with the phantoms of Black liberation.

SWAPO executives themselves were speaking with the measured tones of a shadow Government. The German community was singled out for its racism, its chauvinistic worship of German culture, its tolerance of festivals in honour of Hitler's birthday and the apartheid in German schools; the German Consulate was attacked for its support for apartheid;[3] foreign companies were admonished to recognise the UN status of the Territory, to register and to pay taxes to the UN Council; stern signals to firms violating the British prohibition on the supply of arms to South Africa were put out. SWAPO declared that Vorster was temporizing and they were now contemplating a take-it-or-leave-it deadline. In Katutura support for SWAPO was tangibly on the increase, with crowds of three to four thousand surrounding the ever informal ad-hoc oil drum platforms.

Beyond the borders of Namibia the external wing too appeared to enjoy fate's blessing. In the UN SWAPO was honoured as the sole authentic representative of the Namibian people; in the General Assembly, where the Third World representatives predominated, the majority favoured SWAPO, the 'love child' of the UN. In January 1976 the Security Council passed Resolution 385 requiring free elections under the supervision and control of the UN for Namibia as one political entity, the release of political prisoners, the return of exiles and the withdrawal of South Africa's troops and administration. Later in the year there was speculation that SWAPO might, at the OAU summit in Mauritius in 1976, seek to change its status from that of liberation movement to government in exile. The General Assembly also gave its support to the armed struggle, and accorded SWAPO observer status. In law, SWAPO enthroned as a government in exile could legitimately summon foreign governments to help out in an attack against the illegal South African occupation.

The South Africans were on their own – or so it seemed. The SADF had invaded Angola – their armour was within sight of the capital Luanda in January 1976 – but changed their minds and retreated. The entire venture had taken place furtively, presumably to avoid international protest and embarrassment to South Africa's allies. South Africa's tight censorship prevented all publication of the facts until the Government chose to utter. South African ministers explained that they had entered Angola to stave off Communism but had been let down by pusillanimous – unnamed – allies, understood by all as a reference to the US.

Betrayed by its allies, South Africa's guilty silence and the refusal of the so-called allies to join in combat only served to underline South Africa's seeming isolation. There was open speculation in South Africa on the risk of a SWAPO army stiffened by Cuban advisers and Russian armour entering into conventional conflict with South Africa; Whites were haunted and Blacks stirred by Vietnamese and Algerian parallels.

In contrast to the South African isolation SWAPO had many helpers on the international scene. The Angolan Government had signed an agreement of cooperation with it in Angola; the Russians and Chinese were offering aid and training; the OAU had approved Cuban support for SWAPO; Sweden had donated over $1,000,000 for medical and food supplies, the Dutch $700,000.

President Neto of Angola foreshadowed a final push for liberation in Zimbabwe (then Rhodesia) and Namibia. Nujoma's threat to intensify the armed struggle and vanquish Windhoek by force of arms seemed at the time not unrealisable.

In the north Ovamboland had become a war zone. SWAPO guerrillas now organised in PLAN, the People's Liberation Army of Namibia, crossed the borders in increasing numbers and penetrated to the south as far as Otavi and Windhoek. From the latter half of 1975 there were increasing attacks on Army and police units, pro-Government chiefs and collaborators, and tribal police. More land mines were used and more shops were raided.

The State reacted by imposing an iron code of risk and obligation on the populations of Ovambo, Kavango and Caprivi – in surface area equivalent to half of Namibia. New regulations brought into force on the 19th May 1976 declared the three homelands to be Security Districts; failure to report the presence of strangers or insurgents became a criminal offence carrying severe penalties; the police and Army were granted new powers of arrest, detention incommunicado, search and confiscation. Access to legal advisers was specifically denied. All persons entering or departing from the Security Districts now required permission. The authorities arrogated to themselves power to prevent any 'specified activities' in any particular 'place'; the populations of villages could be moved from one area to another; shops, schools, hospitals and mission stations could now be closed down or uprooted. Such legal firepower was a powerful tool in persuading villagers to opt for the bitter road of counter-insurgency and betrayal. New powers to create no-go military zones were applied to a *cordon sanitaire* one kilometre wide running parallel to the border with Angola. Whole villages and crops were destroyed by the SADF as troops and bulldozers cleared the no-man's-land – a euphemism for a shoot-to-kill zone. In this the Army had the support of the Ovambo Government. In Ovambo and Kavango new battalions of Black soldiers were being trained; a start was made in Rehoboth with the first Baster commando and members of the Cape-Coloured Corps were brought into the operational area. The Army, now responsible for the whole of the border, increased its build up of troop strength. Nujoma accused the SADF of deploying fifty thousand men; a UN research paper put the figure at forty-five thousand; western journalists opted for a range of fifteen to twenty thousand.

South African ministers sketched a vision of a southern Armageddon: the nation was to steel itself for the worst, against an onslaught on a 'total scale' on the economic, political, diplomatic and psychological fronts. The *laager* syndrome prevailed. All able-bodied men were encouraged to volunteer for service. On the border an eight-foot security fence with a wire overlap was put up. On the White ranches agitated farmers, armed with semi-automatic weapons, built security fences and observation towers; women were absorbed into the commandos; White schools practised civil defence methods; senior police officers were called out to allay fears in rural areas and official experts on terrorism moved around the country lecturing to a strained White population. A group of businessmen put up R50,000 as a reward for information leading to the arrest and conviction of guerillas.[4] Namibia, on the verge of war, seemed prey to the same bloody processes that had ravaged Algeria, Kenya, Mozambique and Angola.

Against the totality of counter measures SWAPO miraculously gained ground. The very immensity of South African preparations suggested ironic proof of SWAPO's mysterious vitality. The guerillas struck in many directions: in July 1976 SWAPO guerillas killed Ndjoba's bodyguard; in spite of the massive SADF presence, the Army flew Ndjoba nightly by helicopter to the safety of a fortified compound. Hundreds of students were escorted – the police said they were abducted – across the border to Angola. Teams of workers clearing the no-go zone were harassed and their equipment was damaged or stolen; a large depot at Nkonjo was destroyed. A group of heavily armed guerillas succeeded in establishing themselves in inaccessible mountains near to Otavi a hundred and fifty miles to the north of Windhoek. This caused so much upset that the SADF prohibited press publication of this incursion until the Supreme Court, asked to intervene, set aside the prohibition.[5] In London Peter Katjavivi announced that SWAPO fighters had established themselves in the central area and were poised to attack military installations.

In Ovamboland, a much vaunted Army programme to capture the hearts and minds of the local populace had little success. Doctors, teachers and technicians from the Army were seconded to hospitals, schools and colleges. But the Army's system of search, arrest and interrogation created no friends: too often guerilla contact led to indiscriminate shooting and harassment of Blacks in the vicinity. The Churches reported numerous complaints of rape, indecency and assault committed by the soldiery. With the passage of time the civilian population gave increasing help to the guerillas; the men in the bush, the *domomufitu*, were looked upon as their sons, bound to them in loyalty as members of an extended family and a subjugated people.

The Army's failure in the political war was perhaps less dramatic but by no means less meaningful for the future than its impotence to contain the shooting war. For Blacks in Namibia the *domomufitu* had become a band of legendary figures pushing back the South African juggernaut; even in Windhoek, five hundred miles away from the war zone, some of the power and the glory rubbed off onto the local SWAPO leadership. While enjoying the status of legality – however elusive its value might have been in practice – they were as it were, both comrades and the representatives of the fighters in the north; they had after all at the Walvis Bay Conference once again unanimously elected Sam Nujoma as *their* President. This was not easily reconcilable with an organisation that foreswore complicity in violence, but to thousands of Blacks in Namibia the two 'SWAPOs' converged into a single vehicle of their redemption.

Against the 'SWAPOs' and the mystery of their unsmotherable force, stood only the Turnhalle Conference as a real pretender to national leadership. But this Conference early on lost itelf in a bable of confusion, dishonoured by its attachment to ethnicity, discredited by White manipulation. Its resolution to achieve independence by 1978 was unconvincing and it enjoyed only qualified Western support. Apart from Kapuuo there was no other major Black personality in the Conference with any history of resistance to apartheid. Most of the delegates were unknown quantities; many were well-used collaborators or self-seekers. Preparations for the Conference went hand in hand with immense promises of change which were not fulfilled. The Conference ventured into prolonged debates; from its work came forth confused laborious reports and pronouncements which stood no chance against the elemental rallying cry borrowed from the Angolan revolution – '*a vitória é certa*'.

SWAPO's breakthrough in the south of Namibia came about partly through the 'conversion' of Pastor Hendrik Witbooi. Amongst the Nama tribes the Witboois occupied an illustrious place. They alone had a paramount chief and had earned an honourable historical niche in the wars against German rule.

We have observed how, until the defeat of the Witboois at Naukloof in 1894, Chief Hendrik Witbooi – the Pastor's great grandfather – led the resistance to Leutwein's efforts to establish German hegemony through a system of protection treaties.

After their defeat the Witboois were removed from their land and resettled. In later years, after the crushing of the Nama rebellion, the Namas, at first under the German and later the South African Administration, found themselves steadily deprived of their land. For a people that remembered their kingdom as extending to the hills near to where Windhoek now stands, the shrunken, barren, overpopulated area surrounding Gibeon remains a relentless reminder of their subjugation. It was much the same story with the other Nama tribes – a loose alliance of fourteen Khoisan tribes – that once dominated the south of Namibia. Under South African rule Namaland was designated to accommodate the Namas; such is its sterility that only a third of the estimated fifty thousand Namas are to be found in the Nama homeland; the rest are labourers in White-controlled areas. The Hoachanas – also known as the Rooinasie – had under German rule been granted an inalienable entitlement of fifty thousand hectares of some of the finest agricultural and pastoral land in Namibia. After occupation by the South Africans their land was removed except for a residue of fourteen thousand hectares. 'They simply fenced us in,' said Pastor Markus Kooper, the Hoachanas' spiritual and political leader. 'the Government then gave or sold to the Boers.' This was plateau *hardveld* – ideal for lucrative karakul sheep farming and cattle ranching. Afterwards the South Africans made preparations for a homelands Bantustan-type government and established the Nama council. Most of the Nama headmen were well in their sixties; uneducated, illiterate, and understanding little Afrikaans or English, they had become accustomed, with the incentive of a small monthly stipend, to carry out the administration's wishes. Opposition to the Nama council came from Witbooi, headmen Joel Stephanus and David Goliath – men separated from their colleagues by their relative youthfulness, literacy, experience beyond parochial boundaries and a determination to break from a second-class existence.

Blighted with poverty, malnutrition and a primitive agriculture, the Witbooi community was dependent on seasonal jobs. Pensions for the elderly – at the rate of twelve rand a month – were an important source of income for many of the twenty thousand Witboois housed in iron shanty homes – *hoogoonde* (high ovens) – unbearable in summer, stark and comfortless against the winter. Long before their momentous decision to join SWAPO, the Witboois made their calculation of the regime's intentions and resisted the encroachment of Bantustan structures. On his election as chief, the hard-hitting uncompromising Witbooi was immediately deprived by the authorities of the traditional gun which the Witbooi chiefs had been allowed to keep. Born in 1934, Witbooi qualified as a teacher at the Augustineum in 1955 and later became a school principal at Gibeon. At home in English and Afrikaans, political science and religion, and combining a wry humour with grim insight, Witbooi was an obvious target for Dick van Zyl the BOSS head in Namibia, in his search for Turnhalle collaborators with some halo of legitimacy.

Dick van Zyl's many attempts to win Witbooi over with financial enticement and promises of power were as we shall see, to no avail. According to Witbooi the activities of BOSS, the admixture of intimidation and the strategy of corruption directed at him and other Black leaders, strengthened his vision that his historical duty lay with his people. And if after all this there were doubts lingering in Witbooi's mind, they were swept away by the vision of his great-grandfather which came to him in his dream, a mighty armed equestrian figure, to declare that the time for decisiveness was 'now'.[5]

Witbooi's supporters, aware of the gravity of the decision, joined with him for yet another collective leap in their history. At a SWAPO meeting in Windhoek in November 1976, Witbooi, wearing the traditional homburg of the Witboois – a symbol of tradition and continuity and resistance to German Imperialism – declared their will to throw in their lot with a truly national organisation; in their view, he said, SWAPO alone embodied such a movement. Kooper, Goliath and Stephanus and their followers joined together with the Witboois.[6] Representing in all some fifteen thousand Namibians, the new adherents to SWAPO were in statistical terms of no great moment, but the new alliance did represent serious proof of SWAPO's capacity in future nationwide elections to attract the support of historically and racially disparate groups.

28

Prelude to Turnhalle

The official gathering of multi-ethnic delegations of what was popularly styled the Turnhalle Conference in September 1975 and the constitutional and social changes which ensued in Namibia reflected a new initiative in social and political engineering on the part of the South African Government. The development is of particular interest as it was accompanied by an official assault on some aspects of apartheid. It was paradoxically in Namibia, whose White population was uniquely affected by pro-Nazi Aryan pride and Afrikaner *Herrenvolk* certainty, that a partial dismemberment of the holy cow of apartheid was attempted. It was Namibia's destiny in the 70's to become South Africa's test bed, not only in the field of military and counter insurgency techniques, but also – at least in the perspective of the National Party – momentous social experimentation.

It will be remembered that part of South Africa's conciliatory package to the UN included an undertaking to allow all parties full and free participation in the process leading to self-determination and independence coupled with a Governmental declaration that Pretoria had no intention of delaying the act of self-determination.

From the start it was manifest that the Advisory Council was incapable of taking the lead in any process towards self-determination. Though a breakthrough from the National Party's traditional hostility to multi-racialism, the Council, made up of various invitees from different ethnic groups including the White group – but not the White opposition which had 30% of the White vote – could make no credible claim to be representative. It satisfied no one and, as early as 1973, South Africa's Minister of Foreign Affairs conveyed to Waldheim Pretoria's intention to refashion the Advisory Council into a more meaningful instrument.

The first official glimmerings of a new policy emerged when, early in 1974, Billy Marais, the Prime Minister's special representative in Namibia, called on members of the Windhoek Chamber of Commerce to prepare for 'far reaching changes in the year'. Shortly afterwards Foreign Affairs Minister, Hilgard Muller, released a seven page report to Waldheim promising a liberalisation of racial policies in wages, education and influx control.

But even a more representative Advisory Council was not an adequate constitutional solution for a Territory which, in terms of Vorster's avowed policy, would decide its own destiny without interference from the UN or South Africa. The solution lay in the creation of a Constitutional body in which ostensibly or truly representative Black leaders and spokesmen of the National Party could synthesise a common agreement. It was the Turnhalle Conference which was to develop into this organism; henceforth South Africa's strategy would be to distance itself from its responsibility in Namibia in proportion to the developing experience, authoritativeness and visibility of the men in the Turnhalle.

That the official initiative for the Turnhalle talks should come from within the Territory was an obvious corollary to Vorster's new strategy.

In September 1974 the head committee of the National Party in the Territory made the historic announcement of its intention to hold talks with members of the different population groups. The purpose was to discuss the future evolution of the Territory. Each population group was invited to choose its representatives to the talks where the Whites would be represented by two leading members of the Executive Committee – Dirk Mudge and Eben van Zijl. The Whites, said Mudge, a burly rancher from the Outjo District, were holding out the hand of friendship to the 'non-Whites' in a creative process which would lead to a mutually accepted political dispensation. 'Prejudice and hate must be removed' he declared. From the Whites he called for a changed attitude towards 'Blacks and Browns' and a recognition of the need to concede their dignity and treat them with respect.

The new programme was heralded as the dawn of a new age, but behind the phrase that it was 'up to the Southwesters' to decide for themselves lay a distinct vagueness as to the ultimate direction and purposes of the talks. 'All options are open' was the recurring drift of Vorster's speeches; whether the Constitution would be unitary or federal or whether there would be incorporation within the Republic, were choices which the people of Namibia would have to decide upon.

Vorster also gave the assurance – of cardinal importance to the Whites – that no population group would be forced into a dispensation against its will. This was accompanied by one other conciliatory gesture: ex patriot leaders were invited to return and partake in the political process, though the Government would have to be consulted if they had participated in armed conflict. This move was interpreted as a significant gesture foreshadowing the return of SWAPO leaders in exile and in prison and the release of Herman Ja Toivo. Sean MacBride, the UN Commissioner for Namibia, gave his cautious blessing to the new initiative. Indeed, there was nothing at that stage to suggest that the South Africans, far from contemplating the triumphal return of Ja Toivo and Nujoma, had more amenable figures in mind such as Kerina and Kozonguizi with whom the Government was already in contact.

Prelude to Turnhalle

At first sight the National Party plan placed the Nationalists in a dilemma. Once empowered to vote democratically the overwhelming majority of Namibians would opt for anti-apartheid rule. The very concept of a multi-ethnic conference whose representatives met on the basis of equality presented the South Africans with a somewhat menacing conflict. If the constitutional process was to be successful Black leaders would have to appear credible. But this they could not be if, in common with other Blacks, they were not permitted free movement across the country, nor allowed into cities without permission, and were refused the privilege of living and eating in hotels and restaurants. The problem was that leaders, in order to be credible, had also to be visible. This they could not be – especially the unknown faces from the homelands governments – if they were to be housed in obscure reception centres in the midst of the poverty and squalidness of Katutura where they would be as uncomfortable as they were inaccessible. The opening of hotels and restaurants – also referred to as the abandonment of petty apartheid – to those Blacks who could afford such amenities was a necessary component in the projected scheme of things.

To the outside observer the National Party initiative committed the White man to nothing more than nebulous talks and some humble interference in the prevailing apartheid dispensation. But to most Whites the problem had an altogether different dimension. The ideology of apartheid was absolute in its conception and had for decades been nurtured on the premise that the purity of the White race was co-extensive with its survival. Social contact with Blacks was rigidly controlled; inter-ethnic marriages and sexual contact were prohibited and defined as criminal offences. An unswerving loyalty to the National Party cause was also inspired by the vision of the *swartgevaar* (the Black danger); in the face of an overwhelming Black majority the White man and above all the Afrikaner, who had no country to which he could make his escape, was warned of the need to close ranks and maintain his integrity and separateness against the Black masses. In National Party ideology there was room for the Black man as a guest worker only, a foreign labour unit, imported from the homelands which would be adorned with the trappings of sovereign states.

The calling of the Constitutional Conference and the dismantling of petty apartheid opened potential breaches in apartheid dogma: inherent in the proposed multi-ethnic gathering was the concession that the Black man had some say in Namibia's future constitutional architecture. This, expressed more bluntly, smelt of power-sharing – the antithesis of the apartheid axiom. As for the opening of hotels and restaurants to Blacks, this could be interpreted as a fatal encroachment upon a system of absolute separation, for what was there after all in Afrikaner ideology which distinguished between mingling in bars and restaurants and the ultimate anathema – the common use of cinemas, schools, swimming pools, theatres, hospitals, trains and other public amenities?

Namibia the Violent Heritage

White fears were appeased by categorical assurances that the Conference could never endanger the Whites. 'One man one vote' was 'out'.[1] The fail-safe solution propounded by Mudge was the concensus mechanism: all decisions would have to be unanimous. No ethnic group would be forced against its will to accept any resolution of the Conference. The concensus mechanism was also the key to long-term National Party constitutional thinking: in a federal structure the White homeland, endowed with constitutional power to pass legislation on important topics would, through the protection of the constitutional framework, be preserved in its integrity. The homelands would constitute the second tier in a federal-like structure which bound its components in a loose alliance. In constitutional terms this would represent a variant of the National Party's plans for the creation of independent Bantustans living cheek by jowl with the White homeland. In reality little would be changed and the Black homelands would continue to supply the Whites with the required quota of guest workers.

Bearing in mind that the eleven ethnic groups of Namibia – in National Party ideology they represented eleven different nations – included in their boundaries the haves and the have nots, the landed and the landless, the rich and the poor, the National Party's optimism that unanimity on major decisions could be reached seemed boundless.

Other guarantees were offered in addition to the iron-clad security of concensus: political parties, it was ruled, would not be permitted to attend the Turnhalle Conference. The reason, Mudge elaborated, was that political parties as such were unknown quantities whose leaders were unknown (sic); invitations to political parties would merely lead to a 'Babylonian confusion'. The effect was to exclude Black representatives other than those attached to structures of Homeland government; since Homeland governments and the elections which went with them were unacceptable to anti-apartheid Black political leaders, the greater part of contemporary Black political leadership was, with one single precondition, excluded.[2] The National Party adhered to its exclusionary policy against the suggestion of its own advisor, political science expert Gerhard Tötemeyer of the University of Stellenbosch, who called for the inclusion of SWAPO in the talks.

The immediate rejection of the talks by SWAPO, SWANU, the Damara Council and other outspoken groups confirmed Mudge's assurances that the Conference delegates would not threaten the established order. The National Party finally laid down that law and order would be maintained 'at all costs' throughout the political process and that the solution to social and economic problems was the generation of wealth not its redistribution.

Some months prior to the National Party's September announcement persistent rumours in the White community went far towards preparing Whites for the new shift in thinking. Windhoek abounded with credible rumours that Ovamboland would head for independence after an *Anschluss* with fellow Kwanyama tribesmen on the Angolan side of the border. There was also speculation that the South African Government might assist the new-born state by extending Ovambo territory to include the mineral wealth at Tsumeb. This development, coupled with a strict limitation on the move-ment of Ovambos into the Territory would leave the Whites, then the second most numerous group in Namibia, a freer hand to put the southern house in order. The rumours indeed heralded a shift in official thinking. The South African Government prepared a feasibility study for an independent Ovam-boland, and in October of 1974 Chief Elifas formally proposed the creation of a link up with Kwanyamas in Angola in the constitution of a new sovereign state. This call was taken up by Ovambo Legislative Councillors who moved for a restructuring of the Assembly to allow for an elected majority. Once this was achieved, they said, negotiations would then start up with Portugal in order to obtain her consent to the incorporation.

The carefully martialled arguments and assurances were successful in per-suading many National Party supporters that the Turnhalle Conference was in conformity with the party's basic philosophy. If there were any remaining doubts among White supporters, they were comforted by persuasive con-siderations of *Realpolitik*: the Black homelands were heavily dependent on employment and funds generated by factories, mines, farms and industry in White hands, whilst Namibia as a whole was dependent on the Republic. Once social accord intervened economic confidence would revive and there would be a renewal of investment and prosperity.[3] Even the terminology was appropriately cleansed – no one spoke of a multi-racial conference. The purpose, said the National Party, was a 'multi-national' consultation. The public media were coaxed into supporting the new programme. The prob-lem, Vorster said, pleading for press co-operation was 'delicate'; the issue was not to be handled with 'clumsy hands'. Backed by the Administration's funds the National Party mounted a massive campaign aimed at the reorien-tation of White thinking. Special attention was paid to civil servants; behind closed doors 350 selected officials were introduced to the motives of the Administration.[4] Under the item cryptically formulated as 'dispositions and relations amongst peoples' they were invited to put an end to the abuse of Blacks and the use of incorrect 'forms' of address. At six major conferences of the National Party, held in closed session, the 'big guns' were brought in.[5] South Africa's then Ambassador to the US, Pik Botha, presented an exagger-ated profile of the perils facing Whites in Namibia and went so far as to warn against the danger that the Western Powers and the Socialist Bloc might act in concert against the Republic. He deplored the practices of 'petty apar-theid'; Blacks were no longer to be referred to as 'Kaffirs'; they were to be addressed as 'Mr' or 'Mrs'; the White man's position would never be pre-judiced; on the contrary a multi-ethnic alliance would be able to spearhead South Africa's counter-attack in the world and in the UN; accommodation with Blacks would yield support against SWAPO; the new dispensation, even if unacceptable to the UN, would be defensible in the eyes of South

Africa's friends and trading partners. The Republic was faced by threats of sanctions and the ominous link of Black nationalism and marxism in Africa, Botha added. Nothing could be lost by treating the Black man in a civilized fashion, addressing him as 'Mr' instead of 'Boy' and allowing him entrance to hotels and restaurants.

In addition to the efforts of the public media, an intense campaign aimed at the direct persuasion of opinion-makers was mounted. A specially selected task force of over 100 officials moved around the country addressing teachers, local organisations and farmers' associations. In March 1975 the Legislative Assembly appointed a special committee to investigate 'obstacles' to race relations, whilst the magistracy was involved in an investigation into racial friction between Whites and Coloureds. (The publication of the Theron Commission's monumental and courageous report on the very issue did not deter the magistrates from starting up their own inquiry). SWANU leaders sneered at the bustle of inquiry into 'what everyone knows about'. But the investigations, even though they appeared superfluous, did help create an atmosphere of re-evaluation and re-adjustment. They were busy, commented a member of the Assembly, with a huge human experiment; it was now over to them to 'grow like a snake out of its own skin'.

We have already noted SWAPO's conditional rejection of the Conference. SWAPO emphasised its demand for an unrestricted Conference under UN supervision culminating in UN supervised elections and independence. SWANU's Gerson Veii dismissed the Conference as a 'tribal solution'. The homeland leaders he said had been taught only one phrase '*Ja Baas*' (Yes Sir). As a preliminary to acceptance to the Conference, Veii demanded a probationary period of twelve months without apartheid. Justus Garoeb, the leader of the Damaras, the second largest Black group in the Territory, echoed the insistence on guarantees that elections would be held under international supervision. Garoeb, a former member of the Prime Minister's Advisory Council, had hardened in his attitude towards officialdom. The Government, he said, was 'playing' with Blacks. He and the Damara leaders condemned the Conference as a 'fake' and as 'illegal'. The time had come, declared Garoeb, for the Government to put an end to its 'game' with the Territory. Garoeb was supported in his attitude by the Damara Advisory Council and the Damara Tribal Executive. In the Herero community Chief Munjuku of the Mbandero group – he too had sat on the Prime Minister's Advisory Council but had walked out after the first session – announced the Mbandero's unconditional rejection of the Conference.

Hendrik Witbooi and Nama Chiefs Goliath and Stephanus spurned the Turnhalle Conference and called on the Government to take drastic action to avert conflict. The Government's 'desperate attempts to enforce its will through sly tactics' would bring disaster, they said; the only solution was independence in a unitary state. The Bondels were also not persuaded and, as a precondition to acceptance of a Conference, demanded unconditional

undertakings to restore their lost land. The NNC too opposed the Conference and rejected its ethnic premises. Kapuuo at first denounced the Conference, demanded the inclusion of political parties and the exclusion of tribal
leaders and representatives of the homelands administrations. The 'Voice',
a Nama-supported group headed by K. Conradie, proclaimed the thesis that
the Conference was 'doomed' unless political parties were allowed to participate. They characterised the Conference as a 'resurrection of the Hitler
fantasy . . . ' and as a 'marathon political carnival . . . '.

The Conference organisers were alive to the need to draw in real life political figures such as Garoeb, Kapuuo, Hendrik Witbooi and Chief Munjuku.
Without their participation the Conference was bound to be lacking in legitimacy and would be vulnerable to the 'stooge' sting. The Prime Minister's
Advisory Council had been packed with Government protegés – a primary
weakness which led to its dismal failure. As early as March 1973 Security
Branch officers, emissaries of Jannie de Wet, had secretly offered Kapuuo a
seat on the Advisory Council. Kapuuo rejected the offer. He brushed aside
the Advisory Council as 'illegal' and a 'bluff'; he was not prepared to accept
an invitation delivered by an official who did not recognise his chieftainship.
This informal exchange was notable in the Namibian context: it was the first
attempt to persuade a militant Black opponent to accept service in a Govern-
ment-created Council. Kapuuo's answer also signalled a preparedness to
withdraw from an uncompromisingly anti-apartheid stand.

From the beginning of 1973 it became evident that anonymous interests
were concerned with Kapuuo's political future. With the help of undisclosed
funds he broke out of his modest role of community leader in Katutura to
become a frequent visitor to Western capitals where Conferences and meetings were arranged for him by public relations agents. Public relations agent
Jack Summers, earning $10,000 a month, planned Kapuuo's visit to the
Commonwealth Conference in Jamaica in the middle of 1975 when Kapuuo
introduced himself as a guest of Sir Seretse Khama of Botswana. This was
repudiated and the fiasco ended with Kapuuo's expulsion from the Conference. At the UN Kapuuo agitated against the recognition of SWAPO as the
sole representative of the Namibian people, and objected to the exclusive
funding of SWAPO. After this manoeuvre failed, his attacks on SWAPO
sharpened. It was a tribal organisation bent on imposing its will upon the
Territory; the seeds of reason could germinate; no political organisation had
been banned and the freedom accorded to 'natural leaders' was proof of a
basic rationality. His own favourite themes – police brutality, 'fascist' legislation, the humiliation of Blacks and racist oppression – began to fade. At the
same time that Kapuuo was attacking the Turnhalle Conference ambiguity
crept into his language and, with statesmanlike fairness, he began to welcome discussions for finding mutual grounds of common interest. It was not
too late, he urged, to start improving race relations but there had to be tangible proof of a change of heart. Assuming an unwonted testiness Kapuuo laid

down his conditions precedent: an immediate negotiation for the transfer of power, the abandonment of the homelands policy and the release of political prisoners. He began to propound the thesis that the real danger was that of Ovambo domination. His solution was a prophylactic partition of the Territory. It was finally in June 1975 that Kapuuo, without offering explanations for the abandonment of his conditions and his demand for 'tangible proof', agreed to participate in the Turnhalle Conference on behalf of the 'entire Herero nation'. The Tjamuaha-Maharero Royal House immediately repudiated this gesture on the ground that Kapuuo was merely a self-styled paramount chief recognised by only a portion of the Hereros. Gerson Veii declared that the Herero ancestral warriors would be shocked in their graves by Kapuuo's decision. How was it possible, he asked, for the Hereros to reject the UN in favour of the 'killers' of December 1959 and 1975. A transformed Kapuuo, turned, as we have noted, upon his opponents in SWANU and SWAPO. SWANU leader Gerson Kangueehi was dragged to Kapuuo's house and assaulted; Axel Johannes and Aaron Mushimba were seized in the street, marched to Kapuuo's home, beaten and then finally turned over the police. In the Waterberg Herero reserve Kapuuo's followers organised a boycott of businessmen who had withheld political support, expelled David Meroro's son Ernest, a shopkeeper in the reserve, and put up boycott notices threatening assault on those who defied the boycott order.

Other attempts to win over popular Black leaders were less successful.

The first attempt to persuade Justus Garoeb, the head of the 75,000 strong Damara community, was made by the Prime Minister's personal representative Billy Marais. When Marais' attempt failed, Dirk Mudge joined in and paraded the various advantages of entry into the Conference – the grant of specific salaries, the advantages of official transport and accommodation and national renown. Mudge too was unable to shake the Damara Council's unanimous disinclination.

From the time they took office in August 1972 the Damara Councillors kept their distance from the Administration. At their investiture the Bantu Affairs Commissioner had asked them to denounce the UN. They evaded the issue; they were 'new boys' and much was to depend on South African policy. Their concern, said Garoeb at the time, was some amelioration of their great penury, above all more land for Damaras whose 4.8 million hectares compared poorly with the 37 million belonging to a White community only 25,000 greater in number. Highly articulate in English and Afrikaans, well read and well informed, Garoeb brought a mature vision to bear on the problems of the Damara community. Mudge's efforts to woo him and his councillors were met by an inflexible demand for constitutional development under UN supervision. The Damaras were impressed neither by Mudge's eloquence, nor his arguments that the UN was ignorant of local conditions, nor the fact that he and Marais would turn up for consultations in a private aircraft, nor by the gift of a light delivery truck which Mudge handed over as a donation from the 'White people of South Africa'. When it became clear that nothing would bring the Damaras to heel, officials of the Department of Constitutional Development demanded the return of the vehicle. After Garoeb refused to hand it over it was seized by armed Security policemen in a road ambush.[6]

Anonymous political and financial interests also tried their hand with Garoeb. While in New York, Kerina, purporting to represent the UK businessman James Endicott – a close collaborator with Kapuuo – made an offer of a million dollars for his co-operation. This offer was recorded on a paper napkin which Garoeb brought back to Namibia to be displayed as a derisory exhibit.

The Damara Council's intransigence compelled Mudge to make do with second best which was to invite a struggling businessman, E.H.L. Christy, to represent the Damaras at the Conference. Shortly afterwards a minor moribund organisation, the Damara United Front (DUF), was revived and Party offices were opened at Khorixas, the Damara capital.

It was also in 1975 that regional headquarters of the Security Police were established at Khorigas in Damaraland. From their base, security men moved into the reserve and, according to Garoeb, became an on-going vigilant presence that tirelessly monitored the activities of the inhabitants and worked on the recruitment of informers. The security branch officers applied pressure and persuasion on the community to win support for the Turnhalle Conference.[7] They were not ineffective. Recruits were found and a group of teachers, including Johannes Gaseb and Johannes Skrywer, joined DUF. The new recruits had little political background; none had been prominent in community work. Prior to its involvement with the Turnhalle Conference, DUF had held no public meetings. After the full Damara delegation had been assembled for the Conference the *Windhoek Advertiser* observed that some delegates had been taken from the streets, others from a soccer team. Apart from the embarrassment of being unrepresentative DUF was also a political party. The apparent inconsistency with the Turnhalle exclusionary rule was explained: they were merely acting as 'agents' to arrange the appointment of delegates and not as agents for the party as such.[8] It is not without interest that the first public statement issued by Christy announced the intention of anonymous 'Damara leaders' to attend summit talks. No names were given, perhaps because both Christy and Mudge had then little idea who those 'leaders' would be.[9]

The Administration applied systematic pressure in Damaraland in support of DUF. Officials impressed upon headmen and councillors the need to co-operate with the Conference. They gave various reasons: since Turnhalle represents a peaceful change, its rejection meant increasing violence; violence meant terrorism for which Damaras could be prosecuted and imprisoned. Garoeb and his fellow councillors were dismissed from their posts in the Administration while would-be illegal uncut diamond sellers – 'traps' working with the police – were unusually active in plying Garoeb and his fellow councillors with bargain offers. In the towns the municipalities warned workers to support DUF or face expulsion; farmers were also drawn into the process and gave jobs to DUF supporters. Applicants for passports – unless they were DUF supporters – ran into unexpected complications. Applicants gathered from the security police that it would be easier if they supported Christy. There were also muttered warnings that when Christy 'came to power' he would be in a position to direct the security police to lock up 'this man or that man'. Guns, usually prohibited to Blacks, were more easily available for those who lined up with DUF. Later with the establishment of the Damara Representative Authority in 1977 further measures were taken to consolidate the authority of DUF. Employees of the Authority, including nurses and teachers, were warned of dismissal unless they joined DUF. Headmasters were appointed only from DUF supporters. (Despite the pressures the majority of 200 teachers in Damaraland remained Garoeb supporters.) As for Christy and his collaborators a visible new prosperity supervened and they were provided with White secretaries – previously called 'directors'.

From early in 1975, Dick van Zyl became a frequent visitor to Witbooi's low, squat, metal-roofed home in Gibeon. As head of BOSS, it was not easy to refuse van Zyl access. The approach was blunt and seemingly artless. Van Zyl presented himself as a member of BOSS: 'I am no policeman – merely a friend of the Prime Minister's office.' He profiled the attractions of Turnhalle involvement mingled with a shrewd appeal to Witbooi's patriotic pride and an opportunity to weld the Nama headmen into a power block under his leadership and so renew the grandeur of the house of Witbooi; as a Namibian statesman Witbooi would make frequent visits to great cities overseas to present the truth of Namibia to ministers and opinion-makers of the Western world; his speeches would be reflected in the newspapers, there would be photographs of himself and his family and he would win the esteem of his people and international renown. All expenses would be paid; the salary would be substantial and he would possess a better house and a 'beautiful car.' The offer was sealed with an assurance of indefinite Governmental protection.

For a school principal earning R240 a month, the owner of an ailing five-year-old motor car, the financial advantages were indisputable, but the offer was not taken up.

Witbooi was not invited to the next meeting where van Zijl's prime theme was the dual menace of Communism and tribalism in SWAPO; he conceded that the 'previous road' had not been right, but now the White man offered the hand of friendship; he wanted an immediate positive answer. This time Joel Stephanus voiced objections to the Conference and was immediately accused of being a SWAPO man. 'The front part of your body is in the gathering,' said Eben van Zijl in an effort to isolate his influence, 'but the back part is held by SWAPO.' In the meantime BOSS agents pursued their work of persuasion, flattery and promise; Dick van Zyl, professing an interest in Stephanus's farming operations, asked whether he had enough money for petrol, invited him, in his 'own capacity,' to join Turnhalle; Stephanus was young, there was a long future for him, all expenses would be paid and thousands of rands would be secretly paid to him – a secret to be shared by the two of them alone. Avuncular and protective, van Zyl encouraged him to go back and 'swing' the views of his people back home; once that was done he would personally fly back with a parcel of money.

Neither the Turnhalle Conference nor the Nama Council were to receive support from Witbooi, Stephanus, Markus Kooper, or David Goliath representing the Goliath tribe.

Their stubbornness was to cost them dearly. Witbooi's official powers as chief over Gibeon were eroded, he was removed from his post as headmaster, and official recognition of his captaincy was withdrawn. The collective solidarity of the Witboois merited, it seemed, collective punishment. Word was spread amongst farmers in the surrounding areas that the Witboois were pro-SWAPO; work seekers on the farms were told 'Go home – ask SWAPO for work.' The Administration built offices and homes for teachers and pensioners; the contractors looked elsewhere for labourers, and opted for Ovambo contract labour. Once the homes were ready – grandiose they were compared with the amorphous home-made metal structures – they were allocated to those who had signified their loyalty to officialdom and the Turnhalle.

Later in 1978 Witbooi's punishment was to be arrest and solitary confinement under Section 6 of the Terrorism Act.

The Administration retaliated against Joel Stephanus by summarily withdrawing his appointment; he was threatened with criminal charges; though his followers paid grazing fees – destined to pay for community needs and development – repairs to equipment and the construction of dams ceased, and a number of farms – the 'Odendaal farms' – were withdrawn from their possession. Other screws were tightened. Their water supply was cut off and they, and the Goliath community, were refused branding irons. Given the prohibition against selling unbranded stock, this was a serious blow in a pastoral community.

The tightening of the screws had a logic of its own.

As most Blacks now saw it, no new generous dawn had broken in Namibia.

29

The Turnhalle Exercise

The Conference opened in the Turnhalle, a freshly redecorated German colonial style building on the fringe of the business centre, on the 1st September 1975, against a background of uncertainty. The security police were active, making arrests in the wake of the Elifas assassination. In the north, units of the Army carried out searches and arrested numerous suspects including school children. A general economic gloom prevailed, investment was at a low ebb, property prices had reached their nadir and many Whites had begun to leave.

Nine hotels opened their doors for Blacks, though the reception was not always cordial.[1] One of the delegates, Charlie Hartung, protested that it was pointless to remove apartheid signs from public places and 'hang them on your heart'.[2]

As a preliminary to the commencement of the Conference a twenty-two member credentials committee was formed to examine the credentials of the 156 delegates who presented themselves. The true function of the committee was somewhat obscure since no 'gatecrashers' turned up. Only those delegations which had been invited attended the Conference. The avowed purpose was to check that the delegates were indeed representative of their respective ethnic group but this rule was disregarded in the case of the Damaras and the Bondels representatives, nor was it a question of determining the integrity of delegates, as the committee had no difficulty in admitting a delegation leader who had served a sentence of imprisonment for fraud. It was evidently also not the function of the committee to impose a sense of proportion on the size of delegations; Kapuuo's delegation of 34 was bizarrely disproportionate for a community representing less than 7% of the population.[3] The Ovambos, accounting for almost half the population of the Territory, were represented by one eighth of the delegates. The Whites were at first represented by only two spokesmen.

A discernable function of the credentials committee was the creation of an aura of legitimacy and constitutional regularity. It was an attempt to distance the Conference from the intense negotiations and manoeuvring which preceded it and create the impression that the Conference was indeed a gathering of national leaders on a mission from their respective communities. The committee also functioned as a fail-safe mechanism which would exclude any unwanted representatives who might care to present themselves. The overall strategy aimed at the isolation of the representatives from all influences other than that of the National Party leaders and like-minded civil servants. When members of the United Party set out to meet homelands government leaders Mudge intervened to prevent them from 'peddling' its federal policy before the Black delegates could reach the stage of making a responsible decision. The importation by Kapuuo of US Attorney Schwartz as law adviser led to immediate complications. Though Mr. Schwartz's credentials were politically impeccable – he was an established lawyer in a US firm specialising in New York's theatrical world – his admission was considered a dangerous precedent as other delegations might be tempted to follow suit. The Conference organisers did not welcome the prospect of lawyers whose analytical abilities and legal skills might upset the management of the Conference. But some compromise with Kapuuo had to be found; the solution was to admit Schwartz to a room adjoining the Conference from where he could follow the proceedings through earphones.[4] (Later on in the Conference, when constitutional issues came up, each delegation was invited to make use of the services of lawyers hired by the Government.)

Though the Conference from the outset was held in the glare of public attention covered by scores of South African and foreign reporters, journalists and observers, the paradoxical decision was taken that the proceedings should be held in camera – an unusual procedure for a gathering of constitutional founding fathers. The effect was to immunise the representatives to a large extent from public and private criticism and persuasion. The debates were not published. During the proceedings reporters were reduced to waiting around for Billy Marais' daily disbursement of officially composed information. The *Algemeine Zeitung* complained that journalists were being treated like rabid dogs. The *Windhoek Advertiser* concluded that the Press had no hope of being allowed access to the conference chamber as that would destroy a number of myths[5] and that 'one should not be surprised if some of the news dispatches intimate a system of manipulating people who are supposed to be leaders'.[6] A motion for the admission of Press representatives was moved by the Coloured delegation but was opposed by the Ovambo, Kavango and Caprivi delegations.

After the debate on the Declaration of Intent, steps were taken to intensify the intellectual quarantine imposed upon the delegates. During the debate on this first pronouncement of the Conference, a proposal that the Territory should become an independent confederation was opposed. Arguments centred around the use of vocabulary; there were objections to the word 'peoples' as foreshadowing too great a concession to the homelands principle. A compromise formulation was 'population groups'. In their declaration the delegates expressed themselves to be the authentic representatives, intent on discussing their constitutional future and opposed to the use of force. But despite the supposed compromise on vocabulary, the declaration remained an expression of National Party ideology. The emphasis on a federal alliance of different nations is more than apparent:

'That mindful of the interdependence of the various population groups and the interests of South West Africa in its entirety, to create a form of government which will guarantee to every population group the greatest possible say in its own and national affairs which will fully protect the rights of minorities and which will do right and justice to all.'

But the debate produced friction and irritation and reporters wrote of the possibility of a large scale walkout.[7] This reportage prompted the Conference organisers to move the 'muzzling resolution' which bound delegates to silence. The resolution was officially carried, and was indeed described as an act of consensus; but a number of delegates afterwards complained that only some members of the delegations had had the written resolution before them, that the debate was rapidly disposed of and that most of the delegates had no idea of the precise contents of the resolution passed in their name. Many were appalled when journalists subsequently read out and explained the implication of the resolution. (The incident provides some evidence of manipulation in the Conference itself and also the establishment of 'elite' elements in the delegations enjoying a special relationship with the Conference organisers.)

The delegates were required to pledge their secrecy on oath.[8] The resolution's effect was none the less to create an informer system amongst delegates who entered into furtive communication with journalists.[9] The subsequent leakage of information led to a further bizarrerie – the appearance of the security police on the scene.[10] Henceforth the delegates were compelled to carry on their activities under the watchful eye of security agents who were as we have noted already intimately connected with the proceedings. The first approach to Kapuuo had been made through police officers; they had taken part in the approach to other delegates; they enjoyed a close rapport with chiefs and homelands ministers and had, as we have seen, played an indispensable role in the evolution of the Nama and Damara responses. The awareness of police vigilance was reinforced by the discovery of a 'bugging' device in the private lounge of a hotel shortly before a conference between attorney Schwartz and certain of the delegates.[11] The shadow of the police was understandably disciplining; it also provided a comforting sense of immunity to willing collaborators.[12]

Amongst the delegates themselves a secrecy committee was established to preserve the confidentiality of the talks and to keep a watchful eye on the delegates. A by-product of the secrecy rule – the delegates had no right to discuss the proceedings with *anybody* outside of the Conference – was the implication that the delegates were powerless to report on the proceedings to their own supporters outside of the Conference Hall.[13] But embarrassing reports continued to appear in the Press, and upset the Conference organisers to the extent that Advocate van Zijl in the White Legislative Assembly moved that the Press should be asked to stop writing about the Conference.

The absence of a timetable was a striking feature of the Conference. The organisers spoke of the urgency of the talks and yet the procedural pattern was one of periodic debates separated by long adjournments. Far from being a constitutional conference where leaders debated their aspirations and their constitutional programme, attention was from the outset deflected into prolonged explorations in committee, where chosen delegates were embroiled with problems of 'petty apartheid', pension schemes social welfare and labour laws. The delegates, Mudge explained in the initial session, were not 'keen' to enter into the question of the constitution. One committee researched the merits and de-merits of the abolition of the Pass Laws and the desirability of enforcing the issue of identity documents. Its conclusion – wholly in conformity with National Party thinking – was that some system controlling the movement of Blacks into towns should be maintained, that identity documents reflecting the racial classification of their bearers should be required and that the restructuring of the Pass Laws should be left to the Administration. Other conclusions were: a minimum wage of R106 – to be recommended, not compulsory;[14] equalisation of pay but only after the elapse of six years.[15]

The committee on education, at a time when student revolt against the Bantu education system had set off a concatenation of riots and disturbances in the Republic and Namibia, refrained from calling the system itself into question. It dealt rather with the need not to 'force' education upon ethnic groups; children should not attend school outside the ethnic pale unless authorised by their parents and the education authority.[16]

Viewed in retrospect the delegates made no attempt to stake their claim and win for their impoverished supporters – in so far as they had any – a greater share in the national wealth. The process was rather educative; it provided an ambient culture in which the delegates steadily absorbed the vocabulary and principles of National Party ideology.[17] At the same time most of the delegates – men to whom the luxury of hotels, abundant food and lavish salaries seemed a miraculous gift – came to reflect upon themselves as powerful and meaningful leaders in the community. The occupants of the Turnhalle came to think of themselves as a meritorious elite with a historic duty in the new dispensation. This sentiment was later to be strengthened by serious proposals that the Conference should be transformed into a transitional government.

A handful of delegates who ventured to criticise the draft Constitution as apartheid in disguise were labelled *dwarstrekkers* (squabblers); Charlie Hartung and Krohne, leaders of the National Independence Party, were isolated and out-manoeuvred. (They resigned from the Turnhalle in March 1977.) Dissident delegates were kept out of the committees – the head of each ethnic delegation decided in his discretion who would attend – and were hindered in their attempt to address the Conference. The agenda committee maintained a firm grip on the proceedings; Hartung's motion that political parties should be allowed into the Conference was never allowed to surface. According to Hartung, the Conference organisers were in the habit of hurrying discussions; there was always an excuse; for example that Ndjoba had to attend an urgent meeting in Ovamboland. At the time of the debate on the Declaration of Intent, the leaders attempted to rush it through; they said it was already in Pik Botha's hands at the UN and had to be distributed urgently.

The delegates bowed supinely to the demands of the National Party organisers who, at times, found themselves unable to contain their antipathy. Eben van Zijl gibed in a clash with a Damara delegate: 'You forget that we fetched you Damaras from the mountains, put clothes on you and lifted you up from the mud'. In another exchange he pointed to a Bushman delegate and asked 'That Bushman, how did he get there? It is we the Whites who gave him protection'.[18] The target of Van Zijl's attack, Bushman delegate Zaogub, had to be restrained from assaulting him. After Dr. Ben Africa, the leader of the Baster delegation attended a performance in the Whites only Windhoek Theatre, he was cross-examined by resentful White delegates.

Whatever the delegates might have felt, their hurt feelings were assuaged by the relative luxury in their new surroundings. All the delegates received salaries of approximately R20,000 a year. For most of them, men who had emerged from humble origins, the figure was dazzling. (Some time before the Conference a Bushman delegate was asked what he most wanted in the world; he answered, 'A horse'. His donkey, he explained, was too slow for hunting.) The delegates were housed in hotels, where they enjoyed access to unrestricted quantities of free food and liquor. Some had little idea of what they were about. A Bushman delegate had to be taught to sign his name before the Conference started up. The chief minister of Kavango, Alphonse Mayeuero, in discussion with the Reverend Heinz Hunke, disclosed his categorical demand for a 'confederation', not a 'federation', but conceded his ignorance of the distinction. At the commencement of the Conference one Bushman delegate was apparently so obscure that his surname was unknown. His reported contribution to sessions of the Conference was to say on one occasion 'That is very good,' in the Afrikaans language.[19] During the course of the Conference a number of delegates began to show symptoms of heavy drinking; on more than one occasion some representatives were found asleep on their Turnhalle benches. This excited press comment: it had become fashionable, some journalists noted, for delegates to wear dark glasses during sessions.

The delegates were also cast into an ambassadorial role. Early in 1976 thirty-five of their number were sent to the US in the wistful belief that they could persuade Department of State officials that they were the true representatives. In the UK they were warmly welcomed by Conservative Party back-benchers. Kapuuo, preceded by his PR agent, made the rounds of European capitals, gave Press Conferences and interviewed Ministers. In June of 1976 he was officially invited by the Governor of New York to attend an official fête; not long afterwards Kapuuo threw a party in Manhattan – an extravaganza which reportedly cost his backers $40,000 – with film actress Elizabeth Taylor as his star guest.[20] Journalists speculated on the sources of Kapuuo's fund: US companies operating in Southern Africa, the CIA acting in conjunction with BOSS, and South African mining interests.[21] There were even improbable rumours that the Mafia, based in Miami, was a funding source. This found an echo in subsequent court proceedings where a cheque, made out to cover Kapuuo's air expenses and the cost of flying other delegates around the world, was allegedly traced to known Mafia collaborators in the US.[22]

Diplomatic and propaganda activity by the delegates was reinforced by former disaffected SWAPO members who returned to throw in their lot with the Conference. Kerina surfaced from academic seclusion in New York where he abandoned a teaching post to take up employment as a promoter of the Conference. His reappearance on the scene was prefaced by denunciations of the UN and sensational revelations that SWAPO was planning an invasion in the, then, near future. (He declined to disclose his source of information). At first employed to work for the Pro-SWA/Namibian Foundation, Kerina exacted a salary of R50,000 a year, quarrelled with the Foundation and found himself dismissed. Not long after his arrival he bought a cattle farm for R100,000.[23] Mudge afterwards disclaimed any co-operation with Kerina who subsequently disappeared from the scene.[24]

The South Africans gathered other former SWAPO leaders who, having left the organisation while in exile, had fallen into obscurity and endured financial hardship. After seven years in exile Kozonguizi, a struggling barrister in London, welcomed the opportunity to take up a position with ambassadorial trappings. He became the Turnhalle's roving ambassador in Africa.[25] Appolus, a former SWAPO official, returned to act as PRO on behalf of the Conference; he edited the *Times of Namibia* and lived in a Windhoek hotel with his wife. Others brought back were Jackson Kambode, a former Trades Union organiser then without employment, and Paul Helmudt, a founder member of SWAPO.

All expenses were paid by the Namibian Foundation.

30

The Constitutional Labyrinth

In March 1977 SWAPO's National Conference at Katutura enlarged its executive structure to make room for its new allies; Hendrik Witbooi was appointed to the newly created post of Secretary for Education and Culture; at the age of twenty-nine Dan Tjongarero became the youngest incumbent to the office of Vice Chairman; Pastor Z. Kameeta, former president of the NNC, was appointed Secretary for Health and Social Welfare. Reelected were Sam Nujoma, President, Mishak Muyongo, Vice President and David Merero – now in exile – Chairman. Martha Ford was elected Secretary for the Women's Council of SWAPO, Joseph Kahuika Secretary for the Elders' Council and Milner Mokganedi Tlhabanello the Secretary for Publicity and Information in the place of Tjongarero. The Conference condemned the Turnhalle process, the proposed interim government, Proclamation R17, the Terrorism Act and the 'perpetration of atrocities' as a threat to world peace and a gross violation of human rights. SWAPO reiterated its preparedness to negotiate with South Africa and called on the international community to 'pressurise the illegal occupying regime' into holding fair and free elections under UN supervision and control.

Within a month of the National Conference SWAPO ranks were swelled by the seventeen thousand member Association for the Preservation of the Tjamuuaha-Maherero Royal House, an organisation founded to protect the Herero Royal House against usurpers in the power struggle which ensued after the death of Chief Hosea Kutako. At a SWAPO Press Conference in Windhoek on the 14th April 1977 the Rev. B.G. Karuaera, the Association's Chairman, announced their unconditional resolution to join SWAPO. Their primary motivation, he explained, was the collective desire to achieve national unity and so avoid the fratricidal conflict then bedevilling Angolan history.

The Turnhalle delegates were alive to SWAPO's gathering support; many felt that they were losing credibility, as nothing concrete had been established. At report-back meetings in the Caprivi outspoken elements challenged Turnhalle principles and confirmed fears of SWAPO's widening popularity.[1] The delegates were faced with the unpalatable truth that they had failed to generate a mass following. They were by and large traditional leaders tethered to the Administration, or political homuncules who – with the exception of Kapuuo – could claim no significant fund of popular support. Pastor Ndjoba, Elifas's political heir, like so many other delegates from the homelands, was enmeshed in the alien machinery of Bantustan government. Kozonguizi, Kerina, Appollus and other returned exiles, unknown or barely remembered, had long lost contact with Namibia.

If the homelands delegates were given some public support it was thanks to residual tribal culture. Backing came usually from elderly members, in recognition of traditional loyalty. But 1976, the year of student revolt in the Republic, had left an irreversible mark in Black society. Until then tradition had rendered homage to parental authority; the word of the elders were inflexible law. In 1976 all that changed. The youth took over in Soweto and the Black townships; they fought off the police, organised strikes and destroyed vice dens and liquor stores; they took the initiative, issued orders and suffered the consequences. For months after the disturbances the students wielded internal power in the townships. This social ferment did not bypass Namibia; it was in 1976 that many students in Namibia echoed the seismic convulsions in the Republic, boycotted schools, protested against Bantu education, infected their teachers with their enthusiasm and demonstrated a militancy hitherto unknown in student circles. Many were expelled. In November 1976 there were disturbances at the Martin Luther High School in Omaruru when students protested against Bantu education; teaching staff supported the students and the headmaster announced his intention to close the school indefinitely until an alternative education system had been introduced. Within weeks student trouble spread to other towns including Khorixas, Tses and Windhoek.[2] At the Okakarara Secondary School all political activity was suppressed which was not favourable to the Turnhalle Conference. Seventeen students were expelled for protesting, others were arrested for possessing legal SWAPO publications and membership cards.[3] Tjongarero complained that it had become fashionable in state schools to expel anti-Turnhalle-minded students; the South West African Teachers Association condemned the expulsions.

With the winds of youthful militancy blowing across Namibia, neither Kozonguizi nor Ndjoba nor Kerina nor Doctor Africa were likely to capture the imaginations of students, teachers, businessmen, nurses, clerks and other elites; the traditionalist leaders, more than ever, were likely to be viewed with disdain as some form of primitive political throw back.

What, after all, had the Conference in fact accomplished by autumn of 1977? A Bill of Rights had been adopted but what was its meaning to Black citizens? The various freedoms couched in general and sententious phrases were at first blush not unimpressive; Bills of Rights are easily written – they are less easily upheld; a Bill of Rights without the mechanism of legal enforcement is so much paper. The Turnhalle draftsmen made no provision for legal enforcement of the Bill of Rights; the Courts was given jurisdiction to pronounce upon it, but its judgement was to serve merely as an advisory opinion; the Bill would not be binding on the legislative authorities.[4] The Bill significantly contained a provision that everyone could *possess* land – but this provided no inviolable right to own property, an ominous omission in a country where the good farmland and towns were overwhelmingly the property of Whites.[5]

The draft Constitution presented in March 1977 paid lip service to the principle that discrimination in property right should end – a pioneering concession neutralized by the principle that established rights would be recognised and protected. The draft foreshadowed a central government comprising a president, an executive body called the Council of Ministers and a National Assembly of sixty representatives. The procedure of the National Assembly was to be governed by a unique foundational rule: all decisions and legislation were constitutional only if made with total consensus.[6] No law could be promulgated unless voted by the majority on each of the ethnic delegations. These delegates were to be appointed to the National Assembly by the second tier governments – Bantustan governments for the Blacks and the existing Legislative Assembly for the Whites. The ethnic groups were to be represented as follows: Ovambos twelve, Whites six, Damaras, Hereros, Kavangos, Coloureds, Namas and Caprivians five each; Bushmen, Basters and Tswanas four each. The consensus formula might well have been indispensable for reassuring White voters bewildered by the prospect of sharing parliamentary power with Blacks; its theoretical functioning seemed plausible except that it was doomed in practice to become a constitutional mockery – unless, of course, the consensus was not genuine.

The inadequacies of the Turnhalle Conference led to sharp criticism from right wing nationalists. The HNP (Herstigte Nationale Party), a Party of right-wingers who broke from the National Party in 1969, mounted a campaign of protest against the grand design of multi-racial interim government – for them a serious breach of racial purity – and canvassed energetically around a nationwide petition of protest. (They put out a report that ninety-five per cent of the Whites who had been approached, had given their signatures.)[7] A new movement BOERSWA (Organisation for the Maintenance of the Unbreakable Unity of the Republic and South West Africa) concentrated its opposition against any severance of ties with the Republic, called on Whites to make a stand in a struggle for the preservation of Afrikaans and German purity. An Afrikaner priest, Dominee Jannie Jooste predicted that the white man's destiny was at stake, that the principle of ethnicity – once the Blacks were given freedom of movement – would not protect the Whites and that under the new dispensation the portrait of some Black state president would preside over every classroom and White boys would receive training under Black officers.[8]

In the face of such vociferous disenchantment the Government took the precaution of seeking the explicit consent of the majority of White Namibians. In a dual thrust designed to test the attitude of supporters and generate enthusiasm for a transitional government with Black leaders, the National Party, early in February 1977, announced that Whites would hold their own referendum. The Whites were asked to signify whether they were in favour of 'the establishment of an interim government and independence for the Territory in accordance with the principles accepted by the Constitutional Conference.'[9] (The formula had been drafted with forethought and was to have lasting consequences for the developing tensions in the White population.) Since the draft constitution had been presented as the infant child of National Party principles the chances of a 'Yes' vote seemed favourable and yet little was left to chance. A troubled White population was once again deluged with explanations and exhortations and detailed reasons why the establishment of an interim government would lay the foundation for prosperity and stability, inhibit UN hostility, revive economic confidence and eventually secure international recognition. A 'Yes' vote, it was said, was for the peaceful solution, a 'No' vote meant confrontation. The referendum was held on the 17th May 1977. Only Namibian citizens were allowed to vote; this excluded ten thousand German nationals but gave the vote to thirty thousand South African civil servants few of whom had any intention of staying in the Territory after independence.

The National Party's optimistic predictions were fulfilled with an overwhelming positive return.

31

New Dialogue and the Western Quintet

The internal preparations towards interim government were viewed by Western Governments as a dangerously irreversible path leading away from an internationally acceptable settlement. At the beginning of April 1977 representatives of the US, Great Britain, Canada, West Germany and France met with Vorster to convey their Governments' wish for a solution in terms of Security Council Resolution 385. The Prime Minister's first response was to confer with the Turnhalle Constitutional Committee; from this point onwards the Government would consistently defer to Turnhalle spokesmen in all its dealings with the international community and the Western Five. In the initial round of talks the Western Five representatives – the Contact Group – declined to have any dealings with Turnhalle delegates; later this stance was modified during a visit to Windhoek when the representatives refused to set foot within the precincts of the Turnhalle but signified their preparedness to meet Turnhalle delegates as well as SWAPO, Church leaders and other interested parties.[1] Henceforth the promotion of the Turnhalle delegates – through to their great moment at the Geneva Conference in January 1981 – was to be the cardinal feature of South African diplomatic activity. The genuflexions were sometimes more ostensible than real: during one round of negotiations four delegates on 'stand-by' at a hotel in Capetown where negotiations were in progress, were surprised to hear over the national news that Foreign Minister Pik Botha had conferred with them at intervals during the negotiation process.

Early negotiations centred on the details of an interim administrative authority which would govern in the transitional run-up to election of representatives to a constituent assembly. The Contact Group proposed some form of neutral bureaucratic administration – (One suggestion was to appoint Bishop Auala or Präses de Vries at the helm of a transitional government [2]). The Government in turn submitted the Western proposals to the Turnhalle representatives, only to be turned down.[3] It was then announced that in an effort to break the deadlock the Turnhalle leaders had decided to request the South African Government to appoint an Administrator General to rule the Territory until the completion of elections. Vorster acceded to this request[4] and introduced legislation in Parliament empowering the State President to appoint an Administrator General by Proclamation. In the first week of July 1977 Judge M.T. Steyn was appointed to the office. From the moment of his accession to office he would represent the South African Government and would yet, at the same time, be perceived as the living embodiment of a Turnhalle initiative.

From the outset of the negotiations Vorster rejected the pith and substance of Resolution 385: the *supervision and control* of elections by the UN. But a UN presence in the form of a special representative of the Secretary General who could collaborate with the Administrator General would be considered. Once again the Turnhalle leaders were consulted; they gave their consent, declaring that they wished to gain the widest possible acceptance.

In the succeeding months of negotiations the Contact Group flitted to and fro between the interested parties in an attempt to reconcile the irreconcilable and bind South Africa, SWAPO and the UN with gossamer ambiguous phrases to a common undertaking. From Mudge's quarter there was no fugitive phraseology or painstakingly fostered mistiness. He warranted effective South African control throughout the transitional period; the Administrator General would, he said – this was as early as June 1977 – concern himself with the evolution and control of electoral procedures whilst the Turnhalle representatives, freed from administrative chores, would devote their full attention to election preparations.

Throughout the discussions observers scanned the latest formulations in the international parley in order to divine the direction of progress; few cared to read the future in Mudge's blunt prognostications. With the investiture of an Administrator General endowed with plenary powers the Government readied itself for changes in the Territory; this was a major step in South Africa's two track strategy of distancing itself from Namibian responsibility and at the same time foisting a consciousness of its Turnhalle creations upon a discomfitted international community. Now that they were ready South Africa began to demand speedy development – a remarkable insistence after decades of inertia. The theme of urgency, used so ably to hasten decisions and facilitate pressure in the Turnhalle, was renewed. Any dragging of feet, said the Prime Minister, would not be South Africa's fault.[5] There was one other tactical advantage in hustling the parties into an agreement; if SWAPO put its signature to a settlement it would find itself in a race against time to mount an effective election machine.

In November 1977 the Turnhalle Conference was dissolved. The HNP expressed shock at the new turn of events. After eighteen months of effort, the abandonment of the Turnhalle they argued was inexcusable, a waste of money and effort, a capitulation forced upon the South Africans by – unspecified – 'negro representatives in the US.'

We have noted how the principle of ethnicity and the exclusion of political parties provided an ongoing protection to the Turnhalle delegates against the risk of a SWAPO or NNF intrusion into the Turnhalle. With the dissolution of the Conference Mudge tore through the web of sophistry with the announcement of a new electoral scheme: elections would no longer take place on an ethnic basis, voters would vote for political parties at their nearest polling booths, there would be no constituencies, the names of candidates would not appear on the ballot papers and each party would be allotted seats in terms of a system of proportional representation.

The revelation of such detailed unilaterally drafted plans was a defiant gesture against the backdrop of negotiations and the efforts of the contact group to thrash out details of an agreed electoral system. Mudge's allusion to the new role of political parties seemed curiously premature at a time when the Turnhalle delegates had no such organisation at their disposal; nor did a party with overt racists seem remotely viable. The appointment of an Administrator General, the definitive formulation of electoral rules and Mudge's language were all uncomfortably diagnostic of a basic South African plan – the product of mature aloof reflection – to proceed with internal elections using South African machinery and under South African control, in which SWAPO would not care to participate.

If in May of 1977, Vorster, in reply to a US suggestion that Blacks should participate in the elections to a South African national Government, could say, 'We cannot negotiate on our own destruction even now or tomorrow', he must have given his brethren in Windhoek adequate reassurance that wherever SWAPO might have to be reckoned with, it would not be at the polls.[6] With the unfolding of events more evidence was to emerge to reveal the essential nature and continuity of South Africa's intentions.

After the installation of the Administrator General in September 1977 the stage – but for one final gesture – was set for a new electoral chapter. On the 28th September, after failing to wrest the leadership of the National Party from Du Plessis – he missed by six votes[7] – Mudge and his followers walked out of the National Party Conference. This move, likewise the fruit of prolonged preparations – as early as July 1976 Mudge foreshadowed a multiracial movement[8] – liberated Mudge from complicity with the inflexible racism and embarrassing vocabularly of many of his rivals. Mudge was now free to present a truly *verligte* ('enlightened') countenance and mount an alliance with Black collaborators, which in its purified form, might be more credible on the international and home fronts.

The breakaway party was named the Republican Party; it wooed German-speaking Namibians and members of the Action Group of Percy Niehaus, a former United Party opposition leader in the Territory. The new party opposed discrimination on the basis of race or colour, subject to the somewhat Orwellian qualification that the party did believe in the existence of racial differences. The Republican Party – open to Whites only – declared its support for multi-ethnicity and its determination to combat racial discrimination. The Turnhalle delegates neither laughed nor protested, nor complained that this was the reincarnation of the National Party with rhetorical trimmings. Andrew Kloppers, the leader of the Coloured delegation, applauded and characterised Mudge's defeat in the National Party as a blessing in disguise. Within two days of the walk-out the Republican Party was installed in spacious furnished offices in Windhoek complete with telephones and telecommunications.[9] Shortly afterwards the grand alliance of the Republican Party and the entire phalanx of ethnic leaders was proclaimed and baptised the Democratic Turnhalle Alliance (DTA), with Mudge as its leader. The Vice-Chairmanship went to Barney Barnes, a leader of the Coloured Delegation, and the relatively unimportant ceremonial offices of President and Vice-President to Kapuuo and Ndjoba respectively. Gerson Veii dismissed the breakaway as 'irrelevant' while SWAPO described it as an exercise in opportunism. Du Plessis accused Mudge of planning the walk-out in advance and gave stern warnings of inter-racial strife: job opportunities were weak, Whites were leaving, apartments were empty and, as rentals declined, White sanctuaries would be penetrated by increasing numbers of Blacks in a process which would lead to bloodshed; by seeking to put an end to separate residential areas Mudge had dealt an axe blow at the very root of 'sacred principles'.[10]

On the 6th December the National Party announced the formation of its own multi-ethnic group, AKTUR (Action Committee for the Maintenace of Turnhalle principles).[11] The new organisation would embrace population groups only. Political parties would not be allowed.

In this way Du Plessis readied his faction in the fight for the soul of the Black man.

32

Transitional Rule: Law and Violence under the Administrator General

The accession to office by the Administrator General on 1st September 1977 appeared to mark the commencement of the consummation of internal constitutional development. Armed with untramelled legislative and executive powers – conferred by the State President in Proclamation No. 181 of 1977 – he became for practical and legal purposes the new Government of Namibia, subject in law to the South African Parliament only. Since his appointment was South Africa's proffered solution to the problem of installing an impartial interim government in the pre-election period, there was much emphasis on his neutrality. The appointment of a Supreme Court Judge to fill the role was a shrewd attempt to reinforce the notion of the man's neutrality. Judge M.T. Steyn, son of Colin Steyn the wartime Minister of Justice in the Smuts Government, was with his bland history and jovial manner well cast for the role of benign mediator and midwife to whatever constitutional creature the South African Government might be prepared to authorise. A residence was prepared for him and he and his staff took over two floors of the Kalahari Sands, a modern hotel in the centre of Windhoek. On the same day that he took up his appointment the office of Administrator of Namibia ceased to exist.

Steyn, on arrival, defined himself as wholly neutral. He would facilitate a fair and free election, repeal the Immorality Act, the Mixed Marriages Act and the Pass Laws. All political parties, including SWAPO, were invited to participate in the election process. He set out to meet Church leaders and win their confidence; his protestations of neutral umpireship impressed them. To Sam Nujoma he extended an invitation – with an offer of safe conduct – to meet him in Windhoek.[1]

SWAPO refused to recognise the 'lone presence' of the Administrator General and rejected his involvement in the election. The suggestion that the Administrator General should merely be advised – and not controlled – by an appointee of the Secretary General was unacceptable to SWAPO. A meeting arranged during a familiarisation trip in the north between Steyn and SWAPO's representative, Skinny Hilundua, was cancelled on SWAPO's instructions.

The Churches took the Administrator General at his word – and tested it. After Steyn had issued an invitation to political exiles to return with a 'legal purpose' to Namibia, five Church leaders petitioned Steyn to allow the return of Colin Winter, and pointed out that the Anglican Church had been deprived of the ministrations of its legally elected Bishop, that the expulsion was 'an affront to the integrity and dignity of thousands . . . ' and had created a feeling of alienation from the authorities. A five man delegation of the South African Council of Churches added their voice to the persuasion. A group of White Anglicans in Windhoek cross-petitioned with a prediction that the return of Winter would aggravate deep divisions in the Church.

On the 7th October 1977 Steyn adopted the argument of the cross-petitioners and turned down the request. Though not bound to give an explanation he said Winter's return would deepen the rift between Anglicans. The excuse was clumsy, as squabbles internal to the Church could have had no relevance to the original order of deportation. This explanation – perhaps more than the response – incensed Church leaders. Steyn, representing the secular authority, had no right to control the appointments in the Church, the exclusive province of the Synod. The Churchmen attacked Steyn's administration. Winter said he was acting out a 'complete charade implemented with the name of justice' and had sided with a 'tiny minority' of Whites. In a diatribe sent off as an open letter Black Anglican clergy inveighed against his partiality and wrote that his ruling left them in no shadow of doubt that he had 'special people to please no matter how small they are.'[2]

Criticisms mounted. Lucia Hamutenya, SWAPO Secretary for Legal Affairs, tore at Steyn's legislative output. His very first Proclamation, Proclamation AG1 with the obscure title 'Ordinance for the Regulation of certain matters in connection with a government for and the administration of Rehoboth and of the application of certain laws accordingly' provided for the further development of a Rehoboth Homelands Legislative Council. Far from being impartial, she said, he was endorsing Government Bantustan policy;[3] whilst the 'Pass Laws' had been ended, she pointed out, Katutura residents were arrested for not being in possession of residence permits.

The pattern of arrests had not changed. Steyn's offer of safe conduct to Nujoma was castigated as a stunt since Nujoma's acceptance would involve recognition of South African authority. Steyn's call to SWAPO – while negotiations were still in progress – to lay down arms and fight at the polls was rejected as partisan propaganda making. (Steyn did not conceal his support for the DTA nor his hostility towards AKTUR. He later overplayed his hand; this was followed by his summary recall from the scene.) Federal Party leader Bryan O'Linn urged Steyn to put an end to the daily propaganda churned out by the SABC in favour of the Turnhalle leaders. The request was noted – no significant changes supervened.[4]

Under the aegis of the Administrator General the prohibitions in the

Immorality Act against sex between different races, and the Mixed Marriages Act – outlawing marriage between the races – were repealed.[5] No inroads were made into the Terrorism Act or the Sabotage Act; to the consternation of those who looked forward to his cutting down repressive legislation, he proceeded to fortify his existing arsenal of discretionary powers of arrest, interrogation and detention. On the 11th November 1977 Steyn promulgated the Security District's Proclamation AG9 of 1977 and simultaneously repealed Proclamation R17 of 1972. Proclamation AG9 empowered the Administrator General or any person acting on his authority to control the place of residence of persons in a Security District, to prohibit them from carrying on 'any activity' or from leaving a Security District. A Proclamation declaring Ovambo, Kavango and Caprivi Security Districts placed the entire population of those areas at the mercy of an administration possessed of unlimited power to destroy businesses, hospitals and homes and impose forced removals. This was analogous to the legal plight of citizens under martial law. (The districts of Windhoek and five other major towns were declared Security Districts a few months later.) Commissioned and non-commissioned police and army officers were authorised to search, seize articles and vehicles and arrest persons for interrogation up to ninety-six hours[6] on suspicion that a detainee had committed an offence or intended to do so or possessed information of some other person's offence or intention to commit an offence. 'Offence' could be anything from murder to driving past a 'Stop' street sign. Steyn also granted himself powers to release detainees conditionally.[7] This facilitated considerable inroads into the political life of individuals through the mere process of arrest – without convictions – and conditional release. A clause in the Proclamation now permitted meetings, provided twenty-four hours notice was given to the magistrate of the District. Another Proclamation, AG10, amended the Riotous Assemblies Act by expanding its prohibition to any incitement by which 'grievous emnity would be engendered between different sections of the inhabitants of the territory.'

On the 18th April 1978, during his eighth month of office, the Administrator General promulgated Proclamation AG26, the 'Detention for the Prevention of Political Violence and Intimidation Proclamation,' providing for sweeping discretionary powers of arrest in cases where he was satisfied that any person contemplated or had promoted violence or intimidation. With this Proclamation the Administrator General could sidestep the adverse publicity provoked in the past by the misuse of the Terrorism Act to arrest political opponents who were innocent of the commission of any offence, let alone terrorism. Once arrested, a detainee could be kept at 'any place' for an unlimited period without access to lawyers.[8] Some seemingly ameliorating provisions provided for fortnightly visits by a magistrate and a review by a legally impotent review committee. (It merely had power to advise the

Administrator General. The Courts were specifically excluded from pronouncing on the recommendations of the committee.)[9] But none of these provisions made inroads into the Administrator General's capacity to order detention of a kind reserved for prisoners under the Terrorism Act – in solitary confinement, *incommunicado* and without access to lawyers. Once more the Administrator General empowered himself to impose conditions on the release of detainees, a serious matter for popular leaders who could in this way be silenced on pain of being returned once more to the cells. Within one week of its promulgation the Proclamation was applied to the SWAPO leadership. In the months that followed the Administrator General made liberal use of the Proclamation's facilities and in this way managed to maintain an inhibiting if not paralysing grip on legal opposition without having to fall back on the drastic but internationally awkward step of declaring SWAPO unlawful.

Behind the Administrator General's mellifluous phraseology and public smile there was a determined continuation of South African policy. Suspicions of his partisanship were, in the course of time, confirmed by his direct intervention in the political arena. His early invitations to Sam Nujoma and to SWAPO were followed up by round condemnations. His attacks became indistinguishable from Mudge's. During the negotiations Steyn predicted that SWAPO would launch a massive attack once the SADF had been withdrawn or neutralised by UN troops.[10] Later towards the end of 1978 it was rumoured that Ovambo workers were planning to strike by way of protest against the elections. An agitated Steyn, forgetting his pretentions to neutrality – and his legal training – issued a stern though legally erroneous warning that any strike against the elections would be tantamount to treason.[11]

Steyn's invitation to SWAPO to participate in the elections provided the organisation with renewed possibilities of asserting itself in public meetings and demonstrations throughout the Territory. In setting out to exploit Steyn's newly proclaimed liberalisation programme, SWAPO leaders appreciated their vulnerability to attack from official quarters. There were, however, other dangers.

In August of 1977 DTA vigilantes – most of them were NUDO supporters – attacked a SWAPO public meeting at Katutura. They arrived in vehicles *en masse*, armed with batons and stones. SWAPO supporters fell back in panic and several were injured. SWAPO followers regrouped and retaliated and, in the fighting which followed, motorcars were smashed, and the windows of neighbouring houses destroyed, and a vehicle belonging to NUDO supporters was set alight and gutted. Armed policemen watched the attack from behind the wire grilles of their vehicles. They did not intervene.[12] Similar incidents took place over the same weekend in Tsumeb, Walvis Bay and Luderitz.[13] In the Herero Aminuis Reserve nine SWANU members were injured when fallen upon by a NUDO contingent.[14]

In October 1977 SWAPO obtained permission to hold a meeting at Oshakati – the first official consent in Ovamboland since 1972. Over a thousand attended the meeting in the Black township's football ground. Oshakati had long been regarded as a SWAPO stronghold. Policemen in camouflage uniforms kept watch; a large contingent of soldiers stood by in Oshakati itself.[15] There were Black power salutes, chants of 'One Namibia One Nation' and tributes to Ja Toivo and Nujoma. Judge Steyn himself attracted some vehement oratory. Milton Tlhabanello declared that Steyn would be jailed if he remained in Namibia after SWAPO came to power. Speaker after speaker made grim predictions that the SADF would not withdraw and accused it of training UNITA (National Union for the Total Independence of Angola), a rebel movement in Angola, in the hope of creating a buffer zone in southern Angola.

In November 1977 SWAPO published its blue print for constitutional change. These proposals were similar to the original discussion paper issued in 1975: constitutional guarantees for human rights were emphasised, anti-racist legislation would be brought into force and an ombudsman would protect individuals against bureaucracy. The judiciary was designed to be independent and entrenched. It was up to the nation's representatives to decide whether the economy would be socialist, capitalist or mixed. The constitution was planned to be unitary and democratic with none of the convoluted burdensome and potentially destabilizing provisions thought up by the Turnhalle Conference. The constitutional vision was clearly conciliatory; the interim law would protect vested legal rights and title to property. SWAPO's political aim was a non-aligned state.[16]

In the same month Dan Tjongarero, the Deputy National Chairman, launched an attack on the issue of identity documents which had been recommended by the Turnhalle. The identity documents carried the bearer's racial classification. This contradicted, said Tjongarero, the Turnhalle pretentions to non-racialism. Namibians, he pointed out, were being compelled on pain of losing their jobs to take out identity documents, whilst in the homelands they were prevented from selling their livestock unless able to show their identity papers. Throughout 1977 SWAPO activists seized what opportunities presented themselves to discredit the Turnhalle 'puppets'. Earlier in the year SWAPO and SWANU members participated in demonstrations against the Turnhalle and distributed leaflets. In March 1977 Emile Apollus was shouted down by SWAPO supporters at a Turnhalle report-back meeting at Gibeon. The meeting refused to allow him and Barnes to develop the theme of corruption in SWAPO. There were cries of 'CIA' and 'BOSS'. The meeting was abandoned. At other report-back meetings in the smaller towns there were poor attendances.

Renewed attacks on SWAPO meetings started in December of 1977. Prior to a meeting at Oluno, army units put up road blocks and searched vehicles and passengers. DTA demonstrators attacked the audience, threw sand and hurled insults. The police reaction was to fire tear gas into the crowd. The tribal police immediately followed up, attacked SWAPO supporters, threatened them with hand grenades and rifles and struck out with *makalani* sticks. The DTA, the police and the tribal police, alleged Martha Ford, had mounted a combined operation, and the SADF had seen to it that SWAPO supporters were unarmed. The fracas was proof, Ford added, that no fair and free elections could be held in Namibia in the presence of the security forces.[17] Pastor T. Haita, the acting Chief Minister of Ovambo, said he regretted the incident but noted that such attacks were not surprising when well-beloved traditional leaders were 'run down'.[18]

In February 1978 SWAPO was compelled to abandon a meeting at Katima Mulilo – and its campaign in the Caprivi – after DTA supporters drove two land rovers into the crowds, attempted to address the meeting through loudspeakers, distributed pamphlets, slashed a SWAPO banner and took up a challenging position in front of the platform.[19] They then threw stones and fired shots. Once again there was police intervention, tear gas was thrown and the crowd dispersed. No arrests were made.[20]

The triumph of DTA ruffianism – carried out under the conniving eyes of the police – had perilous implications beyond the effort to nip SWAPO campaigning in the bud. As the year 1977 drew to a close, Herero men increased their attacks on Ovambo compound dwellers and SWAPO supporters in Katutura. Brought in from the reserves on DTA vehicles, they roamed with impunity through Katutura in irregular armed bands, in an atmosphere fraught with the risk of serious inter-ethnic violence. In the developing tension Kapuuo played a dangerous role with demands that Ovambos, housed in single quarters, should be removed to the compound to make way for Hereros.[21] The Administrator General agreed and compelled unwilling municipal officals to carry out the ejectment. On 28th February the first serious clash took place with a Herero attack on Ovambo workers waiting at a bus stop. To protect themselves the hostel dwellers posted guards and would not even allow cleaners into the building which they administered themselves.[22] Ovambos refused to leave the mixed single quarters for fear of their rooms being set alight by roving Herero bands. There were bitter complaints from SWAPO that the police prevented Ovambos in the compounds from going to the aid of their brethren. By the 7th March six people had been killed in the fighting including one SWAPO official.

At the sites of bloodshed DTA members exploiting their own initiative put out posters 'SWAPO murders' and 'DTA free us from murderers.'[23]

The fires of inter-tribal warfare were of profound significance in the Namibian context; serious chronic clashes between Hereros and Ovambos would strengthen arguments for ethnic separation and the need to entrench minority rights in a constitutional dispensation. The phenomenon was deeply divisive, would enfeeble SWAPO's claim to represent a national will, strengthen arguments for the maintenance of a South African military presence and so alter the course of Namibian development. SWAPO reacted with a general call to keep away from incidents which could develop into a 'civil war.'[24] The Churches appealed to the police to disarm private vigilante groups and bodyguards, to apply the law uniformly and disallow weapons on the streets, and called upon the public not to be influenced by 'slanted news reporting and provocative posters which can only generate feelings of hatred.' The tension persisted and was aggravated by the assassination of Toivo Shiyagaya, the Ovambo Minister of Health and Welfare, at a DTA meeting outside the Ongandjero tribal offices in February. The assassin, a young man armed with a Tokarev automatic pistol, was shot down as he tried to run away in broad daylight. On an empty cigarette packet in his jacket were the words 'PLAN . . . destroy all puppets.'[25] SWAPO, immediately accused, denied responsibility.[26] For reasons which were not understood the young assassin made no attempt to shoot far more prominent DTA leaders such as Kapuuo, Ndjoba and Barnes who were on the same platform.[27]

On the 27th March Kapuuo was himself gunned down by assassins – once again armed with Russian weapons – outside his shop in Katutura.[28] His two bodyguards were wounded. Katutura became explosive; hundreds of Hereros armed with sticks, pangas and knives milled around; Ovambos in a hostel could be heard singing and shouting 'Power'. Riot police patrolled the township though no attempt was made to disarm the roving bands. The death toll from street attacks had by now reached ten.

SWAPO, considered a prime suspect, was blamed. Mudge and Steyn expressed shock and lauded the dead man's achievements. SWAPO was roundly condemned, even though Kapuuo had dangerous political rivals amongst the Hereros. SWAPO denied responsibility[29] while Sam Nujoma reflected on Kapuuo's life more with commiseration for someone misled than hostility for an arch rival. DTA supporters in reply promised to assassinate SWAPO leaders and take revenge on Nujoma no matter where in the world he was to be found. In the wake of these threats SWAPO Treasurer Tauno Hatuikulipi, Martha Ford and Milner Tlhabanello left the Territory.[30] On the day of Kapuuo's funeral five Ovambo hostel dwellers were shot down from outside the hostel complex as Kapuuo's funeral cortège passed.[31] Ed Morrow and other Church leaders who visited the scene of the killing found bullet marks on the walls of the hostel near to patches of bloodstained earth. According to an official release, however, the five Ovambos had been killed while attacking the funeral procession. Contingents of extra police were rushed to Windhoek while Pik Botha flew in to confer with Steyn. The Security Police plunged into the investigation of the assassination; they concentrated on the hypothesis that the assassins had executed their mission with the complicity of a SWAPO network within

214

Namibia, but carried out no immediate swoop as in the aftermath of the Elifas assassination.

The timing of the arrests on this occasion was to be conditioned by major political and international considerations.

33

Psychological Warfare

As the political war against the internal wing of SWAPO intensified, the police set out on a course of bold political intervention. The extent of their preoccupation with the growth of SWAPO as a political force emerged in the attempted 'political assassination' of Dan Tjongarero in December 1977.

On Friday 2nd December nine SWAPO leaders travelled in a Kombi to the ELOC youth centre at Ongwediva in Ovambo to attend a seminar on a paper by a political science professor, André du Toit. Amongst them were Dan Tjongarero, Martha Ford, Tauno Hatuikulipi, Simon Hiskia, Bernardus Petrus, Charles Sihani, and Justin Ellis of the Christian Centre.

A little beyond Onamagongwa, Security Captain W[1] and colleagues were waiting. They stopped the Kombi and after a brief search took the passengers to security headquarters at Oshakati where they were detained by Colonel Schoon under Proclamation AG9 on suspicion of being implicated in 'unholy acts of terrorism'. A captain gave notice that if the investigations were not completed within ninety-six hours their status would change to that of detainees under the Terrorism Act. A white constable J remarked that they could be held for ninety-six years. Tjongarero demanded to see his lawyer.

'You can't see anyone, you have no rights as a detainee,' was the Captain's swift reply.

Well before the police separated Tjongarero from his companions the atmosphere became saturated with threat. One officer affecting myopia went up to Charles Sihani and leaned forward to read the inscription 'Captain Zero' printed on Sihanti's T-shirt. 'You have now reached your zero hour,' he growled; derisory schoolboy humour, but it had its effect. Constable J to Tjongarero: 'You look like a chimpanzee, you should have stayed in Windhoek and spoken with Turnhalle people. This evening or tomorrow you are going to get hurt.'

J glowered at Justin Ellis, accused him of being a little '*kont*'[2] and added 'I have been wanting to cut your throat for a long time now.' Ellis was promised a trip '*hel-toe*' (to hell). A tall cadaverous-faced policeman stared fixedly at Martha Ford. 'Martha dear, are you heartsore?' 'No' replied Ford sharply. 'Don't be sad' he rejoined, 'the days of sadness are yet to come.'

The elements of salvation, survival and death were casually implanted in the dialogue. An officer asked Ellis if he would be redeemed.

Ellis: 'Yes I too will be redeemed.'

Officer: 'When will you be redeemed?'

Ellis: 'According to God's time.'

Officer: 'You are going to hell!'

Several hours later the group, after being separated from Dan Tjongarero and Bernadus Petrus, was removed to the Oshakati Military Camp. The security officers carried Russian-made AK47 sub-machine guns, standard equipment in guerilla ranks, fraught with ugly implications in the hands of the police. (The detainees grasped the ominous presence of the 'AKs' which could later turn out to be the weapons 'found' in the Kombi; an assassination in the bush could be remoulded as a sequel to murderous 'infighting' amongst SWAPO factions.) Was it purely fortuitous that a fake SWAPO publication had shortly before then referred to the need to liquidate Tjongarero? As it turned out their stay in the Military Camp was uneventful; the next morning they were returned to headquarters and asked to make a brief statement about their movements prior to arrest. The interviews were brief; there were no suggestions, no violence and no threats. Later at a press conference the police explained that the group had been suspected of associating with armed terrorists. (The detainees discovered this for the first time when they read the newspapers.)

All were released except for Petrus and Tjongarero. About two hours later Tauno Hatuikulipi, the Director of the Council of Churches, returned to the Police offices to recover a diary that had been taken from him. He arrived simultaneously with a police van. Next to the driver sat a person whom he did not recognise immediately; then with shock he realised that it was none other than Bernardus Petrus, dimly recognisable behind swollen features and red puffy eyes.

Senior officers concentrated a different attack onto Tjongerero. Even before Tjongarero was separated from his companions there were allusions to his death. That his national prestige and Vice-Chairmanship of the organisation provided no shield against assault and death was understood by Tjongarero. Three months earlier Steve Biko, a young colossus of the Black Consciousness Movement in the Republic, had died from fatal injuries sustained in police custody. (Biko had believed that the Security Police might assault him but thought that his prestige ruled out a fatal attack). In the eloquent presence of the 'AKs' the officers surrounding him plied him with reminders that blame for his death could be shifted to SWAPO. The accusations went on for hours: he had aided and abetted terrorists, propagated lies against the police, excused violence and plotted terrorism. It was the same formula: tireless badgering, discomfort and threat and no sleep. Tjongarero, young and intellectual, a virtual newcomer to such confrontations, sank into a deepening turmoil. They said he was not cooperative and that meant indefinite solitary confinement. In a master stroke, designed to act on his sensibility, he was put in a vehicle and taken to the scene of a land mine explosion. The expedition to the debris of destruction was hastily organised with South African journalists and photographers to witness the shaken Tjongarero help remove corpses and victims to an ambulance. The next step was to confront him with two 'rehabilitated' SWAPO guerillas to bring home to him (in the words of Tjongarero's 'confession') the 'absolute revelation of SWAPO's senseless murders'. As Tjongarero later explained – after his release – they induced 'a state of disorientation by way of discomfort, menace, threats and unrelenting intimidation.' This process with its associated bombardment of raw images of physical horror produced in him – like the Pavlovian dogs that had taken too much punishment – an abreaction, a vulnerability and a new dependence. Intellectual and physical survival were at stake in a nightmarish episode where judgment was confounded and nothing but self-annihilation and renunciation seemed the way out. He was brought pen and paper for a 'confession' with its 'revelation' of SWAPO's murders, rapes and infanticides – not a war of liberation but a 'manifestation of the animalistic instincts of barbarism'; he personally had been fed with false atrocity stories about the 'Boers' and had unknowingly contributed to the dissemination of fraudulent propaganda. The 'confession' went on to exonerate the police – it also delved into his intimate personal life – and vowed his intention to leave the 'dirty game' of politics, serve the Church and act as a moderating factor *in the Church*. There had been no physical or psychological compulsion he wrote; his monograph at police headquarters was merely a search to rediscover himself, no matter how long his detention might be. In a formal letter to SWAPO – the police said it was Tjongarero's idea – he tendered his resignation from an organisation that he had abruptly 'discovered' to be senselessly murderous, undemocratic and Marxist. They let him go after he signed and immediately organised a Press Conference to trumpet the news of Tjongarero's revelations and repudiations to the world.[3]

For Tjongarero the demoniacal spell vanished at the moment of his release. Though profoundly shaken by his ordeal he took legal advice and swiftly repudiated his resignation: 'It is not and has never been my intention to step down from my post in an organisation which historically and still today strives for democratic participation of all people of Namibia irrespective of race.'

Tjongarero did not resign nor did SWAPO dismiss him. In response to the Security Police initiative the organisation closed ranks. But the episode did introduce strain and suspicion.

A few months later Tjongarero was relieved of his post on the SWAPO executive.

34

'Guernica, Auschwitz . . . Oshakati . . . '

Bernardus Petrus was not released.

On return to Windhoek, Hatuikulipi reported his encounter to Petrus's father and Lutheran Church leaders. No one understood the mystery of Petrus's continuing detention. Manifestly there had been an assault but would the Judges draw the same inference? An application founded on Hatuikulipi's affidavit was in law sufficient to create a *prima facie* case of assault against some members of Col. Schoon's staff, but one foresaw categorical police denials reinforced perhaps by a magistrate's affidavit to say that all seemed well, culminating in a Judge's ruling against the applicant on the ground that there was no direct evidence implicating the police in violence. But the weakness in the applicant's case could be cured by filing evidence of the existence of a system of Security Police brutality at Oshakati. The moment for such an attack seemed appropriate as a number of witnesses – interviewed during defence preparations in the Nkandi trial – were available to testify. Among others there was Lamek Iithete and Pastor Imene[1] who had been in the cells with Nkandi, and Kautwima and others, including young students who had been subjected to electric shock during police investigations of unrest at Ongwediva college. The evidence of such witnesses could clearly authorise the inference that the injuries Hatuikulipi had seen were the result of a system of brutal interrogation. Above all there was Petrus's own safety and survival at stake and the agonising uncertainty felt by his father. The Churches decided on action. Du Preez and I were then hastily briefed to move an urgent application.

From the moment of touchdown at Ondongua Airport – enlarged to accommodate military transport planes –. we were struck by the changed face of Ovamboland. We saw hundreds of riflemen; movement in and out of the Airport was rigidly controlled by armed soldiers; the airstrip had become a sprawling military encampment. There were military patrols everywhere; it was a country at war without – for the moment – visible death and destruction.

Some of the witnesses had to be tracked down in the Ovambo bush, in the wooded easterly plains near Epembe approximately forty miles to the east of

Ondongua. After borrowing a Church vehicle our expedition went off into the bush. It was only then that our expedition discovered an Ovambo reality which bore no relation to the projected image of a country protected and aided by the army where law and order was firmly maintained in the hands of the police. It was our discovery that parts of Ovambo were in fact subjected to the *de facto* control of SWAPO. The expedition found passage along certain roads was barred by an invisible hand; but the Church vehicle guided by friendly unknown villagers – accomplices in an immense secret? – was able to make its way safely along rough uncontaminated tracks where SWAPO land mines were excluded. The revelation was a shock confirmation of what we had been told: that the Ovambo peasants looked upon the guerillas as their kinsmen and gave help with knowledge of the appalling implications. It was a country of extraordinary paradox. The South African Army was everywhere and the skies buzzed with helicopters and spotter planes in ceaseless observation of a gigantic intangible conspiracy. And when night fell SWAPO took over.

The witnesses were gathered together at the Oniipa Mission with the help of Finnish missionary Olaf Eriksson. Each witness was interviewed separately through an interpreter – and painstakingly cross-examined on the context, sequence and details of his or her narrative. The application had major implications for the Security Branch; an intense counter-attack by counsel for the police was to be expected. This was the time to evaluate the integrity of the evidence and excise exaggerations. No one in the legal process is better placed to judge a witness's honesty than his own counsel. An exploration in depth with appropriate investigative surgery – especially on the fringes of events where a mendacious witness might not have thought far enough – will in most cases reveal the failure of honesty or memory on the part of the witness. We started off interviewing the boys from the College, young men of eighteen of nineteen who answered spontaneously, at times impulsively. A dispute had blown up at the Ongwediva College over the wearing of uniforms, a minor internal episode which led to a student boycott. The sequel to this, said the boys, was the intervention of soldiers and security police followed by savage doses of electric shock. It did not sound probable – even in Ovamboland. But their answers were convincingly direct, whether on the minutiae of brutality or incidental discussions leading to a decision to boycott.

When tested their evidence was unshakeable, their demeanour unassailable. They had brought with them the warranty of truth – fresh burn marks below the stem of the penis, in the pubic triangle, on the scrotum and on the leg. The following sums up their evidence.

Hosea Mbandeka was away from home when soldiers arrived and searched for him. On his return he found a message to call at the security police offices at Oshakati. He obeyed the request. On arrival he was arrested and placed in a cell. After three days he was removed by security police and taken in a Land Rover to an undisclosed destination. He was driven along unknown roads in blindfolded darkness. At last the Land Rover stopped. There were no explanations. He was taken out of the vehicle and guided up the steps of an unidentified building. He was then tied to a chair; some object – held in position by a cloth wound tightly around his head – was placed above his left eye. After the cloth was saturated with water – an excellent conductor of electricity – someone attached a clip to his scrotum. An officer, who sounded like a White man, asked why he had left the College. Mbandeka's affidavit recorded the following.

'I said that I had left because of the way in which students were treated. I said the beating of students was inhuman. I then heard what sounded like the whine of a machine and felt a sudden violent burning sensation in my head which I believed to be electric shock. It seemed to kick my head upwards. I could not breathe. I felt confused and frightened and felt that my head was breaking into fragments. At the same time I felt an agonising burn in my testicles. This burning pain ran through my legs, and also went into my stomach. My whole body was jumping. The White officer said that they would burn me in this fashion until my *'gat'* (anus) was broken. When the burning stopped, my jaws shut violently together, so that I bit my tongue repeatedly and it bled. I was also interrogated as to who had tried to set fire to the mattress room at the college. I replied that I had no idea. I said that had happened when I was already back at home. Not satisfied with this, I was burnt again and again, the officer insisting that I knew the names . . .'

When it came to Reinhold Ipinge's turn the interrogators concentrated on his groin: one electrode immediately below the stem of the penis and one on each side of his groin. Two other electrodes were applied to his left and right ankles. According to Ipinge he had been shocked on the 31st October 1977; when we consulted him on the 7th December the marks were still visible. Photographs were taken and demonstrated a crater of destroyed tissue with its aura of burnt skin. We sent Ipinge to Windhoek for medico-legal investigation by Doctor J.T. Wickens, who found the burn injuries to have a central necrotic area with a residue of dry scab and a periphery of new skin. These were signs pathognomonic of burn injury – 'probably caused by a burn of an electrical nature.'[2] Hosea Mbandeka was examined by a Finnish medical doctor at the Mission Station and found to have 'small pappels in his external genitals which were discharging a little bit of blood.' This too was found consistent with the administration of electric shock.

Naboth Imene, an elderly Lutheran Pastor, recounted his experience with electricity and violence in the *waarheidskamer* – the one sheltering behind a red cross on the door – adjacent to the old police station in Oshakati. Electrodes were clamped on each side of his ears. The current passed directly through his head: 'I suddenly felt an indescribable pain which hurt me very badly especially in my head and I fell to the ground.' His unsatisfied interrogators followed up by suspending him from an iron rod, head downwards. 'I was suspended head down and one of the policemen then started swinging me around on the bar. While this was being done, I was repeatedly assaulted. I was interrogated in this room for approximately two or three hours.' Johannes Kautwima confirmed what Nkandi had passed on to us. He recounted his ordeal – electrodes had been placed in his anus and on his penis – with an inexplicable calm. Electrodes were also placed on his ears; they were all operated simultaneously. Like Pastor Imene, he too was suspended from an iron rod and beaten. We also took an affidavit from Willem Imene, an Ovambo peasant who spoke of being beaten and kicked by four White officers at Oshakati. He felt helpless. These were his words:

'I am a small man and am no longer young having grown children but I do not know my age. I was completely defenceless and begged them to believe that I had told the whole truth that I knew. The assault lasted for about an hour . . . Since then I do not feel that I am the same man being crippled by pain in my back, chest and in my right hip.'

There were other witnesses. Lamek Iithete, a battered looking peasant in his fifties, was shocked on the stomach and on his head. 'My body shook violently. I thought I would die and at that moment wished for death.' Afterwards he was taken to an Army Camp and tied to a pole with his arms outstretched. 'My ankles were also tied. I remained in that position the whole night . . . ' Raula Shinbode, a nurse at the Roman Catholic Hospital in Windhoek, was arrested – they said, because she was 'a friend of the terrorists' – and taken by road to Oshakati security headquarters. A policeman named Z took her to another room in the building where, he said, they made people talk. Suspended by her arms, she hung with her feet completely clear of the ground. She did not notice electrodes being placed against her head. 'I suddenly felt the terrible pain and shaking and trembling through one side of my face and my whole body, but was not aware what caused this.' After two hours of suspension she lost consciousness; Z later told her that she had urinated on the floor and ordered her to clean up. Saltiel Endjala, a twenty-four year old farmer, had crossed the border to buy goats. He was arrested, interrogated and released and then rearrested. At Oshakati – in the room 'with blankets over the windows' – a Sergeant ordered him to remove his clothing except for his underpants. He was shocked on the hips: 'My whole body felt as if barbed wire was being pulled through it.' Two other witnesses, Beata Asino and Elise Kadhila, were beyond our reach as they were still State witnesses – the Nkandi trial was not yet over. The problem was, however, simply solved by attaching a certified copy of their evidence in the trial.

The affidavits were served on Schoon in Oshakati. The security police lost no time in contacting lawyers and filed replying affidavits. Schoon, in a sweeping denial, declared that no assault had taken place on detainees during the two years of his command; he was shocked to read the contents of the applicants' papers; he gave the court his assurance that the allegations were devoid of truth. Their intention, he submitted, was to present the Security Branch in an unfavourable light. (He forgot to add a favourite security police sting to the counter-accusation: that the purpose behind fabricated allegations of brutality was to present the security police in an unfavourable light in order to weaken the security of State.) An affidavit from a visiting magistrate, who saw the detainee on the 10th December for the first time, depicted a healthy uncomplaining Petrus with no signs of injury.

The application was heard by Judges Badenhorst and Hart, sitting as a Full Court on account of the gravity of the issues. Advocate F. Botha of the Windhoek Bar represented the Police; I appeared, assisted by Bryan O'Linn, for Petrus's father. Argument had hardly started when the Judges fixed on Petrus's failure to complain to the magistrate. The Court was not moved by argument that a detainee would be afraid to accuse his captors while in their power. In a torrid interlude the Judge President sharply commanded me to remove my hands from my hips while addressing the Court. I refused. My submissions to the Bench, I said, were respectful and in conformity with my duty as counsel; that duty was to protect my client, not to concern myself with the positioning of my hands.

The thrust of the application had nothing new. The same logic had been rejected in the flogging cases: an injunction commanding police officers to refrain from assault could, in the light of police denials, we submitted, in no way prejudice them. The allegations were very serious, the systems of assault were brutal infringements and a threat to life and health which no court could tolerate.

After the completion of argument Judge Hart, relying on the magistrate's affidavit – and a blurred photograph of Petrus being visited by his girlfriend – started to give judgment in favour of the respondents. It was during the delivery of judgment that Du Preez contacted the magistrate and returned to Court with a message that Petrus had been seen once again by the magistrate and had this time reported he had been assaulted. By now Hart had given Petrus's failure to complain as a ground for dismissing the application. It was of course necessary to interrupt the Judge – an unprecedented move in Windhoek courts – in order to convey the new facts to him. This was done and the Court adjourned. When the Court reassembled Judge Hart proceeded with the following extraordinary reasoning: since Petrus had made a complaint, the original ground for dismissing the application had been removed; now the Court found that Petrus was not intimidated and would speak out if he were assaulted – an irrelevant conclusion and a wrong ground for dismissing the application, for the essence of the application was the protection of the detainee, not his right or preparedness to make complaints to a government official. The Judges found a further ground for dismissing the application, (thus committing, as we later submitted a gross misdirection): the case, they ruled, should be dismissed on the ground that it was not urgent. In legal and practical terms this meant that the application would have to be brought in conformity with ordinary procedure, entailing a possible delay of two or three months before the hearing.

The application was dismissed. An application for leave to appeal to the Appellate Division was refused. Echoing the Judge's approach in the flogging case, the court held that there was no prospect of success on appeal and that an appeal would be a waste of time. A petition was submitted to the Chief Justice who granted leave to appeal in March 1978 – on the basis that there *were* reasonable prospects of success.

Petrus had by then been released.

Church leaders were upset by the judgment in the Petrus application. Heinz Hunke, a brilliant Catholic priest, urged that no Judge could act on the presumption that police officers were not likely to assault detainees. Were there not daily complaints in the courts of police assaults? And whilst the accusations of Black criminals and militants might be viewed as partisan, had not the police themselves led evidence of the practice of gross brutality?

In the same year two policemen, Farmer and Dentlinger, were tried before Judge Hart on a charge of murdering two Black detainees at the Rehoboth Police Station. In that trial the police witnesses themselves – as witnesses for the prosecution – testified to the *frequent use* of the 'spook', a piece of rubber tubing which caused suffocation when pulled over a prisoner's head. One of the deaths had been caused by a ruptured liver. To explain this one accused said that he hit the deceased in the abdomen with the heel of his hand, a style he pointed out he had been taught at Police College.[3]

Haunted by the new dimension of brutality and its immunity throughout the Territory, the Churches campaigned strenuously. Torture had reached 'horrifying proportions' was the assertion of an open letter issued by leaders of the Lutheran, Anglican and Catholic Churches in May 1977. Their letter protested against the widespread use of malpractices and singled out the gruesome details: 'beating with fists or rifle butts, being held in an uncomfortable or painful position for long periods of time, sleep deprivation, hung up by their arms, electric shock, burning with cigarettes, solitary confinement, held incommunicado for months.' They deplored torture as a 'step back into the horrors of ancient pagan customs'. This could never be condoned, they wrote, for torture 'starts a chain reaction of brutality and inhumanity . . . '. The whole society – by implication White society – they argued, bore a moral responsibility; it was *their* parliament which had passed the security laws, thus creating immune enclaves where the poisonous fungus of brutality was encouraged to flourish. 'The only conclusion we can come to' asserted the Churches 'is that those who have authority in the South African forces had given their approval to the use of these brutal methods . . . '

No one expected miracles. Aware that their protest would be shrugged off the Church leaders – disregarding warnings to stop meddling in politics – took the extraordinary initiative of compiling and distributing practical hints to their congregants on ways and means of facing up to torture: 'If any officer should show an inclination to maltreat you tell him that you know it is against the law for him to use his powers in this way. This may deter such a person from acting illegally . . . '

Not long after Steyn took up office, Heinz Hunke's petition lay waiting on his desk. It raised many issues: the authentic leaders of the people were in exile or prison; the police had 'special torturing devices', specialist techniques and their own jargon 'for dangerous forms of torture'; a request to Mudge to institute an impartial court of enquiry had been evaded. Hunke's request to the Administrator General was that he should put an end to the practice of torture and give his 'counter-part', the Secretary General of the UN, full access to all police stations and interrogation centres.

The Church leaders attacked the 'unashamed monopoly of legislative, executive and judicial power' wielded by Steyn, the 'superficial manner' in which he handled reports on torture, the biased way police actions and investigations were carried out in the case of riots and disturbances, and the continuation of torture allegations without 'any hope of protection.'[4] When he took office Steyn had wooed the Church leaders and spoke of reconcilia-tion. This they submitted had been welcomed but his recent actions called into question his ability to oversee the Territory with fairness. As for Procla-mation AG26, they disagreed with the Judge's contention that the ordinary laws of the land were insufficient to ensure peace. The imperative need, they urged, was not repressive legislation but urgent steps to prevent 'total and fatal confrontation' within the Territory of Namibia.

The Administrator General dismissed Heinz Hunke's plea: the allegation had been extensively investigated and he was satisfied that there was 'no substance' in Hunke's averments. 'You were undoubtedly ill-served by your informants. You can rest assured that I will never tolerate or condone the infliction of unlawful violence upon anybody, whether detained or not . . . ' His task, wrote the Administrator General, was to quell unlawful violence and it was up to Hunke as a man of God to assist him.

In his last letter to the Administrator General Heinz Hunke replied:

'It is my belief that a large proportion of Christendom is praying to a God who is dead after having been killed in many places like Guernica, Auschwitz, Archipelago Gulag, Katutura, Oshakati, Ohongo, Kassinga. One day we will have to turn and look for another God, a Living One. We could try, just for a change, with the Father of Jesus from Nazareth. That would be quite a revolution.'

35

Diplomacy and Blitzkrieg

The Western Five's diplomatic intervention was not favoured by SWAPO leaders. They condemned it as foreign to the UN and as an initiative that tended to undermine and bypass the UN with the aim of promoting the Turnhalle troupe as an alternative to SWAPO; nothing less than an election firmly embedded within the protective ambit of Resolution 385 was acceptable. Throughout the negotiations SWAPO's suspicion remained unappeased; since the initial agreement between the Contact Group and South Africa involved an acceptance of 'some form' of international involvement, the negotiations at root implied the risk of some dangerous mutilation of Resolution 385.

A free and fair election spared of the scourge of intimidation and fraud raised thorny issues which had to be solved in the practical situation. Legislative and executive power which remained vested in the South African Government or its instrument, the Administrator General, could constitute an all-encompassing intimidatory decor. The maintenance of law and order by South African Army battalions and the presence of thousands of police active within the controlling grid of chiefs' and headmen's power presented significant built-in mechanisms for intimidation within the texture of Namibian society. The ideal solution exacted the retirement of the warring parties from the arena of conflict – the withdrawal of South African troops and police to the Republic and the return of SWAPO guerrillas to their bases. The vacuum thus created would then be filled by a neutral replacement law enforcing agency which would serve to underpin a neutral bureaucracy.

The solution, SWAPO argued, was to vest policy-making powers in the person of a special representative of the Secretary General; on the signing of a settlement the Security Council should then proceed to endorse the agreement and establish a UN military force numbering between four and five thousand troops, to keep order during the transitional period leading to the election and the establishment of a constituent assembly.

The central issue of power was taken up at the beginning of the negotiations by the Contact Group but remained unresolved. One of the suggestions, as we have noted, was that one of the Lutheran Bishops could approp-

226

riately carry out this function. The South Africans did not share this view; their answer was to appoint the Administrator General as a 'neutral' figure in control of a transitional administration. The Contact Group bowed to this *fait accompli*. The compromise plan foreshadowed in later negotiations – that the UN special representative would have to be satisfied at every stage in the evolution of the transitional period with the actions of the Administrator General – was anxiously reviewed by SWAPO. They pointed out that in the ongoing situation the special representative would be bereft of power; the intelligence and administrative apparatus of the administration would not be under his control – worse still it could serve to undermine him. He would be exposed to the risk of a developing friction with the Administrator General. There were other worrying problems: how would the retirement to base of South African troops be monitored? Would the South Africans allow the return of exiles and release Namibian political prisoners?

The South African Government remained adamant on the fundamental question of power and refused to hand over Namibia to the UN or anyone else; nor were they prepared to withdraw their troops. Its military presence they contended was necessary to contain intimidation and guerrilla infiltration and to honour South Africa's undertakings to ensure the protection of homelands government.

By September 1977 SWAPO, the target of increasing pressure from some of the front line states – who had their own problems with South Africa – consented to make significant concessions. Without surrendering their objections to the Administrator General's dominant role, SWAPO now conceded the framework for the negotiations and admitted a preparedness to go through with the proposals provided South Africa's military presence was withdrawn.[1] The collision of wills on this issue threatened to rupture the negotiations, until the South Africans indicated a preparedness to withdraw a part of their armed forces prior to the election, on condition that SWAPO stopped all hostile acts. Troops would be withdrawn within two months after the cease-fire had been honoured, a UN military force would patrol the border and ensure the maintenance of law and order, and a garrison of four thousand troops would be confined at the Grootfontein and/or Oshivello military camps subject to monitoring by UN observers.

SWAPO resisted the new proposals. Not a single South African soldier should be allowed to remain. There was 'not an inch left for negotiations' replied the South Africans who insisted that they had made all the concessions that they were prepared to make, though by January they were willing to reduce the garrison to three thousand.

During the months of negotiations SWAPO viewed South Africa's manoeuvres with growing distrust. The danger of treachery was uppermost in their thinking for SWAPO's military strength lay in the dispersion of their fighters and their capacity to merge with the Namibian countryside and its population. With SWAPO guerrillas assembled in base camps they would overnight become vulnerable to annihilating attack and bombardment. In SWAPO's view the South Africans had from the outset made no important concessions on fundamental themes. While the South Africans loudly proclaimed their generosity, there were at the same time serious indications that their strategy was to go along with the negotiations in the hope that they would fail. Part of that strategy was to inspire distrust in SWAPO ranks and to 'persuade' SWAPO to break off the talks. When the Administrator General took office he outlined plans for an election which would be carried through with speed: no party would be allowed to retard its progress or postpone the election by threats of non-participation was Steyn's warning – a danger sign of South Africa's unilateral intentions. Hand in hand with Pik Botha's emotional insistence that the South Africans could go no further and could not concede their self destruction was a concomitant element of *krag-daadigheid* manifesting a readiness to rupture the dialogue. In September 1977 Vorster gave curt notice of his intention to break off negotiations unless the West stopped disputing South Africa's possession of Walvis Bay – the only deep water port on the Namibian coast.[2] The very establishment of the Administrator General's office was an unequivocal rebuff of the Western initiative on a most sensitive issue: the creation of a neutral bureaucracy. (The transfer of the Walvis Bay administration to the Cape was another *'fait accompli'* answer to UN and SWAPO demands for the port.) The unilateral nomination and appointment of Steyn as Administrator General was a further indication of South Africa's tough approach. When Martii Ahtissari's name was later proposed as Waldheim's special representative the South Africans found fit to object. The process of creating separate homelands had gone on uninterruptedly. The establishment and development of separate ethnic armies were viewed by the Contact Group and by African states as a gratuitously provocative step. The negotiations' prospects were further shaken by the arrest of Tjongarero in December 1977 and the extraction from him of a condemnation of SWAPO; these moves were bound to infuriate the external as well as the internal leadership. In Windhoek Mudge, Barnes and Kloppers repeatedly proclaimed – without contradiction from Steyn or Pretoria – the DTA's determination to go it alone regardless of SWAPO's participation; in Washington, Kapuuo, towards the end of 1977 spoke of an election to take place early in the coming year irrespective of SWAPO's or the UN's utterances; he was echoed by South African newspaper reports that an election would be held in July 1978 whether or not an internationally acceptable agreement had been reached. Whether the Government had such plans for July is not known; but what emerges from the process of South Africa's unilateral actions, diplomatic manoeuvres, the DTA's declamation and police and administrative provocation was that South Africa, while testing out international reaction, habituated the world to the notion of unilateral elections. (By the time South Africa held its unilateral election in December 1978 much of the heat generated by the issue had dissipated.) In the meantime Turnhalle leaders were busy establishing their presence in foreign capitals.

New hope focused on the 'proximity talks' with the interested parties scheduled to take place in New York in February 1978. In preparation the Contact Group was active among front line states leaders. SWAPO executives conferred with their external counterparts in Lusaka and flew to New York to participate in the talks. Negotiations had barely commenced when Pik Botha made an abrupt departure and returned to Pretoria, ostensibly to confer with the Prime Minister.

By March 1978 SWAPO's stance had undergone a considerable revision. A force of fifteen hundred South African troops confined to base would be tolerated provided it was garrisoned as far south as Karasberg and monitored by a UN peace-keeping force.[3] SWAPO also conceded the principle that the South African police, security police and Boss apparatus would continue to function with the proviso that they should be under the joint control of the special representative and the Administrator General.[4] SWAPO's own forces would be confined in bases under the surveillance of UN monitors. As to the size of the UN Transitional Assistance Group (UNTAG) SWAPO was prepared to be flexible; the size would be left to the discretion of the special representative though SWAPO did suggest a civilian component of a thousand persons and a military force of five thousand.[5]

While SWAPO insisted that its concessions were wide-ranging Pik Botha claimed with some ferocity that South Africa had complied with everything that the UN originally asked for, and made dark hints that some Western countries were secretly abetting SWAPO in the hope of putting their money on 'the right horse'. The theme was one of an embattled South Africa surrounded by enemies and compromised by its friends. The propaganda was not always accurate. On one occasion Pretoria put out a broadcast that the Western Five had demanded a complete withdrawal of South African troops from Namibia. This report while successful in helping to generate a general resentment was entirely untruthful. In Windhoek the DTA began to maintain that further delays in the 'democratic process' would bring down catastrophe; the Namibian economy they pointed out was already gravely affected through political uncertainty. This dangerous impasse was, they claimed, largely attributable to SWAPO's unaccommodating and unreasonable attitudes.

Early in April the Contact Group published the text of its proposals. In an introductory note the authors described the initiative as an attempt to bring about a transfer of authority in accordance with Resolution 385. The election would be held throughout the whole of Namibia as one political entity and would be under the supervision and control of the UN *'in that'*, as a condition to the conduct of the electoral process, the elections themselves, and certification of their result, the special representative would have to satisfy himself at each stage as to the fairness and appropriateness of all measures affecting the political process at all levels of administration before such measures took effect. A substantial civil section of UNTAG – no figures were specified – would assist him to carry out his duties. The implementation of the electoral process and registration were to be conducted to the satisfaction of the special representative. Namibian political prisoners would be released and all refugees, whether detained or not outside the Territory, were to be permitted to participate in the election. The elections for a constituent assembly, which in turn would adopt a constitution, would take place after the following sequence: a cessation of all hostile acts; restriction of South African and SWAPO armed forces to base; the phased withdrawal of SADF troops (save for a garrison of fifteen hundred to be stationed at Grootfontein or Oshivello or both) who would be withdrawn after the certification of the election; the demobilisation of citizen forces, commandos and ethnic forces; the return of SWAPO personnel. The proposals provided for the enforcement of the agreement by a military section of UNTAG. Primary responsibility for maintaining law and order would rest with the existing police forces, whose good conduct was to be ensured by the Administrator General, though the special representative was empowered to 'make arrangements' when appropriate to accompany the police forces in the discharge of their duty.

Though there was optimism that SWAPO leaders would eventually put their signatures to the agreement there were many reservations in SWAPO ranks. In analysing the proposals SWAPO pointed out that while the elections purported to be under the supervision and control of the UN the words 'in that' went far to reverse the meaning of the sentence. The control of the elections remained unequivocally, they said, in the hands of the Administrator General. The special representative had no right of veto; his only 'power' was his capacity to refuse certification. In the context of a nationwide election and its dynamics this placed the special representative – SWAPO's shield against intimidation – at a serious disadvantage; there was no limit to the number of South African police, who could be imported in their thousands from the Republic. The same security branch faces – whose indispensable supports of chiefs and headmen – would still be around.

On the 25th April Vorster revealed in the South African parliament his Government's acceptance of the Western proposals and a trinity of assurances which had encouraged South Africa to opt for the proposals. They were: that the Aministrator General would remain at the head of the Administration with the South African police continuing to maintain law and order in the transitional period, that there would be an end of all hostilities before troop withdrawals began and that Walvis Bay would not form part of the proposed agreement.[6] The role of the Administrator General, he added, would remain unimpaired; the special representative would 'cooperate' with Judge Steyn to ensure the orderly transition to independence and there would be no final withdrawal of troops without the request of the newly established Namibian parliament.

Vorster's declaration had the merit of crystallising the language of the proposals. For the South Africans as also for SWAPO the role of the Administration and the police force would be primordial in the transitional period.

The South African acceptance did not herald an easy passage towards agreement. The day before the announcement a contrasting message was delivered to SWAPO in Windhoek in the form of the arrest of twenty-seven leading members, including Festus Nahola, the Party's Secretary for Foreign Affairs, Jason Angula, Secretary for Labour, and Frans Kambangula, Secretary for Transport. The arrests, which brought the total number of detainees to forty, had the effect of demolishing most of SWAPO's internal leadership. The arrests were effected under Proclamation AG26 which had made its appearance in the Government Gazette only six days earlier.[7] In substance the Proclamation provided for nothing new. Its advantage was that arrests now officially carried the imputation that the detainees were intimidators and agitators and a danger to the unfolding of free and fair elections. But it was its timing, at a moment of such fragility, as much as its content, which aroused consternation; the conclusion seemed inescapable that the South Africans, fully aware of their intention to accept the proposals, set out to provoke SWAPO into resiling from the talks.

The West, in particular the US, congratulated the South Africans, and made some effort to appease SWAPO by toning down the South African emphases.[8] The negotiations dragged on; there were predictions that SWAPO would back down, at least temporarily, on Walvis Bay. SWAPO demanded a clarification of the working relationship between the Administrator General and the special representative and called for the disarming of the South African police, the dismantling of Bantustan tribal authorities and the dissolution of tribal armies, commandos and shooting clubs.

While SWAPO argued and hesitated South Africa struck. On the 4th May 1978 South African jets carried out a lightning raid on a SWAPO refugee transit camp near Kassinga, a hundred and fifty miles north of the Namibian border. Sprawled over a large area the camp contained approximately three thousand refugees, many of them children of school age, housed in tents and thatched wooden structures. Isolated permanent buildings served to house classrooms, a clinic and offices. The aerial blitz was followed by the descent of scores of paratroopers who landed with land mines, mortars and machine guns. Defenceless against bombardment the camp dwellers fled towards the bush only to be cut down by gunfire. Most of the dead had been shot at close range, unarmed and offering no resistance to the South African soldiers. When they departed six hundred corpses and a thousand wounded lay amongst the smoking debris. South Africa asserted that it was a military camp. Luanda based reporters flown to the site found mass open graves of young men and women in jeans, shorts, brightly patterned dresses

231

and shirts. A few of the bodies, betrayed by their khaki uniforms, were those of the camp guards.

The SADF carried out a simultaneous attack on a SWAPO military camp at Cuamato thirty-five miles inside Angola.

Initially the raid had its predictable effect: a shocked Nujoma summarily broke off talks in New York and returned to Luanda. (Nujoma had 'played the fool' by leaving the talks was Vorster's characterisation of his departure). During the weeks of deadlock which followed, Don McHenry, the deputy US Ambassador to the UN, described the Kassinga raid as far out of proportion to anything SWAPO had been doing. Vorster retorted that McHenry was attempting to set up South Africa as a 'scapegoat'.

Negotiations with SWAPO continued. Slowly but inexorably SWAPO moved towards acceptance.

Once again the South Africans acted unilaterally, this time with an announcement of their intention to carry out voter registration. On the 16th June 1978 Proclamation AG37, the Registration of Voters (Constituent Assembly) Proclamation, was promulgated by Steyn. Neither the machinery of registration nor the formulation of the regulations nor the timing of the registration – to take place between the 26th June and the 22nd September – was discussed with the Contact Group or the UN.[9] Foreshadowing a boycott campaign against registration the lawgivers provided for severe penalties for the offence of advising or encouraging persons not to register – three thousand Rand or imprisonment for three years or both. The detentions under AG26 continued; thirty SWAPO detainees at Gobabis went on hunger strike in protest. Hendrik Witbooi was also arrested under AG26. While SWAPO attacked the 'undoubted partiality' of the Administrator General, Steyn, in the wake of the Kassinga raid, vowed that SWAPO would be hit and hit hard again until prepared to lay down arms.

In addition to the technique of the blitzkrieg the South Africans carried on a systematic propaganda war against SWAPO. Of the millions of rands admittedly paid out by the South African Department of Information under the direction of Dr. Rhoodie it may be presumed that a slice of the funding found its way into Namibia. From the start of Turnhalle activities a skilled heavily-funded propaganda campaign was waged throughout Namibia. Unseen accomplices produced professionally competent caricatures, comic strips and publications and did not scruple to forge and disseminate fraudulent reproductions of SWAPO's *Ombuze Ya Namibia* and other publications. Carried out on a massive scale the operation was effected with consummate discretion and secretiveness.[10]

The propagandists attacked SWAPO personalities with vehemence. Tjongarero and Nujoma were caricatured as murderous lions devouring children; Peter Katjavivi was depicted as sitting smugly and safely in London ensconced in a mansion with a fleet of motor cars; Nujoma was reported living in luxury with no care to return to the 'crippled land'; Tjongarero had received fifteen thousand rand for his speeches and had an account in Australia; SWAPO leaders lived like 'capitalist barons' in White areas at a cost equivalent to eighteen years of pay for 'one militant'. In a counterfeit letter under the name Martha Ford, the leaders of SWAPO's military wing, PLAN (People's Liberation Army of Namibia), figured as the 'worst thieves', racists and defectors in the history of mankind.[11] Part of the thrust was to sow discord and inflame inter-tribal hostility. Nujoma was presented as weak and fighting only for the benefit of Ovambos; he was growing old and heading towards a fierce leadership struggle. In a fake *Ombuze Ya Namibia* Nujoma, while admitting that SWAPO killed the innocent, appealed for contributions to a non-existent address in London. The postal code – NSW4. SWAPO was sketched as a creature at the mercy of Communist masters: Nujoma grovelled at Castro's feet. Readers were advised that Tjongarero, Martha Ford, Bishop Dumeni and Justin Ellis were to be avoided. SWAPO it was asserted tortured its victims.[12] A cartoon likened its war machine to an elephant which preferred – after a SWAPO soldier had struck it a hammer blow on the testicles – to defecate on Nujoma rather than do battle. (Many wondered whether the cartoonist would have been allowed such crudity in publications destined for White consumption.)

We have already noted how, in the wake of the Elifas assassination, the SADF, according to their claims, had the good fortune to lay hands on diaries which implicated SWAPO guerrillas in the assassination. After the raid on the camp at Kassinga – code named Moscow – and another camp named Mongolia, the South Africans claimed to have captured most revealing documents. The material included the 'Mongolia document' which 'proved' SWAPO's decision to liquidate Whites by armed struggle under the supervision and control (sic) of Soviet officers and to train saboteurs, tank, aircraft and artillery crews foreshadowing a conventional armoured and aviation strike into Namibia. The purpose of the operation: to avoid participation in the elections, to seize power through violence and to liquidate 'puppets' such as Ndjoba and Kapuuo. SWAPO rejected the document as a 'clear forgery'. On 12 March the Johannesburg *Sunday Times* and the Afrikaans Sunday Paper *Rapport* copiously reproduced passages to underscore the Soviet connection, the teaching of Russian and the training of political commissars; Soviet generals were moving into Angola while ships brought in tanks and artillery in preparation for a full-scale war of liberation according to reports given much prominence in the press. Thousands of guerrillas, it was stated, were streaming southwards as SWAPO's answer to the Western Five's proposals. The SA Broadcasting Corporation (SABC) too made its contribution in an edited broadcast of an interview between Nujoma and the Corporation's reporter Cliff Saunders. Nujoma was reported as saying: 'The question of Black majority rule is out. We are not fighting even for majority rule. We are fighting to seize power in Namibia, for the benefit of the Namibian people . . . '. Wrenched from the contextual dialogue the declaration stood in fundamental contradiction to SWAPO's explicit aims. In Windhoek Mokganedi Tlhabanello rejected the report and quoted from SWAPO's constitutional commitment to a 'democratic secular government founded upon the will of the Namibian people'.[13] Although it was clear from the context that Nujoma, in referring to Black majority rule, meant – following Saunders' vocabulary – a majority regime brought to power in unilateral elections, Vorster hastened to say that Nujoma had 'let the cat out of the bag' and had thus confirmed what had always been suspected.

In Namibia the secret propagandists also set their sights on the Church/ SWAPO relationship with travesties of SWAPO attitudes to the Church. One cartoon depicted Nujoma clad in a guerrilla's outfit urinating on a Church labelled Oniipa.[14]

The Churches themselves presented a different image of SWAPO. It was Vicar General Edward Morrow who said 'Let us never forget that it is SWAPO who has been doing the dying for the freedom for Namibia.'[15] Other groups and individuals, he pointed out, had shown courage but only SWAPO had had the capacity to organise peasants, contract workers, students, housewives, nurses, teachers and clergy into an articulate, politically effective force. The Churches struck back at South African propaganda. The guerrillas, they said, were not alien infiltraters who succeeded by force alone; PLAN forces were established in many areas; people felt safer with PLAN troops than with the SADF, although they certainly feared both. The Churches' loyalty was reciprocated. There were three parts to the Namibian liberation struggle, said SWAPO leaders: SWAPO, PLAN and the Churches.[16]

The Churches mourned the slaughter at Kassinga. After the attack Kleopas Dumeni, then assistant to Bishop Auala, lamented the dead and spoke of many mourning families, their bereavement and uncertainty as to the fate of loved ones. (Dumeni's son survived the attack at Kassinga; Bishop Auala's daughter and the children of three other Lutheran Pastors were later reported killed.)[17] Two days later Dr. Carl Mau, the General Secretary of the Lutheran World Federation, in a telexed message to Vorster, stated that the raid raised doubts about the sincerity of the Government in its negotiations and expressed concern that torture and intimidation continued in Namibia despite the assurances of the Administrator General. The message was returned by the Prime Minister's private secretary. An accompanying note explained the return: it was clear that the telegram had been intended for SWAPO. Such was the Prime Minister's response to the anguish of major Churches.

The Namibian Churches intervened in the work of the Contact Group and hotly contested the adequacy of the group's proposals. Their declarations on this issue introduced a sobering – and for many discordant – note in the context of South Africa's sanctimonious and irritable responses. In their 'Maseru declaration' the Anglicans produced in July 1978 an uncompromising critique of the Western proposals: the proposals could no longer be consi-dered a sufficient safeguard in the pre-independence period; the Western Powers were responsible for a blatant attempt to coerce 'those forces which are working for the liberation of our country . . .'[18]

Three days after the 'Maseru declaration' Morrow and his wife Laureen were ordered to leave the Territory within seven days.[19] Though quiet and self-effacing Morrow had come to be respected by visiting Ambassadors, politicians and journalists. An unassuming gentleness concealed an unshakeable determination. As a successful businessman in Durban, Mor-row could have opted for an easier life. When he perceived the source of White affluence to be none other than the starvation wages paid by white firms Morrow abandoned commerce and started a multi-racial construction company for the Anglican Church in Namibia; after pursuing his studies for the priesthood he was ordained and became Vicar-General. Prior to his expulsion threatening telephone calls increased in frequency. After years in Windhoek he shrugged them off, as also the insults daubed on his house, the attempts to tamper with his car and live bullets 'planted' under its floor mat. In any event the experience of an imperilled home was not new to him. During the Second World War the young Morrow and his family had to run the gauntlet of attacks from Afrikaner pro-Nazi neighbours after Morrow's father joined the army.

While in office Morrow had started the Territory's first non-racial play-school for pre-school children in 1976. Like his predecessors he raised his voice in protest on many occasions. One consistent theme undermined and vexed the South Africans: that SWAPO was a major vehicle of political organisation and protest and that there was no reason to believe that it would not establish a democratic society.

Heinz Hunke's notice of deportation – he and the Morrows were dealt with simultaneously – allowed only ninety-six hours.

For the Administrator General, Hunke must have been the incarnation of the meddling priest. Hunke had agitated tirelessly against the practice of brutality. After the Bernardus application he compiled a dossier of the affidavits and together with Justin Ellis published it under the title '*Torture – a cancer in our society*.' Earlier in 1978 he had written to leaders of the Tur-nhalle delegation with a warning that collaborators who had compromised themselves with the injustices of the present system should be left out of the constitutional process. Though the delegates ran the risk of finding their numbers inside the Turnhalle greatly depleted, there were after all many others who could render their country a good service. In a farewell message Hunke politely reminded Steyn that no dictator could deport the truth. The continuing repression, he said, was part of a prolonged colonial war which found its justification in an old form of imperial Christianity that cynically accused a subdued people of being rebellious and violent. 'I am looking out for another Christianity. Goodbye. God lives.'

The Churches remained active on many fronts. They were the first in the Territory to provide multi-racial education; they arranged and paid for family visits to Robben Island; they provided after-hours literacy classes, courses for the British Certificate of Education, University level programmes for students who had been compelled to leave South African Universities, and a 'crash course' in administration aimed at providing administrators for the Territory after independence. They intervened in the 'Shipanga affair' to procure the release of Andreas Shipanga and his co-detainees locked up at the behest of SWAPO.[20] When this was accomplished they turned on the South African Government with demands for the release of Herman Ja Toivo and the rest of the Namibian colony on Robben Island.

Attacks on the Churches emanated not only from official and vigilante quarters but also from fellow Churchmen. One of the most vituperative attacks upon *Torture – a cancer in our Society* was delivered by Dominee AG Yssel who – his logic overpowered by his vexation – declared that the affidavits were lies because they were untested; he regretted that Church leaders should devote themselves to furthering a lie when they should serve the truth. He and other members of the Dutch Reformed Church (DRC) stated that Finnish Missions had lost support because of their involvement with politics and false accusations,[21] while another Churchman Dominee Strauss – somewhat contradictorally – sounded the alarm that the Lutheran Churches in Namibia were on the march, rallying immense support behind a militant Black god.[22] Within the ranks of the Catholic Church there were inherent tensions reflecting the conflicts in Namibian society. When nine Catholic priests – one of them was Hunke – declared in 1975 that the ruling minority should cease 'its use of violence in keeping a majority down' they were called 'SWAPO priests' by the majority of disapproving White Catholics.[23] Caught between an empathy for a people's struggle and the *weltanschauung* of a White Catholic milieu Bishop Koppman allowed himself to be co-signatory, with other Church leaders, of a letter to Kissinger provided that his name was never to be mentioned should the document ever be published. Lukas de Vries, torn between an identification with the 'suffering poor' and the persuasive voice of Mudge – whom he called his 'friend' – was won over to the regime. He became a discordant voice amongst Church leaders. In April 1978, echoing the appeals of Mudge and the Administrator General, he called upon SWAPO to lay down arms, and later pleaded for recognition of the DTA dominated National Assembly which was established early in 1979.[24]

In the north the Churches were drawn willy-nilly into the war. The Lutheran Mission Hospital at Onandjokwe refused to distinguish between guerillas and South African soldiers and publicly said as much. 'It's a human law' decreed Lukas de Vries. SWAPO guerillas were indeed treated, with the inevitable sequel of arrests and detention of nurses and medical staff. The hospital persisted in its policy though not without fear on the part of the

Churchmen themselves. It was de Vries's prediction that with the erosion of free speech Church sermons would soon be taped and Church leaders intimidated to the point of withdrawal. (These prophetic words, we shall see, heralded de Vries's own retreat.)

Ed Morrow was replaced by James Kauluma who had been consecrated Bishop Suffragan in Westminster Abbey, London, on 15th January 1978. While the authorities had been able to keep Ed Morrow out of Ovambo, Bishop Kauluma, being Ovambo born, required no permission. From Ovambo he was able to throw direct light on the circumstantial evidence of Army destruction in Mission buildings. On Ovambo roads soldiers had stopped his vehicle and compelled him at the point of a gun to dismount. 'All the people' that he met shared with him their fear, not of SWAPO but of the South African soldiers. In the face of growing fear and tension he found a strengthening morale in a people hemmed in on the one side by tribal police who distinguished themselves by excessive drinking and firing random shots, and the SADF soldiery who followed up guerrilla contact by a routine of indiscriminate interrogation and aggression in the area.

In contradiction of South African claims that SWAPO, using press-gang methods, had abducted hundreds of youths across the border to be used as cannon fodder, the Churches projected a different perspective. While conceding that there were forced abductions, the Churches declared that the overwhelming majority of those who were 'abducted' were young people and students who dreamt of a different life or wished to join the liberation army and had asked for a guerrilla escort across the border.

Since Church leaders were admitted to SWAPO camps beyond the border – Lutheran and Anglican bishops were allowed to minister freely to camp inhabitants – their testimony was not easily rebuttable.

36

Military Interrogators

As the conflict in the north spread, an ever increasing volume of complaints of army brutality filtered through to the churches. The information arose from scattered areas in Ovambo; as intimidation was rife – the villagers necessarily had to come to terms with the presence of soldiers in their lives – there were few who were not afraid to speak out openly. The reports, the gruesome anecdotes and visible injuries varied but certain themes persisted: the administration of electricity, assaults by enraged soldiers and the suspension of detainees from poles. The Churches decided on investigation by a legal team with a view to bringing injunction proceedings.

Interrogators traditionally and for good reason resort to illegal interrogation and its associated pressures in secret. Their activities are hidden and considerable effort is devoted to covering evidence of violence. Now that the army was implicated the presence of young soldiers on National Service – most of the soldiers were not members of the permanent force – became a salient consideration. They were conscripts: students, apprentices and school leavers bound to perform a year of compulsory national service. Army propaganda represented the fight as a crusading struggle against Communism; reports of SWAPO fatalities were conveyed with the words 'wipe out' and 'liquidated'. And yet, making allowances for a profound sense of solidarity amongst the 'boys on the border', it did seem unlikely that army commanders would allow the use of violent techniques in the sight of soldiers who might not share the outlook of hardened interrogators.

During preparations for Nkandi's defence, consultations were initially held with former security police detainees who had been kept in an army camp. The arrangement between the security police and the SADF was obscure; it was also unclear how far the security police and soldiers collaborated with one another. Though kept in the camp the detainees were removed from the curious eyes of soldiers and camp inmates when taken for interrogation.

B[1] was initially interviewed as a relevant defence witness in the Nkandi case. His evidence was brief, but for legal purposes the ambient facts required evaluation – how he came to find himself in the camp, his own experience, treatment and credibility. After a four months' stay in a military camp he turned out to be a fertile source of information. Slightly built with an immobile wooden face – the seasons had hewn a matrix of deep lines across his forehead – he had found himself surrounded by soldiers while hoeing his fields. He denied he had seen terrorists. Blindfolded with an adhesive plaster bandage and handcuffed he was beaten on his head and body. The assault seemed modest – according to his description. After his arrival at the camp three ribs were shown under X-ray to be broken. Three weeks later while still under treatment for his rib injury, a White corporal led him to a tent at the centre of the camp near to the kitchen. Now it was a different allegation: he had helped terrorists to lay a land mine. He was shocked over a period of four hours with electrodes on his wrists and legs.

It was a prolonged stay in the camp; with the passage of time he managed to communicate with others including J, N, K and H He learned that J had been beaten with rifles – his arm had been broken. A 'burning iron' (an electrode?) had been placed on his one ear, another on his sex. His bladder, said B had 'exploded'. N – from Epembe – had been kept hoisted in a tent in a row with others for seventy-two hours. A companion victim next to him had died. He was unable to identify the dead man – a forensic misfortune as a death would constitute another fact in our constellation of proof. B had seen the corpse taken down and heard instructions for its disposal. He could not remember further details.

The names multiplied. If witnesses were reluctant to come to us, we went to them. Some took heart from the fact that lawyers were openly pursuing their investigations at the Oniipa Mission; after months of reticence they came forward and took us into their confidence. One of them J was a farmer in the eastern area; he and his wife M were arrested together by the soldiers who accused them of possessing a land mine. Darkness enveloped him with blindfolding and lasted four days. Unknown men beat him and cursed. Under some shelter – he presumed it was a tent – his handcuffs were tied above him. He was shocked on his penis; his body contorted from the strength of the current, his wrists scraped against the cuffs which broke through the skin. On the fourth day he was kicked in the abdomen and lost consciousness. He was then taken to the Military Hospital at Grootfontein for an internal injury. After the consultation we sent J for a medico-legal examination. Scars on the leg and right wrist and on the forearm, a hard swelling of the prepuce, a surgical scar on the abdomen and a scar over the left knee which now had limited flexion provided hard corroboration. His wife M could confirm part of the attack on him. Her recall revealed a different perspective and a different sensibility. Soldiers forced her and her husband and children to lie on the ground while the house was searched. This was the simple beginning of her narrative but as she spoke it began to dawn on us that her description was the reflection of an often endured calamity rather than some awful individual encounter. They were questioned about 'people with guns'. They knew nothing and said so; the soldiers struck her husband with their rifle butts, her across the face with their hands. On the way to an army camp she recognised her husband's voice on the vehicle. She too was blindfolded. She heard the sounds of blows. He was screaming. Days later her blindfold was removed. Her eyes opened onto her husband; he was clad in trousers only, his face was swollen, the skin around his wrists torn and bleeding and there was blood from the right side of his chest. Sometime later she saw L suspended overnight from a fence. She herself had not been shocked with electricity but could identify the interrogation tent. Prisoners would emerge pale and unsteady and walked – according to her imitation – with a distinct yawing movement.

F's detention by soldiers was more traumatic. The introductory attack was a blow on the face by a White soldier while a 'boesman' (bushman) kicked her on the thigh. She had seen guerrillas – she admitted this freely; but this admission was not enough. There were other questions. Had she given them food? Had she had intercourse with any one of them? Electric wire was tied to her right ankle and an electrode was applied to her neck below the right ear. Soldiers held her down while she was shocked – altogether six times. Afterwards she was taken to trees. Her handcuffs were tied with rope so that her outstretched arms were aloft secured to overhanging branches. Her captors threw water on her. She remained there the night with other prisoners like wet beasts trapped in branches. The next interrogation was in a different army camp where Sergeant S and white soldiers interrogated her. (This was the first time that evidence implicated soldiers and security police in joint interrogation procedures). They accused her of having sex with guerrillas and brought out the electrical shock apparatus. She was shocked, hoisted, shocked again and hoisted again until she admitted – falsely. She was then released. F's history underscored a striking phenomenon which we were beginning to understand. At an early stage of interrogation she admitted to having seen guerrillas; after that it continued until she conceded – though untruthfully – that she had had intercourse with the guerrillas. After that she was not punished; she was instead allowed to go home. The process of interrogation now, it seemed, had a punitive dimension as well.

P was arrested at Epembe and felled by soldiers who struck him with their rifle butts. He, M and another young man, O, were taken to an army camp where without preliminaries they were beaten and given electric shock in a tent where three White soldiers and a Black soldier – all of them anonymous – administered the treatment. Afterwards the trio was kicked in the direction of a tent which was to serve as their sleeping accommodation. They were given no clue as to what it was all about except for a succession of oaths and mutterings that they were 'SWAPOs'. On his return to the interrogation tent P, left in a shirt only, became the quarry of a triad of electrodes applied to his genitalia, his anus and an ear. Had he seen 'SWAPOs' was the question which thundered between convulsions. The following day he urinated blood. The next episode took place in another Army camp when he, M and O were suspended from poles in a large tent with three other men. All were shocked at the same time, while suspended. Together they yelled and shook while their limbs danced insanely. It was a mad house of despair. This time there was merely accusation: they had all prepared a meal for the *domomufitu.*

V was shocked with electricity in a novel and more dangerous style. He was first of all made to mount a chair; electrodes were then placed above his ankles. With the sudden rush of electricity his muscles collapsed and he fell to the ground as if struck down by an invisible blow. A White captain, his name printed on his uniform, was in charge. V was shocked three times and fell down each time. After that he was kept in the camp close to the interrogation tent. He heard 'everything' around him.

E had the misfortune to be mentally abnormal. Soldiers found his answers meaningless and provocative; a violent attack left him with a broken arm. (A recent fracture of the left forearm was confirmed under X-ray.)

A White soldier pressed an open blade against R's throat with commands to speak the truth. He was blindfolded and held upright for thirty minutes while the fists of unseen assailants sank into his face. He was made to sit crouched on the same spot for three days and nights after his arrival at an army camp. He remained blindfolded throughout; natural functions took place where he crouched. There was no interrogation, merely occasional vilification and 'SWAPO' muttered with vehemence by voices in the vicinity. After three days he was put in a vehicle and taken on a journey, still crouching, to an unknown destination where he was thrown off. Dishevelled and bewildered he felt sand underneath him. The vehicle drove off; unable to walk he moved off, bent over and froglike, away from what he presumed to be the road. He waited, then pulled off the plaster bandage from over his face. His eyes shrank painfully from an overwhelming African sun. He was alone; the soldiers had gone. Then, very slowly, as his eyes adjusted to the light he made out a house partially hidden behind bushes. It was his home.

R, a shopkeeper from the little town of O, was suspended in the same camp until he became unconscious. His interrogation was a token enquiry into his possession of SWAPO membership cards; since these were legal the ordeal seemed to have been visited on him as a punishment for his beliefs and nothing else. During the three days of his suspension, he and those likewise suspended beside him, received no water until one man – here his evidence linked up with N's report – died from the strain. From R's prodigious memory spewed forth new names and identifying features which he had observed with an anatomist's precision.

Our investigation into the physiology of interrogation widened as each witness gave some clue to the identity of other witnesses and victims. Each new statement added coherence to an emergent canvas of cruciform suspensions, electrical assault, protean violence, enforced crouching, exposure to

241

the elements, deprivation, hunger and thirst and the compulsion on some prisoners to urinate or defecate in their clothing.

Witnesses who had never seen one another, many were from different areas of Ovamboland separated by hundreds of miles – some did not know that they would be questioned by us until the consultation started – provided fragments which, once marshalled, presented a cogent picture of the interrogational techniques.

In May and June 1976 South African troops carried out sweeps in Ovambo in a manoeuvre code named 'Operation Cobra'. One of the conscripts, Bill Anderson, while on leave in July 1976, deserted the Army and flew to London where the *Guardian* newspaper published his account of army practices. In law Anderson was a deserter and subject to criminal prosecution on return to the Republic, but there was nothing to prevent his affidavit being used in injunction proceedings.

The son of a marine biologist, Anderson had attended the University of Cape Town where his political awareness matured in a student milieu. His published report had created a stir and was exploited by anti-apartheid groups. It was important to test the accuracy, coherence and reliability of his information; with this in mind I was instructed to consult with him in London in September 1977.

Anderson's battalion, in concert with four other battalions, carried out comprehensive searches for weapons, suspects and signs of guerrilla activity in a predetermined area. According to Anderson, all males – some as young as thirteen – were blindfolded and brought for interrogation. If anyone attempted to flee the orders were clear: shoot to kill. It was a routine procedure to bring suspects to the camp and submit them to an introductory squall of blows, kicks, and beatings with rifle butts. Young conscripts aged eighteen to nineteen carried out this rather general pre-interrogational mauling. Afterwards 'real' interrogation started. A section of the 'ops tent' (operations tent) was set aside for interrogation. The camp was a 'sorting' centre where suspects would either be released after interrogation or referred to the Ondongua Army camp for further investigation. In the first few weeks a group of ten South African policemen interrogated; this was later left to the soldiers although liaison with the South African police force continued.

According to Anderson's estimates one thousand detainees were brought for interrogation within a period of two months. It was particularly at night – after the pub had closed at nine o'clock – that the interrogators, and their admirers, became active. Screams could be heard across the camp. Anderson himself kept away from the 'ops tent'; he heard the screams but left it to his comrades to fill in the details. Many watched the spectacle of interrogation as a nightly recreation, and returned in debate as to the relative efficiency of electrical shock applied to genitals, nipples or ears. They joked and searched for metaphor: the frantic beating movements of prisoners under electrical assault reminded them of trapped insects. With their return home in mind, Anderson's fellow soldiers searched for souvenirs. One of them, a rifleman-driver who had been ordered to take three suspects 'down the river' and shoot them, cut off an ear and sent it home in a bottle of methylated spirits; he tried to cure a scrotum to fit onto his gear lever, but it rotted.

Suspects were also given the 'water treatment'; their heads were pushed into a bucket of water and held until they ceased to struggle. Anderson saw one large suspect struggle so violently that five men had to hold him down.

In the ultimate analysis, the interrogators were bent on mass punishment as much as the pursuit of facts. In many of the cases we investigated the preponderance of interrogations had not been seriously aimed at eliciting information. The purpose was not to seek out and strike the guilty but to deter the innocent. F and her co-inmates were driven to confessions not as a preliminary to trial but as the final punitive dénouement, the entire process to be viewed as an inquisitional procedure designed, through widespread and indiscriminate use, to produce re-education through fear.

The dossier on Army brutality was at last completed. Viewed objectively, the accumulated bulk of testimony, the quality of the witnesses, their reciprocal corroboration, and the objective corroboration from medico-legal examination had created the foundations for a redoubtable legal attack. But from the commencement of preparations the Church leaders had no illusion as to the possible outcome; they were aware that the Army, more so perhaps than the security police, would summon up all its resources to discredit or intimidate our witnesses. Anderson's affidavit was not supported by any other soldiers and Anderson himself had not seen the 'real' interrogation. What was at stake was not simply the image of a law-enforcing organism but the moral image of South African Whites. Little would be more disturbing to South African morale than a finding, Nuremberg Court style, of connivance with brutality on the part of numbers of Army officers, doctors and conscripts.

The Church leaders foresaw an intense and bitter legal battle. Even so they reckoned a failed application would at least make some contribution to the exposure of the truth.

But their resources were limited, the costs of a prolonged trial which could have lasted many months were prohibitive and they had been deeply discouraged by the judgments in the Petrus and Nkandi cases.

After a great deal of anguished debate they finally came to a conclusion – a momentous, unpublished negative decision to take no action.

37

South Africa Breaks Off

In the aftermath of the attack on Kassinga, SWAPO leaders fought for new negotiating parameters. SWAPO's argument was structured on four objections: the persistence of South Africa's entrenched administration, the availability of an unlimited paramilitary police force, the presence of fifteen hundred troops strategically garrisoned at Grootfontein and/or Oshivello in the north, and the concession – albeit tacit – of South Africa's claim to Walvis Bay and the availability of more than a division of South African troops stationed there. If South Africa had its way they argued, members and supporters would be vulnerable to intimidation and violence. Recent events in Namibia, they said, supported their analysis: there had been a wave of violence in the country and forty-eight SWAPO members and supporters had been killed between the end of February and the 24th April while forty-three of its officials and party workers had been detained without trial since the 18th April 1978.

Spokesmen for the Contact Group were not sympathetic. The proposals, they replied, were final because they could not expect South Africa to make further concessions. Further talks ensued directed at persuading SWAPO to modify its stance. McHenry flew to Africa for talks with Kenneth Kaunda who in turn conferred with Angolan President, Agostinho Neto, in Luanda. The Contact Group put up a compromise proposal to South Africa – a plea for one conciliatory granule – that its troops be confined to only one base. The South Africans refused to entertain this suggestion.

On the 12th July 1978, and after two days of talks in Luanda between representatives of the Western Five, the front line states and SWAPO, SWAPO notified its acceptance of the proposals.

The South African Government immediately viewed the acceptance with suspicion and multiplied its reservations. Ministers now laid down that no South African troops would be withdrawn until a 'visible peace' and 'complete peace' reigned and warned that South Africa would reassess its position in the light of the special representative's report.

After his appointment as Special Representative, Martii Ahtisaari visited the Territory on a fact-finding mission. His arrival was greeted by thousands

244

of rejoicing Blacks, and in the north Auala met him with the words: 'Your coming is the answer to many prayers of our Church and people. We believe your mission will be a successful one . . . ' The Churches hastened to inform Ahtisaari that the registration of voters had been pushed through by means of intimidation and fraud; delay in holding the elections, they urged, had become imperative as citizens needed time to become properly informed, reflect maturely on their choice and gain confidence in the electoral process.

Steyn did not share the Churchmen's views on the timing of the election. In a declaration which produced immediate strain between himself and Ahtisaari, the Administrator General ruled that the holding of elections by the 31st December was a 'mandatory stipulation' and that there was no possibility of a postponement. Though SWAPO viewed the latest *démarche* as an affront to the entire settlement – it was then no more than four months from the December deadline – they objected vigorously but did not withdraw. (The Western plan itself envisaged the 31st December as independence day, but only on the assumption that hostilities had ended seven months before, that most South African troops had withdrawn and an election had been held.)

Even before the release of Waldheim's proposals for the UNTAG team's composition the South Africans said that they would not tolerate five thousand UN troops – the contingent favoured by SWAPO. When Waldheim's report was published calling for seven and a half thousand UN troops, three hundred and sixty police and a seven month run up to the elections, the South Africans declared themselves to be enraged and refused to negotiate on the figures.

On the 20th September 1978 Vorster simultaneously announced his resignation from the Premiership and the rejection of the UN plan.

Clarity at last: South Africa would proceed with internal elections in Namibia.

The decision led to an outcry at the UN and a demand for the imposition of sanctions, above all an oil embargo. But the mood of the Western representatives mellowed swiftly and members of the Contact Group declared their readiness to veto rash moves towards sanctions. On the 29th September 1978 the Security Council adopted Resolution 435 in which the Council reiterated its demand for the withdrawl of South Africa's 'illegal adnimistration' and established UNTAG under its authority to assist the Special Representative to carry out his mandate. Waldheim hastened to explain that the figure, seven thousand five hundred, was his upper limit, that over two thousand men would concern themselves with logistics and that twenty per cent of the total UNTAG force would be on leave at any particular time. Western envoys flew to Pretoria and urged South African ministers to call off their plan. The new Prime Minister, P.W. Botha, remained adamant. The elections, he declared, were to be seen as an internal process to elect leaders; after the elections the South African Government would use their best offices to persuade those leaders to consider ways of achieving international recognition.

Members of the Contact Group declared themselves 'obviously optimistic' at the termination of the talks. They spoke of a significant breakthrough and returned from Pretoria with the glad message that all parties in the Namibian conflict would prefer an international solution and that the talks were to continue.

One immediate result of the further round of talks was to stave off an imminent threat to move for sanctions in the Security Council.

Nineteen months earlier the negotiating process had been born of the seminal premise that South Africa and SWAPO both sought an internationally acceptable solution. It was therefore a matter for no surprise if their message sounded like untrustworthy nonsense in SWAPO's ears.

38

The DTA Offensive

Quite independently of the progress of South Africa's negotiations with the Western Five, the DTA pursued an energetic campaign to establish its image in the Territory. A series of meetings was held in Ovambo and in various towns in the south. The propaganda thrust, designed to project the DTA as a potent force for renewal and change went hand in hand with a virulent anti-SWAPO message. 'SWAPO is just a murder organisation that divided the youth from their parents' was a favourite theme in Ovamboland. SWAPO was vilified for shedding blood when freedom was certain; SWAPO was a Communist tool whose leaders, soaked in anti-Christian Marxism, were merely self-centred men in pursuit of pleasure, luxurious homes and Cadillacs. Numerous meetings were chaired by Barney Barnes who enjoyed making jokes against SWAPO in general and Dan Tjongarero in particular. Less time was directed towards the details of the DTA's social and economic programme. Prior to meetings teams of convassers fanned out. In Ovamboland school children predominated amongst the spectators. According to SWAPO they went along for the sausages and the ice cream. The SADF also lent a hand and ferried in delegates in airforce helicopters. (SWAPO Executive Mokganedi Tlhabanello noted the official aid that was given to the DTA and pointed out that SWAPO by comparison had not been allowed a meeting in Ovamboland for more than five years.)

Canvassing for DTA meetings was enormously facilitated by the jamboree atmosphere which would prevail. Spectators were induced to come forward by the organisation of meetings with brass bands, dancing and the liberal free issue of barbecue steaks and *boerewors* (sausage).[1] To a youthful population brought up on a diet of mealie porridge the fare was not easily resistible. Transport to the meetings was free; spectators were plied with DTA stickers and T-shirts.[2] In an attempt to condition in their audiences a behavioural loyalty if not a felt one, speakers called upon the DTA gatherings to repeat the DTA 'V' sign for peace, a loose version of the Churchillian two-finger salute. The request was not always well received; at a meeting at Oluno half of those in the meeting replied by turning their backs on the speakers.

While delivering registration papers in anticipation of elections, DTA canvassers called on individuals to make a cross on a 'mock ballot' which was then sealed. After this so-called poll the DTA declared itself confident of an overwhelming majority.

The DTA also issued membership cards – an apparently innocuous tactic which was to become an effective tool in winning nominal and real support. The carrying of a membership card by an individual was a symbolic act of dissociation from SWAPO; in an ordinary electoral milieu cleansed of an atmosphere of compulsion the distribution of cards would be little more than an organisational gimmick. Not so in a society rent by war, political violence, counter-violence and punishment. In Namibia, Blacks learned willy-nilly that loyalty to the DTA and the possession of its membership card would, in the milieu of fear and deprivation, provide some immunity and some reward. Ovambos were soon to hear that production of the DTA cards was a necessary passport without which labourers might be deprived of their jobs, peasants denied cattle grazing, the aged cut off from their pensions, children excluded from their schools and individuals denied medical facilities. According to churchmen there were numerous reports from congregants of assaults which accompanied attempts to foist membership cards upon unwilling peasants.[3]

Never before had southern Africa seen any political party mount so extravagant a campaign machine. The DTA boasted of a fleet of twenty-two light delivery vehicles, armoured anti-mine trucks, a mine detecting vehicle, and a bullet-proof Mercedes Benz saloon car.[4] Its 'airforce' comprised one helicopter, two light aircraft and a Dakota equipped with a conference room. It arrived together with the services of two pilots. (One of the aeroplanes equipped with a megaphone overflew the countryside booming DTA propaganda from the skies). R150,000 was spent on the purchase of forty video machines and the importation of TV sets, a novelty of modern science that had as yet to penetrate Namibia. TV production teams were brought in to shoot propaganda films.

Not content with such abundant equipment and an army of propagandists and canvassers the DTA also took the precaution of buying up two important White newspapers, the *Algemeine Zeitung* and in particular the *Windhoek Advertiser*, whose challenging editor had consistently exposed the DTA failings and its brazen campaigning. Both editors were replaced.

What was the cost of assembling the DTA campaign machine? Who were those publicity shy individuals, organisations, companies or governments who found fit to make anonymous contributions on a gigantic scale? According to Mudge an undisclosed donor, after enquiring into the objectives of the DTA alliance said, 'Hold your chair', and then offered the Dakota. The bullet-proof Mercedez Benz car was a gift from an anonymous German donor; according to Mudge the donor's identity was unknown. SWAPO made the allegation that R500,000 a month was used to finance the DTA with funds channelled through the *Seidel Stiftung*, a foundation run by the Christian

Social Union of Bavaria headed by former finance minister Franz Joseph Strauss. Pre-eminent amongst suspect donors was the South African Government itself acting through its Department of Information,[5] an organism which had no hesitation in generally buying support and journalistic approval for South Africa's policy, for example, a TV Station in California and an American newspaper.[6] AKTUR attacked the DTA for its use of alien and unknown funds and accused the alliance of accepting funds from a Johannesburg mining company. Mudge refused to name his donors except to say that they were receiving financial backing from multi-national companies in Namibia.[7] The Secretary of the Republican Party said that German right-wing parties were donating money whilst Kozonguizi – perhaps to create an impression of multi-lateral support – implicated the Progressive Federal Party as a donor. Word spread – it was an 'open secret' – that the *Interessen Gemeinschaft*, a Namibian German organisation, had donated R100,000. According to the *Interessen Gemeinschaft* the West German Government had shown considerable interest in Namibian development and had promised aid of 'unforeseen proportions'.

As the movement of money in and out of accounts remains untraced, the major donors remain shrouded in secrecy.[8] But why should there be any mystery? Why should the donors wish to keep their heads down? The DTA after all was merely a political organisation with an ostensibly worthy purpose.

Or was it that the South African Government, funding the DTA on a gigantic scale feared that their approval and support, once revealed, would become for their controversial protégé the kiss of death?

39

DTA Knockout – The Triumph of Electoral Technology

On the 16th June 1978 the Administrator General briefly announced that the wheels for an election had been set in motion. This somewhat scanty pronouncement heralded Proclamation AG37 which, promulgated the very next day, set up detailed regulations and mechanisms for the registration of voters, the appointment of electoral staff, electoral scrutiny and polling procedures, though no date for the election was fixed. All persons born or resident in the Territory for four years before registration were eligible for registration. Three days later a somewhat bewildered Namibia was told that registration would start up the following week and continue through to September.

Registration began in earnest towards the end of June. This was at a time when South Africa still seemed prepared to participate in UN controlled elections. Pik Botha's call to Secretary General Waldheim to despatch a UN emissary to satisfy himself on the processes of registration only served to confirm this impression. It was only on the 20th September – well after eighty-five per cent of the voting population had registered according to the official claims of the Administration – that Vorster swept away the residual traces of ambiguity with a crisp pronouncement that shut the door on UN participation. From the start the Churches, SWAPO and anti-Turnhalle parties complained of deception in the registration process and did their best to be heard against the massive encouragement to register put out by the SABC and the pro-DTA press.

Despite the short notice which the Administrator General chose to give, it was obvious that preparations for the election had long been in hand. A formidable registration machine comprising four hundred registration officers, together with their staff, interpreters and vehicles – the cost of the operation totalled R1,500,000 – was ready to be put into the field for a campaign planned to last three months.[1] In addition farmers and employers associations organised members to bring along employees to registration centres. The Proclamation provided for a fine of R3,000 or imprisonment for three years, for those found guilty of advising voters not to register, harsh penalties which successfully fettered SWAPO's boycott call. At the opening of the registration campaign a SWAPO official was seized and detained under the Terrorism Act; two executive members were taken in with him bringing the total of SWAPO leaders then in detention to twenty-five.

The provisions for both registration and voting were merely facultative, but the chiefs, the Homelands governments and DTA organisers were generally not at pains to explain voters' rights. On the contrary, tribal chiefs and headmen toured villages and towns in Ovamboland with exhortations to voters to do their 'duty'. Throughout Ovamboland the unambiguous order to register and to vote went out from the administrative and tribal hierarchy. Once again the Churches set out to correct the record; one week before polling, from pulpits throughout Namibia, the word was spread that abstention from voting was not an offence.

Within the anatomy of Ovambo tribal communities and the traditional and administrative power structure of chiefs and headmen, these rumours were sufficiently credible for the Administration's purposes. Fundamental to the process was Ovamboland's pyramidal structure of tribal power: in each district chiefs and their councillors wielded through the headmen and sub-chiefs a far-ranging apparatus of power which penetrated into the smallest and the remotest villages. In the language of Bishop K. Dumeni, who succeeded Auala, the chiefs wield a 'fateful power' over their subjects – the power to grant land, grazing rights and rights of residence. The power of expulsion and its aftermath of exile lay in chiefs' hands. Disrespect or disobedience – indistinctly defined concepts in tribal custom – were punishable: fines, the seizure of cattle or corporal punishment, were possible consequences. The chiefs' capacity to help themselves on a lavish scale to these punitive powers at the time of the flogging campaign in 1973 was nowhere forgotten. Their power extended into the personal lives of individuals – no feast could be held without the permission of the local chief. And beyond the chief lay the Administration with its power to control the allocation of contract labour work. SWAPO accused the Administration of orchestrating its pressures in a 'vote or starve' campaign.

We have already noted how the Lutheran and Anglican attempt to set aside the 1975 election was thwarted by the Administration's refusal to allow a legal team to seek out witnesses in Ovamboland. Though other methods of research were tried, the lawyers had insufficient material on which to found an Application to set aside the election. The report of the legal team was, however, unequivocal: the draft affidavits and statements revealed a constellation of techniques applied in the course of a 'systematic campaign' to coerce voters to the polling booths.[2]

The South Africans claimed an overall 55% poll in the 1975 elections. The claimed statistic for Ovamboland proper was 76%; this is to be contrasted with voters' responses in the Ovambo compounds in the south where workers joined in solidarity, and, free from scrutiny and retribution of chiefs and officials, felt confident enough to abstain. Only 4% voted in the south. What other explanation can there be for the electorate's metamorphosis between 1973 and the 1975 elections?

Rumours swept the Homelands well before the start of the 1978 elections. Once again evidence of organised rumour-mongering was traceable: identical rumours started up simultaneously – this time in the various Homelands, unconnected areas often hundreds of miles apart. Rumours moved through the population with the invisible swiftness of earth tremors leaving in their wake hesitancy and demoralisation. The grim whispers were the same: without registration cards work-seekers were doomed to unemployment, pensioners would receive nothing, patients would be kept out of hospitals, and mail – for most this meant postal orders from sons and husbands on contract – would not be collectable. The prediction that chiefs would not allow cardless peasants to plough crossed Ovamboland like a giant shadow.

The 'instant' rumour that registration cards were to be carried *in addition* to identity cards and tax receipts was firmly reinforced by new Security Force procedures. At a road block at Oshakati, the administrative centre of Ovamboland, armed soldiers demanded registration cards: those without cards were warned to register. This procedure was followed at other centres. Soldiers moved around Ovamboland in armoured cars stopping at kraals and shops with the same enquiries.

The population of Ovamboland was in short subjected to a relentless system of conditioning.[3] The DTA membership card – South African soldiers referred to it as the 'Turnhalle card' – provided a companion vehicle in the conditioning process. As early as April 1978 soldiers on patrol in Ovamboland carried out house to house searches in dragnet operations ostensibly designed to flush out guerrillas; but the soldiers now wanted more than the obligatory identity card and tax receipt – they wanted the 'Turnhalle card'. Pastors in the north reported complaints from men who had been beaten for being without the cards.

The conduct of the Army was an unequivocal pronouncement of its partiality to the DTA, government supporters and voters. In Ovamboland where all travellers were subject to inspection, search and interrogation at road blocks, any confrontation with the soldiery was an episode fraught with the risk of detention and its traditional hazards. It was a society in the throes of war; a rider to the conflict was the drastic all or nothing consequence of political choice. In most societies the very convention of electoral procedures implies a social contract to order political life through predetermined democratic mechanisms. It is unusual for a contesting party in an election – including the most ideologically committed – to warn their opponents of liquidation after electoral defeat. This was not so in Ovamboland where the propaganda media studiously identified SWAPO, the overt lawful organisation, with SWAPO maquisards. Participation at the polls therefore came to figure not so much as an exercise in choice as a cardinal sign of collaboration. Conversely a refusal to register or to vote under the watchful scrutiny of soldiers and policemen could figure in the official context as a treasonable gesture. Both the Army and the DTA effectively exploited the dilemma. At an early stage in its campaigning the DTA evolved its Churchillian 'V' for Victory sign – their 'peace' sign – formed by the separation of the index and middle finger; audiences were educated to understand the symbolic implications of the sign. It became central to DTA ritual, repeated by soldiers on patrol in their armoured vehicles and trucks.[4] Their peace sign was not easily ignored by traditionally courteous Ovambo men and women – even less so in the prevailing tension of the north. The greeting was another step in the learning process which taught that overt solidarity with the DTA was good protection against misunderstanding and violence. The lesson was driven home obliquely with few direct assertions. The unequivocal pronouncements came from a different direction.

It was the official voices on Ovambo and Kavango Radio which admitted no uncertainty. Theirs was a plain insistence that everyone should register and vote, an encouragement that went hand in hand with faintly disguised threats such as 'there is no place in this country for you if you do not register and vote'. This theme was underlined towards the end of November by a general appeal signed by the DTA President and Vice-President which read:

'There are various reasons why your participation in the coming December election is of utmost importance. In the first place you will thus show to the world that you totally reject SWAPO, its communist policy and its murder of peace-loving citizens. Should you therefore not vote it could mean that you support SWAPO.'

Little was left to chance. Psychological strategies were followed up by systematic arrangements for the physical collection of voters from their homes or jobs. In the homelands trucks manned by tribal policemen and DTA supporters called at villages and shops where voters were summarily told to climb on. In some cases employers fired their workers for refusing to register. Farmers and employers in the private sector gathered their workers together for expeditions to the registration or voting centres. On the farms and in small enterprises the workers were isolated and dependent. It was otherwise in the compounds and factories where workers' solidarity produced, as it had done in the 1975 elections, a gross disparity in voting responses. According to official figures the registration was highest in Ovamboland. This claim contrasts starkly with Ovambo registration in the south: in Luderitz 30%; at Consolidated Diamond Mining 6%.

The period for registration was extended into a fourth month – until the 20th November. After that the Administration put out the triumphant claim that 95% of the voters had registered. The claim was immediately attacked. The South Africans, the critics objected, had used projections based on the 1970 census; in so doing they had arrived at an estimated voting population of 440,000, compared with the estimate of 600,000 arrived at by the UN Institute for Namibia, whose officials in Lusaka estimated the population to be closer to 1,250,000 (This divergence may help explain the registration statistics in excess of 100% for Kavango and Kaokoveld.)[5]

There was an immediate outcry from political and Church leaders: the authorities had not insisted on identification nor on proof of four years' residence. No voters' rolls had been published for each district in pursuance of ordinary procedure. Had this been done voters could be identified and challenged. Instead the Administration issued registration cards made up in duplicate and, according to its claim, scrutinised the roll by continuous cross-checking.[6] But the system did appear curious, more so since voters were allowed to register and vote in *any* magisterial area in a Territory as large as France and Germany together. (Months later a UN official enquiring into the system, was referred to a room full of unsorted chaotic piles of registration cards. It was estimated that a team of twenty men would require the greater part of a year to carry out a cross-check.) In retrospect the choice of such clumsy machinery lends support to the criticism that the Administration set out to register thousands of Angolan refugees (SWAPO claimed that 60,000 Angolans had been registered;[7] also that DTA organisers entered graveyards and registered dead souls).[8] Andreas Shipanga attacked the intimidation by 'tribal armies' in the north while NNF Secretary Rukoro focused attention on the dragooning of workers.[9]

With the abstention of all major anti-apartheid parties only AKTUR figured as a serious opponent of the DTA. The campaigning in the run up to the election was marked by AKTUR's unequal struggle against the electioneering thunder which the DTA laid on across the country. (The HNP had negligible support; the Namibia Christian Democratic Party (NCDP) and the Liberation Front (LF) were both minor parties established shortly before the elections. They had little following and less resources and eventually succeeded in polling 9,073 and 4,564 votes respectively.)[10]

The DTA's main purpose was to gather a maximum number of votes. These would serve as the future constituent assembly's certificate of legitimacy and be of immeasurable value in the DTA's worldwide propaganda campaign.[11] How else explain the DTA's monumental efforts in Namibia's *drôle d'election*.[12] Over 400 organisers were put into the field, 132 vehicles were purchased, 36 party offices were opened while supporters were collected in different parts of Namibia and bussed in free of charge to rallies.[13]

At the very beginning of the election fourteen people were injured, some seriously, by an explosion in the Nictus shopping centre in Windhoek. SWAPO denied complicity and attributed authorship to *agents provocateurs*. The explosion injured Blacks and Whites alike, was calculated to cause hatred and resentment of the bombers and was foreign to the pattern of SWAPO insurgent activity. SWAPO's denial was not accepted and numbers of leaders and supporters were arrested in the round-up which followed. The atmosphere of threat was aggravated by the Administrator General's warnings that 'dark forces' were combining to kill citizens;[14] newspapers printed reports that alien mechanised troops were preparing to cross the border and reported rumours that SWAPO was planning a general strike in protest against the elections. (This provoked the Administrator General to the ill-considered pronouncement that such a strike would be tantamount to treason.) On the eve of the elections Roman Catholic Priest Father. Kleinhit-pass was ordered out of the country. No official explanations were tendered but fellow churchmen presumed the expulsions to be a retribution for informing church members that the official intimidation was illegal, that no one was compelled to vote and that the elections could in any event not be internationally recognised.[15] Justin Ellis, an outspoken worker at the Christian Centre was also expelled while in the process of collecting evidence of electoral irregularities.[16] There were also official reports of heavy bombardment from Angola into Ovamboland, of SWAPO attacks and of a device exploding near a polling booth, though the chief electoral officer declared himself ignorant of such events.

Polling started on the 8th December 1978 and lasted five days. The provisions of the Terrorism Act, Proclamation AG9 and AG26, remained in force throughout the country. In the north the SADF provided proof of its military might with a massive deployment of armoured vehicles and soldiers. Soldiers manned checkpoints and searched voters on their way to the 129 polling booths in Ovamboland. Helicopters and mirage fighters criss-crossed the skies in sufficient numbers to instil a ubiquitious sense of scrutiny from which no voter could escape. Reporters from the *Rand Daily Mail* and the Johannesburg *Financial Mail* wrote that the White drivers of almost every army vehicle gave the DTA sign; also that the DTA, having borrowed 100 vehicles from the Administration sent out trucks to kraals in Ovamboland to gather voters and bring them to the polls where they joined the queues under the watchful eyes of patrolling armed DTA field workers.[17] The polling booths surrounded by barbed wire were protected by soldiers and policemen. DTA militia[18] armed with automatic weapons patrolled, wearing party symbols on their arms.[19]

Voters who kept away from the booths were flushed out by scores of mobile polling stations which made their way to villages, farms and kraals.[20] The mobile stations were not confined to limited hours; they carried on day and night, and in the remote areas of Bushman land and Caprivi, moved between water posts and kraals to find voters. Their trucks were accompanied by detachments of soldiers in their Hippos – landmine-resistant high-axled armoured personnel carriers built for anti-guerrilla operations with a hideous animal-like iron configuration. Church leaders vainly remonstrated that country folk living near remote water holes or in kraals would be overcome with terror by the sudden invasion by polling officers and soldiers in armoured vehicles.

DTA trucks brought in voters who then queued to receive instructions in the DTA tent; DTA cadres received them, explaining the voting procedures and usually advised them to request assistance in the polling booth. Many were advised to indicate their choice in the polling booth by giving the DTA sign.

On his arrival at the polling station a voter would surrender his registration card after his signature or fingerprints were checked; his fingers were next checked under infra-red light as a precaution against double voting. (Voters were required to dip their fingers into a fluid which remained active and detectable for a period of five days.) A ballot paper, an envelope marked with the voter's registration number, was then handed over.[21] It was only at this point that the voter was allowed into the voting compartment where he could make his cross or ask for it to be placed there on his behalf.[22]

The voting procedure was attacked by critics as depriving the voter of true secrecy. The mere recording of the registration number, it was argued, undermined any confidence that the voter's choice would remain concealed, as most illiterate voters had to speak up and tell the polling officer of their choice.[23]

At the start of the elections Bishop Auala made his diagnosis: throughout Ovamboland, he said, political organisers and officials had emphasised that people should not abstain from voting. This was interpreted to mean an obligation to vote. The poll, he predicted, would be high. Some would vote of their own accord but the rest out of fear. 'The people' explained Auala 'have told me that they have no choice but to vote.[24] Black soldiers and Black civilians of AKTUR and DTA had told them that they would be refused medical attention if they did not vote, that they would be prevented from working and prevented from being educated.'

The South Africans claimed an astounding turn-out of slightly more than 80%. Of 326,264 votes cast, 4,791 were spoilt papers. 268,000 voted in favour of the DTA representing 82% of all votes cast. With this support the DTA earned itself 41 seats in the 50 man Constituent Assembly. AKTUR polled 38,716; NCDP 9,073; HNP 5,781 and LF 4,564.

The unfolding of the elections in the shadow of South African soldiers and policemen poses the dilemma of all elections held in a conflicted society where violence has become the primary language of political expression. The SADF set out to ensure 'the implementation of the registration process' and yet it was these same troops, now called upon to advise, guide and protect Ovambo men and women who, in the eyes of these men and women, were responsible for the burning and bombing of Ovambo villages, attacks on civilians, the desecration and destruction of Churches and Church property.

Viewed in retrospect the very round condemnation of election procedures by the Churches and political leaders contrasts strangely with the findings of foreign journalists and observers invited by the Administrator General to monitor and pronounce upon the elections. These visitors were lodged in Windhoek's most luxurious hotel at the expense of the Administration; they were entertained and guided by police and army officers who conducted them on selected routes of inspection. Their journalistic reports were largely favourable: they found themselves unable to report on evidence of intimidation and irregularity. This was hardly surprising: like official visitors to San Salvador they were not likely to be taken on a tour of inspection of human rights violations. Similar responses were observed in Rhodesia when in 1979 an election was held by the transitional Government then led by Ian Smith. That election embraced arrangements and techniques which bore a striking resemblance to those fashioned by the South Africans in the 1975 and 1978 elections.

In Rhodesia too foreign observers and journalists judged the elections as proper, basing their assessment mainly on the propriety of conduct at the polls. This is of course a relevant feature, but the intimidation process in Namibia was not excrescential – it was inherent in the very tissue of Namibian society. It was a function of a war milieu where political threats were ultimately indistinguishable from the menace of physical retribution. Those who looked for evidence of assaults, of voters being prodded into trucks and dragged to polling booths were misdirected and disappointed. The problem was that the encircling strands of intimidation had been prepared by chiefs, headmen, Radio announcers, officials and DTA field workers long before the arrival of the foreign observers on Namibian soil. Without insight into the conditioning processes, the potency of rumours and the magical protection of registration cards and Turnhalle cards, the compliance of voters could only be interpreted as a voluntary if not spontaneous exercise of the right to vote. The conclusions of the Chitnis report, issued by observers on behalf of the British Parliamentary Human Rights Group in May 1979, were remarkably similar: what had happened at the Rhodesian polls was not a major issue; the merits and de-merits of polling activity were fairly trivial in judging whether the election taken as a whole was fair and free. The election, the observers found, was 'nothing more than a gigantic confidence trick'. The British report found in conclusion:

'Foreign observers were invited in to watch this brilliantly stage-managed performance so that, deceived by political sleight of hand, they could subsequently impress international opinion through their favourable reports. We cannot play our appointed role in this process and endorse this blatant attempt to perpetuate a fraud and justify a lie'.

In the years which followed the 1978 elections the South African Government campaigned on an immense scale for the recognition of the new DTA Government and in full page advertisements in the major papers of Europe and the United States depicted the Namibian Constituent Assembly as the fruit of fair and free elections. In *Le Figaro, The Times* of London and *The New York Times* the argument seemed plausible, the facts unassailable. Neither SWAPO nor the Churches had the resources to reply in kind and on an equal scale. It was precisely with this foreboding that Bishop Richard Wood, himself expelled from Namibia after attempting to mount a legal attack on the 1975 elections, wrote in 1978 of his 'overwhelming apprehension' for the Namibian people and the danger of their 'terrible despair'.

'The South African Government will make its claim that the elections have been free and that people have voted in terms of their own untramelled discretion. The question which remains for me is the extent to which the world will ignore or forget the simple lessons of history. From the invasion of Angola by the South African army to the Kassinga massacre to the Department of Information scandal, the South African government has established a record of proven falsehood. Can the world still allow itself to be moved by such defeated credibility?' . . .

'My overwhelming apprehension and concern goes out to the people of Namibia in this most sombre hour. For a long time now they have been treated with contempt and cynicism. The new elections will be another chapter in their humiliation. I am frightened of the consequences of their anger and hurt. Any recognition of the elections by the western world can only drive them to a terrible despair. I pray that this will not happen.'[25]

40

The Albatross Lives On

The international bluster that followed on South Africa's shock decision to hold internal elections and establish a Constituent Assembly was tempered by Prime Minister P.W. Botha's assertions that the December elections were merely an internal exercise to identify local leaders in a test of strength against SWAPO. (The National Party in Namibia was later to make the reproach that it – like the international community – had been misled by this formulation.) No unilateral declaration of independence (UDI) was contemplated; the Constituent Assembly, the South Africans hastened to point out, was, in terms of Proclamation AG63 merely authorised to 'draw up and adopt a constitution for the Territory with a view to its becoming independent'; it was powerless to establish a constitution or to legislate. Judge Steyn foresaw that the Assembly would guide him and later work in parallel with a Constituent Assembly which would emerge from a UN supervised election. Though this prediction was promptly scotched by the Prime Minister, SWAPO, suspecting the Constituent Assembly to be the wooden horse of UDI, refused to be appeased. But SWAPO's suspicions were not proveable; there was in short, little evidence on the political horizon to suggest that the Constituent Assembly would not carry out its supposed task of drafting a new Constitution and that South Africa's real purpose – shared by Dirk Mudge and the DTA – was by a process of slow legislative accretions to transform a toothless Constituent Assembly into a National Assembly with plenary legislative and executive powers falling just short of a unilaterally created independent government.[1]

As an earnest of South Africa's intentions Pik Botha invited Dr. Waldheim's Special Representative, Martti Ahtisaari, to visit Namibia for discussions on the operational requirements of UNTAG's forces. There was a note of urgency in Botha's message – the election he said had to take place no later than September 30th 1979. The message was interpreted as a tactic designed to cut to a minimum SWAPO's opportunity to organise an effective electoral campaign. The ploy also implied that the South Africans now meant business – small wonder that the world's protest was so muted. International optimism bloomed once again, though not for long. Ahtisaari made his trip and soon found himself confronted by a host of South Africa's 'difficulties'. The problem as to how a 'visible peace' in the operational area could be identified had now become a major obstacle in the way of South Africa's withdrawal. In an apparent attempt to hurry the negotiating process Pik Botha complained that time was running out; in the same breath Botha adumbrated new areas of potential disagreement – details of UNTAG's status, the legal status of its civilian and military components, and the extent to which UNTAG forces would enjoy immunity and claim exemption from local jurisdiction.[2] Botha also demanded that the UN monitor SWAPO bases in Angola and Zambia – a deadlock demand, as sovereign states do not usually agree to the intrusion of a foreign military presence into their jurisdiction.

Though many issues remained unresolved Botha was nonetheless emphatic: the implementation of the plan had to commence in February.[3] No material problems, he insisted, remained in the way of implementation. Whether cunning or naive, his optimism seemed contagious; the Western powers too thought that prospects for a final settlement looked good. Ahtisaari returned and preparations were started up for the massive repatriation of 32,000 Namibian exiles.[4]

The optimistic glow evaporated after the release of Waldheim's detailed plan for the independence process. Paragraphs 11 and 12 of the plan dealt with the issue of SWAPO military bases. No provision for the monitoring of SWAPO bases beyond the border was made; inside the Territory two bases would be established and monitored. Botha was immediately disparaging and rejected the notion of SWAPO bases inside Namibia as an entirely new unwarranted interpretation of the agreement and a breach of Western undertakings to South Africa. Though accused of crude duplicity Western negotiators, in the face of exasperating attacks, declined the invitation to an unproductive wrangle. Who could deny that SWAPO guerrillas were active in the Territory? Logic dictated that they should be confined rather than be allowed to roam during the election season. If the South African army had been unable to paralyse their movements how was UNTAG expected to succeed?[5]

Botha's rejection was followed by further destructive raids into Angola – a military provocation which was bound to set back negotiations with Angola over the monitoring of SWAPO bases within its borders.

From the sidelines DTA leaders, hoping to compensate for the Constituent Assembly's dreary image vociferously rejected any further negotiation on the establishment of SWAPO bases in the Territory. Acting out a charade of governmental potency Mudge said that 'the moment of truth' had arrived, while the Constituent Assembly put the UN on terms to implement its original plan without SWAPO bases.

The DTA's grandiose election promises were not fulfilled. In a flurry of activity the impotent Assembly produced a rash of motions to abolish residential restrictions and attenuate apartheid in public amenities such as rest camps, holiday resorts and country hotels – gestures of futility, as the motions were bereft of legal significance. These motions were in turn referred to the White Legislative Assembly for comment – such was their humble status at the time. Structured along the lines of a provincial council the Legislative Assembly wielded real power in areas which mattered to an apartheid society – local government, public amenities, recreation, education and health. The Assembly made no attempt to conceal its disapproval.

But the DTA leaders had other ideas. They did not regard the Constituent Assembly as a purely advisory, transitional organism. From early in 1979 the Constituent Assembly's leaders affected the style of a legitimate government waiting in the wings with some impatience for the final legal formalities which would endow it with sovereign power. Impotent to make an impact on Namibian reality and the legacy of poverty, inadequate housing and education and rampant unemployment, the DTA demanded independence, irrespective of international recognition, defended itself with vituperative attacks against AKTUR and blamed the obstructionism of officials and the White Legislative Assembly. Mudge's portentous voice promised self-government by May 1979;[6] Black leaders he explained, had become impatient and were no longer prepared to wait. From Pretoria sibylline utterances from the Prime Minister prophesied that Namibia's political future would be decided primarily by the Constituent Assembly.

Then, in the confused wake of the Settlement breakdown, Pretoria seized its opportunity to push through the next critical phase of creeping constitutional advance. On the 14th May 1979 Proclamation AG21 established the National Assembly whose legislative jurisdiction included sweeping powers to repeal or amend all laws in Namibia including South African Acts of Parliament. Some powers were withheld: the National Assembly was not empowered to alter the international status of the Territory or that of the Administrator General. Between fifty and sixty-five representatives were to compose the National Assembly.

Overnight the Constituent Assembly was transformed into a Parliament with ample legislative capacity, subject to the veto of the Administrator General.

On the 21st May 1979 the National Assembly was inaugurated with processional ceremony through Windhoek's streets, with the rumble of South African panzers and the tramping of marching soldiers who presented their salute to Steyn with punctilious solemnity. While most of Windhoek's population kept aloof, the processional route was lined with DTA supporters who had been bussed in for the occasion with new flags shouting 'Victory to the people, a National Assembly is born'. The *Windhoek Observer* under the editorship of Hannes Smith, formerly editor of the *Windhoek Advertiser* described the spectacle as artificial and inane.[7]

One of the first Bills produced by the National Assembly was designed to strengthen the Security Districts Act. This became the Security Districts Act of 1979. The DTA was now at last in possession of a legislative instrument through which its election promises might be realised. The attack on apartheid, ostensibly the primary target, took the form of the Abolition of Racial Discimination Bill which set out to erase apartheid practices in residential areas and public amenities including hotels, caravan parks, restaurants, cinemas and public recreation areas. Once again the apartheid Albatross stirred. The right wing reacted with energy: AKTUR and the HNP fought back with a vehemence which bordered on hysteria; Sarel Becker, the leader of the HNP in Namibia, derided the Bill as a 'piece of treason'; AKTUR declared its implacable opposition; the measure, they predicted, would violate White identity and breed political strife from which SWAPO alone would be the beneficiary.[8]

White demonstrators jeered members of the National Assembly and organised demonstrations which echoed the tramp of jack boots in Germany; members of the Hitler Jugend marched with White right-wingers and denounced the desegregation Bill as a detestable plot concocted by Jews and Zionists.[9] The vision of Black neighbours was perceived as a dire threat and a breach of Turnhalle's unanimous principle that each population group should have its own protected areas. The White man, proclaimed Du Plessis, would lose his distinctive 'right to privacy'; the new Bill was a 'forced opening' of hotels and restaurants, and the free economy was being crushed. From the pulpit Dominee Du Toit of the Windhoek NGK mother church depicted the horrors of integration while the Windhoek City Council petitioned the National Assembly to respect 'protective title deeds'.[10] The National Party published and distributed a booklet setting out their argument: the 1977 White Referendum they reasoned, approved of independence by an overwhelming majority, but only in accordance with the principles accepted by the Turnhalle; this had not been contradicted by the one-man one-vote election in December 1978, which the Prime Minister had declared to be a purely internal process to identify the leaders. The Turnhalle constitution provided, through the consensus mechanism adequate protection for minorities, with a central government comprising representatives appointed by electoral colleges of the different ethnic groups. That was now ignored; the entire fabric of the Turnhalle constitution, the product of years of negotiation and effort, had been quietly dumped. Positive assurances, declared Du Plessis, had been given by John Vorster and reconfirmed by P.W. Botha when he became Prime Minister; there was now concern that these assurances were no longer valid.[11]

The fever of revolt in the White community spread yet further with Mudge's announcement in July 1979 of the DTA's intention to establish second tier Representative Authorities – the equivalent of Homelands government – for each of the eleven population groups. DTA assurances that each group would be empowered to protect its own culture and language were couched in generalities which failed to satisfy AKTUR and the HNP, who had begun to grasp a new major threat to their life style – the legislative invasion of their own legal citadel, the Legislative Assembly. There was nothing in the National Assembly's constitution which limited its range of fire. Given the complicity of the Administrator General, the National Assembly was empowered to hack away the powers of the Legislative Assembly and rewrite piecemeal the Territory's Constitution.

AKTUR counter-attacked with an urgent application which impugned the very legality of the National Assembly. It was their contention that Proclamation AG21 of 1979 was *ultra vires*, that the National Assembly and the Constituent Assembly were one and the same body and that it had never been the lawmakers' intention to invest the Constituent Assembly with lawmaking powers. This argument was rejected by Judge Badenhorst. The National Assembly, he found, was an advisory instrument of the Administrator General; their laws were merely the laws of the Administrator General. (The legal battle was lost but AKTUR was now able to jeer at the National Assembly's governmental pretentions. To refute AKTUR's barbs Steyn took the unprecedented step of entering into the arena with *his* interpretation of the Court's findings.[12]) AKTUR appealed to the Appellate Division only to be confronted with a new proclamation of the South African State President deeming Proclamation AG21 to have been issued by him, thus extinguishing the last glimmer of hope on the legal front.[13]

Du Plessis cried out that the Whites were in despair over the future of the Territory. Pik Botha was accused of surrendering the Whites in the Territory. Far from now enjoying a Turnhalle-like constitutional certainty the Nationalists found their legal fortress imperilled; there was talk of holy war, brotherly treachery and grim warnings of a new great trek of Whites across the Orange River into the Republic. The sense of disenchantment was aggravated by the desertion of approximately 60% of the farms in the area north west of Otavi. Jaap Marais, the leader of the HNP, called for a new preparedness to die. Windhoek witnessed a rightwing renaissance where HNP meetings drew large crowds; supporters waved flags bearing the odal symbol whose incomprehensible geometry they said was Scandinavian in origin.[14] (Was it a coincidence that neo-Nazi groups in Germany have hoisted the same symbol?) There was open sympathy for the emergent White resistance group BLANKSWA and plentiful talk of armed revolt. A favourite aphorism in HNP circles was that there were other ways to deal with Blacks – it was easier to shoot them.[15] Thousands of Whites, many sporting hand guns, gathered with calls for armed action and violent resistance.

The call for violent resistance went unprosecuted and unpunished.

There was of course no risk of a successful revolt – the loyalty of the SADF was not to be doubted – but the death or maiming of foolhardy martyrs could have a disastrous spin off for the Government in its struggle against growing *verkrampte* (ultra-conservative) opposition in the Republic. In the South African cabinet the majority was faced by the wraith of Afrikaner racial purity incarnate in the Prime Minister's rival Dr. Andries Treurnicht, the leader of the Transvaal National Party, who had been relegated to a minor portfolio.

The *verkrampte* outburst loomed ominously on the Republic's western flank for other reasons. In Afrikaner tradition the Church had historically played a leading role in the unfolding of Afrikaner Nationalism. Now its recalcitrant voice in Namibia gave impetus to the rightwingers. The DRC supported apartheid as a necessary social 'scaffold'; it was hostile to mixed-race marriages and opposed to spiritual, social and biological integration. Without exception the dominees, though officially permitted to open their doors to Black congregants, opted to reserve their pews for White use only. A recrudescent struggle for White survival in Namibia could stir powerful prejudices capable of corroding traditional Afrikaner support for the Government. It was with this in mind that the July National Congress set up an information committee to appeal to South African voters and sent a mission to the Transvaal to gather support from fellow Afrikaners.[16]

On the surface the response was depressing. Treurnicht said that the Party would not interfere in the internal affairs of Namibia.[17] At Upington the Prime Minister, in a not too oblique allusion to the new challenge, declared that the Government could not be tied to the same policies for ever.[18] But the National Party foray into South African politics bore fruit; within a fortnight of the mission of angry rightwingers to the Transvaal, the Prime Minister in a shock announcement revealed the appointment of Professor Gerrit Viljoen, a leading Afrikaner theoretician and head of the powerful but secret Broederbond, to the office of Administrator of Namibia, in place of Judge Steyn.[19] Viljoen's political credentials were impeccable in the Afrikaner world. His appointment was at once a gesture of reconciliation and a pretext for getting rid of Steyn, whose rhetoric had become indistinguishable from that of Dirk Mudge.[20] The agitation subsided, the acerbic challenging tones disappeared, and Viljoen's mediation was welcomed with pious expressions of hope that his help would resolve the differences amongst the Territory's Whites.[21]

Unlike his predecessor, Viljoen took note of AKTUR's demands for racial exclusiveness in the areas which mattered – schools, colleges, hospitals, libraries, public amenities and residential areas.[22] Not all the demands were conceded. (The legal colour bar was not maintained for residential areas, but reassuring financial barriers remained – insuperable for most Blacks who, apart from isolated businessmen and DTA leaders, could simply not afford to buy houses in White areas.) The fratricidal strife was largely resolved; AKTUR succeeded on the main issues and the integrity of White society remained intact. Instead of seeking to confine second tier government to 'cultural and traditional' matters, as Steyn was wont to do, Viljoen set out in a businesslike fashion to crystallise the respective functions of central government and second tier ethnic government. At the end of the negotiating process AKTUR was assured that the teachers' training college would remain White and that the fundamental areas of health and education would remain the preserve of the Legislative Assembly. Legislative proposals, finally tabled by Viljoen on the 28 November 1979, embodied the nucleus of a constitution. The jurisdiction of second tier government was defined to embrace education to the level of primary school teacher training, health services, social welfare and pensions, land tenure, and agriculture. These five primary functions were to be entrenched by proclamation preventing any encroachment by the National Assembly. The rider to these proposals was that the Legislative Assembly would lose control of nature conservation, tourism, roads and traffic control.

These were not deemed essential for the maintenance of White exclusiveness. The Albatross lived on.

The Abolition of Racial Discrimination (Urban Residential Areas and Public Amenities) Act No 3 of 1979, was put on the statute book on 11th July, but its penalty clauses, providing for sentences up to R300 or imprisonment for a period not exceeding three months, were to remain unenforceable pending the decision of the Administrator General.

Viljoen's first priority, after settling accounts with the *verkramptes*, was that the National Assembly should be seen as an 'effective governmental organ'.[23] To accomplish this the next step in the process apparently leading to independence had to be taken – the transfer of executive power to a cabinet responsible in law to the National Assembly. There would, he commented, be no UDI as that would be 'a very risky thing'; foreign affairs, defence, import and excise were to remain with the Republican Government.

In March 1980 Viljoen's draft Bill for the establishment of second tier authorities, now baptised Representative Authorities, was tabled, and AKTUR delegates once again took up their place in the Assembly after months of boycotting.[24]

The Representative Authorities, as defined and established by Proclamation AG8 of 1980, represented a continuity of policy based on the Odendaal Commission's conception of Bantustan Homelands self rule. In its pristine form the Development of Self-Government for Native Nations in SWA Act No. 54 of 1968 provided for the creation of six 'native nations' in Namibia, each destined to have its own legislative and executive councils. The provisions of the Act were implemented to the extent that Ovambo, Kavango, East Caprivi and Rehoboth were established as self-governing homelands. Advisory boards were set up for Namaland, Bushmanland and the Coloured population. The Damaras, latecomers in the process, were the recipients of a self-government structure called a Representative Authority. (The Whites throughout had their Legislative Assembly.) With the promulgation of AG8 the legal nomenclature changed, but in contrast to the Odendaal Commission's pattern of Homelands Government, the Representative Authorities were now endowed with an *ethnic* in addition to a geographical jurisdiction.[25] Rules and regulations of the Representative Authorities were to be binding on all members of the ethnic group wherever they might find themselves in Namibia. The theoretical, administrative and legal architecture of Ovamboland would for example apply Ovambo justice and law enforcement as well as medical care, whether the Ovambo subjects resided in the heart of Katutura or in Bushmanland's obscure village capital. All ethnic governments would now be possessed of their own civil services acting in parallel with that of the central government. The far-reaching and bewildering implications of the projected labyrinth of legislative, executive and administrative structures will be examined in a later section.

Subject to the approval of the Administrator General, Representative Authorites could *inter alia* pass ordinances controlling the acquisition, alienation and occupation of land, farming settlements, primary and secondary education and the training of teachers to the fourth standard, health services and social welfare services. The distribution of funds from central Government to the Representative Authorities was to be in the discretion of the National Assembly. Within two months of Proclamation AG8, new Proclamations established Representative Authorities in the place of the White Legislative Assembly, the Ovambo, Kavango, and Eastern Caprivi Legislative Councils; the Nama Council was converted into a Representative Authority while the Damara Representative Authority was revised in conformity with the new legislation. A few months later fresh Proclamations established Herero and Tswana Representative Authorities. In July 1980 the Administrator General's Advisory Council composed of National Assembly members was converted by Proclamation AG19 of 1980 to a cabinet – vaguely obscured by the title Council of Ministers – consisting of twelve men under the Chairman of the Council who was referred to by Pressmen as the Prime Minister, with each councillor representing one population group.[26] As head of the executive authority the Administrator General was vested with discretionary powers to veto decisions of the Council of Ministers and legislative enactments of the National Assembly and the Representative Authorities, with power in times of national emergency to act independently of the Council of Ministers and so revert to the status of Governor. Concurrently with the establishment of the Council of Ministers the existing 'directorates' – the name for government departments that had been transferred to the Administrator General – were renamed Government Departments. These departments now constituted an independent Namibian civil service. In preparation for this move a steady transfer of South African government departments operating in Namibia had been made to the Administrator General's office, leaving, by the end of 1979, only police, defence, national security, external affairs, excise and import duties and railways in the hands of the South African Government.[27]

It was not long before inroads were made into these residual portfolios.

Emboldened by the feeble African and international reaction to South

Africa's triple thrust towards constitutional development – the establishment of the National Assembly, the Council of Ministers and the Namibian Civil Service – Pretoria determined to push rapidly to the point where the National Assembly could no longer be viewed as a constitutional toy inescapably shackled to the Administrator General's veto.

The first move towards the mounting of the South West Africa Territorial Force (SWATF) was made by Prime Minister Botha in May 1980 with the announcement – then expressed somewhat obliquely – that a handover of 'specific defence functions' to the Administrator General would be made.[28] In anticipation of vigorous UN reaction the South Africans emphasised that SWATF would remain part of the SADF until the Territory became independent.[29]

Thus began the Vietnamisation of Namibia, with Black pitted against Black. The move marked a critical stage. For the first time institutionalised indigenous military power was being created which could eventually, under the control of the Council of Ministers or military putschists seize power. SWATF and a projected South West African Police force (SWAP) could provide muscle to a Namibian power structure, whose demands for independence could enjoy some credibility, and enable the South Africans to argue that a continuing denial of independence might lead to bloodshed. Dirk Mudge's anti-South African growling at the Settlement talks in Geneva in January 1981 provides an interesting foretaste of the sort of pre-independence scenario which could be written. Given the possibility of devastating incursions into Southern Angola and the creation of a cordon sanitaire to inhibit the movement of SWAPO insurgents from their Angolan sanctuary might Pretoria not look forward to the day when a home grown Namibian army – with or without the assistance of 9,000 mercenaries and foreigners of the 32nd Battalion – could contain the insurgent tide?

On September 1st SWAP was established as an independent police force. Provision was made for continuity of service in the new force. The introduction of a new rank system with commissioners, superintendents and inspectors provided a change of cosmetic interest only.[30]

After the founding of SWATF a new Conscription Law was passed requiring all males of all races over sixteen to register for army service. The absorption of Blacks into the army was not new. Tribal battalions had been formed as early as 1975 including the 31 Battalion (Bushmen) and 34 Battalion (Kavango), 35 Battalion (mostly Ovambo), 33 Battalion (Caprivian). The nucleus of a Baster commando unit was started in 1976, a Herero commando in 1977. In 1978 a Kaokoland company was formed to absorb recruits from the Herero and Ovahimba ethnic groups.

The Conscription Law shocked the Black community. It was immediately opposed by community leaders, the Churches, SWAPO, the NNF and Shipanga's party, SWAPO-D[31]. A war of liberation they protested was being turned into a civil war. When recruiting started in earnest there were reports that young Blacks had been dragooned into doing their army service. Individuals began to leave. They were followed by others. By the end of 1980 the Churches warned that a new major exodus was in the making.[32]

The DTA's new thrust towards power and independence did not make it more popular. It found itself instead yet more alienated – derided by most Whites, resented by most Blacks.

41

The Road to Geneva

Though South Africa broke off Settlement negotiations in May 1979 the Government gave assurances that the door to further negotiations remained open. It was not long before Dr. Waldheim, an irrepressible suitor, busied himself with the task of pursuing South Africa with a new proffered solution – the DMZ (De-Militarized Zone) proposal.[1] There would be a DMZ 50 kilometres on either side of the border with Angola; no SWAPO bases would be permitted in Namibia nor anywhere else in the DMZ; SWAPO bases in Angola and Zambia would be monitored by Angolan and Zambian government forces acting in cooperation with UNTAG; in the 50 kilometre strip south of the border South African police would act as monitors in collaboration with UNTAG. SWAPO guerrillas would, with the commencement of the cease-fire, lay down their arms under UN supervision and participate in the election or be removed to bases in Angola and Zambia outside the DMZ. South African forces would provisionally be limited to five selected areas within Namibia. UNTAG would deploy 7,500 troops. In Dr. Waldheim's view the DMZ, though covering 140,000 square kilometres, presented no insuperable logistical difficulties to UNTAG.

SWAPO denounced the DMZ proposal as an attempt to negate the achievement of their military struggle; they would not surrender their arms and would not go along with Front Line States when their vital interests were threatened. Nujoma warned that his guerrillas would open fire on anyone attempting to move them from their present bases.

The DMZ proposals more than met South Africa's original objections: SWAPO bases in Namibia were now excluded; those north of the border would now have to be moved more than 50 kilometres away. But South Africa showed little inclination to be accommodating. Previous UN task forces in Saudi Arabia, the Yemen and Indo-China had not been effective, they argued;[2] the proposers, said Pik Botha, seemed unaware of the logistical implications. By August 1979 however the South Africans, after many expressions of hesitation, allowed themselves to examine the plan. Whether South Africa's revived interest was bona fide or not can perhaps be inferred from their ensuing responses. One clue to the motivation for the shift in position might be found in South Africa's assertion that progress could only be made if the West and the UN recognised the December elections.[3]

The Namibian constitutional impasse – the refusal by the UN and the West to recognise the 1978 elections and the validity of the National Assembly – was in the forefront of South Africa's thinking. A primary strategy was henceforth to exact at the very least a *de facto* recognition of the National Assembly as a living reality. The vehicle for the new strategy was South Africa's complaint that the UN 'blatantly' favoured SWAPO's cause. From early in 1980 South African propaganda harped increasingly and relentlessly on the new issue of UN partiality. The diplomatic confrontation of SWAPO and the DTA was taken up with energy. In May Pik Botha formally requested Dr. Waldheim and the Secretariat of the Security Council to abandon SWAPO as the 'sole and authentic representative of the people of Namibia,' an honorific appointment made by the General Assembly, not the Security Council, and to stop funding SWAPO from the UN's regular budget.[4] Botha's request was not consonant with the political realities: Dr. Waldheim was not empowered to rescind resolutions of the General Assembly, nor was the Security Council in a position to divert funds earmarked for SWAPO by the General Assembly. The South Africans demanded that the Namibian internal leadership be included in all Settlement negotiations.[5] At the UN the South African Ambassador called on the General Assembly to refrain from adopting biased resolutions.

Agitation for a joint conference of SWAPO and the DTA gave additional momentum to South Africa's attack.[6] DTA representatives, said Mudge, would be prepared to have discussions with SWAPO provided the talks were held on Namibian soil. On a visit to London in April Dr. Viljoen hinted at a new approach, should the UN fail to resolve the deadlock. He favoured direct South African negotiation with Angola and Zambia. The government he thought might find it useful to hear what SWAPO had to say. The people of Namibia, he said, were impatient, and 'we must try anything possible'.[7] But did the South Africans really want a settlement? Early in 1980 Robert Mugabe led his Zanu Party to victory at the polls in Zimbabwe with a landslide result, which confirmed suspicion that SWAPO would in turn sweep the board in a fair and free election. An all-party Conference at Lancaster House had in the case of Zimbabwe produced a successful independence formula. In the case of Namibia the possibility of a breakthrough in direct negotiations between SWAPO and DTA leaders was bound – even without the hindsight of the Geneva Conference in 1981 – to become deadlocked. What mediation could have served the South Africans in bona fide negotiations better than the services of Dr. Waldheim and the Contact Group's negotiators? South Africa's Ambassador to the UN called for every effort to wipe away the 'enormous mistrust' of the UN. A Conference, he suggested, where internal parties would be present, and given an opportunity to state their case, would be an effective aid. Anyone who ignores the internal parties, he warned, 'is playing with fire'. SWAPO and the UN Council for Namibia rejected this suggestion. Namibia was a UN responsibility. Only South Africa and SWAPO, the only interested parties at war, with one another should meet. From DTA quarters rose a steady stream of vilification against the UN. Dr. Waldheim was deliberately attempting to delay the independence process, said Mudge, declaring that the DTA was tired of 'bending over backwards'.

In its reply to the DMZ proposals South Africa insisted on twenty 'selective locations' for the deployment of its troops during the twelve weeks after the establishment of the DMZ. After this the SADF would pull out of the DMZ and regroup 1500 troops at Grootfontein and Oshivello. (SWAPO dropped its demands to maintain its own bases inside Namibia and was persuaded to vacate the DMZ entirely within fourteen days after its establishment.) The South African demand for twenty bases was considered provocatively high and was at odds with South Africa's acceptance of the initial plan which proposed only two South African bases.

At the UN, US Ambassador Donald McHenry branded South African policy as one leading Namibia to an ill-conceived and doomed internal settlement.[8] He blamed Pretoria for the breakdown in negotiations, listed all the concessions made by SWAPO and hinted that the US should not oppose sanctions. From the very beginning of negotiations South Africa resisted the most fundamental UN demand, namely UN control and supervision of the elections. South Africa got her way. After SWAPO had approved of the very agreement that South Africa had accepted, South Africa then raised the problem of the 'visible peace', then broke off negotiation and went for an internal election. Now after more than three years of negotiation for an election, supposedly under UN supervision and control, South Africa discovered the UN's partiality. In South Africa the English press including the pro DTA *Windhoek Advertiser* was critical: South Africa's main objections had been met; all indictions suggested that the Government was trying to 'stall' the implementation of an election.[9]

In August 1980 Pik Botha invited a team of senior officials to discuss the modalities of implementing the DMZ plan, as also the composition of UNTAG. Later in October a UN delegation headed by Brian Urquhart, the UN Assistant Secretary General for Political Affairs, visited the Republic only to be told that the time frame of implementation and other details could not be finalised without the resolution of the impartiality issue. The South African Government urged the mission to consult with representatives of political parties from Windhoek and propounded the view that, if the problem of confidence were overcome in a pre-implementation meeting, the end of 1981 would be a realistic target date for independence. While Urquhart was in Windhoek Mudge dangled the possibility of an early election date, provided, he said, all parties were reasonable.[10]

South Africa's stick and carrot tactics paid off, and Dr. Waldheim recommended a pre-implementation multi-party meeting to dispose of all remaining problems including the issue of confidence in the UN.

The Conference was arranged to take place at Geneva on 7th January 1981 in the sumptuous decor of the Palais des Nations under the chairmanship of Dr. Waldheim. Utterances from Windhoek and Pretoria were not auspicious of a mood of reconciliation. Prior to the Conference Pik Botha officially announced that the South African Government would definitely not participate. This led to a furoré, upon which Botha modified his stance. The South African Government would be present but in a non-participating advisory capacity – an approach not easily reconciled with bona fide concerns to put an end to the blood letting.[11] The Conference, said Botha, would be primarily between SWAPO and the internal parties.[12] DTA pronouncements were even less accommodating. Because the UN had not as yet shown its impartiality the Council of Ministers gave out that it might not attend the Geneva talks. Later the Council agreed to attend but with a limited purpose: they would take a strong negotiating position and demand the General Assembly's withdrawal of support for SWAPO, the withdrawal of SWAPO's observer status at the UN and the cessation of all financial aid to the organisation. Mudge referred to the Conference as an opportunity to confront SWAPO *vis-à-vis* its Marxist policies.[13] For Kyaimo Riruako, Kapuuo's successor, the conference was frankly to be used as a platform to put across the DTA point of view rather than as a means to reach any final agreement.[14]

Since SWAPO refused to participate in any Conference where the DTA was represented UN diplomats worked out an ambiguous compromise. DTA leaders and representatives of other internal parties would constitute a delegation under the leadership of the new Administrator General, Danie Hough. (Hough was a provincial councillor from Natal. His appointment in the place of Viljoen was considered a deliberate move to downgrade the importance of the Administrator General's office.)

At Geneva the DTA threatened to walk out unless the South Africans left their ranks. Once there they used every available opportunity to puff their views before journalists and observers from all over the world. They protested against the indignity of being obliged to sit together with the South Africans and the smaller parties.[15] (The *Windhoek Observer* poured scorn on the protest as a move 'unmatched when it comes to political chicanery'[16].) Could the 'democratic parties', asked the DTA, be expected to reach a cease-fire within a few days when they had not been directly and formally invited to express their views on these matters? They had only been consulted via the 'back door'; the implementation of the plan, they complained, had been dragged out since 1979 as a result of SWAPO's intrigue while the UN's bias towards SWAPO gave the organisation enormous psychological advantages.

Although the DTA threatened to walk out unless received as an independent delegation, they did not do so. When Nujoma rose to address, his entire delegation stood up with him and with clenched fists gave the power salute with the words 'We are one'. SWAPO, he said briefly, had accepted Resolution 435 and was ready to sign a cease-fire forthwith. It was a matter of regret, he added before sitting down, that the leaders on Robben Island could not be present.

By this time SWAPO had come round to conceding the surrender of its title of sole representative, once an agreement for a cease-fire had been reached. What further concessions had been wrung out of SWAPO?[17] A 500-word document leaked by the Contact Group provided interesting glimpses: the elimination of SWAPO's UN privileges; assurances for minority rights in Namibia;[18] Ahtisaari's resignation as Commissioner for Namibia and an understanding that the General Assembly and other UN bodies would take no steps which would prejudice the holding of fair and free elections.[19]

DTA leaders countered with bewilderingly acrimonious salvos: SWAPO was an organisation of Russian stooges and revisionist murderers: they were racists and Marxist lackeys, and Ahtisaari supported 'rapist thugs'. The DTA would fight on and would beat SWAPO in the 'African way', by eliminating them. (They had not already done so, said DTA leader Katuutire Kaura, because the South African police had prevented them.[20]) '*A luta continua*' (the struggle goes on) chanted the DTA borrowing SWAPO's militant slogan. A cease-fire, Mudge insisted, was now impossible; they were no longer prepared to accept mere assurances; there would now have to be 'demonstrations of impartiality' and the DTA would have to be permitted to address the Security Council and the General Assembly. Every 'vestige' of UN support had to be removed before a cease-fire could be entertained.

In reply UN officials, with commendable restraint, set out the facts and the immense range of consensus.[21] They pointed out that the primary responsibility for law and order would remain with the Namibian police, that South Africa would retain primary responsibility for running the election and that 7,500 troops together with 400 international staff and 1,000 local recruits would have a massive neutralising effect. Ahtisaari vowed to live up to the 'historic nature' of his duties. Irish Chief Inspector, Stephen Fanning, pledged that his 360 police monitors would be handpicked for impartiality. These promises and explanations were shrugged off; the DTA remained undeflected. Mudge maintained his demand that the UN serve a lengthy period of probation to prove its worth. (In private he indicated that eighteen months were needed to tackle SWAPO at the polls and that independence could be scheduled for the latter part of 1983 – a signal of hope? Another pretext for yet another round of negotiation?)

The South Africans complained that the DTA had become headstrong and mistrustful of South Africa. But Western observers noted a different reality behind the rhetoric: when procedural demands were made in the name of the alliance DTA leaders waited while South African officials first consulted their Government.

273

The DTA's unexpected tirade attracted an unusually stern reproach from Brian Urquhart, who made allusions to regrettable comments expressed in terms which, measured by international standards, left much to be desired. The Front Line States and the OAU were more blunt: 'It was clear from the beginning that South Africa was here to wreck the meeting . . . '

DTA leaders were triumphant. The Conference had been their first opportunity to have discussions 'on equal terms'.

Once again Pik Botha emphasised that the door was still open for discussions.

42

Towards Super-Apartheid

The DTA's outburst at Geneva did little to restore its dwindling prestige. Its manoeuvres were, on the contrary, interpreted as an attempt to sabotage the negotiating process and so stave off indefinitely the possibility of fair and free elections under UN aegis. In contrast to their florid election promises, the Administration fought shy of implementing the Abolition of Racial Discrimination Act after its penalty clause was brought into operation in July 1980.[1] (The clause made provision for fines – not imprisonment.) Offenders were not prosecuted, despite the practice of discrimination, especially in the countryside, where hotel and bar owners remained intractable for some time. [2] The continuing dominance of the White Legislative Assembly and the undisturbed survival of its apartheid policies was a living rebuff to the DTA's avowed policy. It stood in robust contrast to the flimsy structures intended to pass as parallel Black Representative Authorities. The White preserve remained substantially unaffected; its efficient systems of social and health services, social amenities, libraries and transport, schools, colleges and libraries were not opened to other groups.[3] On paper there was an equality of Representative Authorities except that the Blacks lacked the resources for development. In 1980 the national budget approved by the National Assembly totalled R520,000,000 of which only R135,000,000 was allocated to the Black Representative Authorities. In this disproportion the traditional racial inequality in Namibia lived on, guaranteeing, whatever the promises had been, that the poor would remain with them. In the DTA itself there was no equal pay for equal work, and Mudge's Republican Party was open to Whites only.[4] The repeal of the Immorality Act, the Mixed Marriages Act and the Group Areas Act, and the operation of the Abolition of Racial Discrimination Act created a world that in law differed from South Africa, where a White is not permitted to escape from confinement within an apartheid system. The new laws were for Namibian society in substance little more than symbolic acts fostering little change in the quality of Black life.[5]

Theoretically Blacks and Whites could dine, sleep with one another, marry and buy a home in any neighbourhood. Physical changes were in fact few – a few Blacks, among them members of the Council of Ministers, bought property in erstwhile exclusively White suburbs. Beyond lay the racial divide.[6]

White schools and colleges remained exclusive. Though private schools were allowed to become multi-racial they were prohibited from competing in sport against White state schools, unless they fielded all White teams. On the level of tertiary education hundreds of Blacks were turned away from the Academy of Tertiary Education, an institution of the Central Government, where there was insufficient room for students. Nearby the Windhoek College of Education, designed to accommodate 1200 Whites, stood nearly empty with 184 White students.[7] The Legislative Assembly refused an exchange. At Otjiwarongo, Dan Seemuller, a four year old child of mixed race, an adopted son of a White German clergyman, was refused entry into a pre-primary school.[8] German clergymen were appalled while DTA spokesmen lashed out against the perpetuation of apartheid.[9] Kaura went so far as to hint at an ultimate resort to force. Mudge ranted over the teachers' college and the Seemuller case, but did nothing about it. Though the prevailing slogan was 'the DTA rules' it had made no serious effort to prove itself on sensitive issues. There was no demand for the removal of the Administrator General nor was there any real confrontation with the South African Government.[10]

And so the symbols of power, the Tintenpalast, the traditional seat of South West African Government and SWA House, the residence of the Administrator, remained, despite the formation of equal Representative Authorities, firmly in the possession of the White Administration.[11] Windhoek's airport was not renamed; it kept the name of one of the Republic's arch racists – J.G. Strydom. Members of the White Representative Authority received heavier pay packets and drove luxurious limousines, unlike their Black brethren who had to make do without status symbols.

White hospitals remained White. A new White hospital built at a cost of R30,000,000 could only be maintained at 30% capacity because of the shortage of White nurses. Black nurses were forbidden. A new White hospital in Keetmanshoop suffered the same fate.[12] As a sequel to constitutional changes a fragmentation of the health services led to their decline. In the new White State Hospital the Administration offered one floor to the Baster and one to the Coloured Administration.[13] At Khorixas hospital, treatment was refused to patients who were not Damaras, while three senior officials were dismissed because they had supposedly undermined the 'authority' of the DTA ethnic government.[14]

The overwhelming poverty of the Black Homelands projected a lurid light onto the functioning of multiple ethnic Representative Authorites. Given its vast surface and scattered population, a rational pooling of resources is a vital precondition to progress in Namibia. The Constitutional structure envisages the contrary – in its definitive form each Representative Authority would provide its own separate clinics, libraries, swimming pools, schools, social welfare facilities and the rest. But each must also maintain a host of Legislative councillors, ministers and civil servants. Each is required to publish its own laws in its official gazette, but the resources for the project simply are not there. Beyond the maintenance of political structures the rest lies within the penumbra of political fantasy. In order to meet the incapacity of ethnic authorities to take on responsibility, legal provision was made entitling each Representative Authority to assume only so much power and function as it wished to handle. So the Nama and Coloured Representative Authorities did not take up the responsibility for health services which remained with the central government.[15] Provision has also been made for the central Administration to second officers and employees to help out. Representative Authorities are also entitled to render services to other similar Authorities. The inevitable effect will be that Black Representative Authorities will provide services for one another while the White Administration and its community maintain their exclusiveness. Windhoek, containing the biggest conglomeration of ethnic groupings, will for the foreseeable future not be possessed of eleven different swimming pools, eleven different libraries and eleven separate hospitals.

The new constitutional dispensation has not helped to build a nation; it has bred a constitutional monstrosity dedicated to notions of super-apartheid – its ultimate achievement a medley of Bantustans together with a White enclave preserved in its privilege and power. It is also a system which lends itself to corruption and petty tyrany.

At Okahandja a grandiose administrative complex for the Herero administration has been planned at a cost of R2,000,000. It includes five houses for the five-man executive committee while Herero children survive semi-naked in the sparse and futureless reserves.[16] Are Namibia's 500 legislative councillors, 60 executive committee members and 50 members of parliament destined to be treated with equal splendour? After winning an election campaign against DUF in the Damara ethnic election in 1981, Justus Garoeb discovered an over-expenditure of R2,000,000. Money and state material had been used to build large houses for some members of the executive committee at a cost of R70,000 each, while R12,000 had been put into the construction of a private shop belonging to one of the ministers.[17] Members of the Representative Authorities and the National Assembly also took the opportunity to buy deserted farms in the drought-ridden north with funds allocated for drought relief by the central Government. These farms were later sold to ethnic authorities for immense profits. While this was perhaps legally permitted more and more people began to question the morality of the practice.[18] The DTA popularity was not enhanced by reports that one of its leaders, affected by much liquor, had demanded the illegal arrest of guests in a Windhoek hotel.[19] An American millionaire openly admitted using his money to buy the goodwill of DTA leaders in Namibia.[20] A United States Oil Company set out to finance a new political alliance to which

R128,000 would be made available every three months.[21] In Hereroland Riruako encouraged, in terms of tribal law, the introduction of public flogging administered on the buttocks of offenders who were often children.[22]

The overall impression provoked by numbers of DTA leaders was that they were personally ambitious with little concern for the plight of their own people. Overcrowding in the cities had become intolerable. Unemployment and its inevitable aftermath of prostitution and violence precipitated frequent police raids. Many were jailed for trespassing or not having ID documents, their children being left to forage for themselves.[23] The Ovambos remained the most abused victims of the migrant labour system in the unalleviated misery of their compounds.[24] In the Homelands poverty drove workers to eye employment in South African mines – amongst the lowest paid in the Republic – with some wistfulness. There were hopes that the deterioration in South Africa's relationship with Zambia and Mozambique would lead to more jobs for Namibian workers. (In 1975 the average income per year per person was R3,300 for Whites and R230 for Blacks. The cash earnings in the Homelands were even less – R100 to R150 per annum per household.[25])

The DTA's defeats in the face of meaningful opposition in the November 1980 elections aroused little surprise. The National Party won the White ethnic election and Justus Garoeb and his party won the Damara election.[26] (Neither SWAPO nor the other centrists parties participated. No elections were allowed in Ovamboland on account of the security situation.) In the DTA there were intriguing signs of strain and disintegration. Two Herero leaders took up their seats as independents in the National Assembly; both were expelled from NUDO. Baster Kaptein Diergaardt quit the National Assembly with his followers; Werner Neef, a member of the Council of Ministers, resigned.[27] Members of the NUDO Youth League who, it was rumoured, had long resented Mudge's leadership, attacked Mudge for his preoccupation with White interests.[28] For too long Mudge had been the spokesman for the DTA.[29] This too generated resentment. Peter Kalangula agitated against the DTA's attachment to ethnicity. Publicity was also given to Ben Africa's sentiments expressed in an interview with a Japanese journalist; according to the report, he said that the South Africans were the scum of the earth and Mudge would not be on the scene for long.[30] In February 1982 Peter Kalangula withdrew from the DTA together with his Ovambo party.

Facing up to the storm Mudge blamed all ills on the DTA's curbed power. More power, he reasoned defensively, would help the Government fight against the right wing officials in the Civil Service who were 'hell bent' on sabotaging the central government.

The DTA adopted other strategems to distance itself from the taint of ethnicity. In September 1981 Mudge announced that the National Assembly would no longer be structured on an ethnic basis. (Until then each ethnic group was allotted one seat, the remaining seats were then distributed in proportion to the size of each population group.) Two thirds of the seats would henceforth be chosen in straight elections, the remainder to be appointed by the eleven ethnic groups.[31] From the Office of the Administrator General another momentous bulletin emerged: except for the portfolios of Constitutional Affairs, Defence and Foreign Affairs, full executive powers were to be transferred to the Ministers' Council. One other modification was revealed by the Administrator General: the National Assembly was to be enlarged from 50 to 70 members, the additional representatives to be nominated by the Representative Authorities.

With these changes South Africa edged its Namibian charge closer to the brink.

43

The Talks of Sisyphus

Angered by the futility of the settlement negotiations and the DTA's provocative performance at Geneva, the General Assembly, early in March 1981, called for mandatory sanctions. The Western Five abstained from voting on the resolution, which they labelled 'inappropriate' and likely to hit South Africa's Black neighbours harder than the Republic itself.[1] (In the past the Western Five had consistently protected South Africa from sanctions, with the exception of the UN arms embargo which was imposed in 1977; by then South Africa had become a major arms manufacturer in her own right.) In the Security Council the Western Five procrastinated, hoping to stave off a sanctions motion. Their arguments, bolstered by hints that new proposals were being prepared, were dismissed. Sanctions resolutions were moved eliciting from the US, the UK and France, a triple veto blocking the imposition of oil and trade embargoes against South Africa. All the other members of the Security Council voted in favour. At the UN this triad of vetoes was seen as a rebuff to Africa and solid encouragement to South Africa to carry on.

In the months which followed South Africa persisted in its attempt to imprint the DTA's legitimacy on the world consciousness. In March a South African delegation took up their seats in the General Assembly shortly before the commencement of debate on Namibia. The team was summarily excluded from the debate.[2] The DTA swiftly responded with a declaration that it was no longer prepared to negotiate a settlement based on UN Resolution 435. The following month Kalangula and Kaura undertook a much-publicised trip to New York to seek audience before the Security Council's meeting on Namibia. (This was the first time that Black DTA leaders had been to the UN unaccompanied by their White colleagues). Though their mission was backed by three permanent Western members, the Security Council refused to grant a hearing. Towards the end of April Pik Botha in a speech made during the South African elections, affirmed that Namibia would not be handed over to the authority of SWAPO so long as the National Party government was at the helm.

Undaunted by South Africa's adamantine responses, Dr. Waldheim, together with the ten-nation European Common Market, appealed to the Government to reconsider. The appeal carried no implication of possible sanctions. South Africa's position remained unchanged – there would be no implementation of the plan until the UN had visibly shed its bias.

In the meantime the Contact Group busied itself with preparations for a new plan designed to meet South African objections more effectively by way of constitutional safeguards for White minority rights, South African economic interests and the enforcement of Namibia's neutral status.

In Washington different approaches were, however, maturing in the corridors of US policy makers.[3] In the eyes of the Reagan Administration, South Africa, despite its repugnant apartheid policies, deserved the hand of American friendship.[4] US officials spoke of the need to cooperate with their wartime allies – forgetting that foremost leaders of the National Party had been interned for their pro-Nazi sentiments during the war. US preoccupation with global dominoes had shaped the belief that the chief threat to regional stability in southern Africa was the Soviet Union's malignant presence. The withdrawal of the 20,000 Cubans in Angola became the central plank of US policy. Early on in the year Washington conveyed the message that it was willing to undertake a special initiative directed towards a negotiated settlement. What emerged was a grandiose US plan with ambitions to free Namibia of South African control, procure the withdrawal of Cuban forces from Angola, together with a commitment from Luanda's leadership to share power with UNITA. Was the new policy an audacious plan to kill apartheid with kindness? In February Chester Crocker, Assistant Secretary of State for African Affairs, commented while on a visit to Capetown, that the SADF was not an instrument of domestic brutality nor the rogue elephant of southern Africa.[5] In March 1981 special arrangements appear to have been engineered by the State Department to facilitate – and conceal – the visit of high-ranking South African military officers, including the Army's Chief of Staff for Intelligence, to the US for top level interviews.

Official US documentation leaked in May 1981 demonstrated the extent to which Washington's political science was affected by South Africa's arguments: that the real enemy was Angola, that UNITA was pushing back the tide of world Communism and that all the DTA needed was another twelve to eighteen months to prepare for an electoral duel with SWAPO. The documentation nowhere reflected preoccupation with the National Party's own internecine feuding nor any perception that the Cubans, having been brought to Angola precisely because of South Africa's invasion in 1975, were in the year 1981 preoccupied with the protection of US oil company installations and were irrelevant to military activities in the south.

Washington's global manichean outlook estranged it from the reality of Namibia's human predicament, its struggles and the elementary fact that SWAPO support was impregnated with a Christian ethic rather than Marxist dialectics. South Africa was handled with delicate care; no pressure was exerted on her except for Washington's expressed determination to pull out of the talks if they turned out to be fruitless. In the view of the Reagan Administration an election should follow on the adoption of a constitution which guaranteed equal rights, including property rights and minority rights. These efforts were endorsed by the South Africans though only in general terms, whilst Mudge's voice – an ample early warning system – now stridently demanded that all SWAPO guerrillas were to be removed from Angola and Zambia to free the negotiating atmosphere from all traces of intimidation.

America's western partners viewed the US proposals with scepticism. They opposed a Lancaster House style conference and all arrangements which excluded the UN. France had in the meantime acquired a socialist government resolutely committed to the implementation of the UN plan. As the months passed it became clear that South Africa was not to be enticed by Washington's proposals.[6] The Contact Group for its part continued to explore measures designed to build up confidence and avoid a 'winners-take-all' dénouement. Early in September 1981 Pretoria indicated once again that it would accept Resolution 435. The following month Prime Minister Botha met the internal parties in Namibia with a view to preparing the way for further deliberations between them and the Contact Group. These deliberations, said the Prime Minister, were the first direct negotiations and represented a major breakthrough. Once again Pik Botha was encouraging; the new talks, he said, were urgently needed to clear up problems which still impeded an internationally accepted solution.

The long-awaited Western proposals finally surfaced in October 1981. A cluster of constitutional guarantees foreshadowed the principle of a minimum two-thirds vote for the adoption of a constitution by the Constituent Assembly, the establishment of an independent judiciary and a Bill of Rights affording protection to personal liberties and the multi-party system. Property would be protected against seizure without just compensation. All private cultural, social, health and educational institutions were to be open to all races.

UNTAG's composition and the impartiality issue remained unresolved items on the negotiators' agenda.

The endless dialogue went on. The DTA complained that no guarantees had been offered to ensure that the constitutional principles would be enforced; the NP, AKTUR and the HNP rejected elections based on universal suffrage. The Contact Group explained that the constitutional principles were merely guidelines. These guidelines, retorted the DTA, were a waste of time without guarantees of UN impartiality.

The new constitutional package did not resolve the deadlock.

South Africa's doors remained 'open' for further negotiation.

44

The Stench of War

Alive to the fragility of Namibia's new constitutional structures the Government increased its efforts to weaken SWAPO's organisation inside Namibia. By the time the National Assembly was formed most of SWAPO's top officials, with the exception of National Vice-Chairman Dan Tjongarero, were locked up under Proclamation AG9 or AG26. Threats of death abounded. Tjongarero, concerned for the safety of SWAPO workers, closed down their offices in Windhoek.[1] (SWAPO leaders suspected that the Security Police left him at large in order to create suspicion against him.) The internal leadership remained in detention for the greater part of 1979. In August more than seventy detainees went on a hunger strike by way of protest against their continued imprisonment. Pastor Witbooi, Axel Johannes and Tlhabanello were also caught in the swoops. Though the offices remained shut, SWAPO survived without its executive;[2] on May 6th 1979 it in fact held its largest political rally ever. (For his pains Tjongarero was relieved of his duties by Administrative Secretary Moses Garoeb in Lusaka in September 1979 on the ground that his closure of headquarters had been unconstitutional.[3])

A medley of individuals from all walks of life were taken in periodic waves of arrests which succeeded the establishment of the National Assembly. Included were Pastors of the Lutheran and Anglican Churches, nurses, teaches and businessmen.[4] Reverend Philip Shilongo of the Anglican Church's St. Mary's Mission was held under AG9 and then released by the police with the official comment – calculated to create suspicion – that he had 'responded to questioning'. ELC's Chief Editor, Philip Tjerije, was held incommunicado for 296 days then released without charge.[5] Doctor Naftali Hamhata, the head of the Lutheran Medical Mission in Ovamboland, was kept in solitary confinement for two months; he was allowed no change of clothes; there was no running water and he was fed on dry porridge.[6] Liberation from detention was for many SWAPO detainees a bitter beginning of a different experience. They were released subject to conditions restricting them to their homes except during working hours. Henceforth they had to live without visitors, remain at their homes at night and during the weekends, and keep away from gatherings and political activity. The word 'banned' was nowhere used, but the restrictions were identical to those used to throttle political opposition in the Republic. Many SWAPO officials found increasing difficulty in maintaining or finding jobs. Arthur Pickering, formerly of the Windhoek Bar, lost his job at the Rossing Uranium Mine after his arrest. The restriction orders isolated SWAPO officials and militants, whose overt activity was otherwise allowed by law. It was evident that the Government, without banning SWAPO, sought the same effect by subjecting supporters to the threat of unremitting arrest, solitary confinement and suffocating restriction orders. The punitive element was not hidden. The Prime Minister said that SWAPO could not have the best of both worlds, whilst Steyn, during his period of office, explained that some had been arrested because they had failed to 'mend their ways.'

In the state of prolonged semi-siege SWAPO held sporadic meetings with varying success and suffered periodic incursions from police or DTA quarters. A mass meeting of more than 4,000 people gathered to celebrate SWAPO's Namibia Day celebration, bridled, but kept calm in the face of DTA provocation. DTA supporters on a truck equipped with loud-hailers let loose with anti-SWAPO slogans in an attempt to drown the speeches. Equally serious were the DTA's attempts to arouse inter-ethnic animosity – Hereros at the meeting were told to leave immediately whilst one of the occupants of the truck threw stones at the crowd.[7] This took place in the presence of the police who later, using riot vehicles and thunder flashes, broke up a march of 4,000 supporters.[8]

In the courts SWAPO accused were sentenced with severity. In the regional courts 13 years were imposed for inciting others to go for military training. Pastor Imeni was jailed for five years for aiding insurgents. A sentence of seven years imprisonment was imposed on a woman for a speech at Luderitz which encouraged aid for insurgents. A shopkeeper who handed over provisions at gunpoint was sentenced to eight years in Windhoek. (The Appellate Division found that he had acted under compulsion and set aside the conviction.) A semi-literate Black farm worker was sentenced to death by Judge Strydom for helping armed insurgents who had called at the farm. (The Appellate Division converted this sentence on appeal to 18 years imprisonment.) A White accused, Louis Nagel, who shot and killed a waiter in a Windhoek street for calling him a 'Boer', was found guilty of culpable homicide. His effective sentence was three years' imprisonment.[9]

Clearly a disabled and discredited SWAPO would allow Mudge broader freedom to negotiate with and win over the centrist parties, in the hope of lending colour to the DTA's wasting legitimacy. To attract them Mudge depicted a 'government of national unity' and attempted to lure the centrist parties by the offer of seats in the National Assembly. He was not successful. A link-up with the DTA was an unacceptable compromise for the NNF, SWANU, Shipanga, the Federal Party and the NIP. There had been high hopes that SWAPO-D under Shipanga's leadership would take the initiative, seize the leadership of the struggle, gain mass support tor the National

Assembly and so certify its legitimacy. But SWAPO-D, despite generous infusions of money from major companies, showed no sign of vitality and won little support. Patterns of new constitutional alignment are more likely to embrace SWAPO. Whatever their formal structures the Namas under Hendrik Witbooi, together with a minority section of the Hereros led by the Society for the Preservation of the Royal House of Tjamuaha/Maherero under the leadership of Reverend Bartholomew Karuaera, SWANU and the Damara Council are more likely to join with SWAPO. In the prediction of experts SWAPO would win an internationally supervised election.[10] The realisation that no peace is viable unless the guerrillas are part of the solution would, as it did in Zimbabwe, strongly influence the electorate. (Support for this prediction has emerged from an unexpected source – ex-BOSS agent Ivan Himmelhoch who reported that it is BOSS's assessment that SWAPO would have an 83% win.[11])

There is other evidence to support this prognostication.

The mainsprings of Namibian history remain shrouded in their own unfathomable mystery. The widening swathe of suffering cut across the Territory by the official campaigns of violence, prosecution, imprisonment and restriction, has had the curious effect of doing more to invigorate the spirit of resistance than to destroy it.[12] With the spreading stench of war over Namibia, the calamities of death, injury or prosecution have become, in the eyes of many Black Namibians, incontravertible testimonials of honour. A team of British churchmen who visited the Territory in 1981 found that the security forces' practice of dragging the bodies of guerrillas through villages behind their vehicles was a totally counter-productive desecration of the dead. The photographs of mauled dead SWAPO warriors, their armaments and their obliterated bases have served to inspire solidarity with the dead – and the dead were generally young. The sense of identification amongst schoolchildren ran deeply; at Keetmanshoop 134 children were expelled from their school after their participation in a procession and a memorial service to those slain at Kassinga. A churchman on a visit to Namibia tested the clenched fist salute on a group of young children; clusters of raised fists answered with a single reflex. As for the anti-SWAPO propaganda, it emanates from newspapers and radios from the other side of the racial divide, its credibility poisoned at source.

Throughout Namibia the very presence of South African forces, whether in Ovamboland or Windhoek or on the rooftops of dormant villages, has hardened the belief that the South Africans are faced with a growing invisible challenge. The SADF's refusal to publish casualty statistics reinforced the belief that South African propaganda is to be disbelieved and that SWAPO bullets take a heavy toll. Throughout Namibia the sentiment is rightly or wrongly cherished that guerrillas are in charge of enclaves within the operational areas, that those enclaves are spreading remorselessly and that the ultimate future remains with the *domomofitu*.

45

Towards the Apocalyptic Siege

In the ranks of South Africa's White population the war has figured as a proxy struggle for South Africa's survival. From the time of the Angolan débâcle of 1976 South African propaganda has sedulously prepared soldiers and citizens for the apocalyptic siege; South Africa now had to brace itself for the new total strategy, withdraw intellectually and emotionally into the atavistic laager and grapple with its own resources in order to survive in a climate of military, political and psychological threat. The army's propaganda releases contrasted their soldiers' simple heroism with the wanton cruelty of guerrilla cowards. South Africa's generals have also busied themselves with the shaping of this propaganda and taken it upon themselves to share the 'lessons' of the war – that SWAPO is a purely Ovambo organisation, unwilling to share power and serving as willing bondsmen of Soviet imperialism. Regular releases of SWAPO 'kills' have become a caressing accompaniment to the theme of South Africa's invincibility. In 1978 the annual kill was put at 97; the toll for 1980 rose to 1500. Beyond the statistics no details were supplied, never the names of the dead, nor a reference to the village or area of action – merely the cryptic allusion to the 'operational area'. South African journalists drew the appropriate conclusion and predicted the extinction of the SWAPO guerrilla.

The stubborn facts would suggest otherwise.

An examination of SWAPO's strikes, as reflected in the South African press, itself provides a sobering insight into the depth and range of SWAPO's southern penetration. By the middle of 1979 large groups of insurgents had started to operate in the vicinity of Grootfontein. By 1981 an alarming abandonment of farms in the Outjo district, a front line area, had taken place. One third of the farms in the district had become unoccupied,[1] and the town of Kamanjab had approached the Administration to buy up the entire town as it 'could no longer go on.'[2] Road and rail links north of Otjiwarongo were increasingly cut, while chronic sabotage to power lines from Ruacana compelled the Administration to forge a costly link with the Cape grid. Road travel north of Otjiwarongo became dangerous, necessitating the organisation of convoys under armed escort. The redeployment of

PLAN forces on the eastern flank of the Etosha Pan became a perilous strategic threat to road transport to Ovamboland, Okavango and the Caprivi strip. The 'triangle of death' (Otavi Grootfontein Tsumeb) embraces a significant number of mines and ranches. Though attacks were scattered SWAPO's presence became more tangible. This syndrome was a distinct revival of early symptoms in Mozambique and Zimbabwe.

On the border with Angola, guerrilla mobility and infiltration remained unfettered, hundreds of students were escorted across the frontier each year and members of SWAPO's external executive have visited Ovamboland on occasions. Significant parts of Ovamboland are effectively controlled by SWAPO whose guerrillas move around with impunity in the daytime. There have been reports of executions of informers carried out in daytime, the seizure and interrogation of a businessman who was released unharmed after two days, and incidents which have taken place within a few hundred yards of army bases and administrative areas suggesting that the battle for 'hearts and minds' is far from being won.[3] Official attempts to protect chiefs and cabinet ministers have not always been successful. Ministers are obliged to live in forlorn little compounds surrounded by fences and sentries. (Army officials have described their morale as 'wobbly'; they were even reluctant to travel in army mine-protected vehicles.[4]) Attacks on policemen and soldiers include the following: five policemen, seconded to protect a senior headman, machine-gunned; a South African police base at Ongandjera attacked with mortar bombs and RPG rockets, killing two soldiers and injuring others; in January 1981 a bridge between Oshakati and a SAAF airfield blown up; the following month a rocket attack carried out with 120mm calibre rocket launchers – the launching apparatus alone requires seven men to lug it into position – unleashed onto the administrative centre at Oshakati. Seven rockets landed, one of them on the old post office; the next month insurgents operating half way between Ondongwa and Oshakati attacked a unit of the police force. In 1981 more mines were laid, and more telephone poles, water pipes and bridges blown up than the year before.

According to General Geldenhuys between 8,000 and 10,000 SWAPO recruits were under training in 1980. Asked at a press interview about the 'depressing' picture of PLAN successes told to journalists by the 'troopees' he replied that individual soldiers lacked a precise understanding of what was happening in the field. He also thought that the number of accidents in the SADF – accidents accounted for a large number of fatalities – was not disproportionately high.[5]

With an enemy supposedly on the verge of extinction, the SADF nonetheless took the precaution of augmenting its military might in Namibia. In mid-1981 860 hectares of land were acquired from the Windhoek City Council to construct a huge base linked by rail to the capital.[6] The overall impression is one of increasing army activity, of increasing numbers of new military vehicles heading northwards. Roads in Ovamboland are heavily tarred to discourage the planting of landmines. Army bases have been constructed near most Namibian towns. Oshakati's Black township is surrounded by high wire with watch towers and machine guns. No movement is allowed after 6 pm. South African soldiers are not seen on the back roads used by the locals and SWAPO.[7] (On the reports of churchmen, the South Africans mine the back roads so that civilian casualties can be attributed to SWAPO.) A prevalent complaint from army commanders – not involved in propaganda exercises – is that the 'locals' do not usually give information on the enemy,[8] and that the enemy is 'getting to the people'. A letter to the *Windhoek Observer* corroborating the dire descriptions of churchmen, had the following to say: 'Today's stories from the north are incredible. They tell of villagers being rounded up and men and women of all ages made to lie on their stomachs in long queues for hours and innocent people being beaten up mercilessly and houses burnt to ashes'.[9] Army contact with insurgents lead less to follow up operations than to reprisals on the civilian population. The pattern of SADF reprisal in the north has included the destruction of houses and agricultural land, designed to force peasants to give up their land and move near to South African army bases.[10] In the words of Pastor Albertus Maasdorp, the then General Secretary of the Council of Churches in Namibia, 'the SADF is not protecting us. It is causing great suffering to the Namibian people. Just recently we heard of a co-worker in our church whose house was burnt by the SADF. I have seen it myself . . . '[11]

The little publicised disappearance of PLAN prisoners of war has become an enveloping source of anguish. From time to time segmental evidence has emerged of the liquidation of SWAPO detainees after interrogation; shallow graves have been uncovered; many have disappeared after arrest by the Security Forces.

In the aftermath of the Kassinga raid in May 1978 the army detained more than 100 captured SWAPO prisoners – the majority were young girls – at a prison camp near Mariental south of Windhoek. Though the camp was in fact visible from a public road, the authorities denied this detention until early 1981. The official admission was then made that the army was holding 117 members of SWAPO captured in the raid. The Churches agitated for the release of prisoners' names to put an end to the agony of uncertainty for those families whose children were thought missing or dead. Prisoner of war status in terms of the Geneva Convention was not accorded – this would have compelled the release of the names. (To this day it is unknown whether Nashilongo Taaipopi, former leader of the SYL, is alive or not. His body was not found at Kassinga.) Fears for their safety arose after the release of 63 other prisoners shortly after their return from Kassinga. Interviewed by Reverend Heinz Hunke, many accused the Security Forces of brutality;[12] they had been shocked with electricity and beaten and kicked on their 'kidneys and genitals and/or other parts of the body'.[13] But the enigma of Mariental prompts other disquieting questions. Mariental inmates are the outcome of a single raid. If, from the totality of army and police action in 1980, 1500 SWAPO fighters were killed, how many were taken prisoner? In ordinary combat the captured prisoners usually outnumber the enemy's dead. It was within five months of the Kassinga episode that reports on Mariental reached churchmen. As we have seen, the authorities in later years, by their admissions, confirmed these reports of the camp and its inmates.[14] For Namibia the contemporary agony is the prevailing silence, the absence of reports or even rumours of other such camps or prisons. In a country so sparsely populated concentration camps and prisoners of war camps cannot be hidden indefinitely. Information releases from the SADF only aggravate the fear; no reference to captured SWAPO prisoners was made until September 1981, and then only after an official of the Red Cross had commented on the curious absence of prisoners of war. Then on 11th September the Minister of Police announced that 23 SWAPO prisoners had been taken between July and September; an army release referred to the capture of 85 members of SWAPO.

Death has come to stalk Namibia in multiple forms. The phenomenon of the pro-governmental death squad – in the central and southern American republics it has become a major instrument of terror – has reared its head in Namibia. Rumours relating to certain members of a special police operations K-unit, code-named Koevoet (crowbar), have been rife. A three-page death list including businessmen, pastors, evangelists, and professional men appeared early in 1978. Koevoet members came into public focus after attacks were made on wealthy Black Namibian businessmen who had reportedly passed on large sums to SWAPO. David Sheehama, reputedly a millionaire who owned a supermarket, a general wholesale and other businesses, was ordered by a death squad made up of White and Black attackers to lie on the floor prone before being shot in the head. (On a previous occasion, after his home had been bombed, Sheehama spoke up and said that the bombers' footprints were those of soldiers.) In September 1981 a posse of Black and White soldiers, dressed as SWAPO guerrillas, executed Ovambo businessman Israel Jona's security guard after ordering him to lie on his stomach in the veld.[15] After the seizure and disappearance of her husband Rachel Nakaua brought a fruitless court application against the SADF.[16] With the arrival of the Ondjambas (elephants), army mine-proof trucks, men armed with South African army rifles broke down the door and removed her husband who was never seen again. The police and the army denied responsibility for his arrest. Rauaha Ashipembe was held for 30 days after enquiring at army and police headquarters at Oshivello into the disappearance of her husband.[17] During her imprisonment no questions were put to her and no explanation was given for her detention. (Her husband's truck had also disappeared without trace.) After the slaying of Thomas Philippus, one of the wealthiest businessmen in Ovamboland, his two daughters were killed by a parcel bomb filled with 3 kilograms of high explosives.[18] According to SWAPO reports a mass grave had been discovered at Okatope to which 'truckloads' of corpses had been taken. Was it Koevoet members or soldiers who, with the dexterity of professional demolition experts, blew up the Lutheran Printing Plant in November 1980 – and before then in 1973? Prior to the explosion, a movement of military vehicles and unidentified armed men, operating under cover of curfew, were seen near the plant. After the explosion the police were informed at 1.30 am – they arrived at 10 am. Was it Koevoet members who systematically destroyed St. Mary's Mission in June 1981? Once again a squad boldly appeared in vehicles during the curfew, made no attempt to conceal their preparations and proceeded to demolish the entire seminary, the chapel, the classrooms, dormitory and library. A flare commonly used by the SADF was picked up at the devastated site afterwards. On this occasion the police arrived five hours after a report had been lodged.[19]

On numerous occasions Anglican and Lutheran services were broken up by military action, congregants were ordered to leave the church premises and made to identify themselves. There were often arrests. Church leaders received daily reports of members murdered by the soldiery. Numbers of churchmen died in ambushes and land-mine incidents. The dignity of office provided no deterent. Bishop Kleopas Dumeni's wife was compelled by the soldiery to dig a latrine and use it in the presence of gun toting servicemen. Bishop James Kauluma, consecrated Bishop Suffragen of the Anglican Church in 1978, was stopped and searched by soldiers during a visit to the north. During questioning they 'poked their guns in my mouth' he reported.

The SADF's embroilment in a widening process of counter-insurgency has been associated with a diligent development and refinement of its equipment and techniques. After South Africa's hasty withdrawal from Angola in 1976 the SADF developed its own rocketry and weapons and evolved a new breed of panzer vehicles better adapted to the southern African terrain.[20] From SADF research arose the new R4 rifle, new communications equipment, and mineproof armoured personnel carriers including the Ratel, the Casspir, and the Buffel. In 1981 Armscor's turnover was more than one billion rand.[21] Embargoed war material was procured;[22] hand guns – presumably intended for South Africa–backed insurgents in Mozambique and UNITA – were imported, in breach of UN sanctions, through Danish and West German shipping companies. The weaponry included American and Eastern Bloc manufactured assault rifles, grenades, rockets and anti-tank mines. Through corporations in Canada and the US the components of a highly sophisticated 155mm NATO cannon were smuggled into the Republic.[23]

The SADF has also absorbed into its battalions former Rhodesian Selous scouts, veterans from the civil war in Zimbabwe, and mercenaries. Advertisements published abroad have invited mercenaries to join in the action in Namibia: a R2,000 prize per insurgent's head was one of the incentives put out.[24] South Africa's 32nd battalion comprises 9,000 troops made up of black refugees from Angola and white mercenaries. Detachments of this battalion, equipped with East European weaponry and unmarked uniforms, have carried out prolonged missions into southern Angola. The men are equipped with boots which are not regular South African Army issue; the Whites blacken their faces before going into action.[25] These detachments have been used in the process of depopulating SWAPO's sanctuaries; according to reports, their instructions were to destroy public buildings, schools and hospitals and wipe out civilians in designated areas.[26] In an interview with the BBC, former Lance Corporal Trevor Edwards said, 'Our main job was to take an area and to clear it. We killed everything . . . we killed cattle, we killed goats and we killed people. Half the time the civilians don't know what is going on.'[27] Corroboration for his narration of atrocities has been provided by other witnesses. Captain Belmundo, a mercenary captured during action in Angola, testified before an international commission of inquiry chaired by Nobel Prize-winner Sean MacBride. 'We had precise instructions' said Belmundo 'to destroy schools, hospitals and houses and to wipe out the civilian population and its cattle.'[28]

Even so the fortunes of war did not change. The army's intensified efforts failed to push back the guerrillas. While the 'kill' statistics would suggest unacceptably cruel losses, South Africa's figures for slaughtered guerrillas are inextricably confused with the victims of wild reprisals. But whatever the losses might have been South Africa's military might has been unable to staunch the persistent infiltration of groups who sleep in dugouts in the bush or merge with the village populations wearing civilian clothing by day, politicising and organising their fellow countrymen by night. South Africa's generals have recognised that they are not winning the hearts and minds of the Namibian people and that there can be no military solution. The recognition that South Africa's military juggernaut is at grips with unconquerable elements was spelled out by Major General Charles Lloyd in a BBC interview in March 1981: 'We can actually destroy our military enemy. But this is not to say that we will destroy SWAPO. SWAPO is a political thing as well that is in the minds of the people. Bullets kill bodies not minds . . . '

Powerless to grasp and break its elusive enemy in Namibia the SADF chose to counter-attack with military strikes on SWAPO bases in southern Angola. Since the massacre at Kassinga, however, SWAPO has moved over to a loose deployment of its forces. Its camps, stripped of permanent buildings, were no longer easily detectable under aerial reconnaissance. Detachments of men were spread over wide areas without protective but tell-tale trenches and fortifications, while bunkers were built underground with access only through small concealed openings. Continued raids inflicted severe damage on SWAPO bases, but the organisation's momentum and its capacity to regroup and carry on seemed unaffected, despite the length and tenuousness of the supply lines from Luanda, in drought-ridden provinces which were themselves threatened with famine. It was this resilience on the part of SWAPO fighters which prompted the South Africans to readjust their strategy in southern Angola. The pattern of lightning sorties gave way to periodic invasions with deep thrusts to the north. In the latter half of 1980, during Operation 'Smokeshell', the attack, spread out over hundreds of square miles, led to the death of over 400 persons and the destruction of numerous SWAPO bases. South Africa simultaneously occupied Huila Province and a number of towns including Katomba, Kuomato and Naulilia, and clashed with detachments of the Angolan army (FAPLA).[29] The SADF afterwards returned with 350 tons of equipment, weaponry, heat-seeking missiles, trucks and armoured personnel carriers.[30]

In July 1981 South African soldiers backed by jets and helicopters launched a further invasion, involving one infantry brigade and three battalions. Numbers of towns including Evalo, Ndova and Chana were occupied; the village of Mutaco was destroyed. South Africa's new strategy, said General Lloyd, was to destroy the wasps' nest rather than the individual wasps. In the words of the SABC, the army's cardinal aim was the 'total destruction of SWAPO's military strength'. In August the South Africans met international criticism with a claim that they were pulling out. They were in fact preparing a renewed offensive. In September the provincial capital Ngiva was reoccupied together with Xangongo, Cahama and Mongua. An estimated force of 9,000 troops transported in Ratels – 16 ton, three-axle driven armed troop carriers – attacked in tightly coordinated land and air strikes. After the operation, code-named 'Protea', the South Africans claimed that a thousand Angolans and SWAPO personnel had been killed.

The prime targets for destruction in Southern Angola were bridges, hospitals, factories, schools, public buildings and transport. The calamitous consequences of invasion were inevitably to drive away the populations from the southern provinces by terror and starvation. In regions already beset by famine South African troops carried out systematic pillaging operations in livestock, tractors, bulldozers and vehicles.[31] High quality timber was loaded onto trucks and removed to Johannesburg;[32] animals which could not be transported were destroyed. Former US Attorney-General Ramsay Clark found a prevailing atmosphere akin to a 'state of war'; there were networks of trenches and bunkers and reports of daily attacks by South African soldiers and aircraft, with a pattern of helicopter assaults carried out under cover of heavy fire. During his visit, a car in the vicinity was fired upon – the occupants were seven nuns. In the fields he saw dozens of carcasses of cattle. There was, he observed, a method in the madness: to stampede the populations from the southern provinces. The roads from Angola to Ngiva have been described by visiting foreign journalists as resembling a scene from a war movie, with refugees and vehicles been harried by ambushes and constant air attacks, in an atmosphere of undeclared war.[33] In October 1981 a British international law expert, Reg Austin, found that the South Africans had come to stay; through its continuous aerial presence the South African air force assumed authority over huge areas in the southern provinces where those who remained behind lived in 'constant terror'. Ordinary civilian traffic was regularly subjected to attack though less often if vehicles displayed a white flag. The constant danger hindered travel south of Lubango, situated 200 kilometres north of the Namibian border. At Cahama only 10% of the buildings in the main street remained intact; the hospital, the dispensary and a food distribution centre had been destroyed. Between those homes that had survived bombardment residents had dug slit trenches to serve as air raid shelters. At Chiulo, two Catholic mission workers reported the attack on a bus by two South African aircraft, at the moment of its emergence from the Chiulo Hospital, killing two passengers and wounding twenty seven others.[34]

According to the Angolan Government the South African Army became more aggressive and 'arrogant' since the advent of the Reagan Administration. Angola accused South Africa of deploying 45,000 troops in Operation 'Protea'.[35] If this is true the South Africans resorted to a monumental 'overkill', carried out in the hope of deterring Angola from providing SWAPO with a sanctuary. The attacks made serious inroads into Angola's economic infrastructure necessitating the diversion of more than 50% of Angola's budget to defence. The devastation in the southern provinces led to acute famine and major population upheavals; emergency food supplies were required for the Kunene, Huila and Cuando Cabango provinces. A UN mission to Angola estimated that 130,000 persons became homeless refugees as a result of South African attacks in 1981.[36] Since 1975 more than 600,000 people became dependent refugees as a sequel to South African and UNITA military activity and drought.[37]

It is not without reason that Namibia, the cockpit of struggle between the UN and South Africa, has been described as Africa's hinge of fate. Now the unendurable flames of warfare have spread from Namibia to southern Angola. Where will Africa burn next?

46

Postscript – Machtpolitik and all that

Since the completion of the manuscript in March 1982, significant changes have taken place in Namibia and Angola. Above all the shifts in the military and socio-economic situation in southern Africa feature prominently as a guide to the future evolution of events.

In the aftermath of Operation Protea – the invasion of southern Angola in August 1981 – the SADF remained in effective control of extensive areas of southern Angola. Over 5000 soldiers were – according to the Angolans – stationed on Angolan soil, their battalions established in Kunene Province, and in the areas of Ngiva, Xangongo, Evale, Kuamato and Mupa. From that time onwards, the army carried out periodic thrusts deeper into Angola. In Operation Daisy, in December 1981, an army attack upon Chitequeta, 250 kilometres north of the border, 71 guerrillas were killed.

In July and August of 1982 major attacks were directed against the towns Cahama and Tchimbemba which were bombarded from the air. This time South Africa's official assessment of SWAPO losses was put at 345 dead. Later in November 1982, two vital bridges across the Giraul River near to Namibe (formerly Mocamedes) were blown up by South African commando units. South African statistics for 1982 put SWAPO losses at 1268 against the death of 77 South African soldiers. (The figure of 77 seemed curiously low in comparison with 259 other soldiers who died – in the words of General Malan – as a result of accidents not associated with 'enemy action'.[1])

Military activity continued into 1983; in Operation Askari, launched in December of that year, South Africa claimed 500 SWAPO and FAPLA deaths with the loss of 21 of their own men. This attack, carried out at the time when South Africa was offering a ceasefire, was recounted by some South African newspapers in a glow of triumphant chauvinism with much emphasis on the war booty, the great quantities of Soviet made tanks, missiles and weaponry seized in a conflict which was described as a 'pitting of Russian against South African military commanders'.[2]

The succession of incursions, carried out in concert with UNITA forces, increasingly took their toll. Faced with overwhelming fire power and air superiority. Angola's strategy was to withdraw its troops as far as possible without exposing centres of strategic importance such as Lubango. South Africa, said General Magnus Malan, was geared to take drastic measures against neighbouring states harbouring guerrilla movements. His message, we shall see, was not lost on the Angolans. At what point would Angola reach breaking point and accept South Africa's offer for a 'ceasefire' – a diplomatic euphemism for submission to South Africa's demands that SWAPO activity be curbed?

The hurt inflicted upon Angola's socio-economic structures was painfully evident. By the end of 1982, Angola assessed the total damage caused by South African attacks, in the region of US$10 billion. The economy was in a dismal state. Southern regions were in ruin with a central government able neither to maintain administration nor generate social and economic reconstruction. Precious hard currency earned through the exportation of oil from the Cabinda enclave was steadily drained in payment for supplies and weaponry and the maintenance of Cuban troops and Eastern Bloc advisers.

While havoc spread in southern Angola, what was the effect of the mauling endured by SWAPO? South African spokesmen claimed that SWAPO lost 20% of its fighting force in 1982 and that their supply lines were destroyed in a way that the American B52 bombers never managed against the Vietcong, with SWAPO bases along the length of the operational front shattered and many of its veteran officers lost. Perhaps. But the facts are not easily reconcilable with repeated SADF claims to have delivered decisive blows against SWAPO's war effort. In northern Namibia SWAPO's political influence did not weaken. In spite of South Africa's repeated onslaughts SWAPO mounted 'Operation Volcano', their biggest offensive in the sixteen year war, in March 1983, and infiltrated – according to the Administrator General – over 600 men across Kaokoland, Ovamboland and Western Kavango, with penetration as far south as the Tsumeb-Grootfontein triangle.[3] Infiltrators blew up the Oshakati post office and a service station; a major bridge near to Oshakati was sabotaged and eight members of the Ovambo Special Constabulary and two soldiers guarding a farm in the Tsumeb district were killed. Motorists using the Great North Road to Ondongua were requested to make use of the regular convoy system escorted by armoured troop carriers. Over one hundred recruits were escorted back into Angola. By September 1983, 800 insurgents were reportedly operating permanently in the Kavango and Ovambo war zones.[4] Farmers in the Tsumeb district continued to pull out; in one sector, the population of farmers dropped from 57 to 4. Those who remained were under persistent strain and kept radio contact with defence headquarters. At the end of 1984 SWATF claimed the virtual elimination of all SWAPO guerillas in the war zone.[5] This claim did not, however, square with a number of facts: on the admission of SWATF itself, SWAPO's acts of sabotage – overt actions which are not easily concealed from the public – had doubled in 1984 compared with 1983; in October 1984 the introduction of compulsory military service for all males between the ages of seventeen and fifty-five was announced; in Kavango the curfew was re-introduced; early in 1985 the entry of civilians into Ovamboland, Kavango and other areas without police permission was prohibited on the ground that their safety could not be guaranteed; in 1984 a new "crack unit" of SWATF was formed in order to meet SWAPO penetration in white farming areas; in January 1985, South Africa complained that SWAPO activity had not declined since the signing of the Lusaka agreement.[6]

The scale of SWAPO's 1983 offensive produced a measure of panic in the north. The SADF responded with a fierce censorship on all reports of SWAPO activities, other than those authorised by military censors.[7] The stubbornly critical *Windhoek Observer* went to press with blank spaces where censored articles had to be struck out; its offices were raided, its reporters searched and photographs and material were confiscated. A number of issues were later banned and in December 1984, Gwen Lister, its defiant political editor, was prosecuted, in the event unsuccessfully, in terms of the Official Secrets Act. In South Africa, official steps were taken against newspapers after publication of Archbishop Hurley's broad condemnations of SADF and police malpractices in the operational areas.

Prior to 1980, Kaokoland and Kavango were both substantially free of guerrilla activities, but during 1982 it had become all too evident to the South African security forces that all was not well in these areas and that, despite the acclaimed mastery of the SADF, SWAPO's clout in the north was increasing. In December 1981, a dusk to dawn curfew was imposed on western Kavango; in May 1982, South African soldiers and a police station were attacked at Nkurenkuru; policemen and soldiers travelling westwards from Rundu, the Kavango capital, did so only in armoured vehicles.[8] As the tension tightened in Kavango, members of the DTA drew up an elimination list and called for the summary shooting of SWAPO sympathisers. Waves of detentions solved nothing, whilst the spectrum of those detained – government officials, accountants, school teachers and priests, businessmen and farmers – was yet further evidence of SWAPO's underlying support.

Now it was the turn of travellers from Grootfontein to Rundu to make their way in escorted convoys. Towards the end of 1983, a vast defoliation project, designed to strip all vegetation along the highway to Rundu, was announced. Yet another counter-insurgency measure was the large scale uprooting of Kavango inhabitants – thousands were involved according to Hans Rohr, the leader of the NCDP – and their forcible resettlement along the Kavango River close to SADF bases. In court hearings at Rundu, police witnesses spoke of the unco-operative attitude of the local population. As far as the police were concerned, the entire western Kavango was politically speaking 'rotten'.[9]

In Kaokoland, the modest administrative capital Opuwo became transformed into an armed camp surrounded with barbed wire and protected throughout by uniformed men carrying assault rifles. The presence of a very large number of panzer vehicles, policemen and soldiers implied the invisible, unacknowledged, proliferation of SWAPO maquisards. A new airstrip designed to accommodate heavy aircraft was built near the town. According to the Chief of Police insurgents were at one stage so active, holding meetings and distributing leaflets with a network of helpers, that it was near to impossible to cope with the situation.[10]

The guerrillas it seemed, often fought and lived with much impunity. Pupils and their teachers have been repeatedly 'abducted' in broad daylight from their schools; the abductions were often reported to the authorities only days after the event.[11] Policemen have testified that SWAPO insurgents at one time acted freely in Kaokoland as if there was 'no security force in the area'. According to Hans Rohr, guerrillas walked around in Kavango in uniform in broad daylight, enjoying the assistance of the inhabitants. Leaflets directed at soldiers were distributed in Ovamboland 'under the noses' of the security forces.[12] Armed in the early days mainly with handguns, guerrillas were now in possession of anti-aircraft weapons, rockets, bazookas and mortars. SWAPO uniforms were customarily worn though, not infrequently, the fighters donned civilian garb and travelled freely, sometimes taking advantage of the accommodation offered by municipal hostels.

In the south, on the other hand, the officially legal 'Internal Wing' of SWAPO tried to avoid confrontation. The provisions of new security legislation in the form of AG22 of 1981 effectively silenced SWAPO's overt voice. No public meetings could be held without prior notice being given to a Magistrate who could then call upon the meeting's organisers to state whether or not they favoured the overthrow of present authority by means of force. The trouncing of a SWAPO demonstration with pick-axe handles and batons at the time of the UN Secretary General's visit in August 1983 added to the discouragement. But SWAPO nevertheless managed to carry on. In 1983 Dan Tjongeroro was re-elected as Deputy Chairman. David Meroro was elected the Chairman of SWAPO both in and outside of Namibia; the Reverend Witbooi was appointed Vice President. Spokesmen inside Namibia and overseas pursued SWAPO's conciliatory theme: there was room for private enterprise; Mugabe's conciliatory example would be followed; SWAPO was committed to racial conciliation and economic pragmatism. Released prematurely in March 1984, Ja Toivo returned to the struggle with unabated eagerness.

The years of battering and vilification had not destroyed the movement. Impartial observers – according to the South African press – agreed that SWAPO would, in a nationwide election, win 75% to 80% of the votes.[13]

As for SADF and police activity in the north, an analysis would suggest the development of new patterns of organisation: Koevoet, it would seem, has been allotted the primary responsibility for counter-insurgency whilst the SADF directs its energy towards securing a buffer zone in southern

Angola, in particular in the Cuando-Cubango and Kunene provinces.[14] The activities of Koevoet have increased considerably over the last two years and their numbers have been swelled by new adherents. A disturbing new feature of police activity is the unashamed, unconcealed, deployment of brutality against suspects. Sensing some immunity from official retribution, certain Koevoet members, often acting in large squads, have openly hunted and beaten suspects to death in the presence of members of the public. Some episodes have given rise to Court cases where the murderous quality of their techniques and training have come into public focus. A striking example relates to the arrest and assault upon Kaduma Katanga, a farmer in the Kavango operational area, in November 1982. In a search for other suspects, Katanga was compelled to run from house to house followed by a squad of Koevoet members in their Casspir vehicles and beaten with an ox-yoke in public until he lost consciousness.[15] One year later, in the trial of two Koevoet policemen, a magistrate found that other unspecified members of Koevoet had killed Katanga. (The Court expressed its awareness of the difficulties encountered in the field by the police; here they had acted over-enthusiastically and the two accused – against whom the prosecution was able only to muster evidence of a blow and a slap – were collectively fined R.90) The death of a school principal, Jona Hamukwaya, also aroused widespread concern. Arrested by a convoy of Koevoet vehicles, he was taken to a river and beaten to death. Persons in the vicinity, including Hamukwaya's wife who was fetching water, heard the blows and his screams which slowly grew quieter and then stopped. 'All teachers are SWAPO' his attackers shouted. Their accusation: he had given food to SWAPO guerrillas.

The overt savagery in this and other instances elicited protest from unexpected quarters: the local chief spoke out in spite of warnings from the security forces to keep silent; Rudolf Ngondo, a former member of the Minister's Council said that Hamukwaya and Katanga had been killed off 'like snakes being crushed with sticks'.[16] In its memorandum to the Van Dyk Commission, appointed to probe Namibian security legislation, the Namibian Bar Council submitted that there were too many unsolved disappearances and too few political detainees who were brought to trial. The Council had many concerns: deaths in detention, malicious destruction of private property and the abuse of power. The rule of law was in jeopardy and legislative amendments to do away with the wide immunity granted to members of the defence force in terms of the Defence Act of 1959 were needed. After the disappearance of Johannes Kakuva from the Opuwo Police station, proceedings were opened by his widow against the Minister for Police in the Supreme Court. At the conclusion of a prolonged investigation into security police methods of interrogation Judge Mouton found that detainees had been treated with systematic brutality. Suspects had been detained in a gas cylinder cubicle – some for as long as six days – and thrashed with considerable violence.[17] Witnesses were able to demonstrate 'tram-line scars' on their bodies. After a beating, one witness, a sixty-nine year old herdsman, suffered temporary insanity and urinated involuntarily in his cell. In November 1983, an urgent application was brought by Sabine Nestor to protect her husband who had been arrested. Affidavits disclosed the existence of a secret interrogation camp in the Namibian countryside where detainees were caned, beaten on the soles of their feet and subjected to electric shock. According to the allegations – all of which were denied by the police – interrogation was compounded with obscenity and sadism. One detainee said that a fluid which smelt of spirits was poured into his anus. The full Court, led by the newly appointed Judge President, Hans Berker, analysed the issues with painstaking care and – for human rights lawyers – a refreshing anxiety for the fate of detainees held incommunicado under AG9.[18] In April 1984, the Minister of Justice acting in terms of the Defence Act No. 44 of 1957 nullified proceedings in the Windhoek Supreme Court for the release of the Marienthal detainees. This led to a storm of protest and the subsequent release of the detainees who were, after six years in custody, now officially considered no longer to constitute a security risk.[19] But one very worrying question remained. Given the official count of SWAPO guerillas killed, where were the hundreds, if not thousands of guerillas taken captive? Apart from Onaimwandi, a "rehabilitation camp" near Oshakati, no other concentrations of prisoners were known.

In yet another hearing, a businessman sought Court protection against extortion and the threat of murder by a member of Koevoet. It was part of the applicant's case that he could not look to protection from ordinary members of the South African Police who he said, were afraid of Koevoet. This theme was repeated in a trial against Koevoet member Jonas Paulus who was indicted on multiple charges of murder, robbery and rape. Called to give evidence in extenuation, Paulus' commander confirmed one of the worst fears: members of Koevoet were trained to be 'killing machines' and would show no mercy to SWAPO soldiers. Their overriding aim was the 'extermination' of the enemy.[20]

The massacre of twelve people, including children, in the village of Oshipanda was perhaps one of the worst of the publicised atrocities carried out under cover of counter-insurgency. In inquest proceedings, a magistrate found that SWAPO guerrillas had lined up the victims against a wall and shot them dead. A different story was uncovered by the Windhoek Observer: the killing was the work of members of the security forces who, having helped themselves to money and clothes belonging to the villagers, then summarily shot them to simulate insurgent activity. The assault rifles used at Oshipanda were AK47s – standard guerrilla equipment now in regular use by members of Koevoet in field operations.[21]

For many in the north, members of Koevoet have come to figure as the real terrorists. The widespread fear was pithily expressed by one victim at a press conference in Tsumeb: 'For a Black man to talk about what is happening in the north is to sign his own death warrant.'[22] That the security forces are perceived as an occupying power by the black populace was the finding of Bishop Desmond Tutu and Rev. Peter Storey of the South African Council of Churches after their visit to northern Namibia in February 1983. Another tough critic of the new style of blatant violence has been Hans Rohr, the chairman of the NCDP and member of the National Assembly: taking advantage of his constitutional status, Rohr has exposed malpractices, cases of killing and abduction by security force members dressed as SWAPO fighters and arranged press conferences for victims of police and army brutality. He has produced poignant examples: an elderly Kavango headman who had been beaten and robbed; a headmaster whose ribs had been broken; a social welfare worker who was gratuitously shot in the leg; an elderly chief who had been assaulted with demands that his wife be handed over for sexual purposes; four school teachers who had been blindfolded and shocked, then beaten violently with a spade.

The flagrant violation of human rights in the north and the ensuing outcry prompted the SADF to mount a special liaison committee under the chairmanship of an army brigadier to investigate complaints of atrocities; in July 1982 SWATF established an office in Windhoek to investigate allegations of maltreatment. The SADF committee, organised with the co-operation of Peter Kalangula, then proceeded with investigations which were shrouded in obscurity. In an attempt to enhance its image it was announced that the liaison committee comprised representatives of the army, the Ovambo government, local businessmen and church leaders. The churches promptly denied any involvement and stressed their unwillingness to give credibility to a tribunal which represented both judge and accused.

An army spokesman later declared that the rate of atrocities was very low 'considering the conditions and number of troops'. Forty allegations were said to have been investigated; in Ovambo only one of twenty-four allegations had not been solved; several soldiers, it was announced, would be prosecuted for offences (which were not specified) and a public, eager for information, was told that one person, (who was not named), had already appeared in court.[23] The investigation did not make its mark on Namibian judicial history. Given the secrecy in its proceedings and the preposterous generalities of its reports the entire exercise was from the start wedded to futility.

The establishment of the liaison committee with Peter Kalangula represented, however, more than an attempt to ward off criticisms of army misconduct; it was also part of the army's new strategy of attempting to draw Kalangula and his following into collaboration with the generals. By the end of 1981 South African army chiefs had come to regard Kalangula as the only credible Black leader outside of SWAPO capable of supplanting a declining and ineffective DTA leadership. It was with this in mind that army chiefs encouraged Kalangula to break with the DTA and rename his party – in order to escape ethnic undertones – the Christian Democratic Action for Social Justice (CDA).

Of yet greater importance was the evolution in the South African Government's attitude towards the DTA leadership under Mudge. In the course of 1982 Pretoria's attitude underwent a dramatic transformation. Before then all diplomatic steps were taken in consultation with the DTA; by July this ritual was no longer pursued;[24] Mudge began to hint at the possibility of South African betrayal and denounced the setting up of the liaison committee by the SADF.[25] The responsibility for policing, he complained, was that of the central government and no one else.

Not long after, an unbelieving DTA leadership learned that the Administrator General had entered into unilateral negotiations with ethnic government leaders with a view to forging an entirely new political dispensation.

The DTA as ruling party undoubtedly enjoyed its apogee in 1980. But important processes were at work, gnawing at its raison d'être, weakening its influence and corroding its image. It became increasingly evident that the heady promises from the days of DTA campaigning would not be fulfilled; the grand design of apartheid remained unaffected. If anything, the promotion of Namibia's constellation of ethnic governments enhanced the archetypal features of the apartheid structure. As late as 1983 the DTA central government had not succeeded in taking over the municipalities in the territory; Blacks remained effectively excluded from libraries and swimming pools; apartheid in government schools remained untouched and white public schools were still barred from taking part in inter-racial sports competitions. Though official statistics suggested that equal sums were being spent on children of different races, an analysis of the true figures indicated otherwise – that R1500 was spent on each white child, approximately seven times more than that spent on black scholars.[26] Though hotels and restaurants were open to Blacks, apartheid facilities remained intact at many service stations and episodes of violence directed at inter-racial couples and Blacks left no doubt as to the surviving vigour of racism in the territory. Apartheid remained the rule in hospitals and cemeteries. In Katutura the misery remained unalleviated and periodic raids for trespassers did not cease. Community workers in Katutura estimated that over 10,000 children went to bed hungry at night. Conditions generally were aggravated by the decline in the economy and rising unemployment.

The essential flaw in the DTA was that it had been, from its earliest beginnings, a synthetic organism, the offspring of political machination. Dominated by white interests, it had neither the will nor the capacity to perform necessary surgery on Namibian misery. This incapacity was compounded by the division of its political power on ethnic lines; it was this ethnic character which from the beginning pervaded its entire structure and provoked a failure of legitimacy. Conceived as a political force in the black community, it failed to forge an ideology of liberation – on the contrary, its policy was fundamentally one of collaboration on all matters with Pretoria, especially on the key issue of security. It supported strikes into Angola, made no protests against inroads into human liberty and was itself instrumental in passing legislation which gave wider powers and greater protection to the security forces. The impunity with which DTA members had so often broken up opposition meetings was neither forgiven nor forgotten; as late as August 1982 hundreds of DTA members, bussed in from Windhoek, attempted to break up a meeting of the Damara Council, while an aeroplane flew low overhead dropping its load of derogatory pamphlets. The revelation that the DTA was the recipient of an annual cash donation of approximately R120,000 a year from the Hans Seidel Foundation in West Germany did not improve the party's image.[27] The growing corruption in the ranks of ethnic governments only added to the DTA's embarrassment. Evidence before the Thirion Commission of Enquiry into corruption and mismanagement produced lurid details of organised corruption, theft, the purchase of non-existent materials, the purchase of farms without prior evaluation and the diversion of public money for the private use of individuals.

As the DTA star faded, the leadership cast around for popular support and directed strident rhetoric against the South African government which was accused of blocking their course towards a true democracy. A Bill designed to abolish public holidays, imposed on Namibia by South Africa statutes, brought the DTA into direct conflict with right wing Afrikaners who complained that the legislation was an attack on the cornerstone of their cultural heritage. The National Party petitioned the Administrator General to stop the legislation. Their petition was successful. The issue did not seem to be important. It was in fact a turning point.

The DTA's season of withering was associated with a powerful revival of right wing Afrikaner sentiment. This was sparked off by the very notion of multi-racial government, the risk of further inroads into white privilege and Pretoria's announcement that phase one of the settlement plan leading to an internationally supervised election had been accepted by the South African Government. The very idea of central government takeover of municipalities sent 'cold shivers' – according to the right wing press – down the spines of Afrikanerdom. The primary fear was that any black resident who merely possessed a 'few zinc sheets and a rooster' would be granted voting rights and the power to do what he wished with white tax payer's money. (The true solution, argued the Nationalists, was the establishment of three municipalities.) There was talk of violence, the taking up of arms and the possibility of riots; moves were made to form a grand alliance with the National Party, the HNP, the Conservative Party and the extremist WWB. Whites were urged to unite and 'fight as never before'; there were accusations of betrayal – betrayal of white traditions and of the young men who were giving their lives on the border; once again there were threats of a great trek back into the Republic.[28] They warned that the DTA was in disarray, that SWAPO would inevitably take power in the framework of a multi-racial constitution and introduce the final anathema, the destruction of the apartheid life style.

With a major referendum looming in the Republic, Pretoria could not afford to disregard the tumult of voices in Namibia. The referendum, destined to be held in November 1983, was designed to test the wishes of the white electorate on the acceptability of a proposed tricameral parliament made up of whites and representatives from the coloured and Indian com-munites. For the South African Government the issues of internal self gov-ernment of Namibia, the implementation of Resolution 435 and the conduct of the war were inextricably interlinked. Apart from the threats of right wing Afrikaners in Namibia, the Government also had to face up to the harsh sig-nificance of opinion polls in South Africa which revealed over-whelming white support for a tough policy: 80% supported military attacks on guerrilla bases in neighbouring states; 60% opposed direct negotiations with SWAPO 71% believed that blacks had no cause to take up arms against the Govern-ment.[29] The government in Pretoria found itself confronted by numbers of contradictions – many of their own making. It was the government itself which had rejected out of hand the notion of a 'red flag' over Windhoek; it was on more than one occasion that Pik Botha had said, 'We cannot negotiate with leaders who use communist weapons'. If Pretoria refused to have truck with Moscow's supposed surrogates, how could it ever dare to justify their domination over white communities in Namibia?

It was at a meeting with the Prime Minister in Pretoria in July 1982 that the new plans to put an end to DTA hegemony and the National Assembly were presented to Dirk Mudge. It was the view of the South African government, he was informed, that the National Assembly should become more rep-resentative. The new blueprint for constitutional change foreshadowed the inclusion of leaders from various ethnic groups and from the private sector in a reconstituted government.

Forgotten was Pretoria's oft repeated postulate – that the people of Namibia would decide their own fate. It was of course true that the DTA rul-ing party had come to be less representative; they had lost the white election and were beaten by Justice Garoeb's party in the Damara election. The Baster and Coloured segments broke with the DTA; with the defection of Peter Kalangula and the CDA, the entire DTA leadership faced elimination as rul-ing party in any future elections. It is part of the ordinary democratic process for ruling parties to lose in popularity and eventually find themselves thrown out of office. Similarly in Namibia the natural cure lay in the holding of new elections, not the scrapping of an entire constitution, which had been operated by a party brought into power in elections which the South African government themselves claimed to be thoroughly democratic. What super democracy did Pretoria now have in mind? How would the intrusion of ethnic leaders and representatives from the private sector add in any way to the democratic process? Pretoria's justification for a constitutional mutation was threadbare. Namibia had become an economic millstone: according to the Prime Minister, South African assistance, apart from the cost of defence and security, approached a billion rands. Since South Africa paid, it had the right to make decisions.

On his return to Namibia an infuriated Mudge ranted against Pretoria's 'treachery'. Mudge now accused Military Intelligence of engineering the new constitutional strategy as well as the defection of Peter Kalangula. At the conference in Pretoria, army Brigadier Theo May and an officer of South African Military Intelligence had been present, said Mudge, thus confirming evidence of the growing influence of the generals in the South African government's decision making process. An undignified exchange broke out between Mudge and the Administrator General. Mudge made the charge that the approach to ethnic leaders had been carried out secretively; the betrayal, he declared, was nothing but an attempt to win internal support from Transvaal right-wingers who had traditionally strong links with the National Party in Namibia.

On the 20th of November 1982, Pretoria decreed a three month extension of the National Assembly's life, instead of the usual period of six months. For the DTA this seemingly unmomentous act was the official herald of its doom. On the 19th of January 1983, the National Assembly was formally dissolved leaving the Administrator General – in conformity with the National Party's demands – in the position of an all powerful governor. With one legal stroke, an entire constitutional chapter, introduced with much flourish and pomp, into which many millions of rands were invested and which for years was glorified as the incarnation of the popular will, was thus definitively closed. One month later, the Administrator General, Danie Hough, was replaced by Dr Willie Van Niekerk. Dr Van Niekerk arrived at a time of considerable acrimony between the DTA and Pretoria; as a snub to the new incumbent the DTA restricted its welcoming delegation to a lone – former – Bushman representative. Not long after his arrival Dr Van Niekerk formally proposed the setting up of a State Council comprising fifty representatives to be drawn from the internal parties and the private sector; its duty would be to act in an advisory capacity and formulate a new constitution which would be put to the electorate in a referendum. Each ethnic group, he ruled, would be accorded the right of veto. The consensus mechanism, so dear to the hearts of the National party, had at last made its reappearance.

The promulgation of the State Council in July 1983 seemed destined however to be premature. The CDA, an indispensible participant in any credible constitutional structure, declined to participate; conditional acceptance only was given by the National Party, the Labour party and the NCDP. SWAPO, SWANU, SWAPO-D, the NIP and the HNP gave it the cold shoulder. Unwilling to lose further political credibility through participation in a discredited constitutional chimera, the DTA requested that its implementation be delayed until the political parties in the territory had been given an opportunity to come up with alternative ideas. Months later, after a flurry between various parties and much negotiation, the Multi-Party Conference of internal parties was launched in September 1983.

From its debut there seemed little likelihood that the Multi-Party Conference would fructify in meaningful developments, given the disparate nature of its constituent elements. A gamut of discordant opinions ranged from SWANU members on the left wing, some Maoist in tendency, through the radical NIP to the Damara council (which considered itself close to SWAPO,) through the DTA and the Rehoboth National Liberation Front to the arch *verkramptes* and neo-fascist elements on the rightwing. As if re-enacting the first stages of the Turnhalle Conference, they established committees to investigate economic, political and social problems and showed an immediate disinclination to debate contentious subjects.[30] At its conference in Windhoek in February 1984, various spokesmen presented a ragbag of rhetoric; some spoke as if they constituted an interim government, others as if they were already in opposition. Nothing of promise emerged from the debate and some political observers wrote off the episode as a complete 'farce'.

Whether farcical or not, however, the South African Government readily perceived the utility of the Multi-Party Conference, both as an interim solution to a constitutional impasse and as representing, however incoherently, an internal leadership which could serve South Africa's purposes.

We have already noted how the South African government, some months after the débâcle at Geneva in January 1981, once again indicated a willingness to implement an internationally supervised election in Namibia. Pretoria's new diplomatic approach was disarmingly simple: a solution was needed 'urgently' but white fears had to be appeased. It was very much with the small but crucial rightwing Afrikaner electorate in mind that the Western Five set to work to forge new constitutional proposals which were put out in October 1981 and provided for significant constitutional guarantees. The election plan was designed to unfold in three phases: firstly the determination of a constitution and electoral mechanisms by a constituent assembly; secondly the implementation of a ceasefire and a withdrawal of the warring parties and finally phase three, a seven month period of preparation leading to the election itself.

The new proposals, as we have seen, met with unanimous disapproval from the DTA, the NP, AKTUR and the HNP.

In a further gesture of reassurance to Namibian whites, a revised plan projected a two tier electoral system. Each voter would exercise two votes, one for a candidate in his constituency and one for a party of the voter's choice.

Experts on Namibian demography considered that the mechanism was orientated to minimising SWAPO's electoral strength. This time it was the turn of SWAPO and the front line states to object.

Once again the settlement negotiations floundered. In the meantime South Africa extended its presence in southern Angola while its air force steadily widened the ambit of aerial destruction. The anxious prospect for Angola was that of a long and bloody stalemate. Despite the input of Soviet-bloc military assistance, the Angolan army showed itself no match for the SADF. Backed by South Africa, UNITA, a movement with significant support in Angola, manifestly deepened its inroads into the interior. (UNITA maintained that it too should be involved in any international settlement of Namibia).

It was in June 1982 that South Africa again opted for a startling initiative. It now declared itself ready to proceed with phases one and two of the election plan, provided Cuban forces withdrew from Angola. Once again the matter was one of urgency, with South African demands that an election under UN supervision (sic) should be held by no later than March 1983.[31]

The demand for a Cuban withdrawal was not new; it had been raised by South Africa and the DTA in the early stages of negotiations though it appears to have been forgotten subsequently.[32] Now all the anxiety which had ostensibly obsessed Pretoria over a period of five years had suddenly evaporated. Anxious to achieve a diplomatic coup before the next presidential election in the United States, Dr Chester Crocker, Assistant Secretary of State for African Affairs, urged that the focus had come to rest on the Cuban link because all other problems had been solved. This proposition was by no stretch of imagination true as neither the constitution, nor phase one, nor the issue of UN impartiality, nor the size and composition of UNTAG, major obstacles upon which the earlier negotiations had foundered, had been resolved. But now the South Africans appeared to be in earnest: Pretoria expressed concern to establish an international fund to support the constitutional principles; UN General Chand was invited to draw up plans for the redeployment of UN troops within a period of two months and the US embassy took up offices in Windhoek on behalf of UNTAG. (Who would have guessed that UNTAG would be dissolved by December 1982?) Concerted pressure was exerted by the US on the Angolan government, SWAPO and the front line states. This time African solidarity was able to withstand the western diplomatic offensive. The Cubans were necessary for Angola's defence, declared the Luanda government and would depart only after the exercise of Angola's 'sovereign decision'. Despite the rebuff, the US State Department maintained its support for Pretoria's demands and brushed aside criticisms of African statesmen and US critics led by Howard Wolpe, Chairman of the House Foreign Affairs Africa sub-committee, that the Cubans were nowhere involved in the turmoil on Angola's southern border and that it was indeed South Africa itself which was at the heart of southern African regional instability.

In striking contrast to US benevolence towards South Africa, the US administration presented SWAPO with a somewhat severe countenance. In May 1982 SWAPO's UN representative, Theo Ben Gurirab, was temporarily blocked from entering the USA. SWAPO's activities were also subjected to intense scrutiny by a US sub-committee on security and terrorism followed, in August 1982, by an investigation carried out by the US Justice department. In its attempt to favour UNITA, the Reagan administration tried but failed to secure a repeal of the Clark amendment forbidding the grant of US aid to any group in Angola. (Such was the intimacy between Pretoria and the US, that – according to a 'leaked' secret document from the State department – the Reagan administration knew in advance of South Africa's 1982 invasion plans.[33]) And yet with all the expressed enthusiasm and confident thrusting aside of detail did the Pretoria government desire a definitive settlement? In the midst of fragile negotiating processes South Africa, as we have noted above, carried out one of its most punitive raids into Angola in August 1982. The raid once again fortuitously led to 'discovered' documents whose drift, if true, could not have been more damaging to SWAPO's cause, including as they did a hit list, and plans for murdering political leaders, stock piling of arms and the outbreak of violence on the signing of the ceasefire.

Was there not after all an underlying logic in the chain of contradiction? While South Africa set out to improve its image in the world with reasonable sounding diplomatic gestures, was the real dialogue not pursued through the barrel of a gun? Inevitably, Angola would be brought to the point where its concern for survival would of necessity have to be weighed up against solidarity with SWAPO. Parallel with the patter of diplomatic negotiations and the threatening military, social and economic collapse in Angola, the South African government chose to engage the Angolans in an exercise with a difference.

It was early in December 1982 that the South African Foreign Minister Pik Botha met Angolan ministers in the Cape Verde Islands and presented South Africa's ceasefire proposals. The proposals foreshadowed the withdrawal of South African troops from Angola, the simultaneous withdrawal of Cuban positions north of the 14th parallel and the creation of a buffer zone, coupled with an Angolan undertaking to prevent infiltration by SWAPO.[34] The proposal was not taken up. One year later, in December 1983, and while South African forces were pursuing Operation Askari, Pretoria offered a thirty–day period of disengagement commencing as from the 31st of January 1984, on condition that Angola and SWAPO did not exploit the situation. Since South Africa had never admitted the continued presence of its troops in Angola, the language of the proposal in itself constituted an interesting *démarche*. The rejection of this proposal by both Angola and SWAPO in the context of South African allegations that near to a thousand SWAPO fighters were moving southwards towards Namibia provided South Africa with a golden pretext to develop a most crushing operation upon Angolan soil. Then on the 31st of January and at the time when the SADF assault was at its height, Pretoria announced that it had unilaterally begun to 'disengage' its forces in southern Angola as a preparatory step towards an eventual ceasefire. The decision to disengage, it was explained, was taken on the basis of assurances received through the American government.[35] Dr Chester Crocker praised the South African offer as a 'window of opportunity' which could lead to a long term solution of southern African problems. There was intense diplomatic activity. For the Angolans, the proffered carrot was the possibility of US economic aid and recognition, and the termination of South African support for UNITA. On the Angolan side there were interesting signs of softening attitudes. President Dos Santos told the Angolan Peoples Assembly that he was convinced that direct discussions between South Africa and SWAPO would lead to the implementation of Resolution 435.[36] From South African quarters, there was merely the comment that talks with SWAPO were possible provided they were conducted with the Administrator General at the head of a delegation of political parties, in the event the Multi-Party Conference.[37]

It was against this background that Angola announced its acceptance of the principle of a thirty day truce with South Africa – provided Pretoria promised to initiate the process of Namibian independence within fifteen days of the commencement of the truce. Though no such undertaking was given by South Africa, Angola, early in February 1984, issued a portentous statement: it now declared itself to be willing to 'test' South Africa's truce offer of the 31st of January.

A pivotal decision had been taken in Luanda. Angola's insistence on a South African undertaking to implement Resolution 435 had been quietly dropped.

Finally, in mid-February 1984 – while Sam Nujoma was steadfastly demanding that South Africa should enter into direct negotiations with SWAPO – the Luando government and South Africa, with the US acting as mediator, met at Lusaka and agreed on the formation of a joint monitoring commission (JMC) with a view to 'monitoring the disengagement progress'. The unexpressed essence of the agreement, however, was the understanding that SWAPO guerrillas would no longer be allowed to move through areas vacated by the South African army. The agreement carried with it the necessary implication that the Angolans would on the morrow find themselves combating SWAPO on behalf of the SADF. Though the accord figures as an apparent breach of African solidarity, President Kaunda of Zambia chose to characterise it as an 'historic opportunity to make progress'.

SWAPO itself was not represented at the conference; though Angola declared the Lusaka agreement to be the forerunner of direct negotiations between SWAPO and South Africa 'without intermediaries', the inherent assymetry of the agreement was patent: South Africa had committed itself to nothing, neither an undertaking to implement an internationally supervised election nor to terminate its support for UNITA nor to enter into direct negotiations with SWAPO. In Windhoek, the Americans immediately opened a monitoring centre; Angola and South Africa mounted joint patrols with a view to monitoring the South African withdrawal and enforcing a cordon sanitaire which, if effective, would sever SWAPO's logistical arteries.

By March 1984 the JMC had – according to South African sources – clashed with SWAPO guerrillas on at least three occasions resulting in the death of eight SWAPO guerrillas and two members of the JMC.

Pik Botha declared himself to be personally satisfied with the co-operation between Angolan and South African elements in the JMC.

The unobtrusive manner in which Angola entered into the fateful Lusaka agreement is to be contrasted with a parallel development on South Africa's 'eastern front' where, in the same month of February 1984, Samora Machel and the South African Prime Minister entered into a non aggression pact on the common border at Nkomati. In terms of the accord Mozambique, in effect, undertook to put an end to the operation of ANC guerrillas on Mozambican soil. Pretoria for its part, effectively agreed to stop support for Mozambican rebels in the Mozambique National Resistance Movement (MNR). (South Africa has never admitted any involvement in the organising, arming and funding of the organisation until April 1985.) Originally the cat's paw of Ian Smith's Rhodesian government, the then minuscule rebel group was vigorously revived after Robert Mugabe's election victory. Backed by South Africa, the MNR inflicted immense damage on bridges and rail and road communications in Mozambique and progressively extended their presence in the countryside. Mozambique, like Angola, was brought to its knees – partly as a consequence of its own ill-conceived policies, severe drought and floods as well as the successful rebel operations. Like Angola, Mozambique was militarily no match for the South African army and found itself subjected to humiliating raids including a land strike into the suburbs of the Mozambican capital of Maputo. After years of support and expressions of solidarity with ANC guerrillas, Maputo found itself economically and militarily subdued and driven to submission at Nkomati where, putting on a brave face, Samora Michel, clad in full military uniform, signed the accord and shook hands with the South African Prime Minister in an elaborate decor with military bands playing the national anthems in the presence of more than a thousand guests, including representatives from African states and the Soviet bloc. The accord, declared Machel, represented a 'definitive break in the cycle of violence'. Amongst the Mozambicans the treaty was enthusiastically reported as a win for Maputo over the anti-government rebels. In South Africa, the Nkomati accord, an artifact of South African

Machtpolitik, was acclaimed as a major diplomatic triumph for the Republic and as evidence that Pretoria, pursuing a process of internal and external reform, deserved to be rehabilitated and re-admitted to the community of nations. Amongst many whites there was a sense of euphoria; they perceived the Nkomati agreement as the promise of stability, heralding a new epoque of co-operation with neighbouring Black states and the emergence of the apartheid pariah from its state of almost universal exclusion.

Not long after the signing of the accord, Mozambican police carried out raids on homes occupied by members of the ANC, in search of arms, in terms of an undertaking to 'eliminate' all arms depots which might be used by guerrilla elements. Like their Angolan counterparts, the Mozambicans also entered into a joint monitoring commission described as the Joint South African–Mozambican Security Commission.

In January 1984, in the month preceding the signing of the Nkomati and Lusaka accords, leaders of the MPC were invited to take part in talks between Chester Crocker and representatives of the South African Government in Cape Town. The meeting was of no particular moment but for one fact: the absence of ethnic, business and other community leaders to whom the South African Government appeared to have attached so much importance at the time of the dissolution of the National Assembly.[35]

Later, in February 1984, a distinctly revised approach to the MPC emerged from Prime Minister P.W. Botha's pronouncements. The MPC leaders, he said, were to assume direct responsibility for the future; South Africa wished to solve the Namibian issue "in one way or another as soon as possible".[36] Once again, the theme of urgency informed the South African stance: the MPC leaders were now required to present comprehensive proposals by no later than March the 15th 1984.[37]

The political choreography in which the MPC would be required to serve became clearer from other pronouncements of the Prime Minister. If the MPC leaders, he said, wished to discuss the problems of Namibia with SWAPO in a regional conference outside the UN framework, the South African Government would not stand in their way as the Government felt that Southern African leaders should solve the region's problems by themselves at a conference which should be held in an African country and which included UNITA and the MPLA.[38] In conformity with the bland objectivity of this approach, the MPC leaders toned down their vituperation against SWAPO and issued a call to the organisation to join them in a government of national unity. In March of the same year, the MPC published a Bill of Fundamental Rights and Objectives. Black MPC leaders called for the scrapping of ethnic governments, the opening of schools and hospitals, the release of political detainees and a cutting down of security legislation.[39]

Flushed with the success of their peace accords with Angola and Mozambique, the South Africans were once again on the diplomatic offensive. The Government explained their new strategy: it was imperative that South

Africa should rid itself of the Namibian burden as soon as possible as Namibia had become an economic millstone; the cost of implementing Resolution 435 was prohibitive and the Resolution had in any event become outdated.[40] The South African Government referred to a growing willingness on the part of the internal parties to seek a solution with SWAPO; SWAPO had been mauled militarily and was being restrained by Angola and, with every prospect of military annihilation, should opt for peace and enter into discussions like any other party. This in turn would avoid the need for a very costly contingent of UNTAG troops. For Angola, there was also some inducement: if peace were established through a regional conference, South Africa might not object to the Cubans remaining in Angola.[41]

South Africa's strategy clearly had as its aim the destruction of SWAPO's legitimacy as also its title of "sole authentic representative".[42] Instead of negotiating the issues of peace and independence with South Africa, SWAPO would, in terms of South Africa's grand design, merely participate in constitutional discussions "like any other party."[43] But the political and diplomatic disadvantages inherent in such a conference were not, however, likely to be accepted by SWAPO, unless of course SWAPO itself was driven to the conference tables by the front line states themselves on some of whom SWAPO was vitally dependent for the maintenance of bases and its logistical infrastructure. If, for the sake of limiting Rhodesian attacks against their soil, President Kaunda and President Machel were able to coerce Robert Mugabe and his ZANU party to submit to a compromise at the Lancaster House conference in December 1979 against ZANU's will, President Dos Santos and President Kaunda, on both of whom SWAPO depended could, in effect, repeat the process. All of the front line states were economically dependent on South Africa, in particular Zambia with its run down economy and critical shortage of vital commodities, food and foreign exchange.[44] In the face of South African attacks, ominous advances by Unita forces and economic disintegration, President Dos Santos needed above all to come to terms with South Africa. President Dos Santos, as we have already noted, had already begun to refer to future talks between SWAPO and South Africa with optimism whilst President Kaunda, expressing the view that P.W. Botha was a sincere man, declared himself in February 1984 to be interested in meeting MPC leaders.[45] By then South African secret diplomacy had won over Togo, Senegal, and the Ivory Coast – all of them in the throes of a debt crisis – together with Gabon to support the proposed regional conference. Later in May, South African military and diplomatic activity bore fruit with the announcement that a conference was to take place between SWAPO, the Administrator General Willie van Niekerk and an MPC delegation in Lusaka. This announcement followed a breakthrough meeting in which a reluctant Sam Nujoma was persuaded to go to the proposed conference by Prime Minister Mugabe and the front line Presidents.[46] SWAPO declared that as far as it was concerned, the meeting was merely between SWAPO

311

and the Administrator General representing South Africa and that it was for them a matter of indifference as to who appeared as part of the Administrator General's delegation. This declaration is to be contrasted with Pretoria's official attitude, namely, that the talks had really nothing to do with the South African Government as such.[47] The South Africans had their way: before the meeting began, SWAPO submitted to pressure from President Kaunda to take part in a conference in which his co-chairman was none other than Willie van Niekerk.

Like its Geneva predecessor in January 1981, the meeting achieved nothing. The South African delegation pressed for a joint declaration, insisted on the removal of the Cubans and showed little interest in discussions on substantive issues. The Administrator General himself had no mandate to negotiate.[48] What happened at the time of the conference was, however, not without interest. The Damara Council led by Justus Garoeb, a section of SWANU and the Mbanderu Council joined the SWAPO delegation which now had as one of its members a White Windhoek advocate, Anton Lubowski.[49] At a secret meeting between General Hennie van der Westhuizen, Chief of South African Military Intelligence and Sam Nujoma, SWAPO was invited to join a government of national unity in which the portfolios of defence, security and internal affairs would be held by MPC ministers. The purpose of such a caretaker government would be to negotiate a future Namibian constitution with South Africa before the holding of elections. The offer was not accepted.[50]

After the Lusaka conference, the MPC delegation flew off to pre-arranged meetings with government officials in Paris, London and Washington. They also met with the US Secretary for the State, George Schultz, as well as the Heads of State of Gabon, Senegal, Ivory Coast and Togo. Later in July, South Africa, represented by the the Administrator General, met a SWAPO delegation in Cape Verde though without members of the MPC being present.[51] The offer of a ceasefire unrelated to Resolution 435 was once again made. Apart from widespread publicity, nothing else was achieved. The only purpose of the meetings, SWAPO complained, was to sustain myth that South Africa wished to solve issues peacefully in Southern Africa; as for SWAPO, they had made all possible concessions.[52]

On the 17th June 1985, the MPC was finally installed as a government with wide legislative and executive powers. The formal ceremony was preceded by a military parade past P.W. Botha, now the South African State President, in which drum majorettes and a host of panzer vehicles took part in what seemed to be a reproduction of the DTA regime's inauguration ceremony in May 1979. In terms of Proclamation R101, 1985, the new government would at all times be subject to the State President's authority. The MPC's Bill of Fundamental Rights and Objectives was indeed enshrined in the constitution but provision was made for the maintenance of the entire existing web of security legislation. The formulation fo the Bill also clearly indicated an intention to protect existing apartheid structures including segregation in schools and hospitals. Though a majority was sufficient for any cabinet resolution, any member of the cabinet could in terms of Section 27 of the Constitution effectively, even though temporarily, paralyse action by submitting the issue for adjudication by the Courts. Bearing in mind the lengthy delays involved in litigation, the provision went far towards the re-introduction of the consensus principle.

Neither the wealth of publicity nor the flurry of international activity nor the grant of governmental power proved however to be of much help to the MPC in its quest for legitimacy. At the time of the MPC's accession to power, the Damara Council, the overwhelming majority of SWANU members, the Mbanderu Council, the NIP and the NUDO Progressive Party had with SWAPO, grouped themselves into a broad "patriotic front" the People's Consultative Conference, against the MPC government. The dearth of support remained the MPC's primary obstacle to legitimacy; according to NP commentators, the MPC had no more than 15% popular backing.[53] The core of Black support in the MPC comprised NUDO supporters led by the DTA president, Kuaimo Riruako, a minority group of SWANU supporters led by moderate Black leader and former Maoist, Moses Katjiuongua, a very small party SWAPO-D – it had held no public meetings in the last five years – led by Andreas Shipanga and the Rehoboth Liberation Front whose highly conservative leader, Hans Diergaardt, had in the past, on occasions, aligned his organisation with the NP.

The ramshackle contradictory quality of the MPC was publicly reflected in their campaigning. Whilst Moses Katjiuongua called for the opening of schools to all races and for the abolition of ethnic authorities established under Proclamation AG8, NP leader Kosie Pretorius avowed, without denouncement from Black leaders in the MPC, that there would be no opening of schools and the NP organ, *Die Suidwester*, assured its members that ethnic authorities would be preserved by the new constitution.[54]

The events of the 17th June 1985, the day on which the MPC was installed in government did not augur well for a party in search of popular backing. On that day, 4000 persons attended a meeting called by the People's Consultative Conference in Katutura in protest against the MPC government. After the meeting, 600 demonstrators marched peacefully – though illegally – through the streets of Katutura. They were then set upon by members of Koevoet, clubbed and teargassed. Many supporters were women who were beaten, some, while they were on the ground. Seventy-one people were injured. This assault took place on the same afternoon that doves of peace were released in Windhoek as part of the official inauguration ceremony.[55]

The deterioration of the South African Government's image was a further embarrassment to the MPC. By June 1985 the credibility of the South African Government had, since the time of its successes in February 1984, been seriously eroded. More than a year had passed since the signing of the Nkomati and Lusaka agreements which had been represented as a turning point in South African internal and external history. But the Nkomati agreement had not brought peace to Mozambique. On the contrary, the MNR, which had received a massive stockpile of arms and supplies from South Africa in the weeks immediately prior to the signing of the Accord, continued to receive support from South African soil. In May 1985, a SADF sabotage squad was caught in the Cabinda enclave. The squad had instructions to destroy Angola's refineries, the jugular vein of the Angolan economy. (Apart from sabotage equipment, squad members carried leaflets purporting to be issued by Unita.[56]) There was worldwide protest. The South Africans said that their men were monitoring ANC or SWAPO activities in the enclave. Since there was no ANC or SWAPO presence there, the explanation was not credible. A month earlier, South Africa's credibility had been further tarnished by Pik Botha's bold admission in the South African parliament of South Africa's past support for the MNR, a fact that South Africa had steadfastly denied for years. In the Republic itself, there were serious political convulsions. Black townships had become increasingly restive in 1984 and 1985. Throughout South Africa, protesters were confronted by the police; between September and April, three hundred and eighty-one people had been killed by police action.[37] At Uitenhage, a town near Port Elizabeth, in the Eastern Cape, twenty participants in a funeral procession were killed by machinegun fire on the 21st March 1985. Most of the dead had bullet wounds in their backs.[58]

Instead of the vision of enlightenment and accommodation promised by Pretoria, the reality was death and violent repression.

In the ultimate analysis, South Africa's diplomatic successes associated with the Lusaka and Nkomati Accords and the Lusaka conference of May 1984 did not represent a *rapprochement* born of a new spirit of reconciliation. All three events rather reflected a reluctant submission to South Africa's will, a bitter accommodation imposed by overwhelming economic and military superiority. Though all three events had the trappings of international diplomacy, they were in fact an extension of South African internal policy. They will not help to solve the Southern African crisis; they will be remembered as the inglorious fruits of violence, violence driven by its own inexorable laws into ever-widening conflict and havoc. Neither the deployment of Angolan and Mozambican forces in the role of South Africa's policemen nor the coercion of SWAPO to the conference tables can, in the long term, contribute to a golden age of co-operation so much as to the spread of anti-apartheid hatred beyond the borders of the Republic. As for the future of Southern Africa, little is predictable except for one fact: the Republic of South Africa, the economic heart of Southern Africa will continue to be tormented by bloodshed and instability as long as the millions of Blacks in the Republic and Namibia are required to submit to the twin fate of helotry and discrimination. In the end, the essence of the South African tragedy is attributable neither to SWAPO nor the ANC nor Mozambique nor Angola but to the philosophy and practice of apartheid, perceived in Southern Africa as the ultimate political evil, capable of survival only through the exercise of violence and the abuse of power.

NOTES

Abbreviations: The following abbreviations are used:

R.D.M.   Rand Daily Mail
S.A.L.R.   South African Law Reports
W.A.   Windhoek Advertiser
W.O.   Windhoek Observer

CHAPTER 1

1. Now known as Lüderitzbay.
2. Drechsler, Horst, *Let us die fighting*. Zed Press 1980 p. 23.
3. Leutwein, Theodore, *Elf Jahre Gouverneur in Deutsch Sudwestafrika*. Berlin 1906 p. 13
4. The Hereros, composed of nomadic pastoral tribes, were divided into two main groupings: the Mbanderu and the Ovaherero. The Namas, occupying land to the south of Hereroland, were likewise nomadic, cattle owning tribes; they had migrated into Namibia from the Cape in response to European expansion. The most numerous and powerful of the indigenous tribes, the Ovambos, had settled in the north and remained in substance unaffected by German penetration.
5. Rorbach, Paul, *Deutsche Kolonialwirtschaft*. Berlin 1907 p. 218.
6. Drechsler. op. cit. p. 71.
7. Bley, Helmuth, *South West Africa under German Rule*. Heinemann Educational Books Ltd. London 1971. p. 14.
8. *Report on the Natives of S.W.A. and their treatment by Germany*. H.M.S.O. London 1918 p. 20.
9. Bley. op.cit. p. 31.
10. Report. op.cit. p. 10.
11. Bley. op.cit. p. 68.
12. Ibid. p. 138.
13. Applied to the Protectorate of S.W.A. by a decree of the Governor dated 8th November 1896.
14. Report. op.cit. pp. 156-159.
15. Bley. op.cit. p. 140.
16. Report. op.cit. p. 53.
17. Dove, Karl, *Deutsch-Sudwestafrika* p. 10.
18. Report. op.cit. p. 58.
19. Ibid. p. 56.
20. Ibid. p. 63.
21. Ibid. p. 65.
22. Goldblatt, I, *History of South West Africa from the Beginnings of the Nineteenth Century*. Juta & Co. Capetown 1971. p. 132.
23. Hunke, Heinz, *Namibia I.D.O.C.* International. Rome 1980. p. 84.
24. Ibid. p. 84.

CHAPTER 2

1. Report. op.cit., p. 23.
2. Goldblatt, op.cit., p. 21.
3. Hunke, op.cit., p. 82.
4. Nachtwei, Winfried, *Namibia – Von der anti-kolonialen Revolte zum nationalen befreiungskampf*, Sendler Verlag, Mannheim 1976. p. 32.
5. Hunke, op.cit., p. 85.

316

Notes

6. Hellberg, C, *The Voice of the Voiceless*, Verbum, Stockholm, p. 26.
7. Hunke, op.cit., p. 85.
8. Bley, op.cit., p. 213.

CHAPTER 3

1. Wellington, J.W., *South West Africa and its Human Issues*, Oxford University Press, 1967, pp. 270-271.
2. 1922 Administrator's Report.
3. Ibid, p. 279.
4. Article 22 of the Covenant of the League of Nations.
5. Fraenkel, Peter, *The Namibians of South West Africa*, MRG, Report No. 19, p. 11.
6. First, Ruth, *South West Africa*, Penguin African Library, 1963, p. 107.

CHAPTER 4

1. First, Ruth, op. cit., p. 197.
2. Cronje, Gillian and Suzanne, *The Workers of Namibia*, IDAF, London 1979, pp. 32-34.
3. *To be Born a Nation*, Department of Information and Publicity, SWAPO of Namibia, London 1981, p. 172.
4. *Breaking Contract – The Story of Vinnia Ndadi*, L.S.M. Press, Canada 1976.
5. *To be Born a Nation*, op.cit., p. 177.
6. Carlson, Joel, *No Neutral Ground*, Thomas Y Crowell Company, New York 1973, pp. 167-170.
7. Ibid., p. 207.
8. Ja Toivo was released in March 1984.

CHAPTER 5

1. The population of each ethnic group according to 1981 official figures: Ovambos 516,600; Damaras 76,800; Hereros 77,600; Kavangos 98,000; Namas 49,700; Coloured – persons of mixed race – 43,500; East Caprivians 39,500; Rehoboth Basters 25,800; Tswanas 6,800. No figures are available for the Kaokolanders (7,000 according to the 1974 official estimates) nor for the Bushmen (26,000 according to the 1974 official estimates). According to the 1981 figures the white population was 75,600.
2. Hunke, op.cit., p. 83.

3. de Vries, J Lukas, *Mission and Colonialism in Namibia*, Ravan Press, Johannesburg 1978, pp. 147-149.
4. Tötemeyer, G, *Namibia Old and New*, Hurst 1978, p. 50.
5. Winter, Colin, *Namibia*, Lutterworth Press, Guildford & London 1977, p. 24.
6. *Diocese of Damaraland*, Bishop's Charge, Windhoek, 3 October 1969 p. 2.
7. Winter, Colin, op.cit., pp. 67-68.

CHAPTER 6

1. Winter, Colin, op.cit., p. 112.
2. Ibid., p. 114.
3. Serfontein, J.H.S., *Namibia*, Fokus Suid Publishers, Randburg 1976, p. 201.
4. de Vries, J. Lukas, op.cit., p. 202.
5. Cone, James H., *Black Theology and Black Power*, Seabury 1969.
6. Carlson, Joel, op.cit., p. 200.
7. Osmers, John, *Bishop Colin Winter and the Anglican Church in Namibia*, Paper 1976.

CHAPTER 7

1. Booth, William H, *Report on a visit to Namibia*, Criminal Court, City of New York, March 1972, p. 3.
2. Serfontein, J.H.S., op.cit., p. 219.
3. Kane-Berman, John, *Contract Labour in S.W.A.*, S.A. Institute of Race Relations.
4. The South African Rand was at the time approximately the equivalent of 1 US Dollar.
5. Voipio, Rauha, *Kontrak – soos die Owambo dit sien*, E.L.C., 1972.
6. L.S.M. Information Centre, op.cit., p. 75.
7. Moorsom, R., *Under-development, Contract Labour and Worker Consciousness in Namibia*, Journal of Southern African Studies, 1977.
8. Kane-Berman. J., op.cit., Appendix 11, p. viii.
9. Government Gazette, No. 3377, 4 February 1972.
10. Rogers, B, *Namibia's General Strike*, Africa Today, Spring 1972.
11. Booth, William H, op.cit., p. 140.
12. Winter, C., op.cit., p. 5.
13. Ibid., p. 148.

14. Ibid., pp. 144-147.
15. Booth, William H., op.cit., p. 4.
16. Winter, C., *Diocese of Damaraland*, Circular, Windhoek, 2 February 1972.

CHAPTER 8

1. Serfontein, J.H.S., op.cit., p. 71.
2. *RDM* 28.4.73.
3. Serfontein, J.H.S., op.cit., p. 75.
4. *The Star*, 13.10.73.
5. *Financial Mail*, 13.4.73.
6. *RDM*, 17.8.73.

CHAPTER 9

1. *The Star*, 12.5.73.
2. Serfontein, J.H.S., op.cit., p. 207.

CHAPTER 10

1. Tötemeyer, G., *SWA/Namibia*, Fokus Suid Publishers, Randburg, 1977, pp. 122-123.
2. Nuukwawo and Nangutuuala vs The Ondongwe Tribal Authority. Affidavit of Johannes Nangutuuala, p. 65.
3. Wood & Others vs The Ondongwa Tribal Authority, Affidavit of Nestory Shanyengana, p. 107.
4. Ibid., Affidavit of Nathaneel Homateni, p. 101(a).
5. Ibid., Affidavit of Franz Nangutuuala, p. 126.
6. Ibid., Affidavit of Franz Nangutuuala, p. 128.
7. Ibid., Affidavit of Elise Nghilwamo, p. 173.
8. Ibid., Affidavit of Elise Nghilwamo, pp. 35-36.

CHAPTER 11

1. 1972, S.A.L.R., (3), p. 934 (W).
2. 1975, S.A.L.R., (2), p. 294 (AD).

CHAPTER 12

1. *Die Suidwes Afrikaner*, 27.11.73.
2. *The Windhoek Adveriser*, (W.A.), 25.7.73.
3. National Unity Democratic Organisation.
4. W.A., 13.11.73.
6. *Algemeine Zeitung*, 22.1.74.

7. W.A., 10.9.73.
8. W.A., 27.8.73.
9. W.A., 4.9.73.
10. S21, General Law Amendment Act 76 of 1962.
11. *Die Suidwester*, 25.1.74.
12. W.A., 7.6.73.

CHAPTER 13

1. W.A., 13.11.73.
2. W.A., 12.11.73.
3. W.A., 13.11.73.
4. W.A., 19.11.73.

CHAPTER 14

1. W.A., 15.1.74.
2. *Die Suidwester*, 14.1.74.
3. W.A., 14.1.74.
4. W.A., 18.1.74.
5. *Die Suidwester*, 12.2.74.

CHAPTER 15

1. Act 83 of 1967.

CHAPTER 16

1. Neither the initials nor the ranks attributed to the officers referred to in this or later chapters bear any relationship to their real names or ranks.
2. The initials attributed to the doctors referred to in this chapter do not correspond to their real names.

CHAPTER 17

1. *Die Suidwes Afrikaner* 16.7.74.
2. R.D.M. 17.9.74.
3. R.D.M. 10.8.74.

CHAPTER 18

1. W.A., 24.9.74.
2. W.A., 10.2.75.
3. W.A., 8.4.75.
4. Serfontein, J.H.S., op.cit., p. 18.
5. *Sunday Times*, (Johannesburg), 30.10.74.
6. W.A., 11.4.74.
7. SWAPO Press Release, 17.1.75.
8. *Die Suidwes Afrikaner*, 3.12.74.
9. SWAPO Press Rlease, 29.11.74.

10. *Financial Mail*, 24.1.75.
11. *Sunday Times*, (Johannesburg). 19.1.75.
12. W.A., 23.4.75.
13. R.D.M., 1.5.75.
14. W.A., 29.5.75.
15. *Sunday Express*, 4.5.75.

CHAPTER 19

1. W.A., 23.5.75.
2. W.A., 5.6.75.
3. W.A., 12.2.75.
4. W.A., 12.6.75.
5. W.A., 12.6.75.
6. *Die Suidwes Afrikaner*, 17.7.75.
7. W.A., 16.6.75.
8. *Die Suidwester*, 18.6.75.
9. *The Cape Times*, 24.6.75.
10. *Die Suidwester*, 1.8.75.

CHAPTER 20

1. Issued in terms of the Undesirables Removal Proclamation No 50 of 1920.
2. R.D.M., 2.6.75.
3. W.A., 16.7.76.
4. W.A., 20.8.75.
5. An open letter by Pastor Kameeta.
6. Kameeta, Z., *Church and Nationalism in South Africa*, Ravan Press, 1975.
7. Ibid.
8. *Guardian*, 17.6.75.
9. W.A., 13.1.75.

CHAPTER 21

1. Neither the initials nor the ranks attributed to the officers referred to in this and later chapters bear any relationship to their real names or ranks.
2. Rossouw vs Sachs, S.A.L.R., 1964, Volume 2, p. 551, A.D.

CHAPTER 22

1. An obscene mode of address – literally, womb.
2. A mixture of pidgin English, Afrikaans and Zulu.

CHAPTER 23

1. A vulgar allusion to female genitals.

CHAPTER 25

1. Neither the initials nor the ranks attributed to the officers referred in this chapter bear any relationship to their real names or ranks.
2. A black Angolan.

CHAPTER 27

1. W.A., 2.9.76.
2. W.A., 19.10.76.
3. *Cape Times*, 1.6.76.
4. W.A., 24.2.76.
5. *Guardian*, 24.6.76.
6. W.A., 5.11.76.
7. W.A., 1.11.76.

CHAPTER 28

1. R.D.M., 18.9.75.
2. Landis, Elizabeth, *Southern Africa in Crisis*, Editor G. Carter and P. O'Meara, pp. 184-186.
3. W.A., 4.4.75.
4. *Sunday Times*, 18.5.75.
5. Serfontein, op.cit., pp. 254-255.
6. W.A., 11.8.75.
7. W.A., 28.8.75.
8. W.A., 28.7.75.
9. W.A., 26.8.75.

CHAPTER 29

1. W.A., 6.12.75.
2. R.D.M., 7.6.75.
3. *Cape Times*, 30.8.75.
4. W.A., 4.9.75.
5. W.A., 13.11.75.
6. W.A., 5.9.75.
7. *Sunday Times*, 11.9.75.
8. R.D.M., 2.6.76.
9. R.D.M., 12.9.75.
10. W.A., 8.8.76.
11. W.A., 3.9.75.
12. *The Times*, 4.9.75.
13. *Cape Times*, 12.9.75.
14. W.A., 5.3.76.
15. W.A., 4.3.76.
16. *The Star*, 13.3.76.
17. R.D.M., 17.3.76.
18. R.D.M., 20.10.76.
19. *The Daily Telegraph*, 2.9.76.

20. W.A., 7.10.76.
21. R.D.M., 14.10.76.
22. *Die Suidwester*, 16.11.79.
23. W.A., 29.8.77.
24. W.A., 4.4.78.
25. *Guardian*, 13.3.76.

CHAPTER 30

1. *Cape Times*, 1.11.76.
2. R.D.M., 16.11.76.
3. W.A., 14.21.76.
4. R.D.M., 10.3.77.
5. *Cape Times*, 18.3.77.
6. R.D.M., 10.3.77.
7. W.A., 28.4.77.
8. W.A., 15.2.77.
9. W.A., 11.2.77.
10. W.A., 4.4.77.
11. W.A., 25.2.77.

CHAPTER 31

1. W.A., 9.5.77.
2. W.A., 6.6.77.
3. *Financial Times*, 11.6.77.
4. *Guardian*, 11.6.77.
5. W.A., 15.6.77.
6. *The Observer*, 22.5.77.
7. W.A., 28.9.77.
8. W.A., 26.10.77.
9. W.A., 6.12.77.

CHAPTER 32

1. W.A., 8.9.77.
2. W.A., 18.10.77.
3. W.A., 22.11.77.
4. R.D.M., 17.9.77.
5. Proclamation AG64 of 1977.
6. Altered to thirty days by Proclamation AG23 of 1979.
7. Proclamation AG27 of 1979.
8. Section 3(i) of Proclamation AG26 of 1978.
9. Section 7 of Proclamation AG26 of 1978.
10. W.A., 8.9.78.
11. *The Times*, 27.6.78.
12. W.A., 29.8.77.
13. R.D.M., 31.8.77.
14. W.A., 2.9.77.
15. W.A., 11.10.77.

16. W.A., 25.11.77.
17. W.A., 21.12.77.
18. W.A., 21.12.77.
19. W.A., 30.1.78.
20. W.A., 6.2.78.
21. W.A., 3.3.78.
22. W.A., 7.3.78.
23. W.A., 2.3.78.
24. W.A., 2.3.78.
25. W.O., 2.12.78.
26. R.D.M., 9.2.78.
27. W.A., 8.2.78.
28. *Sunday Times*, 9.4.78.
29. *Morning Star*, 29.3.78.
30. *Sunday Times*, 2.4.78.
31. R.D.M., 17.4.78.

CHAPTER 33

1. The initials and ranks attributed to officials in this chapter bear no relationship to their real names or ranks.
2. W.A., 6.12.77.

CHAPTER 34

1. Pastor Imene was sentenced to imprisonment for five years under the Terrorism Act No 83 of 1967 for the offence of aiding guerrillas.
2. Affidavit of Dr J.W. Wickens.
3. W.A., 9.3.77.
4. *L.W.F. News Service*, 18.5.78.

CHAPTER 35

1. *The Times*, 13.10.77.
2. *The Times*, 17.9.77.
3. W.A., 12.2.78.
4. W.A., 1.3.78.
5. W.A., 12.8.77.
6. *The Times*, 26.4.78.
7. *Financial Mail*, 21.4.78.
8. R.D.M., 28.4.78.
9. *The Times*, 21.6.78.
10. *Morning Star*, 30.11.77.
11. W.A., 10.1.78.
12. W.A., 8.12.78.
13. W.A., 2.3.78.
14. W.A., 3.6.77.
15. *The Observer*, 3.9.78.
16. *The Observer*, 3.9.78.
17. W.A., 20.6.78.

Notes

19. The expulsion order was issued on the
14th July in terms of the Undesirables
Removal Amendment
Proclamation AG50 of 1978.
20. *L.W.F. News Service*, 16.8.78.
21. W.A., 25.1.78.
22. W.A., 3.3.78.
23. R.D.M., 6.12.75.
24. W.A., 10.4.78.

CHAPTER 36

1. The initials attributed to this and other
persons in this chapter do not, for their
own protection, correspond with their
true initials.

CHAPTER 38

1. *The Times*, 13.10.78.
2. *The New Stateman*, 3.11.78.
3. R.D.M., 29.6.78.
4. *Africa*, Volume 85, September 1978.
5. Dirk Mudge denied involvement by the
Department of Information.
6. W.A., 10.11.78.
7. *Financial Mail*, 4.8.78.
8. W.A., 24.10.78.

CHAPTER 39

1. W.A., 21.6.78.
2. Ellis, Justin, *Elections in Namibia?*
British Council of Churches and
Catholic Institute for International
Relations, Nottingham, May 1979, p. 21.
3. *Financial Mail*, 7.12.78.
4. W.O., 9.12.78.
5. Ellis, Justin, op.cit., p. 25.
6. W.A., 11.8.78.
7. Ellis, Justin, op.cit., p. 25.
8. R.D.M, 20.11.78.
9. W.A., 25.11.78.
10. W.O., 7.10.78.
11. *Africa*, Number 87, November 1978.
12. W.O., 9.12.78.
13. R.D.M., 30.11.78.
14. W.O., 2.12.78.
15. Ellis, Justin, op.cit., p. 30.
16. W.A., 29.11.78.
17. W.O., 13.12.78.
18. *Die Suidwester*, 5.12.78.
19. *Financial Mail*, 5.12.78.

20. W.O., 13.12.78.
21. W.O., 9.12.78.
22. W.O., 2.12.78.
23. Ellis, Justin, op.cit., p. 29.
24. *The Times*, 5.12.78.
25. Wood, Richard, Statement by Richard
Wood, Assistant Bishop of Damaraland
(Namibia), *The Namibian Elections – 4
December 1978*, London, 1978.

CHAPTER 40

1. W.A., 20.4.79.
2. W.A., 22.1.79.
3. *Financial Times*, 22.2.79.
4. *The Star*, 10.2.79.
5. *Financial Mail*, 9.3.79.
6. *The Star*, 12.5.79.
7. W.O., 26.5.79.
8. W.A., 11.6.79.
9. *Financial Mail*, 15.6.79.
10. R.D.M., 12.6.79.
11. *Sunday Express*, 5.8.79.
12. W.A., 27.7.79.
13. Proclamation 172 of 1979 issued on the
13th August 1979.
14. W.O., 3.3.79.
15. *Die Suidwester*, 22.5.80.
16. *Guardian*, 25.7.79.
17. *Guardian*, 25.7.79.
18. *Sunday Times*, 29.7.79.
19. *Sunday Express*, 5.8.79.
20. *The diplomatic report*, New York,
February 1979.
21. W.A., 7.12.79.
22. R.D.M., 22.9.79.
23. R.D.M., 25.10.79.
24. W.A., 5.3.78.
25. Abrahams, K., *Representative Authorities
and Ethnic Elections*, The Namibian
Review, July/August 1980.
26. W.A., 31.8.81.
27. R.D.M., 25.10.79.
28. R.D.M., 2.8.80.
29. *The Citizen*, 5.7.80.
30. W.O., 4.4.81.
31. W.O., 17.1.81.
32. W.O., 24.1.81.

CHAPTER 41

1. The DMZ plan was first proposed by
Angola. The UN proposal based on the

321

DMZ plan was never formulated in an official document though a confidential proposal was circulated freely.

2. W.O., 4.9.80.
3. *The Daily Telegraph*, 16.8.79.
4. W.A., 13.5.80.
5. *Sunday Post*, 21.9.80.
6. *Cape Times*, 6.10.80.
7. R.D.M., 1.4.80.
8. W.A., 10.9.80.
9. R.D.M., 18.11.80.
10. *Sunday Times*, 26.10.80.
11. W.A., 3.12.80.
12. *Guardian*, 26.11.80.
13. W.A., 8.12.80.
14. W.A., 20.11.80.
15. W.O., 13.12.80.
16. W.O., 17.11.81.
17. *Africa*, Number 112, December 1980.
18. Rotberg, R.I., *Christian Science Monitor*, 5.1.81.
19. R.D.M., 23.1.81.
20. R.D.M., 21.1.81.
21. Thornberry, C., Paper for the Scandinavian Institute of African Studies, 1981.

CHAPTER 42

1. W.A., 25.6.80.
2. W.O., 15.8.81.
3. W.A., 26.8.80.
4. W.A., 26.1.79.
5. W.A., 5.6.81.
6. *New York Times*, 31.12.80.
7. *Financial Mail*, 27.3.81.
8. *The Citizen*, 7.5.81.
9. W.A., 19.5.81.
10. W.O., 6.6.81.
11. W.A., 18.5.81.
12. R.D.M., 29.1.81.
13. *The Citizen*, 18.7.81.
14. *Die Suidwester*, 15.4.80.
15. W.A., 30.9.81.
16. W.O., 7.3.81.
17. W.O., 21.3.81.
18. R.D.M., 13.10.81.
19. W.O., 7.3.81.
20. R.D.M., 20.5.81.
21. W.A., 24.7.81.
22. W.O., 4.7.81.
23. W.O., 4.4.81.
24. W.O., 15.8.81.

25. Thomas, W.H., *Economic Development in Namibia*, Kaiser Grünewald, Munich, 1978, p. 284.
26. W.A., 10.11.80.
27. W.A., 29.6.81.
28. W.O., 4.4.81.
29. W.A., 22.5.81.
30. W.O., 5.9.81.
31. *The Star*, 30.5.81.

CHAPTER 43

1. Johnson, L.D., *Sanctions and South Africa*, Harvard International Law Journal, Fall 1978, p. 887.
2. The credentials of the South African delegation had not been renewed for several years and were found to be not in order.
3. The US was South Africa's number one trading partner in 1980.
4. *Namibia Update*, Washington 17.6.81.
5. R.D.M., 7.2.81.
6. *The Christian Science Monitor*, 9.10.81.

CHAPTER 44

1. *New African*, November 1979.
2. *Daily Despatch*, 16.10.80.
3. *Sunday Post*, 30.9.79.
4. *Focus*, I.D.A.F. Number 31, 1980.
5. Ibid., Number 33, 1981.
6. W.O., 4.10.80.
7. *Cape Times*, 31.8.81.
8. W.A., 3.9.81.
9. W.O., 7.3.81.
10. R.D.M., 7.5.80.
11. *The Star*, 21.8.80.
12. *New York Times*, 6.1.81.

CHAPTER 46

1. *The Star*, 12.4.83.
2. *Sunday Times* (SA) 8.1.84.
3. W.A., 21.2.83.
4. R.D.M., 13.9.83.
5. *The Star*, 5.3.83.
6. W.A., 17.5.82.
7. W.A., 20.10.83.
8. W.O., 7.5.83.
9. R.D.M., 19.2.83.
10. W.O., 23.4.83.
11. *The Star*, 25.9.82.

12. *Work In Progress*, 29–1982.
13. W.A., 21.10.82.
14. W.O., 27.11.82.
15. Judgment of the Supreme Court Windhoek, 14.6.83.
16. Since the detainees were released shortly after the application was launched, the Court was not called upon to make findings on affidavits which alleged mistreatment of other detainees.
17. W.O., 7.5.83.
18. W.O., 28.2.82.
19. *Guardian*, 15.11.83.
20. R.D.M., 5.6.82.
21. W.O., 31.7.82.
22. W.O., 29.10.83.
23. R.D.M., 26.4.82.
24. R.D.M., 2.7.82.
25. *The Star*, 20.11.82.
26. W.O., 26.11.83.
27. *Financial Times*, 18.6.82.
28. W.O., 26.6.82.
29. *Washington Post*, 13.9.82.
30. *International Herald Tribune*, 29.1.83.
31. *Le Monde*, 2.2.84.
32. *West Africa (Nigeria)*, 6.2.84.
33. *The Times*, 10.2.84.
34. *The Star*, 9.1.84.
35. W.O., 28.1.84.
36. W.A., 2.2.84.
37. *MPC Proposals on the Issue of the Independence of South West Africa/Namibia 27.3.1985.*
38. *The Times*.
39. W.A., 2.4.85.
40. *Current Affairs*, 18.5.85.
41. *International Herald Tribune*, 19.9.84.
42. *The Times*, 13.4.84.
43. *Facing Reality* by Sean Cleary. *Leadership South Africa* Second Quarter 1984, Vol 3 No. 2.
44. *Namibia Review* No. 31 January/September 1984.
45. W.A., 28.2.84.
46. *The Times*, 11.5.84.
47. *The Times*, 11.5.84.
48. *The Guardian*, 14.9.84.
49. W.O., 19.5.84.
50. *The Times*, 16.5.84
51. *MPC Aide Memoire*, 15.2.85.
52. *The Star*, 17.9.84.
53. *The Economist*, 27.4.85.
54. *Namibia Review* No. 31 January/September 1984.
55. *Statement of the Council of Churches of Namibia*, 21.6.85
56. *The Times*, 24.5.84.
57. *Business Day*, 19.6.85.
58. *The Star*, 12.6.85.

Index

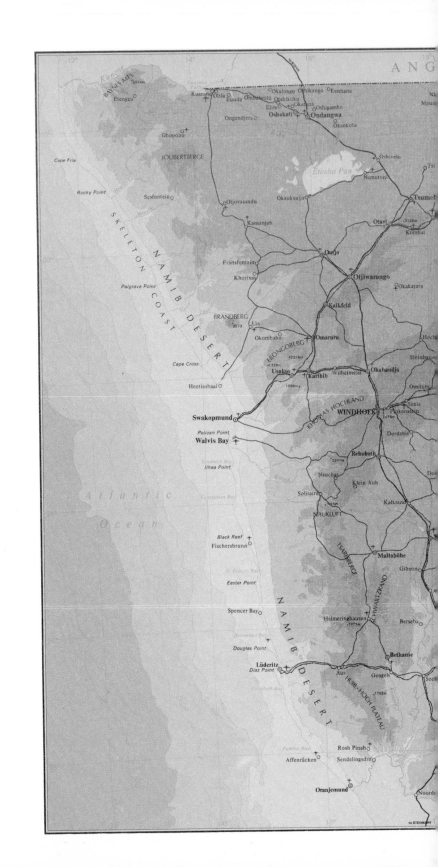